A Commentary
on the
New Taxa

described in

The Botany of Captain Beechey's Voyage
by W. J. Hooker and G. A. Walker-Arnott

H. J. NOLTIE

EDINBURGH: Royal Botanic Garden Edinburgh
MMX

First published by the Royal Botanic Garden Edinburgh, 2010
20a Inverleith Row, Edinburgh, EH3 5LR
www.rbge.org.uk

Copyright © Royal Botanic Garden Edinburgh, 2010

All rights reserved. No part of this publication may be reproduced, stored in a retrieval system or transmitted, in any form, or by any means, electronic, mechanical, photocopying, recording or otherwise, without the prior written consent of the copyright holders and publishers.

ISBN: 978-1-906129-68-2
Designed by: Fakenham Photosetting
Printed by: Martins the Printers, Berwick-upon-Tweed

Contents

INTRODUCTION v
   1. Specimens at Edinburgh (E) vii
   2. Specimens at Kew (K) vii
   3. Beechey specimens in other herbaria x
   4. Typification xi

Chapter 1. HISTORY OF THE *BLOSSOM* VOYAGE 1
   1. Personnel 3
      1.1.1 The Captain: Frederick William Beechey 3
      1.1.2 The Surgeon: Alexander Collie 5
      1.1.3 The Naturalist: George Tradescant Lay 7
      1.1.4 Other Officers 8
   2. The Voyage 9
      1.2.1 The South Seas 9
      1.2.2 Northern latitudes 14
      1.2.3 The Pacific again 15
      1.2.4 Second Alaskan visit, and return to Britain 18
      1.2.5 In Britain: division of the spoils 19

Chapter 2. THE SUPPLEMENTS AND OTHER CHINESE
COLLECTIONS 21
      2.1 California: David Douglas 21
      2.2 The 'California' collections of 'Tolmie' 23
      2.3 Mexico: Andrew Sinclair and H.M.S. *Sulphur* 24
      2.4 China: Charles Millett & the Rev. G.H. Vachell 25

Chapter 3. THE HOOKER & ARNOTT COLLABORATION 27
      3.1 Arnott's contribution 27
      3.2 Hooker's contribution 28
      3.3 Publication history 28
      3.4 Dates of publication 34

Chapter 4. ALPHABETICAL LIST OF NEW TAXA 35
      4.1 Phanerogams 35
      4.2 Cryptogams 187

Appendix I. Collectors of new taxa 195
Appendix II. Details of collecting localities 199
Appendix III. Original drawings by W.J. Hooker 203
Appendix IV. Taxa for which no original material found 209

Acknowledgements 211

References 213

Index of Scientific Names 215

Illustrations

Fig. 1. Original material of *Leptopetalum mexicanum*.

Fig. 2. Original material of *Layia emarginata* showing examples of handwriting of Hooker and of Arnott.

Fig. 3. H.M.S. *Blossom* off the Sandwich Islands.

Fig. 4. Captain Frederick William Beechey.

Fig. 5. Map of the Pacific Ocean showing the route of the *Blossom*.

Fig. 6. Landing in Bounty Bay, Pitcairn Island

Fig. 7. Interior of Pitcairn Island

Fig. 8. Attack upon Lieutenants Wainwright and Belcher by natives of the Gambier Islands.

Fig. 9. Crew of the *Blossom's* barge erecting a post for Captain Franklin near Refuge Inlet, Alaska.

Fig. 10. Original drawing of *Cerasus ilicifolius* by William Jackson Hooker.

Fig. 11. Engraving of *Cerasus ilicifolius* by Joseph Swan.

Introduction

The Botany of Captain Beechey's Voyage, as stated on its title page, is primarily an account of the plants collected on the voyage of H.M.S. *Blossom*, under the command of Frederick William Beechey in the years 1825, 1826, 1827 and 1828. The collections were made largely by two of the ship's officers, the naturalist George Tradescant Lay and the surgeon Alexander Collie, though the latter was by far the more assiduous of the pair. At the request of Beechey (with the permission of the Admiralty, effectively that of the redoubtable John Barrow) the collections were sent for study, identification, and description, to W.J. Hooker in Glasgow, who was then working on his *Flora Boreali-Americana*, which treated the botanical collections of Richardson, Franklin, Drummond and Douglas. Hooker enlisted the help of George Arnott Walker-Arnott and the work appeared in ten parts between 1830 and 1841. Hooker himself drew the 100 plates, which were engraved by Joseph Swan. The *Blossom* specimens were found to be by no means of the highest quality, limited in quantity when it came to making duplicates, and with minimal locality details (some of which were mistaken). The publication of the *Botany* was organised in geographical sections – Chile, Mexico, California etc., and, due to the amphi-Pacific range of the voyage, included a large number of taxa, many already known, but many new to science, from ten countries in present-day terms. In undertaking such a wide-ranging floristic work, it was impossible for two knowledgeable botanists not to draw upon other collections, especially as the region as a whole had been previously visited by some of the great voyages of discovery – by Captains Cook (with Banks and the Forsters) and Vancouver (with Menzies), by the French, the Russian voyage of Kotzebue, and specific areas had more recently been investigated by terrestrially based collectors such as John Gillies (Chile) and Charles Millett (coastal China). As work progressed two important further collections became available and were treated by Hooker & Arnott in supplements to the Californian and Mexican sections – those of David Douglas (with some by John McLeod), and Dr Andrew Sinclair, surgeon of H.M.S. *Sulphur*, respectively.

The structure of the *Botany* has led to various problems in identifying the original material on which new taxa were based, and monographers have not always noticed important details hidden in introductory material to the sections. Other important information, including protologues of new species, is sometimes embedded in footnotes, and, on p. 201, is an important statement that after finishing the Chinese Asclepiadaceae, all the specimens described up to that point (i.e., other than those kept in Hooker's and Arnott's own herbaria), were returned to the Admiralty and subsequently 'presented to private individuals', so the rest of the China section had, perforce, to be based on other material in Hooker's and Arnott's herbaria (mainly that of Millett and Vachell). The title of the work, and the (potentially misleading) annotation 'Beechey' on many of the specimens has not infrequently led to the collector of a particular specimen being cited in floristic and monographic works as Beechey himself. This is despite the prominent statement on the title page that the collections from the *Blossom* (i.e., the majority of the work) were made by 'Messrs Lay and Collie'. Likewise, some authors have failed to notice introductory statements to the Supplements, with the information that the Californian one, 'where not otherwise mentioned', was based on Douglas collections, and that the collector of the specimens in the Mexican one was Dr Sinclair.

The reason for undertaking the present work is that the author has long been aware that the set of 'Beechey' specimens in Arnott's herbarium (which came on permanent loan with the University of Glasgow herbarium (GL) in 1966) was one of the most important in the herbarium of the Royal Botanic Garden Edinburgh (E), that it was rich in original material, but that most had never been identified as such (types were eventually found for c. 250 of Hooker & Arnott's names, of which only 64 had previously been so recognised). Arnott's herbarium is of enormous taxonomic importance but to a very large extent has been overlooked. In fact, Arnott's set of Beechey plants is one of very few cases where Stafleu & Cowan (1979: 291) drew attention to its significance, which has led to a small number of monographers borrowing and annotating material. The statement in 'TL 2':

Arnott's herbarium is at GL (now E). Asa Gray states that the Beechey plants are in Arnott's herbarium. Hooker also owned a set, which may in part also still be at GL (now E)

is, however, misleading and requires modification. Hooker's herbarium is, of course, entirely at Kew, where he took it on leaving Glasgow in 1840, being purchased for the nation in 1866. The source of Gray's comment is a paper on European herbaria resulting from a tour during which he visited Scotland (Gray, 1840). On 7 December 1838 Arnott wrote to Hooker (KDC 10 f. 18) that 'I expect him [Gray] to spend some time with me in my wilderness', a reference to Arnott's country estate of Arlary, Kinross-shire. Gray was struck both with Arnott, 'this sagacious botanist', and with his herbarium, which, while richest in 'East Indian plants is also interesting to the North American botanist, as well for the plants of the *Botany of Capt. Beechey's Voyage*, &c., published by Hooker and himself'. Gray was also, inevitably, impressed by Hooker's herbarium in Glasgow 'the largest and most valuable collection in the world, in the possession of a private individual': that he did not specifically mention the Beechey specimens therein is probably simply because there was so much else that was noteworthy.

Having searched for the original material of all the new 'Beechey' taxa at both Kew and Edinburgh it is clear that Hooker's and Arnott's collections are of equal importance. It is impossible to know which author did particular pieces of the work. Some of the earlier taxa have annotations of MS names attributed to Hooker alone, but many of the sheets in Hooker's herbarium have tickets attached annotated in Arnott's hand, and it seems possible that Arnott did a greater share of the work as Hooker became busier during the course of the 1830s.

1. Specimens at Edinburgh (E)

As was common practice at the time, Arnott mounted on a single sheet specimens of what he considered to belong to the same taxon, no matter their origin. The Beechey specimens thus commonly share a sheet with other material, e.g. Cuming or Bridges specimens in the case of the South American collections. The relevant specimens are labelled in Arnott's hand with the name (followed by 'H & A' in the case of new taxa) the locality and 'Beechey' (FIGS 1, 2). There are also some duplicates from Arnott's herbarium, with a printed label which probably came to E from Glasgow University herbarium on 5 February 1902 (RBGE Donations to Herbarium). It is not known why this group was split from the main part of Arnott's herbarium, and some are clearly original Beechey specimens, with Arnott's own annotations. Arnott gave some duplicates from his set to William Gourlie, which (via Trinity College Glasgow) ended up back in GL and thence to E.

2. Specimens at Kew (K)

The multiple mounting on sheets in Hooker's herbarium at Kew is much more extreme than that on any of Arnott's. They are annotated in a similar way to Arnott's, but it is sometimes hard to be certain which annotation belongs with which specimen. For this reason (and when specimens have been found not to be conspecific) some sheets have been dissected and remounted, often with loss of information written only once on the original sheet (this unfortunately sometimes includes the species name) – that the locality has not been transferred with the correct fragment is always present as a nagging doubt. Sometimes Beechey material at K is not duplicated at E, and *vice versa*. Some of the Hooker sheets at Kew seem to have been mounted at a considerably later date than that of the publication, as they have tickets annotated in George Bentham's hand with the name and collecting details, and may have been curated when Bentham was working on the *Botany of H.M.S. Sulphur*. Care is required with sheets bearing a Hooker & Arnott name, but which have collectors or localities different from those of the protologue: some such,

Fig. 1. Original material of *Leptopetalum mexicanum*.
A typical 'Beechey' sheet from Arnott's herbarium – labelled beneath the specimens in Arnott's hand; the description on the ticket is also in Arnott's hand. Though labelled 'Mexico', this is one of the collections that actually came from Bonin.
Royal Botanic Garden Edinburgh.

Introduction

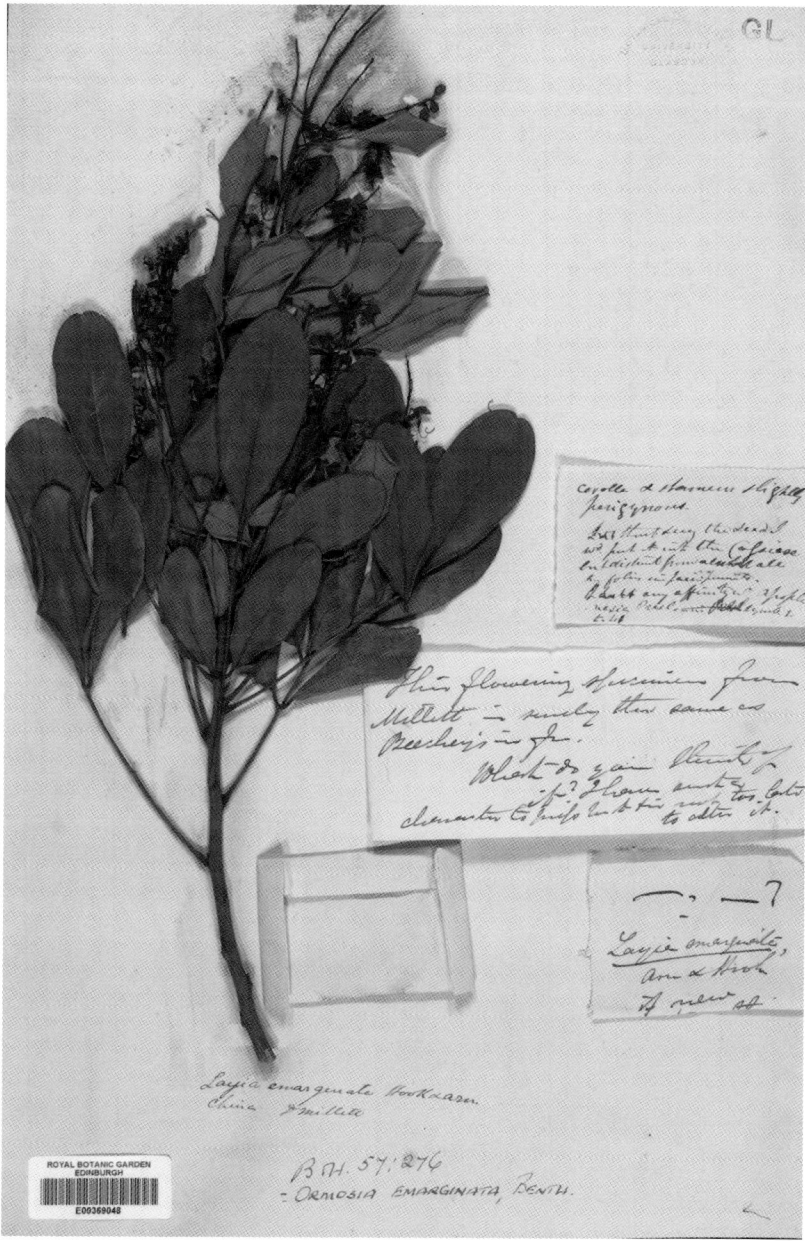

Fig. 2. Original material of *Layia emarginata*, showing examples of handwriting of Hooker and of Arnott.
This is a specimen in Arnott's herbarium, collected by Charles Millett in China, and sent to Arnott by Hooker. The annotation beneath the specimen is in Arnott's hand, as is the uppermost ticket on the right-hand side; the lower two are in Hooker's.
Royal Botanic Garden Edinburgh.

which are not part of the original material, have been (over-enthusiastically) put into type covers, the apparent Hooker & Arnott annotation merely representing a later identification.

3. Beechey specimens in other herbaria

Original material of about 52 taxa has not been found either at Edinburgh or Kew (see Appendix IV). Clearly some may well be lurking in these herbaria but have been overlooked due to misfiling (either taxonomic or geographic); others may have been lost (e.g., lent to researchers in other herbaria and not returned). Given the large number it nevertheless seems that some material might genuinely be missing. Did this, perhaps, include material sent back to the Admiralty by Hooker & Arnott c. 1837 (see footnote on p 201 of the *Botany*) and subsequently 'presented to private individuals'? This cannot be known, though it seems a little unlikely given Hooker's acquisitiveness (in the name of Science). Surely he would have kept a duplicate of all the new taxa (if ever so small – and some specimens are!), and, where possible, given one to Arnott? It is hoped that this publication, by drawing attention to what is missing, may allow the errant specimens to be found, whether at Edinburgh, Kew, or in other herbaria.

An unquantified amount of Beechey material is known to be at the Natural History Museum, London (BM) and at Geneva (G). The history of these is explained in Miller's account of the Lambertian herbarium (Miller, 1970: 514). These specimens were sent by Hooker to London around 1834 and split between Robert Brown and Aylmer Bourke Lambert. The former are now at BM; the latter were sold to Obadaiah Rich at the Lambert sale, subsequently sold to Benjamin Delessert, and have ended up at Geneva. The fact that these specimens were duplicates, sent by Hooker, makes it almost certain that they will not include material not retained by himself and/or Arnott, so cannot account for the 'missing' types. The present author in December 2009 searched for 36 of the 'missing' types at BM and found none, nor indeed encountered a single Beechey specimen suggesting that the total number of specimens given to Brown was not large.

In a letter to Hooker (KDC 61 ff 16–7) Beechey said that he had promised Collie a set of specimens, and this may well have been effected as at E are some fern specimens in the herbarium of Archibald Menzies labelled 'Otaheite. Mr Collie', which Collie must have given personally to Menzies.

Bryophyte collections are much more easily divisible than those of flowering plants, and Hooker appears to have been generous in doing so. The monographer of *Jungermannia conchifolia*, cited types at the Natural History Museum (BM), Harvard (FH), Helsinki (H), New York Botanical Garden (NY) and Paris (PC). The same may well apply to other mosses and liverworts.

4. Typification

Except in rare cases where descriptions are said to be based on a single collection, or in the case of Millett and Vachell for which numbered collections are often cited, it is impossible to be sure of the precise collection(s) on which new taxa were based. In certain cases (e.g., *Antigonon leptopus*, *Erythraea macrantha*, *Ficus beecheyana*, *Sicyos pachycarpus*, *Quinchamalium chilense*) it is clear that mixed gatherings were involved, suggesting multiple gatherings included under a single name by Hooker & Arnott. The collecting 'localities' (usually large areas) are often denoted merely at the start of each geographical section and some of these are misleading (e.g., the use of 'Society Islands' for collections made between Easter Island and Tahiti (with a few specific exceptions), on the grounds that 'As many of the plants of these Islands appear common to the whole group, we have rarely thought if necessary to mention the particular stations of the species'. It is noteworthy that Hooker & Arnott had little concept of local endemism. Individual numbered collections are never cited for the 'Beechey' taxa, though in some cases a particular place-name (and/or collector) is referred to after the description. Other collections (e.g., earlier ones of Menzies) are sometimes also discussed and can also represent part of the original material for 'Beechey' names. For this reason the term 'original material', rather than 'syntype', has been used throughout the present work, and it is up to monographers to lectotypify from among this material. No taxa have been typified here, but references to earlier type citations encountered during the nomenclatural and taxonomic research have been given (though many such typifications doubtless remain to be discovered).

It is unfortunate that some twentieth-century authors cited specimens in publications as 'type' (i.e., effectively lectotypified a name) but did not annotate the relevant herbarium sheets. In these cases it is doubtful if the author actually saw the material, and merely presumed that it 'should be' at K, or, in the light of the statement in TL2, at E (GL). Citing a collection without seeing it is particularly unhelpful in the case of sheets in Hooker's herbarium, most of which, as noted above, bear multiple collections by different collectors, so that it is necessary to be very precise as to particular specimens when choosing a lectotype.

CHAPTER 1
History of the *Blossom* voyage

Probably because Captain Beechey himself saw the *Botany*, along with the *Zoology* (Richardson *et al.*, 1839), as supplementary to his own *Narrative* of the voyage published in 1831, nothing was provided by Hooker & Arnott in the way of introductory material to their work. Valuable supplementary details to those in the *Narrative* are to be found in the unpublished correspondence between Beechey and Hooker – details relevant to the collections themselves, and to the extended history of their publication.

In order to understand the context of the botanical collections it is appropriate to provide here a summary of the history and route of the voyage taken from Beechey's *Narrative*, with brief biographical details of Beechey, Lay and Collie. Short biographical details of the other collectors whose work was used by Hooker & Arnott are provided in Appendix I, and co-ordinates for the collecting localities in Appendix II.

The voyage of the *Blossom* under Beechey has been very largely forgotten. There have been several exceptions to this, including the belated publication of Lieutenant George Peard's journal of the voyage, with valuable introductory material by Barry M. Gough (1973). Susan McKelvey treated the American parts in her extensive *Botanical Exploration of the Trans-Mississippi West 1790–1850* (McKelvey, 1955), and Professor A. Lincoln wrote on the exploration work (geographical and natural historical) undertaken during the two Californian sojourns, which he considered 'more productive scientifically than that of any previous expedition to Northern California' (Lincoln, 1969 a, b). Also noteworthy is Fergus Fleming's highly readable *Barrow's Boys* (1999), which, while giving only the briefest of mentions of the voyage, provides a detailed picture of its wider context. The story, however, is well worth telling; the reason for its invisibility being largely due to that of its conception – embedded in its subtitle 'to the Pacific and the Beering [sic] Strait'. It was, in fact, an episode in one of the 'great games' of the nineteenth century – the search for a Northwest (Northeast if you were Russian) Passage around the coast of the North American continent. In the present age of satellite imagery and advanced telecommunications – to say nothing of global warming – it is easy for this to seem a faintly ludicrous pursuit, but at stake were dreams of new global trade routes, in Britain's case the search for a quicker route to the riches of the Orient. By 1825 several relevant pioneering expeditions had already been mounted, and Beechey himself had been to the Arctic under

Fig. 3. H.M.S. *Blossom* off the Sandwich Islands, 1826 or 1827. Watercolour by William Smyth (PAF 5964).
© National Maritime Museum, Greenwich, London.

John Franklin in 1818, and with William Edward Parry in 1819. But in 1824 John Barrow, the influential and long-serving (if persistently wrong-headed) Second Secretary to the Admiralty, together with Parry and Franklin, planned a two-pronged attack – to find a sea route, and to explore and map north-western Canada in an attempt to strengthen British interests against those of the Russian-American Trading Company. The former expedition was to be under Parry, with the ships *Fury* and *Hecla*; the latter, under John Franklin, was to follow the Mackenzie River, with the aim of reaching the coast of Alaska.

Beechey's command was to the frigate *Blossom*, a 26-gun ship (FIG. 3), reduced for this service to 16 (14 eighteen-pounder carronades and two six-pounders), thereby technically rendering the vessel a 'Sloop of War'. In the summer of 1824, at Deptford, it was fitted out for surveying work, its sides 'strengthened so as to be able to bear a shock from Ice'. A 38-foot, 'schooner-rigged, copper-bottomed Barge' was built to take along for coastal exploration (FIG. 9). Beechey's orders, signed by Robert Dundas, second Viscount Melville, First Lord of the Admiralty, were to go via Cape Horn and the Pacific (where he was to discover if Ducie's and Elizabeth Island were the same or different, and to deliver despatches to the British Consul in Hawaii), and reach a rendezvous on Chamisso Island, Kotzebue Sound, on the Bering Strait in Alaska. He was to arrive there not later than 10 July 1826 (a date slightly modified in discussions between Beechey and Franklin), 'for the purpose of affording such assistance as may be required, either by Captain Parry or Captain Franklin, should one or both of those officers make their appearance in that neighbourhood'. Should the Arctic explorers fail to appear, Beechey was to spend the winter and spring of 1826/7 undertaking surveying

History of the Blossom voyage

work in the Pacific, return to Alaska in late summer 1828, and only then to return to Britain.

Hardly surprisingly neither Parry nor Franklin did 'make their appearance', though it would later emerge that the latter had, at one point, been a mere 146 miles from a surveying party sent by Beechey that reached Point Barrow, the extreme north-western tip of the American continent. In this respect, the trip might be seen as an heroic failure: but this would be to overlook much that was achieved in its pursuit. Beechey's skills as a captain and navigator were of the highest order. He reached Chamisso Island a mere 14 days after the date agreed with Franklin, a date hatched more than a year earlier, from the security of the shores of the distant Thames. In his summary of achievements of the voyage, Beechey, with understated modesty, allowed the statistics to speak for themselves: 73,000 miles covered in three years, charts made of 14 harbours (two of which were new), of 40 islands (six new) and of 600 miles of coast (one fifth not previously delineated). In addition to his own elegant, two-volume *Narrative* (in octavo and quarto editions, 1831), illustrated with engravings from drawings made on the voyage by William Smyth, Beechey himself and his brother Richard, two substantial works on the natural history of the voyage were eventually published (though both in tiny editions) – the botanical one here under consideration by Hooker & Arnott (1830–41), and a zoological one (with fifty coloured plates) in 1839 by John Richardson (mammals), N.A. Vigors (birds), E.T. Bennett & G.T. Lay (fish), Richard Owen (crustacea), J.E. Gray (reptiles and amphibia), and J.E. Gray & G.B. Sowerby (molluscs). The *Zoology* also included a chapter on geology and mineralogy by the (diversely zoophagous) Rev. William Buckland, based on notes by Belcher and Collie. In respectful tones, Beechey had also to report the human cost of his venture: of the 100 men who set out, 15 did not return – lost to sickness, shipwreck or other misfortune.

It took Hooker & Arnott thirteen years to complete their work on the plants collected on the *Blossom* voyage, and their statistics can be added to Beechey's geographical ones: the new taxa amounted to (approximately) 12 genera and 290 species of flowering plant and conifer (of which about 143 are still recognised either under the original name or under a new combination); 20 ferns; one clubmoss; six bryophytes, two algae; one parasitic fungus, and two lichens. Barry Gough (1973: 46) rightly praised the *Botany*, 'like the volume on zoology ... [as] a testament to the toils of the Royal Navy in the pursuit of science'.

1.1 Personnel

1.1.1. The Captain: Frederick William Beechey

Frederick William Beechey (1796–1856) came of an extremely artistic family and himself made competent topographical drawings on the voyage (FIGS 6, 7). His father was the excellent, but under-rated, portrait painter Sir William Beechey, his mother Anne (*née* Jessop) a painter of miniatures. His

Chapter 1

Fig. 4. Frederick William Beechey in his Captain's full dress uniform. Oil portrait by his brother George Duncan Beechey (BHC 2543). Started before the *Blossom* voyage (c. 1822–5), but completed after it and exhibited at the Royal Academy in 1828.
© National Maritime Museum, Greenwich, London.

brother George Duncan was also a portrait painter (FIG. 4), who emigrated to India, to the Court of Awadh at Lucknow, where he married a daughter of the king. A younger brother, Richard Brydges, as a midshipman made drawings on the *Blossom* voyage (FIG. 8) and later became a distinguished marine painter.

The following summary of Beechey's life is based largely on Lambert (2004). Given the early start of naval careers (in his case at the age of ten) Beechey was, by 1825, already an experienced officer and hydrographer; his early service had been in the English Channel, Portugal and the East Indies, and he had seen active service off the coast of Madagascar in 1811. He had also served in North America and in 1818 was appointed to serve on an Arctic expedition under Franklin on the *Trent*, and the following year he had taken part in Buchan's attempt to reach the North Pole (they got as far as Spitsbergen), serving under Parry on the *Hecla*. In 1821 and 1822 he was involved in a survey of the north coast of Africa under W.H. Smith, and in the latter year was promoted Commander. The *Blossom*, in 1825, was Beechey's first major command and while on this, in 1828, he was promoted Captain. Of the officers and crew chosen by Beechey for the *Blossom*, the most relevant to the present work were the surgeon Alexander Collie (whose assistant was Thomas Neilson, 'a dashing young man from Glasgow'), and the naturalist George Tradescant Lay.

It has been said that Beechey was not particularly well liked by his staff, and Collie before the start of the voyage described him as 'a little, sharp faced, reddish haired, rather inconsequential buck'. But this should probably be put down to intemperate youth trying to amuse or impress his brother. Something similar might be said of an impression of Beechey at a dinner party in 1824 recorded by Jane Griffin (later Lady Franklin) as 'a prim looking

History of the Blossom voyage

little man ... [who] was very silent'. In later life Beechey was seen as a reliable hand, ending up as President of the Royal Geographical Society, and the figure that emerges from his long correspondence with W.J. Hooker is that of a likeable character, concerned (but not obsessively so) with accuracy and fairness to the efforts of his officers, and anxious for publication of their discoveries.

Although the primary aim of the voyage was to meet the Arctic travellers, geographical surveying and natural history were important corollaries. The Admiralty's instructions stated:

> As we have appointed Mr. Tradescant Lay as naturalist on the voyage, and some of your officers are acquainted with certain branches of natural history, it is expected that your visits to the numerous islands of the Pacific will afford the means of collecting rare and curious specimens in the several departments of this branch of science. You are to cause it to be understood that two specimens, *at least*, of each article are to be reserved for the public museums; after which the naturalist and officers will be at liberty to collect for themselves. You will pay every attention in your power to the preservation of the various specimens of natural history, and on your arrival in England transmit them to this office. (Beechey, 1831 1: xii).

Beechey himself collected a very few 'plants in a folio vol: but they were all examined by Collie who took out two or three specimens which had not been collected by any other person and put them in the public collection' (KDC 44 ff 39–40); his other botanical contribution was a drawing of the bizarre, and aptly named fungus, *Phallus daemona*, engraved as plate 20 of the *Botany*. Hooker & Arnott named three plants for Beechey (an *Eryngium*, a *Ficus* and a *Panicum*), and several later authors have added to the tally. He is also remembered zoologically in the Beechey or California ground squirrel (*Spermophilus beecheyi*), a common Californian mammal, named by Sir John Richardson in 1839 based on Collie's notes.

In September 1835 Beechey was appointed to H.M.S. *Sulphur* (a sixth-rate warship) to survey parts of the coast of South America, with her consort the schooner *Starling* (continuing the work of Fitzroy and the *Beagle*), but he became ill and returned to Britain from Valparaiso in or shortly after June 1836 and was replaced (after an hiatus during which H. Kellett acted) by Edward Belcher who joined the ship at Panama in February 1837 – the *Sulphur* botanical collections will be discussed below. In 1837, and for the next ten years, Beechey commanded ships (including H.M.S.V. *African*) involved in anti-smuggling activities around the Irish coast. Some of this was based at Stranraer, from where, in November 1839, he sent a broken barometer to Hooker to be repaired in Glasgow (KDC 63 f. 21). Beechey became a naval elder statesman, a Rear Admiral of the White, who served on the Arctic Council, advising, among other things, on the Franklin searches.

1.1.2. The Surgeon: Alexander Collie

Given the pre-eminent role of Collie in making the botanical collections on the *Blossom* voyage, it is appropriate to include a summary of his life, based on the work of Gwen Chessell, who has recently rescued him from oblivion (Chessell, 2008). Alexander Collie (1793–1835) was born on the farm of Wantonwells at Insch, Aberdeenshire. From 1808 to 1812 he studied for an arts degree at King's College, Aberdeen, while concurrently acquiring a practical medical training as an apprentice to Dr William Dyce. Collie must have known Dyce's eponymous son (born 1806) as an infant, little knowing what a distinguished artist he would become. Rather than pursue medical training in Edinburgh, Collie went to London to study at the hospitals of Guy's and St Thomas's, attending lectures by Sir Astley Cooper. He passed his exams at the Surgeon's Hall in January 1813, and became an assistant surgeon in the Royal Navy, posted to H.M.S. *Doris* on a three-year voyage to India and China. Collie returned to London in 1816, was promoted to Surgeon, and spent the winter of 1816/17 in Edinburgh attending courses in Military Surgery (John Thomson), Chemistry (Thomas Charles Hope), Obstetrics (James Hamilton) and Practice of Medicine (James Gregory). Collie's medical ambitions must have been serious and in November 1817 he travelled to Paris for further medical study with another Edinburgh student, Andrew Combe who (with his brother George) was to gain renown (verging on notoriety) as a leading phrenologist. Collie shared this interest and, with Combe, attended lectures given by Johann Spurzheim; the Scots pair also attended lectures on geology and botany at the Jardin du Roi – the latter presumably given by the great Antoine-Laurent de Jussieu. After a four-month tour to Switzerland and Italy, Collie returned to London where he was appointed Surgeon to H.M.S. *Gannet*, which spent three years chasing smugglers off the coast of Ireland (1821–4). At this point Collie was appointed Surgeon to the *Blossom*, but though his credentials for the medical posting are understandable, what is not clear from the slender surviving evidence is how or where he obtained his botanical expertise and experience. This must have been considerable as he was put up for the Linnean Society in May 1824, giving botany as his main interest – his proposers were Archibald Menzies (in whose Pacific wake he would be following), W.J. Hooker, Robert Brown (whose path he would later cross in Western Australia) and J.E. Bicheno. In October 1824 Collie knew that he was to be posted as Surgeon to the *Blossom*, and made appropriate preparations – his friend Combe asked him to bring back human skulls and measurements.

After the *Blossom* voyage, in January 1829, Collie was appointed to H.M.S. *Sulphur*, as surgeon in charge of troops accompanying the party going out to found the Swan River Colony in Western Australia. The *Sulphur* accompanied the more commodious *Parmelia* on which travelled James Stirling, the incipient colony's Lieutenant Governor, and James Drummond who would become the colony's official botanist (many of whose Swan River specimens came into Arnott's herbarium and are now at Edinburgh). Collie stayed on in Western Australia, being made Government Resident and magistrate at Albany in 1831, and Colonial Surgeon, based in Perth, in 1833. By 1835 the tuberculosis from which he had suffered for many years had worsened to the

History of the Blossom voyage

point where he decided to return home and boarded a ship to return via Sydney. It was too late; he was landed at Albany, where he expired on 8 November. During his time in Western Australia Collie collected plants, but these fared no better than his journals from the *Blossom* expedition. His sister-in-law, a frugal and clearly exceptionally philistine, Aberdeenshire farmer's wife used the vellum from these precious volumes as jam pot covers, their paper pages for making spills for singeing chicken carcasses! The botanical collections Collie sent to the Linnean Society were auctioned off in 1863 and are now dispersed, and those sent to his patron Dr (later Sir) William Burnett at the Haslar Hospital were almost certainly destroyed in bombing during World War II.

The destruction of the notes and diaries from the *Blossom* (to say nothing of his early death and lack of material from his later Australian period) means that it is impossible to make a fair assessment of Collie's abilities as a botanist and he can really only be remembered as a collector, which probably fails to do him justice. Despite these collecting efforts Collie is commemorated in only a single plant name – and even that is no longer in use. Due to the existence of John Lindley's *Collea* (named for Thomas Colley) in the family Orchidaceae it was not possible for anyone to name a genus for Alexander Collie, as it would have made something perilously close to a homonym. It is very odd, however, (not to say decidedly ungenerous) that Hooker & Arnott failed to name so much as a single species for him, and it fell to the Viennese botanist Stefan Endlicher to do so in 1836. This was the grass *Panicum colliei*, collected by Lay or Collie on the Sandwich Islands, a renaming of Hooker & Arnott's *P. affine* (because the epithet was found to have been previously used), but sadly this is no longer recognised as distinct from *P. pellitum*. With Lay, his name is, however, remembered in California in a vernacular name for *Castilleja affinis*, which is sometimes known as the 'Lay & Collie Indian paint-brush' – cumbersome it may be, but slightly better than nothing! Collie is also remembered as a small footnote in the annals of British horticultural history, as the introducer of that most handsome of ornamental gooseberries, the 'fuchsia-flowered' *Ribes speciosum*, from seed collected at Monterey, the story of which will be given below.

1.1.3. The Naturalist: George Tradescant Lay

Though the parents of the ship's official Naturalist clearly had some interest in natural science (or at least antiquarianism), rather little of this seems to have rubbed off on their son, George Tradescant Lay (1799–45). Little is known of him, but Collie in a letter to his brother George (quoted by Chessell, 2008: 60), dismissed him as 'a learned pedant, a most erudite classical scholar but little versed in natural history'. It cannot be accidental that in Beechey's acknowledgements in his *Narrative*, while paying particular tribute to Collie's contribution, there is no mention of Lay's.

More is to be found about Lay's failings in a private letter from Beechey to Hooker replying to one in which Hooker had clearly complained of the inadequacies of the botanical collections. Beechey wrote:

I am extremely sorry to find that our collection of plants has turned out so indifferently and that the duplicates are so few. I cannot in any way remove the blame ... from the shoulders of our collector [Lay], whose chief recommendation from Mr Barrow was that "he was a collector and not a finished naturalist". He had nothing to do but to collect ... [but was] over fond of the violin (if indeed he had any knowledge at all of procuring botanical specimens) for I really believe there were not ten days throughout the voyage on which he did not, when he was able, play seven hours at least, much to the annoyance of those who were within reach of his music. I believe him to have been a very unfit person for the situation as I have heard as loud complaints from other quarters, of his ignorance in particular, as from yourself. This need go no further as I should be sorry to do Mr Lay any injury (KDC 61 ff 16–17).

So Lay fiddled while Collie collected! Admittedly, the Naturalist did become ill in the Pacific and had to be left behind in Hawaii for the whole of the first summer, where his illness continued and he did nothing. The frustratingly little anecdotal botanical information cited by Hooker & Arnott is all taken from Collie's notes (sadly no longer extant, as noted above), and it seems likely that very few of the botanical collections are due to Lay, whose only contribution to the natural history of the expedition is as joint-author of the fish account in the *Zoology*. Despite his feeble efforts (for which he received an annual salary of £110), Hooker & Arnott made not one, but two, attempts to commemorate his name in a genus *Layia* (FIG. 2).

Lay's later life was spent in China, where he went as Agent for the British & Foreign Bible Society, and in 1843 became British Consul at Canton. At least during this period he seems to have taken natural history rather more seriously, sending plants to the British Museum and publishing numerous articles on China, some of which included botanical and natural historical material (see Bretschneider, 1898: 290 for further details).

1.1.4. Other officers

Beechey was scrupulously fair in the matter of who actually collected the botanical specimens on the voyage of the *Blossom*. Hooker must have asked for a definitive statement, to which Beechey replied:

the collection is, I believe, the joint labour of the naturalist [i.e., Lay], and officers of the ship though Mr Collie undoubtedly gathered more than all the others put together; and perhaps some of the officers furnished nothing at all that was new. I think if would be proper, all things considered, to say the collection was made by Mr Lay (Naturalist) and the officers of the ship in general, but in particular Mr Collie the surgeon, who during the absence of Mr Lay zealously undertook the care of the department with which he was entrusted ... but we must not call Mr Collie a Naturalist or deprive the officers of the little merit that may be due to them (KDC 44 ff 20-1).

Among the other officers who collected the odd plant was almost certainly the Assistant Surveyor, Lieutenant Edward Belcher. Though Belcher was notoriously unpopular ('perhaps no officer of equal ability has ever succeeded in inspiring so much personal dislike'), Collie seems to have got on well with him, and he helped Collie with his geological work, including the excavation of mammoth bones at Escholtz Bay, Alaska. As noted above, it was Belcher who took over Beechey's command of the *Sulphur* in 1837. Lieutenant John

History of the Blossom voyage

Wainwright was primarily interested in astronomy, but also had pteridological interests as Beechey later told Hooker (KDC 44 ff 39–40) that Wainwright had made a 'private collection … consisting entirely of ferns'. Lieutenant George Peard in his journal makes the occasional anecdotal reference to plants, but was more interested in geology and zoology (especially shells and birds).

1.2 The Voyage

The *Blossom* sailed from Spithead on 19 May 1825, making for Rio de Janeiro, which was reached on 8 July. Although a month was spent there the botanical collections made were later found not to be worth describing. The ship headed round Cape Horn, reaching Concepción in Chile on 8 October. Here Beechey was struck by some familiar temperate European genera, and commented on the *panque* (*Gunnera scabra*), eaten in strips with cheese and wine after dinner, or in rhubarb-like tarts. Lay & Collie did not collect the *panque*, but they made specimens of about 165 species of flowering plant during their twelve days at Concepción, of which 43 were new to science. The ship headed north, and two days were spent at Valparaiso before heading westwards to Easter Island. At Valparaiso Beechey took on a man to assist Lay in making botanical collections – his name is not recorded, but he 'had been accustomed to collect in N[ew] S[outh] Wales', and his recruitment had been 'much against the rules of the service as he was over aged and no seaman' (KDC 61 ff 16–7).

1.2.1. The South Seas

No plants are specifically mentioned from Easter Island, but the landing party under Lieutenant Peard (which included Collie) had to beat an undignified retreat under a hail of stones lobbed by angry natives. This was despite the Admiralty instructions that Beechey was 'particularly to impress on the minds of … [his] officers and men the necessity of being extremely guarded in their intercourse with the females of those places so as to avoid exciting the jealousy of the men'. Unfortunately, collections made between Easter Island and Tahiti were all described by Hooker & Arnott under the blanket (and inaccurate) heading 'Society Islands', so localities for particular plants are impossible to ascertain other than the few cases where a specific island is named. At the end of November and start of December Beechey found that Ducie's and Elizabeth (which he noted should, on grounds of priority, be called Henderson's) Islands were distinct: the former a coral atoll; the latter girt with fifty-foot cliffs. Pitcairn Island was reached on 4 December 1825 (FIGS 6, 7), and they stayed there almost three weeks, being the last voyagers to interview John Adams (1763–1829), the only extant survivor of the notorious *Bounty* mutiny of 37 years previously, and sire to a race that exists to this day. Touchingly Beechey regularised the uxorial relationship between Adams and his blind, bed-ridden consort; the young Richard Beechey

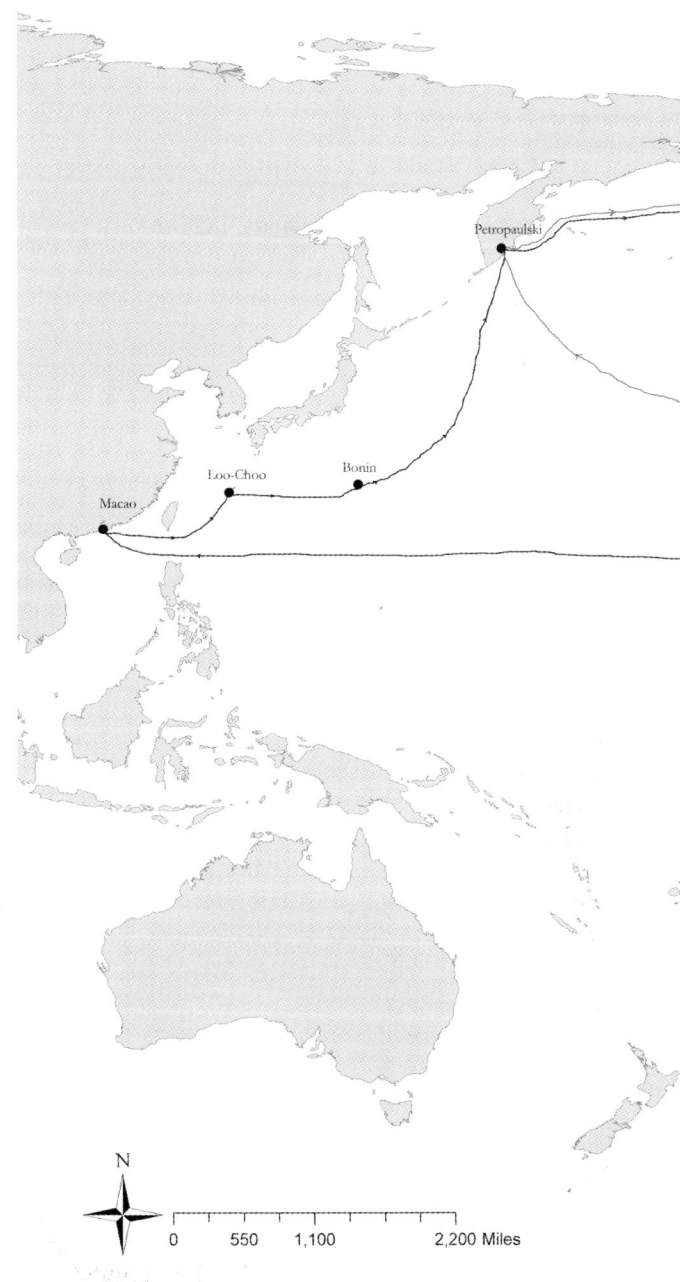

Route 1825-6
Route 1826-7
Route 1827-8

Fig. 5. Map of the Pacific Ocean showing the route of H.M.S. *Blossom* (in slightly simplified form).
Drawn by Alan Elliott.

History of the Blossom voyage

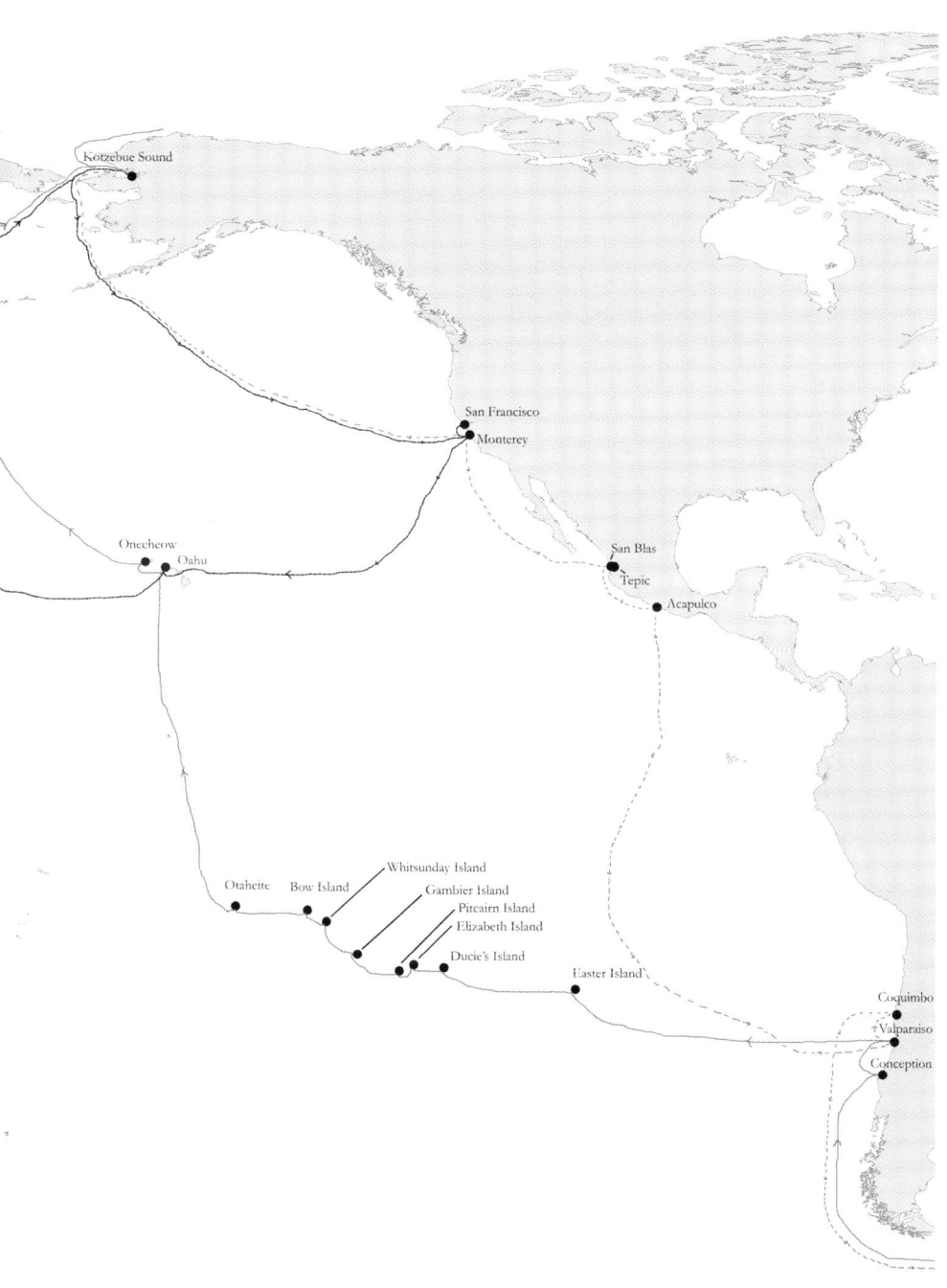

Fig. 6. Landing in Bounty Bay, Pitcairn Island
Steel engraving by Edward Francis Finden, after a drawing by Frederick William Beechey, from the octavo edition of Beechey's *Narrative*. London 1831.

Fig. 7. Interior of Pitcairn Island
Steel engraving by Edward Francis Finden, after a drawing by Frederick William Beechey, from the octavo edition of Beechey's *Narrative*. London 1831.

History of the Blossom voyage

Fig. 8. Attack upon Lieutenants Wainwright and Belcher by natives of the Gambier Islands. Steel engraving by Edward Francis Finden, after a drawing by Richard Brydges Beechey, from the octavo edition of Beechey's *Narrative*. London 1831.

drew Adams's portrait, and Collie gathered data on the pulse rates of the inhabitants.

The *Blossom* sailed west and the next islands encountered were the Gambier (Mangareva) group, where they stayed for two weeks over the New Year: a diamond-shaped fringing reef encloses a lagoon that Beechey named after his vessel; the islands after his officers – the southernmost, uninhabited, one being dedicated to Collie. *Metrosideros obovata* was collected and Collie undertook ethnographic work and poked around in a mummy. The islanders warmly rubbed noses with the Europeans, but, as on Easter Island, the encounter turned sour and ended in violence (FIG. 8). Before reaching Tahiti on 18 March 1826, two more small 'coral islands' of the Tuamotu group were visited: Whitsunday Island (now Pinaki) on 23 January, where they ate *Pandanus* leaves that tasted to Peard like 'mustard & cress', and where the novelties *Myoporum* (now *Nesogenes*) *euphrasioides* and *Heliotropium anomalum* were collected; and Bow Island (now Hao), from 14 to 20 February, where wells were dug for fresh water that Collie analyzed chemically.

As have other Europeans, before and since, Beechey and his crew found Tahiti a 'delightful island' – they stayed for almost five weeks in March and April; the natives were friendly and the officers hobnobbed with the royal family – six-year old Pomarree III, his mother, and aunt who acted as Queen Regent. The British Consul for the Sandwich, Society and Friendly Islands, Richard Charlton and his family, were also on a visit and the crew, after a long diet of bread and flour, was pleased to feast on breadfruit. Beechey presumably presented the young king with the 'fowling piece embossed with silver' sent by the Admiralty. On the voyage between Tahiti and the Sandwich Islands (Hawaii), dysentery struck – two died, and Tradescant Lay was affected. They arrived at Honolulu, on Oahu, on 20 May 1826, and stayed for eleven days. The island the voyagers found barren compared with lush Tahiti but they collected plants, made astronomical observations, and again met royalty – the sixteen-year old Tamehameta III (to whom they hopefully gave the second of the Admiralty's presentation guns), his guardian/Prime Minister Karaimoku, known as 'Mr Pitt', and John C. Jones, the American Consul.

When it came to sailing, Lay, who had still not fully recovered from dysentery, 'conceiving he should be able to make some valuable discoveries & better promote the ends of science, got leave to remain behind'. Collie officially took over as Naturalist until they returned to Oahu eight months later. Having failed to get adequate supplies of bread on Oahu, the ship headed north-west stopping for a day on the small island of Oneeheow (Ni'ihau) to pick up 60 barrels of yams, and 20 of sweet potatoes that they had ordered and paid for, but had to make do with 20 barrels of the former. Here they collected a grass that Hooker & Arnott would later name after the captain as *Panicum beecheyi*.

1.2.2. Northern latitudes

The *Blossom* arrived at Petropaulski on Awtaschka Bay of the Kamchatka peninsula on 28 June 1826, where the party regained health – aided by fresh food and a week of Russian hospitality under the Russian governor Captain Stanitski. In Peard's words they were uplifted by 'the Note of the Cookoo [which] was most grateful to our ears, and put us in mind of old England'. It was here, however, that they received a letter that revealed that half of the reason for their trip, the Parry expedition, had already given up – the *Fury* abandoned at Somerset Island in August 1825 and the party retreated to London on its consort the *Hecla*. But there was still Franklin who might require help, so they sailed for Alaska on 5 July via St Lawrence Island, reaching Chamisso Island in Kotzebue Sound on 25 July, a mere ten days after the date agreed between Beechey and Franklin. There was no sign of Franklin so they left supplies and headed northwards up the coast in the *Blossom* for a month's surveying, launching the barge, under the charge of the Ship's Master Thomas Elson, to investigate the shore-line. In Escholtz Bay Collie, with Belcher's help, investigated the strange frozen cliffs, full of fluvio-glacial deposits rich in the bones of bison, deer, horse and mammoth tusks, discovered by Otto von Kotzebue in 1816 (during the Russian expedition of 1815–18, on the ship *Rurik*, with the naturalists J.F. von Eschscholtz and Adelbert von Chamisso, whose collections were frequently referred to by Hooker & Arnott). The Esquimaux were friendly, though the exotic food that they offered (blubber, walrus and 'unicorn [i.e., narwhal] flesh') was loftily dismissed; supplies (with marker posts) for

History of the Blossom voyage

Fig. 9. Crew of the *Blossom's* barge erecting a post for Captain Franklin near Refuge Inlet, Alaska.
Steel engraving by Edward Francis Finden, after a drawing by William Smyth, from the octavo edition of Beechey's *Narrative*. London 1831.

Franklin were deposited at various points (FIG. 9), and at Cape Krusenstern Beechey commented on the buttercups, vaccinium, saxifrages, crucifers and poppies. The *Blossom* reached as far as the Icy Cape, but the barge reached Point Barrow, a further 126 miles to the north-east. The two vessels were reunited at Chamisso Island in early September, where they waited for Franklin for a further month, the danger of becoming ice-bound getting ever greater, before sailing for San Francisco on 14 October. It later emerged that on 18 August Franklin and his party had reached 'Return Reef' a mere 146 miles east of Port Barrow only five days before Elson's party reached the latter with the barge; Franklin had turned back to over-winter at Fort Franklin on the Great Bear Lake, then headed south and met up with John Richardson at Cumberland House in June 1827 and returned to Britain.

1.2.3. The Pacific again

The *Blossom* entered the Golden Gate of San Francisco, then part of Mexico, on 7 November 1826 and stayed for seven weeks, where they were greatly helped by William Hartnell, a British merchant who had become a naturalised Mexican. The ship's supplies were low, and little was obtainable at San Francisco, so Collie, with one of the ship's clerks, John Evans, and the purser, George Marsh, were despatched the 120 miles to Monterey on a six-day expedition by horseback, to try to obtain medicines and stores for the boatswain and carpenter. It was probably on this excursion that Collie collected seed of the spectacular, scarlet, fuchsia-flowered gooseberry, *Ribes speciosum*, which had first been collected hereabouts by his predecessor Archibald Menzies, surgeon on Vancouver's voyage, around 1793 and described by Friedrich Pursh in 1814. It is not known if very many seeds were collected by Lay or Collie, but it is recorded that in 1828 the latter gave these highly desirable ones from Monterey to the botanist Aylmer Bourke Lambert; the shrub flowered in Lambert's garden in 1832 whence they were described and illustrated by John Lindley the following year.

The *Blossom* stopped off at Monterey from 1 to 5 January 1827 to pick up stores that had been arranged by Hartnell (cocoa, sugar, salt beef and potatoes), augmented by 920 gallons of rum brought from the American brig *Harbinger*, but Beechey had decided to cross the Pacific to get the much needed medicines and ship's supplies at Macao, stopping off at Hawaii for nearly six weeks *en route*.

The ship reached Oahu on 26 January where the party was reunited both with Lay, who had collected nothing during his Hawaiian sojourn, and with the British Consul Richard Charlton who had returned from Tahiti. While on Oahu Collie treated a sailor suffering from an unpleasant skin complaint, of the legs and feet, with the local plant 'ava' (*Piper methysticum*), of which he took supplies for future use. Almost no details are known of where particular botanical collections were made, but from the details given for the cucurbit *Sicyos pachycarpus* it is clear that Collie visited the volcanic Diamond Head Crater (Leahi) on one of his visits to Oahu, either in 1826 or 1827. The majority of the Hawaiian collections were presumably made on this longer, second visit, amounting to 160 species of flowering plant, of which Hooker & Arnott described 41 as new; it was also by far the most productive 'locality' of the trip for ferns (and fern allies), with 53 species collected, of which 14 were new. It was either on this or the previous visit to Hawaii that 'many of the specimens were ... packed in cases ... [in a] whale ship that brought them home' (KDC 44 ff 34–5). It was to their remaining for three years in these cases that Beechey later attributed 'the bad condition of part of the collection'.

On 1 March the *Blossom* sailed from Hawaii, heading due west. They anchored at Typa, the outer harbour of Macao, on 11 April, but their reception by the Chinese Hong merchants was frosty – their ship was not a merchant one, but an armed British warship, and the sailors were considered 'barbarians'. During the almost three weeks spent there, despite an unhealthy climate, and being the only accessible, and therefore best known part of China, some interesting plant collections were nonetheless made. These included almost 30 new species and two new genera. The latter included the legume genus, with a single species, that Hooker & Arnott named after Tradescant Lay – *Layia emarginata*, a large, evergreen shrub with yellow flowers (FIG. 2). Hooker & Arnott had earlier, but provisionally, named a Californian genus of Compositae

History of the Blossom voyage

after Lay, and, paradoxically, it is this that has been 'conserved', the legume now being known as *Ormosia emarginata*. With a certain amount of diplomacy between British East India Company officials and the Chinese authorities in Canton, Beechey was able to obtain food, water and medicines, and set off north for a second summer of waiting, and exploring the Alaskan coast.

En route for Kamchatka they stopped at the Loo Choo (Ryukyu) islands, at the harbour of 'Napa-kiang' (now Naha) on the island of Okinawa, and at the Bonin Islands or Yslas del Arzobispo (now the Ogasawara-gunto Group). They spent nine days in May based at Naha taking on water, refitting the ship, and to allow the recovery of some of the sailors from sickness contracted in China. The Loo Choo inhabitants were hospitable and, in addition to plant collecting (about 120 species, of which about 11 were new), the party took a great interest in the culture of the island (written about by Basil Hall who had visited in 1816); Collie, remembering his promise to Andrew Combe, measured the heads of some of the natives. The only new marine alga of the trip was collected here, the brown seaweed *Dictyota spinulosa*. From 9 to 16 June Beechey explored, and claimed for Britain, the Bonin Islands – anchoring in a harbour he named Port Lloyd (after the Bishop of Oxford), on what he named Peel Island (after the then Secretary of State for the Home Department), now Chichijima, the largest of the group, then uninhabited. The harbour abounded in green turtles and the party observed columnar basalt like that of the Giant's Causeway. George Peard recorded that 'our botanists met with a number of rare plants' – about 42 species of flowering plant were collected (which subsequently became mixed with the Mexican ones), of which 12 were new – including *Carex boottiana*, a handsome sedge of rocky coasts. The party also cut down (but failed to make herbarium specimens of) some 20 to 30 foot palms, *Clinostigma savoryana*, which Collie described as a 'cabbage tree', an excellent antiscorbutic, the 'top shoot' of which, when boiled, tasted like sea kale or asparagus.

On 3 July the party was back at Petropaulski, where they stayed for two weeks. George Peard recorded a botanical ramble made with Collie on 12 July 'over the hills and through the woods by the sea shore to Avatcha, a village ... where we were hospitably entertained by Mr. Tolman an American Settler'. Though 'one of those Serpentine districts said to be inimical to Vegetation ... the ground was covered with beautiful wild flowers of different kinds, and the shrubs, plants, grass &c were growing in great luxuriance. We observed a species of Cedar tree (the Pinus combra), two kinds of Willow, and the alder, but the common tree of the country is the Birch'. Peard also noted that the 'root of the Saranna' (*Fritillaria kamtschatcensis*) was 'in general use and held in great estimation either plain boiled as a Vegetable, or forming a component part of bread. Various kinds of Wild berries grow in abundance, and an indifferent wine is made from them. The Wild Garlic gives a very disagreeable flavour to the milk and butter'. During the two visits to Kamchatka some 88 species of flowering plant were collected, though of these the only novelties were two species of *Carex* and a *Potentilla* variety.

The party once again set sail for Chamisso Island, which they reached on 4 August, and though the 'cotton grass [was] in full bloom' the weather was to prove far worse than in the previous year.

1.2.4. Second Alaskan visit and return to Britain

There was no sign of Franklin's party, so Beechey continued his explorations of the Alaskan coastline, with the help of the barge this time under the command of Edward Belcher, the *Blossom's* Assistant Surveyor. Tragedy struck when the barge was wrecked – three sailors died and Belcher (for the second time on the trip) was lucky to escape with his life. On 27 September Collie, with Wainwright, Marsh, Lay and Peard went ptarmigan shooting, but it was not only birds that were killed – there were several unpleasant incidents with the Esquimaux, at least one of whom was shot. The party stayed around Kotzebue Sound until 5 October. Between the two visits to Alaska the party collected 191 species of flowering plant, but, given the earlier North American collections worked on by Hooker, very few of these were new to science (one new species of *Salix*, and varieties of an *Anemone*, a *Saxifraga* and an *Artemisia*).

The *Blossom* sailed to California, landing at Monterey on 29 October. They made a trip to San Francisco, where they stayed for two weeks, before returning to Monterey from where they sailed on 5 January 1828, for San Blas in Mexico where they learned of Franklin's safe arrival at Liverpool on 26 September of the previous year. To the annoyance of Collie and the crew, Beechey decided to stay for three months in Mexico, ostensibly surveying the coast, but really to load up with 'specie' – silver ingots, raw silver ('plata piña') and dollars – on which the captain (alone) would receive a commission of 1½ percent on that safely returned to Britain. Beechey justified this as due to the disturbed political situation and the doubtless genuine desire of British merchants, under the consul George Barron, to get their wealth shipped out of Mexico. During a trip up the coast, more dollars were collected from Mazatlan. Time was spent at Tepic, a commercial town 40 kilometres inland from San Blas, and at the adjacent town of Xalisco (spelt 'Talisco' by Hooker & Arnott) at the foot of Mount San Juan. Collie was upset by the delay and what he considered the base motive for it, but he put the time to good use, and from Tepic and Talisco almost 80 new species (including *Antigonon leptopus*, the ice-cream creeper, now a pantropical weed) and five new genera were collected, before the departure of the silver-laden *Blossom* from San Blas on 8 March. Acapulco was the next port of call (12 to 18 March) where the ship's bowsprit was mended and turkeys taken on board.

The crew must by this time have been glad to leave North America, reaching Valparaiso in Chile on 29 April. They remained here three weeks, taking yet more cash on board, strangely, from Collie's old ship the *Doris*, and it was here that Beechey heard of his promotion from Commander to Captain, by order of the Duke of Clarence, Lord High Admiral (later King William IV,

History of the Blossom voyage

his father's patron, to whom Beechey would in due course present copies of his own account of the voyage and of the first part of Hooker & Arnott's *Botany*). Although they had been here for two days in October 1825, it was probably on this occasion that the 32 species of flowering plant (13 new to science), were collected from Valparaiso. A trip to Coquimbo followed, 350 km north up the coast, where they felt an earthquake – to pick up more silver, which by this time amounted to 1.5 million dollars! The riches of this penultimate stop, however, were not limited to precious metal, for Coquimbo is in one of the richest areas of Chile for endemic plants, and though Lay & Collie collected only 28 species of flowering plant during their eleven days here, 17 of these were described as new. These included a mistletoe, parasitic on cacti, described as *Loranthus cactorum* (now known as *Tristerix aphyllus*), *Cordia decandra*, which is now a threatened species due to its use for making charcoal, and the strange, hemiparasitic *Krameria cistoidea*. From Coquimbo the *Blossom* sailed on 3 June; there was a final stop at Rio, and after a transatlantic crossing of 49 days the *Blossom* was paid off at Woolwich on 12 October 1828.

1.2.5. In Britain: division of the spoils

1828 was an epic year for the arrival of large and exotic botanical collections in London: in July Nathaniel Wallich had arrived from Calcutta with the vast treasure of the East India Company's S and SE Asian herbarium, and these were closely followed by the Pacific collections of the *Blossom*. Hooker evidently lost no time in writing to Beechey offering to describe the latter, working as he was on Franklin's and Richardson's North American collections for his *Flora Boreali-Americana*. Beechey consulted Barrow and both agreed that Hooker was the best man for the job but, being tactful, Beechey warned of 'a delicacy in at once depriving' Lay of the opportunity of so doing (KDC 44 f. 9). The specimens were duly packed up and sent to Hooker by 31 October, and it was 'Mr Barrow's wish that you [Hooker] would select one specimen of each kind for the British Museum, one for Edinburgh [i.e. for Robert Jameson's University Museum], one for yourself, and return the others to me' (KDC 44 ff 12–3). This division of the spoils is not exactly what happened, and when (soon afterwards) Beechey discovered from Hooker how sparse the duplicates were he asked for these to be returned to Barrow, where hopefully the set he had promised to Collie could be separated (KDC 61 ff 16–7). Beechey was at this point wildly over-optimistic in hoping that the botanical work 'should appear by the middle of March next [i.e. 1829]'! The intention was that the *Botany* would accompany Beechey's official 'publication of the Voyage', which he initially hoped would be published by John Murray, but which appeared an impressively short time later (in 1831) under the imprint of Colburn & Bentley.

Beechey undertook the publishing negotiations – with the Treasury, for a grant to cover preparation and engraving of illustrations, and the ticklish task of finding a publisher for a specialist scientific work. He was quickly successful with the first (KDC 44 ff 15–6), and by 28 May 1829 had obtained a grant of £700 to cover the plates of the botany and zoology volumes, of which Beechey thought £250, later raised to £300, could be spent on the *Botany* – giving Hooker discretion over what to illustrate but asking that they should be rare or new plants not included by Franklin. To do justice to the plates the format of the work was to be *quarto*. Hooker intended to draw the plates himself (probably a way of making at least a little pin money), but had not explained this to Beechey. Not knowing this Beechey must have queried the cost and Hooker taken offence, leading to an outpouring of mortification from Beechey's pen – fearing Hooker might have understood it as an accusation of 'connecting your own advantage', that is, over-charging for his own work (KDC 44 ff 17–8). The question of finding a publisher will be discussed below.

CHAPTER 2
The supplements and other Chinese collections

In addition to the *Blossom* collections, starting in the seventh part of the *Botany* (1838), Hooker & Arnott extended the scope of their work, with two substantial supplements dealing with related material. The first treating David Douglas's later Californian collections; the second Mexican specimens collected by Andrew Sinclair. As noted in the Introduction 'non-*Blossom*' material was also used in the section on China.

2.1 California: David Douglas

The renowned plant collector David Douglas was one of William Hooker's most successful and devoted protégés. His story has often been told (Hooker, 1836; Harvey, 1947; McKelvey, 1955; Mitchell & House, 1999) and the following account relies heavily on Harvey's account. Although the twenty-four year old Douglas left Glasgow Botanic Garden in 1823 to work for the Horticultural Society of London, he continued to repay his perceived debt to Hooker with information and specimens from his three American expeditions (though little, if any, from his first to north-eastern USA and Ontario, as this was primarily horticultural). The second expedition to the Columbia River, thence overland to Hudson's Bay, was a different story, and the collections from that trip, along with those of Thomas Drummond and John Richardson, formed the basis of what is considered Hooker's finest solo botanical work on flowering plants, his *Flora Boreali-Americana* (1829–40) treating the plants of the part of North America under British sway (through the medium of the Hudson's Bay Company). Douglas was no 'mere' collector: he named and described plants, and provided detailed background information in his diaries, those of the second trip eventually being published in 1914.

The third trip of 1830–4 is the one with which we are concerned here, as the collections from it form the basis of Hooker & Arnott's 'California Supplement'. The trip famously ended in tragedy in a bull pit in Hawaii, but there were other disasters before this, of which the worst was the destruction of Douglas's Californian botanical notes and diaries. For this reason it is impossible to know the collecting details for the considerable riches of this trip beyond the stark 'California' on the specimens in the herbaria of Hooker, Arnott and others.

In 1827 Douglas had returned in triumph from his second trip – to adulation in metropolitan horticultural circles on account of the large number of outstanding plants successfully introduced into cultivation. He then spent two increasingly unhappy years in London, before being sent to California by the Horticultural Society (on an annual salary of £120), with additional support from the British Government and the Hudson's Bay Company, and training in surveying from Captain Edward Sabine, brother of Douglas's friend and supporter Joseph Sabine, Secretary of the Horticultural Society. Douglas went by ship via Cape Horn and spent six months in the Pacific Northwest (Columbia River and Blue Mountains) before sailing for Monterey in California, which he reached on 22 December 1830. He was to spend the next 19 months there, far longer than he initially intended.

Hooker & Arnott (p. 316) stated that Douglas's Californian collections were made 'chiefly at Monterey and San Francisco, (at no great distance from the coast)'. Despite the tragic loss of Doulgas's relevant notes and diaries, from letters to his brother John, to Hooker, and to George Barnston, McKelvey (1955: 399–405) and others have been able to piece together something of the dates and itineraries of Douglas in California in 1831. Douglas was based in Monterey where he was greatly assisted by the British merchant W.E. Hartnell, who had been so useful to Beechey in San Francisco in 1826; Douglas was also greatly helped in California by Franciscan brothers at their network of mission stations. In February 1831 Douglas made an expedition to the east and north of Monterey, including San Juan Bautista, Santa Cruz and Santa Clara during which he saw the coast redwood (*Sequoia sempervirens*). In May a trip south to Santa Barbara was made, and in July/August an excursion to San Francisco and the Mount Diablo part of the Coast Range, in which he reached as far north as Fort Ross. The collections, amounting to about 500 species, were made largely between March and June after which the vegetation, especially the colourful annuals, became completely burned up; in November 1831 he met up with Thomas Coulter who was in Mexico collecting for A.P. de Candolle. Douglas appears to have collected much less in 1832, due at least in part to the disturbed political situation in the early, botanically productive, part of the year – though he continued to study conifers, one of his greatest interests. It should be noted that while in California Douglas received a copy of Beechey's recently published *Narrative*, but took issue with its negative account of the Franciscans.

Douglas left Monterey on 18 August 1832, to return to the Columbia River via Hawaii. From Honolulu he sent 19 bundles of his Californian collection of dried plants, to be split between the Horticultural Society and Hooker, but it was here that he discovered the difficulties that had recently beset the Society and resigned from its service. Hooker was thrilled with his share and wrote 'what a glorious collection has Douglas sent to me from California! ... I think I scarcely ever in a collection of such an extent saw so much that is new and

The supplements and other Chinese collections

rare'. Douglas reached the Columbia River (for the third time) in October 1832, and from here, in March 1833, started a great journey to the north (to the area known as New Caledonia, in what would become British Columbia), intending to reach the Russian settlement of Sitka and return to Britain overland through Russia. This was not to happen, and in June he turned back from Fort St James, and it was in a boat accident on the Fraser River on 13 June that Douglas lost his botanical notes, diaries, and collections representing 400 species. He returned to Fort Vancouver in August 1833, where he met up with two of Hooker's pupils working as Hudson's Bay Company surgeons – Meredith Gairdner and William Fraser Tolmie. Douglas then sailed for Hawaii, which he reached in December, and where he was killed the following July.

Location of Douglas material

At Edinburgh are duplicates sent by Hooker to Arnott; there are also some in R.K. Greville's herbarium, probably sent him by Bentham. There are also Douglas specimens in Lindley's herbarium at Cambridge (CGE). At Kew not all of the Douglas material described in the California Supplement has been found. The material at Kew includes the specimens sent directly by Douglas to Hooker, but there is also much in Bentham's herbarium, presumably duplicates retained by him from the set of the Horticultural Society (of which he was Secretary from 1830), many with a printed 'Douglas California, 1833' label – the date presumably referring to the date they were received from Hawaii. Many of the Douglas sheets from Bentham's herbarium had not previously been recognised as types. Perhaps, being duplicates, they tended not sent to be on loan to monographers and therefore missed being annotated, and doubtless many were not picked up when the great sweeping into red covers that took place at Kew in 1940 (prior to the partial evacuation of the herbarium), when Hooker material was perhaps considered more important than Bentham's. The Horticultural Society's own set (1460 specimens) was sold to the BM in 1856, and should still be there, though it has not been searched for in the research for the present work. Douglas material is also to be found in Asa Gray's herbarium (Harvard, GH), in John Torrey's herbarium (New York Botanical Garden, NY), in the Komarov Institute, St Petersburg (LE), and the Fielding-Druce Herbarium at Oxford (OXF).

In the *Botany of Captain Beechey's Voyage* Hooker & Arnott described about 65 species, and five genera, of Douglas's Californian collections as new.

2.2 The 'California' collections of 'Tolmie'

The other important collection used by Hooker & Arnott for their 'California Supplement' was made neither in the place, nor by the person in whose name the specimens were recorded! This is the 'Californian' collection of W.F. Tolmie. As explained above Tolmie was a pupil of Hooker, who met Douglas at Fort Vancouver in 1833. The collection was made four years later, by a 'friend of Mr Tolmie' whose name Hooker & Arnott did not record (and may not have known). They were, however, aware of the circumstances during which this small, but exceptionally rich collection was made. The occasion was the 1837 'meeting of the [Hudson's Bay Company] Beaver Trappers, who, to the number of 500 or 600, are scattered through the Rocky Mountains and adjacent country ... held that year in the valley of the "Green River" [now in Wyoming], a stream which is considered to be probably the main branch of the Rio Colorado'. Tolmie's friend had travelled to this extraordinary annual rendezvous (the thirteenth such event) from Fort Vancouver, via the Blue Mountains [in present day Oregon], and the Snake River [largely in present-day Idaho]. With considerable powers of detection Susan McKelvey (1955: 627–635) was able to piece together the story of this collection – the collector proving to be a Hudson's Bay Company fur trader called John McLeod; McKelvey even found a list of the collection numbers and localities. Hooker & Arnott neglected to transfer the numbers to the specimens, though as some localities provided only a single collection, the numbers for at least those can be deduced. Of a mere 77 collections at least 20 were described as new species.

2.3 Mexico: Andrew Sinclair and H.M.S. *Sulphur*

The third of the major collections treated in the *Botany of Captain Beechey's Voyage* is that in the 'Mexico Supplement' (part 9, 1840) made on the voyage of H.M.S. *Sulphur* between December 1837 and February 1838. In fact, some of these were made at Realejo – then in 'Guatemala', now in Nicaragua. As with the South Sea collections Hooker & Arnott had little idea of the importance of accuracy in the matter of plant distribution and thought that the flora of Guatemala and Mexico were so similar 'judging from what little we know of it ... that we have no hesitation in including all under the general head of Mexican Plants'. The other collecting localities (San Blas, Tepic, Acapulco) had previously been visited on the *Blossom* voyage.

The reason for the inclusion of these plants is that the *Sulphur* was initially under the command of Captain Beechey, undertaking survey work on the western coast of the Americas. Beechey had learned a lesson from the poor quality of the *Blossom* specimens and this time 'built a place [on the ship] ... for the preservation of specimens'; he asked Hooker's botanical advice 'Is there anything worth looking for upon the Falkland Islands?' (KDC 62 ff 13–4), and (having clearly read Humboldt) on indicator species he should look out for that might provide useful information on altitudinal zonation (KDC 62 ff 19–20). Hooker was not quick enough to recommend his own surgeon-naturalist, but the appointment of Andrew Sinclair as surgeon, and Richard Brinsley Hinds (1811–46) as his assistant, as reported to Hooker by Beechey in September 1835 (KDC 62 ff 13–4), proved satisfactory. At the request of King William IV a 'collector (a better sort of gardener) from Kew' (KDC 62 ff 19–20) was added to the complement in the person of George Barclay. Due to illness Beechey had to return home in, or soon after, June 1836 (after only six months of the voyage), but he made arrangements with Sir John Barrow

The supplements and other Chinese collections

that 'Dr Sinclair shall collect specimens of Botany for you [Hooker] – and Mr Hinds for Professor Lindley' (KDC 62 ff 21–2), later asking Barrow that Barclay's plants should also go to Hooker (KDC 63 ff 23–4).

After Beechey's departure, the command of the *Sulphur* was given in 1837 to Edward Belcher. In 1839 Sinclair also had to leave the voyage due to ill health, when the ship stopped surveying the American coast and was ordered to cross the Pacific. Here it became embroiled in the first Opium War with China and the *Sulphur* was not to reach England again until July 1842 having been away for seven years. Belcher published a 'Narrative' of the voyage in 1843. Oddly, it was only a very discrete part (in terms of date) of Sinclair's collections that were treated in the 'Mexican Supplement', the other botanical collections of the *Sulphur*, made by Hinds and Barclay, were described between 1844 and 1846 by George Bentham in *The Botany of the Voyage of H.M.S. Sulphur*. Hinds was interested in physical influences (climate and soil) on plant distribution and wrote an account along these lines, 'Regions of Vegetation', for Belcher's *Narrative* (also issued as a separate) and several 'spinoff' papers in Vol 1 of *Hooker's London Journal of Botany* (1842), and in Vols 9 (1842) and 15 (1845) of the *Annals and Magazine of Natural History* (one of the botanical editors of which was J.H. Balfour). Charles Darwin may have considered Hinds's work 'pompous and very poor' (letter to Hooker 19 iii 1845) and others have rated them no higher, with the result that they have been almost entirely overlooked. This biogeographical approach, however, was a striking advance compared with Hooker & Arnott's lack of interest in such matters with regard to the *Blossom* collections.

In total Hooker & Arnott described about 40 species, and two genera, of Sinclair's Mexican collections as new.

2.4 China: Charles Millett & the Rev. G.H. Vachell

With the return of specimens to the Admiralty, while in the middle of their Chinese account, Hooker & Arnott decided to make use of additional material from China in their own herbaria, largely that of Charles Millett and the Rev. George Harvey Vachell. Millett was an East India Company official who worked in Ceylon, and at Canton and Macao. Little is known of him, but Wight & Arnott dedicated a well known leguminous genus to him, and several species, including *Cleyera millettii* and *Caesalpinia millettii*, were named for him in the present work. Equally little is known of Vachell, a chaplain to the East India Company factory at Macao from 1828 to 1836.

The Millett specimens were given to Hooker, who passed duplicates of them to Arnott – these latter (at E) usually do not have Millett's name, just the details 'Canton, Dr Hooker'. The Vachell specimens came 'through the medium of the Rev. Professor Henslow of Cambridge', who seems to have sent them independently to Hooker and to Arnott (and also some to R.K. Greville, which have also ended up at E). It should be noted that original material of several taxa based on both Millett, and Vachell specimens, has not been found at K.

CHAPTER 3
The Hooker & Arnott collaboration

3.1 Arnott's contribution

References to his work on the *Botany of Captain Beechey's Voyage* are scattered through Arnott's letters to W.J. Hooker. The first to imply his involvement is on 20 February 1830 (KDC 1 f. 8), when Hooker was getting material ready, and Beechey was still trying to find a publisher. On 10 Mar 1832 (KDC 3 f. 18) Arnott thanked Hooker for getting 'the Beecheyan No. [part 2] finished'. On 7 Jan 1833 Arnott was putting off an intended visit from the Indian botanist Robert Wight for a week, in order to 'let me attend a little to Beechey next No. [part 4]' (KDC 3 f. 41) and on 10 February, he was working specifically on Beechey's [Californian] Compositae (KDC 3 f. 43). In July 1833 Wight had written to Hooker begging him to take off Arnott's hands 'the remainder of this number [part 4] of Beechey' so that he could concentrate on helping Wight with their joint *Prodromus Florae Peninsulae Indiae Orientalis* (KDC 3 f. 58). On 19 January 1834 Arnott told Hooker he would 'with pleasure work with you at Beechey or the [Botanical] Miscellany' when the *Prodromus* was published (KDC 3 f. 59), which duly occurred in August 1834. 'From Novr. 1 1834 to the middle of May 1835' (KDC 3 f. 95) Arnott was back at work on Beechey, which must refer to part 5, on China, not published until 1836. In 1838 are several references – on 4 Mar (KDC 10 f. 5) Arnott was working on the Loo Choo and Bonin plants (for part 6), with the help of Thunberg's *Flora Japonica*, and probably on 7 March (KDC 10 f. 6) he was returning the Loo Choo and some of the Mexican specimens to Hooker in Glasgow; on 5 June 1838 Hooker evidently had enough material to finish a part [6], but Arnott considered that he ought to work on Wight's vast influx of specimens from India, rather than on Beechey (KDC 10 f. 9). On 31 Oct 1838 (KDC 10 f. 15) Arnott had been 'three days hammering away at the Mexican Corolliflorae [for part 7]', and on 20 July 1839, Arnott was working on what must have been part 9 (KDC 12 f. 17). It must be emphasised that these references were picked up when scanning the Arnott correspondence primarily for his collaborative work with Robert Wight and much may have been missed. In particular it is inconceivable that Arnott was not heavily involved in the final, tenth, part published in 1841, but prepared at a time when Arnott was working exceptionally hard for Hooker – lecturing and editing in Glasgow, while Hooker was in London canvassing for the Kew job.

3.2 Hooker's contribution

Unfortunately there is no source of information on the parts on which Hooker worked, though he certainly did his share, concurrently with his solo work on *Flora Boreali-Americana*. Many specimens in Hooker's herbarium (K) bear a ticket annotated by Arnott with the name and collecting details ('B' for Beechey), sometimes with rough, as opposed to Hooker's fine, drawings, suggesting that Arnott did the work on these taxa, and returned them (sometimes unicates) to Hooker. Some specimens at K have manuscript names attribute to Hooker alone, not the 'H & A' of the later ones. Some specimens at E bear bits of letters from Hooker to Arnott commenting on specimens (FIG. 2). One important part of the work that can unambiguously be assigned to Hooker, however, is the making of the drawings for the 100 plates of the book (FIGS 10, 11). Details of the surviving original drawings are listed in Appendix III; those of new taxa being of particular importance as they form part of the original material of those species.

3.3 Publication history

The protracted publication history of the *Botany* can, as noted by Stafleu (1965), be tracked in letters from Beechey to Hooker between 1828 and 1843 in the Director's Correspondence at Kew. This is not, however, always easy to follow – not so much from Beechey's bad handwriting (though bad it is), as from his maddening habit of dating many letters with the day and month, but not the year, and their resultant subsequent binding out of chronological order. What is revealed is the previously unrecorded fact that no fewer than four publishers (and three printers) were involved. The correspondence resonates strongly to this day – both with the difficulty of finding a commercial publisher willing to take on a specialist publication with a limited market, but also the long timescale required for such projects and wildly unrealistic initial estimates as to timescale!

At the start Beechey hoped that the eminent publisher John Murray would take on his own *Narrative* of the voyage, and the related volumes on natural history. Murray prevaricated, but in November 1829 declined 'having anything to do with the Botany' (KDC 44 f. 22) on the grounds that he had 'not sold thirty copies of Franklin's Zoology', at which point Beechey seems to have asked Hooker to find his own publisher. At this time Hooker was using Treuttel & Würtz for his and Greville's *Icones Filicum* and for his own *Flora Boreali-Americana*, but Beechey himself persisted; in December 1829 he approached Adolphus Richter, the London manager of Treuttel & Würtz, but Richter was unwilling to take it on until he saw how Hooker's other *Flora* would sell (KDC 44 ff 23–4). The persistence bore fruit and on 5 Feb 1830 Beechey could tell Hooker (KDC 44 ff 26–7) that 'I have at last found a Publisher for the Botany,

The Hooker & Arnott collaboration

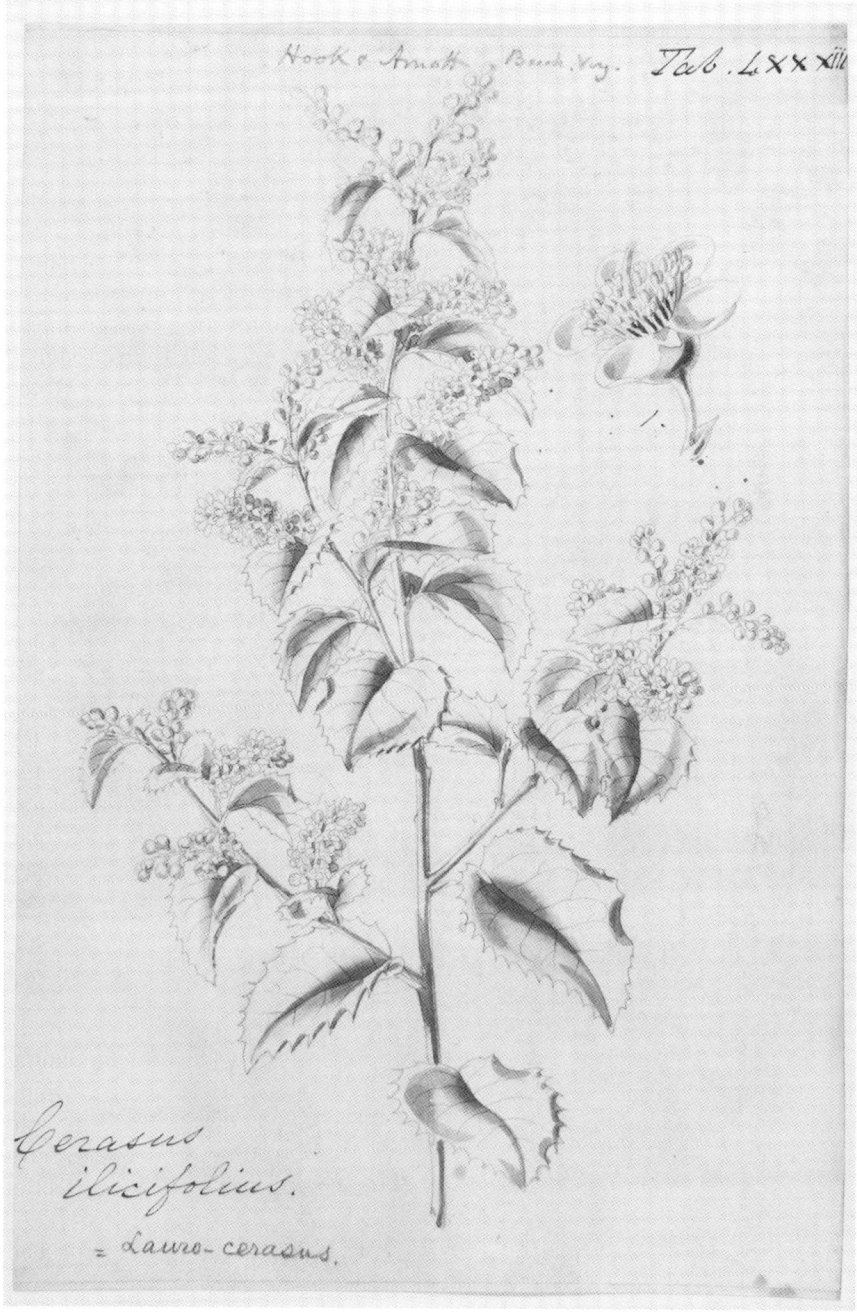

Fig. 10. Original drawing of *Cerasus ilicifolius*, by W.J. Hooker (pencil and sepia wash). Royal Botanic Garden Edinburgh (from the collection of H.F.C. Cleghorn).

30 Chapter 3

Fig. 11. Engraving of *Cerasus ilicifolius* by Joseph Swan, Tab. LXXXIII of the *Botany of Captain Beechey's Voyage*.
Royal Botanic Garden Edinburgh (from the copy owned by H.F.C. Cleghorn).

The Hooker & Arnott collaboration 31

in Messrs. Colburn and Bentley', of New Burlington Street, the terms having been arranged the previous month: 'I am to furnish them with the M.S.S. and plates ready for issuing – they are to pay for the paper of the engravings and all other outgoings' (KDC 44 f. 25).

Busy as he was, it seems that Hooker did not actually start work until he received this news, as on 12 February 1830 he asked Beechey for confirmation of details including the format; that there was £300 to cover the drawings and plates; and that the publisher was merely paying for the 'printing & paper & the necessary expenses of getting the book [out]' (KDC 44 f. 28). Hooker later (KDC 44 ff 39–40) stated that £300 would cover the cost of drawing and engraving 100 plates, the number finally made; the £30 per part was apparently the only payment he received for his work. For ease of supervision and proof-reading Hooker insisted that the printing of both letterpress and plates was done in Glasgow. Part 1 was printed by the firm of Curll & Bell, Parts 2–4 by Bell & Bain, and probably most of the remainder by Edward Khull the University Printer; the plates were all engraved by Joseph Swan (FIG. 11). Hooker undertook to 'supply the Mss as fast as it can be printed' and told Beechey that 'I have procured the assistance of a zealous Botanist'. No mention of poor Arnott's name here or at any other point in the entire correspondence between Beechey and Hooker! In March Beechey confirmed that Richard Bentley had agreed to the work being printed in parts in Glasgow, and that the print run would be 250 copies 'after which the plates are to be sold, and the money to be appropriated to the liquidation of a debt which must be incurred' (KDC 44 ff 30–1). Hooker was to receive 12 complimentary copies and Beechey had earlier asked for a similar number to present to 'heads of Departments &c' (KDC 44 f. 22).

Now that work was underway it became obvious that the *Botany* was going to be a far more substantial work than originally envisaged – clearly more than 200 pages, and eventually 485. This started the first warning bell ringing for Bentley who agreed to continue only if Beechey could get the 'Government to take fifty copies' (KDC 44 ff 7–8) – this probably happened, as, despite further negotiations with Treuttel & Würtz, Part 1 was published by Colburn & Bentley (as were both quarto and octavo editions of Beechey's *Narrative*, in 1831). Beechey had received his copy of Part 1 by 14 December 1830 (KDC 61 ff 18–9), having the previous month urged Hooker to produce it by 1 December as 'I purpose about that time presenting a copy of the other two volumes [presumably the *Narrative* and *Zoology*] to His Majesty [King William IV] and it is very desirable that a specimen of the Botanical part should accompany them'. The first part was too much for Colburn & Bentley and having 'discovered that the letter press has very far exceeded the limits proposed, have unceremoniously refused to proceed with the publication' (KDC 61 ff 18–9). This is probably not surprising as Henry Colburn and Richard Bentley, better known as publishers of novels, were in 1831 on bad terms and in financial difficulty, their partnership being dissolved the following year. Beechey presented a handsomely bound copy of the first part to the King at a *levée* some time before 25 February 1831 (KDC 61 ff 37–8), but sadly this copy is no longer in the Royal Library (Emma Stuart, pers. comm.).

An hiatus in publishing the *Botany* followed. Beechey returned to Adolphus Richter of Treuttel & Würtz who in January 1832 agreed to continue the publication 'on the same terms as Messrs. Colburn & Bentley, except that the coppers of the engravings are to be their property ... The work is to appear in 10 Nos. of 6 sheets each, and from nine to eleven plates in every No ... You are to have 13 copies ... [but] there are to be only 125 copies printed in future' (KDC 61 ff 26–7). Under Richter's management the British branch of the distinguished Paris and Strasburg house of Treuttel & Würtz (based at 30 Soho Square) was an altogether more suitable publisher for a scientific work – as noted earlier they were already publishing Hooker's *Flora Boreali-Americana* and *Icones Filicum*, and other major works including Wallich's *Plantae Asiaticae Rariores*, J.E. Gray's *Illustrations of Indian Zoology* and H.T. De La Beche's *Geological Notes*. Richter behaved handsomely and even offered to pay for colouring of the botanical plates, but this was scarcely possible, being made from dried specimens; optimistically Beechey 'pledged myself that the numbers shall succeed each other as expeditiously as possible, and I hope you [Hooker] will assist me in fulfilling my engagement'! The printer had clearly not been told of the change in publisher, and there is reference to reprinting the covers of a part with Colburn & Bentley's name (KDC 61 ff 26–7), which must refer to Part 2. Beechey had not yet received his copy of this second part on 7 Feb 1832 (KDC 62 f. 25), though must have done so shortly thereafter as he had reimbursed Hooker's expenses for it (£30/3/10) on 2 February (KDC 61 f. 34). On 17 June 1832, in view of his promise to Richter, Beechey was chivvying Hooker for the third part 'as some of his subscribers have threatened to withdraw their names unless the Nos. follow more closely upon each other', though Hooker (not forgetting the elusive Arnott) were still ahead of the zoologists – no part of the *Zoology* had yet appeared and Beechey had been 'waiting sixteen months for Mr [J.E.] Gray's shells' (KDC 61 ff 28–9). Beechey received copies of Part 3 on 13 November 1832 and thought the publishers must be 'well pleased with the spirited manner in which the engravings have been got up' (KDC 61 ff 30–1). Hooker's expenses on Part 3 were reimbursed on 17 Nov 1832 (KDC 61 f. 34) and at this point he was working on Part 4, which appeared a year later, in October 1833 (paid for on 5 December 1833 – KDC 61 f. 34). After this part followed another hiatus due to Richter's financial difficulties and on 29 September 1835 (about to leave on the voyage of the *Sulphur*) Beechey wrote to Hooker 'As regards our publisher I have been waiting month after month in the hope of being able to acquaint you with his recommencing business, but he has not yet arranged his affairs' (KDC 62 ff 13–4). By October 1836 Richter had at least temporarily recovered and 'was going on again' (KDC 62 ff 8–9), and issued Part 5 (which treats Chinese plants) before November 1836, despite the date of this part given by Stafleu (1965) and Stafleu & Cowan (1979) as 'Jul–Aug 1837'.

However, 1836, the traditional date of Part 5, given by Jackson (1893 – on the basis of dates of generic names published by Pfeiffer), under various plant names in *Index Kewensis*, on annotations on the copies in New York Botanical Garden, and by Rickett (1945), is undoubtedly correct. Beechey's reference to the part is in a letter of 15 November that maddeningly has no year (KDC 62 ff 21–2). But on circumstantial grounds it is far more likely to be 1836 than 1837. This letter was written from his father's house, 18 Harley Street, but Beechey stated that he was about to go to Worthing, almost certainly referring to a recuperative stay after his illness on the *Sulphur*, referred to in a letter from Worthing dated 24 October 1836: by autumn 1837 Beechey was returned to health and on duty in the Irish Sea on H.M.S.V. *African*. Stafleu (1965) made no comment on the change of the date, which, given its previously universal citation as 1836, makes it virtually beyond doubt that it is a typographical error (another striking one on the same page is that Jackson's initials are given as 'D.D.' rather than 'B.D.').

Part 5 was still published by Richter, but his financial troubles were far from over and he was 'bankrupted before the copies came from Glasgow' (KDC 69 f. 25). Beechey, had, therefore, once again, to find a new publisher for both 'his' *Botany* and *Zoology* (KDC 62 ff 17–8). This time it was Henry G. Bohn of 4 York Street, Covent Garden, who took them on and Bohn had published Part 6 of the *Botany* by July 1838. From his ship at Rostrevor, on 12 June 1839, Beechey acknowledged a letter from Hooker informing him of the publication of Parts 7 and 8 (KDC 63 f. 25). The implication is that the two parts had been published together, but this may have been a misunderstanding and Stafleu gave Dec 1838 for Part 7, and Jan–May 1839 for Part 8. In the same letter Beechey was pleased to hear of Joseph Hooker's appointment to the 'South Polar expedition'. By January 1840 only £160 of the original £700 Treasury grant was left, which would allow for plates for only two more parts of the *Botany* (£60), as Bohn was asking for the remaining £100 'for remuneration of expenses he has been at in getting the work (Zoology and Botany) together and bringing it forward' (KDC 63 ff 23–4). Because the scope of the work had by now stretched to include other material, especially that of Sinclair from the *Sulphur* also under Beechey's patronage, Beechey bargained with Bohn over the publication of further parts, but this was not possible. The Treasury money was exhausted and the final numbers of the *Botany of Captain Beechey's Voyage* were Part 9 in Feb/Mar 1840, and Part 10 in Jan/Jun 1841.

As already noted the original print run was, even for the date and nature of the work, exceptionally small, but it was not until 1965 that Stafleu published a facsimile edition. However, in the meantime, some of the plates had been re-issued in lithographic facsimile. Some of these are present in the 'Plates Collection' at the Natural History Museum, and plates 80–100 of the Linnean Society of London's copy of the *Botany* are represented by these facsimiles.

The binding of this copy appears to be nineteenth-century, so these plates probably date from the latter-half of that century – the original printing of some of the engravings would appear to have become exhausted and lithographs made to enable copies of the whole work to be made up.

3.4 Dates of publication

Various attempts have been made to ascertain the important matter of the publication dates of the various parts, notably Benjamin Daydon Jackson (1893); H.W. Rickett (1945) and Frans Stafleu (1965). Important also are the manuscript notes on J.H. Barnhart's copy at New York Botanical Garden where copies of the first four parts in their original covers (dated to year) fortunately survive. Stafleu also used the Beechey/Hooker correspondence at Kew (but made no comment on their problematic dating).

Part 1. pp 1–48, tt. 1–10. Dec 1830 [cover dated 1831] (published by Colburn & Bentley, London; printed by Curll & Bell, Glasgow). Edition 250.
Part 2. pp 49–96, tt. 11–20. Jan/Feb 1832 (published by Treuttel & Würtz, Treuttel Jun. & Richter, London; printed by Bell & Bain, Glasgow). Edition for this and subsequent parts 125.
Part 3. pp 97–144, tt. 21–29 *bis*. Oct/Nov 1832 (published by Treuttel & Würtz, Treuttel Jun. & Richter, London; printed by Bell & Bain, Glasgow).
Part 4. pp 145–192, tt. 30–39. Oct 1833 (published by Treuttel & Würtz, Treuttel Jun. & Richter, London; printed by Bell & Bain, Glasgow).
Part 5. pp 193–240, tt. 40–49. Jul/Aug 1836* (probably published by Treuttel & Würtz, Treuttel Jun.,& Richter, London).
Part 6. pp 241–288, tt. 50–59. Jul 1838 (published by Henry G. Bohn, London).
Part 7. pp 289–336, tt. 60–69. Dec 1838 (published by Henry G. Bohn, London).
Part 8. pp 337–384, tt. 70–79. Jan/May 1839 (published by Henry G. Bohn, London).
Part 9. pp 385–432, tt. 80–89. Feb/Mar 1840 (published by Henry G. Bohn, London).
Part 10. pp 433–485, tt. 90–99. Jan/Jun 1841 (published by Henry G. Bohn, London; printed by Edward Khull, Glasgow).

* Note – a correction to TL2.

CHAPTER 4
Alphabetical list of new taxa

Layout of entries:
Name, authority, place of publication. Date. (CURRENT FAMILY PLACEMENT).
 N.B. Only names attributable to Hooker & Arnott are treated, those attributed by them to other authors (e.g. Bentham, Nees) though first published in this work are only included if they have in the past been (mistakenly) attributed to Hooker & Arnott, or for other specified reasons. These 'non-Hooker& Arnott' names are enclosed in square brackets, and names that are not validly published in double quotation marks.
Original material cited.
 Original material seen at E (barcode cited, where present).
 Original material seen at K (barcode cited, where present).
Notes. References to relevant literature are cited in abbreviated form within the text (rather than in a separate bibliography).
Accepted name.

4.1 PHANEROGAMS

ANGIOSPERMS
Abutilon albidum Hook. & Arn., Bot. Beechey Voy. 6: 278. 1838, *nom. illeg.* (MALVACEAE).
Original material: Tepic, Mexico, Lay & Collie.
 None found at E or K.
Note. Although the synonym 'Sida albida Willd.?' is cited, the expression of doubt means that this should be treated as a new species based on the Beechey material, rather than as a new combination. It is, however, an illegitimate homonym of *A. albidum* (Willd.) Sweet (1826) (based on *Sida albida* Willd., from the Canary Islands).
 Not treated by P.A. Fryxell in his Malvaceae of Mexico (Syst. Bot. Monog. 25. 1988), and merely listed as a name in his *Abutilon* nomenclator (Lundellia 5: 82. 2002).

"*Acacia cavenia* Hook. & Arn.", Bot. Beechey Voy. 1: 21. 1830. (LEGUMINOSAE). Although Hooker & Arnott intended to make a new combination citing 'Mimosa Cavenia. Molin. [Sag. Stor. Nat.] Chil. [354. 1782]', this is an

orthographic variant of *M. caven* on p. 174 of the same work, to which exactly the same diagnosis was applied, so Hooker & Arnott are considered to have published the combination "*Acacia caven* (Molina) Hook. & Arn." ('*cavenia*'). However, this is a later isonym of *Acacia caven* (Molina) Molina, Sag. Stor. Nat. Chili, ed. 2, pp 163, 299. 1812. A neotype for *Mimosa caven* Molina was designated by J. Aronson in Ann. Missouri Bot. Gard. 79: 963. 1992. (J. McN.).
Note. Sometimes placed in the genus *Vachellia* as *V. caven* (Molina) Seigler & Ebinger.
= ***Acacia caven*** (Molina) Molina

Achyranthes velutina Hook. & Arn., Bot. Beechey Voy. 2: 68. 1832. (AMARANTHACEAE).
Original material: 'Bow Island', Lay & Collie; specimens from Owhyhee collected by Mr Menzies, and ones from Oahu collected by Mr Macrae are also mentioned.
 At E: a sheet ex herb. Arnott (E00369197), annotated by him with the name and 'Bow Island – Beechey' – this was annotated as isotype by J. Florence in 1998.
 At K: a sheet ex herb. Hooker bears two specimens and it is not entirely clear to which the tickets belong, though both are original material; the one in Arnott's hand annotated with the name and 'Bow isld., Beechey' perhaps belongs with that on the left; the other is the Menzies collection and is annotated in an unknown hand with the name and 'A.M.'. The Beechey specimen was annotated 'lecto[type]' by J. Florence in 1998, but it is not known if this typification has been published.
≡ ***A. aspera*** L. var. ***velutina*** (Hook. & Arn.) C.C. Towns.

Adenostoma Hook. & Arn., Bot. Beechey Voy. 3: 139. 1832. (ROSACEAE).

Adenostoma fasciculatum Hook. & Arn., Bot. Beechey Voy. 3: 139, t. 30. 1832 (as '*fasciculata*'). (ROSACEAE).
Original material: 'Sandy plains in the Bay of Monterey', California, Lay & Collie.
 A sheet at E, ex herb. Arnott (E00369051), annotated by him with the name and 'California', though lacking the name 'Beechey', may be original material (if it were a later Californian collection it is likely to have been annotated as having come from Hooker).
 No Beechey material at K, where in the type cover are only later collections of Douglas and Coulter; there is one earlier one 'California at Monterey 1792', possibly a Menzies specimen, but this is not original material.

Alphabetical list of new taxa 37

Adesmia angustifolia Hook. & Arn., Bot. Beechey Voy. 1: 19. 1830. (LEGUMINOSAE).
Type: 'Valparaiso. *Mr. Bridges*'.
  No type material at E: those ex herb. Arnott and annotated by him with this name are other collections: *Mathews* 181, *Cuming* 617 (1831).
  Type at K: the central specimen (K000328011) on a sheet ex herb. Hooker annotated by him with the name and 'Chili, Bridges' (the other specimens are King, and Cuming, collections).
= **Adesmia tenella** Hook. & Arn.

Adesmia conferta Hook. & Arn., Bot. Beechey Voy. 1: 20. 1830. (LEGUMINOSAE).
Type: 'Chili. *Mr. Cruckshanks*'.
  No type material at E: those ex herb. Arnott and annotated by him with this name are other collections: *Bridges* 9 (1832), *Cuming* 296, 297 (1831).
  Type at K: the central specimen (K000329287) on a sheet ex herb. Hooker annotated by Hooker 'Chili, Mr Cruickshanks', it does not bear the name in Hooker's hand, but has a later annotation 'presumably the type of Adesmia conferta Hook. & Arn.', which, indeed, it is.

Adesmia glutinosa Hook. & Arn., Bot. Beechey Voy. 1: 19. 1830. (LEGUMINOSAE).
Original material: 'Coquimbo', Chili, Lay & Collie.
  None found at E.
  At K: the upper specimen (K000222500) on a sheet ex herb. Hooker annotated by him with the name and 'Beechey's Voy.' – it was annotated 'type' by I.M. Johnston, but it is not known if this has been published (the other, Gay, collection is not original material).

Adesmia microphylla Hook. & Arn., Bot. Beechey Voy. 1: 19, t. 9. 1830. (LEGUMINOSAE).
Original material: 'Valparaiso', Chili, Lay & Collie. A specimen of Menzies is also mentioned. It is also noted that 'it has also been gathered by Mr. Macrae', though no specimen of his is cited.
  At E: a specimen on a sheet ex herb. Arnott, annotated by him 'Valparaiso, Beechey' (the other two specimens on the sheet, *Mathews* 220, *Cuming* 609, bear the name in Arnott's hand, but are not original material).
  Of the numerous collections on the four sheets in a type cover at K probably none represents original material. Two of these sheets bear the name and reference in Hooker's hand: each of these bears two collections – one has Bridges and Mathews material, the other Bridges and Cuming; the two other sheets do not have the name in Hooker's hand and bear collections by Harvey, Macrae, Cuming, Coppinger: of these only the Macrae might possibly be considered original material.

Adesmia tenella Hook. & Arn., Bot. Beechey Voy. 1: 19. 1830. (LEGUMINOSAE).
Syntypes: 'Chili. *Mr. Cruckshanks*. Hills near Valparaiso, *Mr. Bridges*'.

A sheet at E, ex herb. Arnott, has two specimens both annotated by him with the name, but neither can be a type – although the left-hand one is annotated 'Valparaiso, Bridges 1832. No 8' it cannot, from the date, be a type, neither can the other specimen (*Cuming* 618).

Two sheets, ex herb. Hooker at K bear types. On one, bearing the name in Hooker's hand, the upper specimen (K000328006) is a syntype annotated by Hooker 'Chili, "Leg. biarticulatum" Mr Cruickshanks' (the lower specimen, *Cuming* 618, is not a type). The central specimen (K000328008) on the second sheet is probably the other syntype, though the ticket bearing the name and 'Valparaiso, Bridges', in what is probably Arnott's hand, is placed ambiguously and is closer to one of the other two specimens (ex herb. Martius) that are not types and were identified by Skotsberg as *A. angustifolia*.

Alisma andrieuxii Hook. & Arn., Bot. Beechey Voy. 7: 311. 1838. (ALISMATACEAE).
Original material: Tepic, Mexico, Lay & Collie; '*Andrieux Pl. Mexic. Exsicc. n. 91*'.

None found at E.

At K: two sheets, both ex herb. Hooker, both remounted. One (K000098521) bears a leaf and an inflorescence, and a ticket cut from the original sheet annotated by Hooker with the name and 'Mexico, Beechey'. The other (K000098522), bears a whole plant and part of an inflorescence, and has the Andrieux field ticket with number '91'.

Note. Althought the wording of the protologue (and the epithet given) is ambiguous Fassett (Rhodora 57: 176. 1955) was probably correct to take the Beechey material as that on which the description was chiefly based. He had seen a drawing of the Beechey specimen at K and effectively lectotypified on this; the sheet was accordingly annotated 'lectotype' by L.B. Holm-Nielsen & R.R. Haynes in 1988.

However, Hooker and Arnott also stated 'the same species was found by M. Andrieux about Tehuantepec of Oaxaca', for which they cited the number '*Andrieux Pl. Mexic. Exsicc. n. 91*' – so this must also be considered as part of the original material. The Andrieux sheet at K was mistakenly annotated 'holotype' by C.S.K. Rataj in 1967, and (correctly) as 'syntype' by Holm-Nielsen & Hayes in 1988.

≡ ***Echinodorus subalatus*** (Mart.) Griseb. subsp. ***andrieuxii*** (Hook. & Arn.) R.R. Haynes & Holm-Niels.

Alisma virgata Hook. & Arn., Bot. Beechey Voy. 7: 311. 1838. (ALISMATACEAE).
Original material: Tepic, Mexico, Lay & Collie.

Isolectotype at E: a sheet (E00369232) annotated by Arnott with the name

Alphabetical list of new taxa 39

and 'Mexico, Beechey'. This is one of the sheets given to E by GL in 1902, with a printed 'Herb. Walker Arnott' label.

Lectotype at K: a sheet (K000098919) ex herb. Hooker, annotated by him on the sheet with the name and 'Mexico, Beechey' – this was annotated 'holotype' by C.S.K. Rataj in 1967, and was published as 'holotype' by Hayes & Holm-Nielsen (Fl. Neotropica 64: 65. 1994).

≡ *Echinodorus virgatus* (Hook. & Arn.) Micheli

Allium falcifolium Hook. & Arn., Bot. Beechey Voy. 9: 400. 1840. (ALLIACEAE). Original material: 'collected by Douglas in California'.

None found at E.

At K, two possible sheets. One ex herb. Hooker bears a ticket of drawings annotated with the name by Hooker and must surely be original material, but it does not have Douglas's name and the other ticket attached to the sheet, also with the name in Hooker's hand, gives the collecting details as 'Snake Country, Tolmie'. A sheet ex herb. Bentham, bears two collections: the left-hand one, bearing a printed Horticultural Society label 'Nova California, Douglas 1833', must be original material and closely resembles those on the Hooker sheet (the right-hand specimen, *Rattan* s.n., is not original material).

Allocarpus scabrifolius Hook. & Arn., Bot. Beechey Voy. 7: 300. 1838. (COMPOSITAE).
Original material: 'Talisco', Mexico, Lay & Collie.

At E: a sheet ex herb. Arnott (E00369135), annotated by him with the name and 'Talisco in Mexico, Beechey'.

None found at K.

≡ *Calea scabrifolia* (Hook. & Arn.) Hemsl.

Alyxia sulcata Hook. & Arn., Bot. Beechey Voy. 2: 90. 1832. (APOCYNACEAE). Original material: Sandwich Islands, Lay & Collie.

At E: two sheets, both ex herb. Arnott (E00098772, E00098773), annotated by him with the name and 'Oahu, Beechey' – these are isolectotypes (see below).

D.J. Middleton (Blumea 47: 56. 2002) designated a specimen at K (that can no longer be found) as lectotype, with an iso[lecto]type at G.

= *Alyxia stellata* (J.R. & G. Forst.) Roem. & Schult.

Amirola glandulosa Hook. & Arn., Bot. Beechey Voy. 1: 12. 1830. (SAPINDACEAE).
Original material: 'Coquimbo', Chili, Lay & Collie.

None found at E.

At K, the top left-hand specimen (K000586268) on a sheet ex herb. Hooker is annotated by him 'Conception, Beechey' – although the locality disagrees with that in the protologue, beside this specimen is a ticket with drawings annotated by Arnott 'Amirola glandulosa n. sp. Conception, Beechey' strongly

suggesting that this is original material (collections of Cuming, and of Bridges, mounted on the same sheet are not).
≡ ***Llagunoa glandulosa*** (Hook. & Arn.) G. Don

Amsinckia vernicosa Hook. & Arn., Bot. Beechey Voy. 8: 370. 1839. (BORAGINACEAE).
Original material: California, Douglas.

At E: a sheet ex herb. Arnott (E00288414), annotated by him with the name and 'California. D[avid] D[ouglas] per Hooker' – this was annotated '(?iso-)type' by Per Lassen in 1985.

At K, two sheets. One ex herb. Hooker with two specimens – the left-hand one, annotated by Hooker 'Amsinckia' to which someone has added, in pencil, the epithet and 'California, Douglas', beside it a ticket with drawings by Hooker and annotated by him with the name – this was annotated 'lectotype' by P. Lassen in 1981, but it is not known if this has been published (the other specimen, *Coulter* 496, is not original material). The second sheet is ex herb. Bentham, bearing a printed 'California, Douglas 1833' label, annotated with the name and reference by Bentham – this was annotated 'isotype' by P. Lassen in 1986.

Andropogon tahitensis Hook. & Arn., Bot. Beechey Voy. 2: 72. 1832. (GRAMINEAE).
Original material: 'Society Islands', Lay & Collie.

None found at E.

At K: a sheet ex herb. Hooker, bearing a ticket annotated by Arnott with the name and the collecting details 'Coral isld., Beechey'; also attached is a ticket with drawings annotated by Hooker 'Andropogon'.
= ***Cymbopogon refractus*** (R. Br.) A. Camus

[*Andropogon vachellii* Nees [var. α], in Hook. & Arn., Bot. Beechey Voy. 6: 243. 1838. (GRAMINEAE).
Note. Not being enclosed in square brackets by Hooker & Arnott, both the description and name of the typical variety, α, are attributable to Nees, though it has been cited in Index Kewensis and elsewhere as 'Nees ex Hook. & Arn.'
= ***Bothriochloa bladhii*** (Retz.) S.T. Blake].

Andropogon vachellii [var.] β *perfectior* Hook. & Arn., Bot. Beechey Voy. 6: 243. 1838. (GRAMINEAE).
Original material: Vachell n. 50 [in part]; specimens from Mr. Millett.

At E: a sheet ex herb. Arnott bearing two specimens. One (E00369234) is annotated by Arnott '*Andropogon vachellii* β. Macao; Revd. Mr Vachell, [n.] 50, per Prof. Henslow'; the other (E00369235), 'Canton; [per] Dr Hooker', is doubtless the Millett specimen.

At K: a remounted, partial, Hooker sheet bearing a printed Vachell label, lacking a number, with the details 'About Macao Nov–Dec 1830', annotated

Alphabetical list of new taxa 41

with the species name in a later hand – it appears to be the form with a more branched inflorescence, and therefore original material of var. β.
= ***Bothriochloa bladhii*** (Retz.) S.T. Blake

Anemone narcissiflora L. [var.] β *uniflora* Hook. & Arn., Bot. Beechey Voy. 3: 121. 1832. (RANUNCULACEAE).
Original material: Kotzebue's Sound & American coast of Behring's Strait, from lat. 67° to 71°, Lay & Collie.
 A sheet at E (E00369001), ex herb. Arnott, bears three specimens: the top left-hand one is original material, annotated by Arnott '"Anemone narcissiflora" Kotzebue Sound Beechey' (the others, from Siberia and the Pyrenees, do not belong to the same subspecies).
 No original material found at K – a Beechey specimen annotated 'Kodiak, NW A[merica]' is a multi-headed form.
= ***Anemone narcissifolia*** L. subsp. ***sibirica*** (L.) Hultén

Anemopsis Hook. & Arn., Bot. Beechey Voy. 9: 390. 1840. (SAURURACEAE).
Coined as a new name for 'Anemia [sensu] Nutt.' [1829], i.e., non O. Swartz (1806).

Anemopsis californica (Nutt.) Hook. & Arn., Bot. Beechey Voy. 9: 390, t. 92. 1840. (SAURURACEAE). [California].
Basionym cited: '*Anemia californica* Nutt. in Tayl. Ann. Nat. Hist. I *p*. 136. [1838]'.

"*Anguria dubia* Hook. & Arn.", Bot. Beechey Voy. 7: 292. 1838. (CUCURBITACEAE).
The name is written as '*Anguria*? *dubia*?', followed by a description and it seems doubtful that this was intended as a binomial – rather as a strong expression of doubt as to whether the relevant specimen actually belonged to the genus. Although it is given as a name in Index Kewensis, it is not validly published, and later (l.c., p. 424) Hooker & Arnott renamed it *Bryonia attenuata* (see below).
 No cited material (Tepic, Mexico, Lay & Collie) found at E or K.
= ***Cayaponia attenuata*** (Hook. & Arn.) Cogn.

Anisopappus Hook. & Arn., Bot. Beechey Voy. 5: 196. 1836. (COMPOSITAE).

Anisopappus chinensis Hook. & Arn., Bot. Beechey Voy. 5: 196. 1836. (COMPOSITAE).
Original material: Chiefly ... about Macao, Lay & Collie.
 None found at E. A specimen at E annotated by Arnott 'Anisopappus chinensis H & A, Verbesina chinensis Willd. Canton, [per] (Dr Hooker)' is likely to be a Millett specimen, and although it bears the name in Arnott's hand is not original material.

None found at K.

Note. This has generally been taken as a new combination based on *Verbesina chinensis* L., Sp. Pl. 901. 1753) – apparently first by Bentham (Fl. Honkong. 180. 1861), more recently by Jarvis (Order out of Chaos 917. 2007). However, the synonymy was queried: 'Verbesina Chinensis. *Linn.*?', and given the query Hooker & Arnott's name cannot be assumed to be based on *V. chinensis*. The ICBN establishes that inclusion of a synonym with an expression of doubt does not make the new name of a new taxon nomenclaturally superfluous (Art. 52 Note 1), but does not specifically refer to a potential basionym cited with an expression of doubt. However, a proposal made to the Nomenclature Section of the XIV IBC in Berlin to treat such a name as a new combination was rejected. Consequently *A. chinensis* should be taken as a new species, validated by the generic description and not as a new combination, even though the two names apply to the same species. (J. McN.).

Note. If no original material comes to light, it would be possible to select as neotype the Osbeck specimen ('habitat in China') at LINN that Wild (Kirkia 4: 51. 1964) selected as type of *A. chinensis*, thereby ensuring that the two names were homotypic. It might, in fact, be argued that Wild (l.c., p. 50) has already done this by citing this specimen as type of *A. chinensis*, even while treating that name as based on *V. chinensis* L. (J. McN.).

Anoda lanceoloata Hook. & Arn., Bot. Beechey Voy. 9: 411. 1840. (MALVACEAE).
Original material: 'Tepic to San Blas', Mexico, Sinclair.
   None found at E.
   At K: the left-hand specimen (K000528407) on a sheet ex herb. Hooker, with a ticket annotated by ?Arnott with the name, and in pencil, in another hand, 'Tepic to San Blas Mexico' – this was annotated 'type' by P.A. Fryxell in 1980, and lectotypified (as 'holotype') by him in Syst. Bot. Monog. 25: 94. 1988 (the other specimen is a later, non-type, Anthony collection).

[*Anthistiria caudata* Nees, in Hook. & Arn., Bot. Beechey Voy. 6: 245. 1838. (GRAMINEAE).
Original material 'Prope Macao et in vicinis insulis, *G.H. Vachell, n.* 46 (ex parte)'.
Note. Although in Index Kewensis this name was cited as 'Nees ex Hook. & Arn.', Hooker and Arnott cited 'N. ab E. in Herb. Lindl.' after the first short Latin description, implying (by analogy with *A. vachellii*) that the description and name are by Nees (i.e., Nees in Hook. & Arn.), as was understood by e.g., N.L. Bor (Grasses Burma Ceylon India Pakistan 250. 1973).
≡ ***Themeda caudata*** (Nees) A. Camus].

Antigonon leptopus Hook. & Arn., Bot. Beechey Voy. 7: 308, t. 69. 1838. (POLYGONACEAE).
Original material: Tepic, Mexico, Lay & Collie.

At E: a sheet ex herb. Arnott (E00369199), annotated by him with the name, reference, and 'Mexico, Beechey'.

At K: a sheet ex herb. Hooker annotated by him 'Mexico Beechey'. It bears three specimens and an early curator has noted that these represent two different taxa – the two left-hand are annotated only with the generic name 'Antigonon'; that on the right (K000585041) is the original material, annotated 'Antigonon leptopus Hook. et Arn. Beech. tab. 69, vix Benth.'

Note. This shows that the 'original' material was not always a single collection.

Antigonon platypus Hook. & Arn., Bot. Beechey Voy. 7: 309. 1838. (POLYGONACEAE).
Type: '*Andrieux Plant. Mexic. exsicc. n.* 117'.
Not found at E.
Type at K: a sheet ex herb. Hooker, annotated by him with the name, and bearing a field ticket 'G. Andrieux, P. Mexic. exsicc. no 117'.
= **Antigonon cordatum** Mart. & Galeotti

"*Aquilegia macrantha* Hook. & Arn". Bot. Beechey Voy. 8: t. 72. 1839. (RANUNCULACEAE).
This name is not validly published – it appears on the plate but was not accepted by the authors in the simultaneously published letterpress – clearly the plate was engraved before the authors realised that the plant was *A. caerulea* Torr. & A. Gray.

Arabis blepharophylla Hook. & Arn., Bot. Beechey Voy. 7: 321. 1838. (CRUCIFERAE).
Original material: California, Douglas.
None found at E.
At K: the upper specimen on a sheet (K000075450) ex herb. Hooker annotated by him with the name and 'California, Douglas' (the lower, Bolander, collection is not original material); the upper right-hand specimen on a sheet (K000075452) ex herb. Bentham with a printed 'California, Douglas 1833' label, annotated by Bentham with the name and reference (the three other collections on the sheet are not original material).

Arbutus furiens Hook. & Arn., Bot. Beechey Voy. 1: 33. 1830. (ERICACEAE).
Original material: 'Conception', Chili, Lay & Collie.
None found at E or K.
= **Gaultheria insana** (Molina) D.J. Middleton

Arbutus punctata Hook. & Arn., Bot. Beechey Voy. 1: 33. 1830. (ERICACEAE).
Original material: 'Conception', Chili, Lay & Collie.
None found at E or K.
= **Gaultheria insana** (Molina) D.J. Middleton

Arbutus pungens Hook. & Arn., Bot. Beechey Voy. 3: 144. 1832. (ERICACEAE).
Original material: San Francisco (or Monterey Bay), California, Lay & Collie.

At E: a sheet ex herb. Arnott (E00369154), annotated by him with the name and 'California, Beechey', and by him later 'Arctostaphylos Hookeri Don DC 3'.

At K: a remounted partial sheet ex herb. Hooker, not annotated with the name, but bearing the details 'California, Beechey' in Hooker's hand is probably original material.

= ***Arctostaphylos hookeri*** G. Don

Aristolochia taliscana Hook. & Arn., Bot. Beechey Voy. 7: 309. 1838. (ARISTOLOCHIACEAE).
Original material: 'Talisco', Mexico, Lay & Collie.

At E: a sheet (E00369200) annotated by Arnott with the name and 'Mexico, Beechey' – this is one of the sheets given to E by GL in 1902 with a printed 'Herb. Walker Arnott' label.

At K, two sheets. One ex herb. Hooker, bearing two collections, the left-hand one has a ticket annotated by Bentham with the name and 'Talisco, Beechey' and is the original material – it was identified as this species by F. Gonzales in 2000 but he failed to notice its type status (the other specimen, *Barclay* s.n., though also annotated with the name by Bentham is not original material). The second sheet is ex herb. Bentham and also bears two collections: the right-hand one (given him by Hooker in 1845) is original material, and is annotated by Bentham with the name and 'Talisco, Beechey' – F. Gonzales also saw this but failed to annotate it as a type (the other collection, *Lamb* 386, is not original material).

Note. H.W. Pfeifer (Ann. Missouri Bot. Gard. 53: 151. 1966) cited 'Type: Lay & Collie *s.n.*, BM'. Given the lack of other types found at BM this requires checking in case the herbarium citation is a mistake.

Artemisia borealis Pallas [var.] β *lanuginosa* Hook. & Arn., Bot. Beechey Voy. 3: 125. 1832. (COMPOSITAE).
Original material: Kotzebue's Sound & American coast of Behring's Strait, from lat. 67° to 71°, Lay & Collie.

At E, a sheet ex herb. Arnott, bears three specimens: the upper right-hand one (E00369142) is original material, annotated by Arnott 'Artemisia borealis β. Kotzebue Sound, Beechey' (the others are annotated: 'Art. borealis γ wormskioldii. Cape Krusenstern, Beechey' (E00369143); and '"A. borealis α Purshii, A: spithamaea Psh., Arctic Sea, Fr[anklin] Exped.' (E00369144) and are not original material).

None found at K.

?= ***Artemisia borealis*** Pallas

Alphabetical list of new taxa 45

Arundinella glabra Hook. & Arn., Bot. Beechey Voy. 5: 237. 1836. (GRAMINEAE).
Original material: 'Prope Macao; *G.H. Vachell*, "T"'.
 None found at E or K.
Note. This name has been attributed (e.g., in Flora of China 22: 568. 2006) to 'Nees ex Hook. & Arn.', but the name is in square brackets, signifying (see note p 220) an addition solely attributable to Hooker & Arnott.
= **Arundinella nepalensis** Trin.

Arundo henslowiana Hook. & Arn., Bot. Beechey Voy. 6: 248. 1838. (GRAMINEAE).
Type: 'In insula "Danorum" dicta, infra Cantonem; *G.H. Vachell*, in *Herb. Henslow, n.* "U"'.
 Not found at E or K.
= **Neyraudia reynaudiana** (Kunth) Keng ex Hitchc.

Asclepias vestita Hook. & Arn., Bot. Beechey Voy. 8: 363. 1839. (APOCYNACEAE [ASCLEPIADACEAE]).
Original material: California, Douglas.
 None found at E.
 At K, two sheets. One, ex herb. Hooker, bearing two collections: the two left-hand specimens are annotated by Hooker with the name and 'California, Douglas', and attached is a ticket with drawings (the other collection, *Lobb* 55, is not original material). The second sheet is ex herb. Bentham, with a printed 'California, Douglas 1833' label, annotated with the name by Bentham.

Aster filaginifolius Hook. & Arn., Bot. Beechey Voy. 4: 146. 1833. (Generic placement queried). (COMPOSITAE).
Original material: San Francisco (or Monterey Bay), California, Lay & Collie.
 At E: a sheet ex herb. Arnott (E00369115), annotated by him with the name and 'California, Beechey'. It also bears a ticket annotated by Nees von Esenbeck: 'Species valde insignis ad Galatallas accedens sed haud eius generis'. It was annotated 'holotype' by J.P. Saroyan in 1976, but it is not known if this typification has been published.
 None found at K.
Note. Sometimes placed in the genus *Corethrogyne* as *C.filaginifolia* (Hook. & Arn.) Nutt.
≡ **Lessingia filaginifolia** (Hook. & Arn.) M.A. Lane

Aster tomentellus Hook. & Arn., Bot. Beechey Voy. 4: 146. 1833. (Generic placement queried). (COMPOSITAE).
Original material: San Francisco (or Monterey Bay), California, Lay & Collie.
 None found at E or K.
= **Lessingia filaginifolia** (Hook. & Arn.) M.A. Lane

Astragalus didymocarpus Hook. & Arn., Bot. Beechey Voy. 7: 334, t. 81. 1838. (LEGUMINOSAE).
Original material: California, Douglas.
  None found at E.
  At K: three sheets are in a type cover, but of these only one is original material – this is ex herb. Bentham with a printed 'California, Douglas 1833' label annotated by Bentham with the name and reference (the other sheets bear Coulter, and Palmer, collections).

Astragalus ervoides Hook. & Arn., Bot. Beechey Voy. 9: 417. 1840. (LEGUMINOSAE).
Original material: 'San Blas to Tepic', Mexico, Sinclair.
  At E: a sheet ex herb. Arnott (E00369037), bearing a label annotated with the name by ?Hooker, to which Arnott has added 'H & A, Bot. Beech. voy. Supp. San Blas to Tepic (Dr Sinclair)'.
  At K: a sheet ex herb. Bentham (K000478288) with a ticket annotated by Bentham with the name, reference and 'San Blas to Tepic, Sinclair'. In a type cover there is also a sheet (K000478289) ex herb. Hooker annotated by him with the name, but the collecting details are 'Acapulco, Beechey' so it cannot be original material.

Astragalus procumbens Hook. & Arn., Bot. Beechey Voy. 1: 18. 1830, *nom. illeg.*, non Mill., 1768. (LEGUMINOSAE).
Original material: 'Conception', Chili, Lay & Collie.
  None at E: those ex herb. Arnott, bearing the name in his hand, are all later collections (*Cuming* 137, 501, 881; *Mathews* 247; *Bridges* 1832 no. 42).
  None of the collections on any of the three sheets ex herb. Hooker in the type cover at K have the correct details. I.M. Johnston (J. Arnold Arb. 28: 377. 1947) stated that he could not find the type at K.
= ***Astragalus amatus*** Clos

Astragalus prostratus Hook. & Arn., Bot. Beechey Voy. 1: 18. 1830, *nom. illeg.*, non Scop., 1787. (LEGUMINOSAE).
Original material: 'Conception', Chili, Lay & Collie.
  None at E: those ex herb. Arnott, bearing the name in his hand, are all later collections (*Cuming* 734, 736, *Bridges* 1832 no. 46) and belong to a different taxon, having been redetermined by I.M. Johnson as *A. berterianus* (Moris) Reiche.
  At K: a sheet (K000502728) ex herb. Hooker, annotated by him with the name and 'Conception, Beechey', was annotated 'type' by I.M. Johnston, and determined by him as *A. filifolius* Clos; by time he published this typification (J. Arnold Arb. 28: 382. 1947) he had reduced these names to the synonymy of *A. berteri* (the other sheets in the type cover are not original material).
= ***Astragalus berteri*** Colla

Astrephia mexicana Hook. & Arn., Bot. Beechey Voy. 9: 431. 1840. (VALERIANACEAE).
Original material: 'Talisco', Mexico, Lay & Collie – specimens previously identified by Hooker & Arnott as *Valeriana ceratophylla* Kunth; 'San Blas and Tepic', Sinclair.

Specimens of both collections at E, both ex herb. Arnott. The first (E00369106) is annotated by Arnott 'Astrephia mexicana H & A. Talisco, Beechey, "Valeriana ceratophylla" Hook. & Arn. non HBK': this is probably an isolectotype (see below). The later collection (E00369107) has a label annotated with the name by ?Hooker, to which Arnott has added 'H & A, Beech. voy supp. San Blas to Tepic, Dr Sinclair.'

At K: a sheet ex herb. Hooker with a ticket on which the name 'Valeriana ceratophylla HBK' has been crossed out and bearing the details 'Astrephia Mexicana H & A. Talisco, Beechey' in Arnott's hand – though not annotated by F.G. Meyer, it is presumably the sheet he intended as lectotype (cited by him as 'T: *Lay* s.n.! (K)' in Ann. Missouri Bot. Gard. 38: 450. 1951). This Beechey sheet was incorrectly annotated 'paratype' by F.R. Barrie in 1988; the one (K000588338) annotated by Barrie as 'holotype' is not a type – though bearing the name in Hooker's hand it was collected by Barclay at Tepic. Note. This is the earliest description of the taxon at specific rank, but the epithet cannot be transferred to *Valeriana* due to *V. mexicana* DC. (1830).
= **Valeriana apiifolia** A. Gray

Atenia Hook. & Arn., Bot. Beechey Voy. 8: 349. 1839. (UMBELLIFERAE).
= **Perideridia** Rchb.

Atenia gairdneri Hook. & Arn., Bot. Beechey Voy. 8: 349. 1839. (UMBELLIFERAE).
Original material: California, Douglas; 'dry grounds by the Columbia River', Dr Gairdner.

At E: a sheet ex herb. Arnott (E00369082), annotated by him with the name, reference, and 'California & Columbia, [per] Hooker'. There are two specimens on the sheet, and it is not clear whether or not one is from each of the localities. The sheet was later annotated by Arnott 'Edosmia Gardneri [sic] Torr. & Gray'.

At K, two sheets. On a sheet ex herb. Hooker (bearing three specimens belonging to two collections) annotated by him with the name and reference, to which is attached a ticket with drawings possibly by Hooker – the left-hand specimen is original material, annotated by Hooker 'California, Douglas' (the right-hand collection cannot be the Gairdner one, as the field ticket has the locality '… meadows all round Vancouver …'). The second sheet, ex herb. Bentham, also has two collections – the right-hand one, with a printed 'California, Douglas 1833' label, annotated with the name by Bentham, is original material (the other, *Geyer* 576, is not).
≡ **Perideridia gairdneri** (Hook. & Arn.) Mathias

Baccharis absinthioides Hook. & Arn., Bot. Beechey Voy. 2: 57. 1832. (COMPOSITAE).
Original material: 'Conception', Chili, Lay & Collie; 'Valparaiso. (Mr. Bridges)'.
The Lay & Collie material was designated [var.] 'α', the Bridges material [var.] 'β', but neither was given a varietal epithet.

A sheet at E (E00369119), ex herb. Arnott, bears two specimens of what is original material; these probably represent a single collection – against one is a small slip with the Bridges number '56', against the right-hand specimen is Arnott's annotation 'Baccharis absinthioides β. Valparaiso, [per] Dr Hooker' (there are two other sheets, bearing later Tweedie, Gillies and Cuming specimens, annotated by Arnott with Candolle's new combination *Tessaria absinthioides*).

At K: no Beechey material, but two sheets of probable Bridges original material, both ex herb. Hooker. One annotated by Hooker 'Valparaiso, Bridges' has a field ticket initially annotated 'Baccharis gnaphalioides H & A mss' to which Hooker has later added the epithet 'absinthioides H & A'. The other bears two specimens, the left-hand one from Valparaiso has a field ticket for *Bridges* 55, annotated by Arnott 'Pluchea absinthioides H & A' (the other specimen, *Cuming* 822, is not original material).

≡ **Tessaria absinthioides** (Hook. & Arn.) DC.

Baccharis mucronata Hook. & Arn., Bot. Beechey Voy. 1: 30. 1830, *nom. illeg.*, non Kunth, 1820. (COMPOSITAE).
Original material: 'Coquimbo', Chili, Lay & Collie.
This name was illegitimate when published, so when Hooker & Arnott believed they were transferring it to *Diplopappus* (Comp. Bot. Mag. 2: 48. 1836; citing additional specimens *Cuming* 73, *Macrae* s.n.), they were actually making a new name.
The name *Diplopappus mucronata* Hook. & Arn. should be typified on the Beechey material, but as none exists at E or K, the other material becomes significant

At E is a sheet ex herb. Arnott with two specimens: one is annotated by him 'Diplopappus mucronatus H & A, Baccharis mucronatus H & A in Beechey. Valparaiso, ([per] Dr Hooker)', which may be a Macrae duplicate; the other is annotated by Arnott 'Valparaiso. Herb Cuming. no. 73 Horses eat this' – this is an isoneotype (see below). Also at E is a duplicate of *Cuming* 73, ex herb. R.K. Greville. The latter two are isoneotypes (see below).

At K are three relevant sheets, two ex herb. Hooker, one ex herb. Bentham. Of the former, one (K000221497) is annotated 'Diplopappus mucronatus H & A' by Hooker, and 'Valparaiso, Macrae' (it also bears another collection); the second sheet (K000221500) is annotated with both names by Hooker and has the details 'Chili, Cuming'. Bentham's sheet bears two collections: the upper

Alphabetical list of new taxa 49

(K000221498) has a printed 'Herb. Soc. Hort. Lond. Propè Valparaiso, Chili, Macrae 1825' label; the lower (K000221499) is a duplicate of *Cuming* 73 with a printed label annotated by Bentham with the name and reference 'Comp. Bot. Mag. 2. 48'. This latter is annotated 'neotypus' and was published as such by L. Klingenberg (Bibliotheca Botanica 157: 161. 2007, with iso[neo]types at BM, FI-W, P).
≡ ***Haplopappus mucronatus*** (Hook. & Arn.) B.D. Jacks.

Baccharis obovata Hook. & Arn., Bot. Beechey Voy. 1: 30. 1830. (COMPOSITAE). Original material: 'Conception', Chili, Lay & Collie.
　None found at E.
　At K: despite a discrepancy over the locality, a sheet ex herb. Hooker, annotated by him with the name and 'Beechey, Valparaiso', is probably original material – it was annotated 'lectotype' by F.H. Hellwig and published as such by him in Mitt. Bot. Staatssamml. Munch. (29: 217. 1990).

Baccharis rigida Hook. & Arn., Bot. Beechey Voy. 2: 57. 1832. (COMPOSITAE). Original material: 'Valparaiso', Chili, Lay & Collie. Material of Cruckshanks and Bridges is also mentioned.
　None found at E or K.
= ***Baccharis oblongifolia*** (Ruiz & Pavon) Pers.

Baccharis rosmarinifolia Hook. & Arn., Bot. Beechey Voy. 1: 30. 1830. (COMPOSITAE).
Original material: 'Conception', Chili, Lay & Collie.
　At E is a sheet annotated by Arnott with the name 'Baccharis rosmarinifolia Hook. & Arn.', to which he has later added the reference 'DC. n 157' and the name 'B. montevidensis Bert. (not Spreng.)'. This is probably not original material as it is not identified as a Beechey collection and bears another, enigmatic, annotation in Arnott's hand '"Eranthium" Chili, Auth'.
　F.H. Hellwig in Mitt. Bot. Staatssamml. Munch. (29: 133. 1990) designated a lectotype as 'Valparaiso, Captain BEECHEY' at K, but this cannot now be found – none of those annotated by Hellwig at K is marked by him as lectotype, and none with the locality Valparaiso is annotated 'Beechey' (the type locality should, in any case, be 'Conception').
= ***Baccharis linearis*** (Ruiz & Pavon) Pers. subsp. ***linearis***

Bahia gracilis Hook. & Arn., Bot. Beechey Voy. 8: 353. 1839. (COMPOSITAE). Type: 'Snake Fort, Snake Country [Oregon/Idaho border]. [John McLeod per] *Mr Tolmie*'.
　Not found at E.
　A. Cronquist in Intermountain Flora (5: 110. 1994) cited 'holotype at K!' but no such specimen can be found.
= ***Eriophyllum lanatum*** (Pursh) J. Forbes

Barnadesia ulicina Hook. & Arn., Bot. Beechey Voy. 1: 29. 1830. (Generic placement queried). (COMPOSITAE).
Type: 'Coquimbo', Chili, Lay & Collie. Hooker and Arnott stated that this was based on a single specimen ('the only specimen we have ever seen'), but this appears to have been divided as there is material at E and K.
　At E, on a sheet ex herb. Arnott, the bottom left-hand specimen (E00249655) annotated by him with the name, reference, and 'Coquimbo (Beechey)' is part of the type. (The two other collections on the sheet are not types of *B. ulicina*: *Bridges* 1423 (E00249654) is a type of *Chuquiraga revoluta* Fielding & Gardner; and *Cuming* 877 (E00249653) of which there is another sheet at E, ex herb. R.K. Greville).
　Type at K, the top left-hand specimen (K000527893) on a sheet ex herb. Hooker beside which is a ticket annotated by Arnott 'Chuquiraga incana Don affinis Barnadesia? ulicina Hook. & Arn. Coquimbo, Cap. Beechey' – Ezcurra (Darwinia 26: 272. 1985) cited this as 'holotype' but did not annotate the sheet. (The other specimen, *Bridges* 1433, is not a type).
≡ ***Chuquiraga ulicina*** (Hook. & Arn.) Hook. & Arn.

Bartonia micrantha Hook. & Arn., Bot. Beechey Voy. 8: 343, t. 85. 1839. (LOASACEAE).
Original material: California, Douglas.
　At E: a sheet ex herb. Arnott (E00369080), annotated by him with the name and 'California' is probably original material.
　At K: the left-hand specimen on a sheet ex herb. Hooker, annotated by him with the name and 'California, Douglas', is original material (the right-hand specimen, *Elmer* 3233, is not). A specimen ex herb. Bentham with a printed 'California, Douglas 1833' label, despite not being annotated with the name, is doubtless original material.
≡ ***Mentzelia micrantha*** (Hook. & Arn.) Torr. & A. Gray

Berberis andrieuxii Hook. & Arn., Bot. Beechey Voy. 7: 318. 1838. (BERBERIDACEAE).
Original material: 'Andrieux … "*Plantae Mexicanae exsicc. n.* 469"'.
　None found at E, but there is a specimen ex herb. Arnott annotated by him with this name, which is a type of 'B. fraxinifolia Hook. ic. [pl. 4:] t. 239[/30. 1841]', with the collection details 'Jalapa, Galeotti, per Hooker'.
　At K, two type sheets: one (K000497238) ex herb. Hooker annotated on the sheet 'B. inermis Hook., B. Andrieuxii in Bot. of Calif.' with a ticket 'G. Andrieux, Pl. Mexic. exsicc. No. 469. Locus proprius incertus'; the other (K000407237) ex herb. Gay, with a copy of the same Andrieux label.
≡ ***Mahonia andrieuxii*** (Hook. & Arn.) Fedde

Alphabetical list of new taxa 51

Berberis glomerata Hook. & Arn., Bot. Beechey Voy. 1: 5. 1830. (BERBERIDACEAE).
Original material: 'Coquimbo', Chili, Lay & Collie.
   None found at E.
   At K: the lower specimen on a sheet ex herb. Hooker annotated by him with the name and reference 'in Beechey's Voy.' (the upper specimen, collected by E.C. Reed, is not original material). C.K. Schneider in 1906 annotated the sheet 'B. glomerata Hook. et Arn. species mixta est ... species in Coquimbo collect. ad B. zahlbruckneriana pertinent' – clearly this is not only incorrect, but makes no sense, as the single collection from Coquimbo in Hooker's herbarium can be taken as the type, and the species to which Schneider referred it is one of his own, published only in 1905 (the only explanation is that Schneider incorrectly took the second element on the sheet also to be a type, and that it belongs to a different taxon, presumably his own concept of '*C. glomerata*').

Bidens paniculata Hook. & Arn., Bot. Beechey Voy. 2: 66. 1832. (COMPOSITAE).
Original matieral: Society Islands, [by implication Otaheite, Mr. Collie].
   None found at E.
   At K: a sheet ex herb. Hooker annotated by him with the name and 'Tahiti, Beechey'.
= *Bidens australis* Spreng.

Bignonia obovata Hook. & Arn., Bot. Beechey Voy. 10: 439. 1841, *nom. illeg.*, non (Kunth) Spreng., 1825. (Generic placement queried). (APOCYNACEAE).
Original material: 'Realejo', Mexico [now Nicaragua], Sinclair.
   None found at E.
   At K, two sheets: a sheet ex herb. Hooker (K000587861) bearing a ticket annotated by Bentham 'Stemmadenia pubescens, Bignonia? obovata Hook. et Arn. Realejo, Sinclair' – annotated 'holotype' by A.J.M. Leeuwenberg in 1990. The other sheet ex herb. Bentham (K000587860) has the same details and was annotated 'isotype' by Leeuwenberg.
Note. A.J. M. Leeuwenberg (Rev. Tabernaemontana II & Stemmadenia 423. 1994) published the above holotype (though not the isotype), but failed to realise that Hooker & Arnott's name was an illegitimate homonym and that their epithet could not be transferred. Bentham (Bot. Voy. Sulph. 125. 1845) had, however, provided a new name for Hooker & Arnott's plant in *Stemmadenia* (and attributed their misplacement as to family, as due to extraneous fruit/seed material on the Sinclair sheet)
≡ *Stemmadenia pubescens* Benth.

Blumea chinensis Hook. & Arn., Bot. Beechey Voy. 5: 195. 1836, *nom. illeg.*, non DC., 1836. (COMPOSITAE).
Original material: Chiefly ... about Macao, China, Lay & Collie. Hooker &

Arnott also stated that 'It [i.e., their *Blumea chinensis*] is Vachell's n. 202', so this could also, perhaps, be considered original material.

At E: no Beechey material, but a duplicate of *Vachell* 202, ex herb. R.K. Greville, with a printed label, to which has been added the details 'Lappas Island on the Peninsula ... 14 May 14 June [1830]', to which Greville has added 'Prof. Henslow. no. 202'.

None found at K.

Note. It would appear that Hooker & Arnott had not yet seen Vol. 5 of Candolle's Prodromus (1836) as they here referred to that author's earlier treatment: 'This [i.e. their *Blumea chinensis*] ... certainly belongs to De Candolle's genus Blumea, (see Wight's Contrib. p. 13, and Guillemin's Arch. de Bot. 2. p. 514)'. In the Prodromus (p. 366) Candolle had created the genus *Duhaldea* for the plant treated here (and had used the name *Blumea chinensis* for a combination based on *Conyza chinensis* L., p. 444).

= **Duhaldea chinensis** DC.

Boehmeria albida Hook. & Arn., Bot. Beechey Voy. 2: 96. 1832. (URTICACEAE). Original material: Sandwich Islands, Lay & Collie.

At E: a sheet ex herb. Arnott (E00369214), annotated by him with the name and 'Oahu, Beechey'.

At K: a sheet ex herb. Hooker bearing a ticket annotated by Arnott with the name and 'Oahu, Beechey' – it was annotated '♂ type' by C. Skotsberg in 1931.

≡ **Pipturus albidus** (Hook. & Arn.) A. Gray

Boehmeria densiflora Hook. & Arn., Bot. Beechey Voy. 6: 271. 1838. (URTICACEAE).
Original material: 'Loo Choo', Lay & Collie.

At E: a sheet ex herb. Arnott (E00369216), annotated by him with the name and 'Loo Choo, Beechey'.

None found at K.

Borkhausia lessingii Hook. & Arn., Bot. Beechey Voy. 4: 145. 1833, *nom. illeg.*, (*Troximon apargioides* Less. cited as synonym). (COMPOSITAE). [California].
Note. This name is to be typified by Lessing's, but of the material from which Hooker & Arnott made their description is a specimen at E annotated by Arnott 'Borkhausia Lessingii H & A, Troximon apargioides Less. California, Beechey', and later by Arnott 'Macrorhynchus Lessingii H & A. Bot Beech Voy. p. 361'.

≡ **Agoseris apargioides** (Less.) Greene

Bouvardia discolor Hook. & Arn., Bot. Beechey Voy. 9: 428. 1840. (Generic placement queried). (RUBIACEAE).
Type: 'Between Tehuantepec and Voca del Monte, Province of Oaxaca. *Andrieux, Pl. Mexic. exsicc. n. 334*'.

Not found at E.

Type at K: the right-hand specimen on a sheet ex herb. Hooker with Andrieux's field ticket, to which Hooker has added the epithet and reference – this was cited as 'type' by W.H. Blackwell in Ann. Missouri Bot. Gard. (55: 28. 1968), but the sheet is not annotated by him; in 1992 D.H. Lorence annotated this sheet as 'lectotype' of *Rondeletia dubia* Hemsl. (the left-hand specimen, *Seeman* 2057 is not a type).
= **Rondeletia leucophylla** Kunth

Bouvardia scabra Hook. & Arn., Bot. Beechey Voy. 9: 427. 1840. (RUBIACEAE). Syntypes: 'Between San Blas and Tepic', Mexico, Sinclair; '*Hartweg Plant. Mex. n.* 99' (identified by Bentham as *B. obovata* Kunth).

At E are sheets of both syntypes ex herb. Arnott. One (E00369093), bears a label annotated by ?Hooker 'Bouvardia scabra. obovata Benth.', to which Arnott has added 'H & A Beech. voy. Supp. San Blas to Tepic Dr Sinclair'. The other (E00369094), is annotated by Arnott 'Bouvardia scabra H & A. Bolaños, Mexico, Hartweg No. 99, B. obovata [sensu] Benth. vix HBK'.

At K is a sheet ex herb. Hooker, bearing three collections, annotated by him with the name and reference: the left-hand specimen (K000173699) is annotated 'Tepic, Sinclair' and in 1966 this was annotated 'holotype' by W.H. Blackwell, though when he published this (Ann. Missouri Bot. Gard. 55: 27. 1968) he took the locality from the protologue rather than what is actually written on the sheet; also on this sheet is a specimen of *Hartweg* 99 which is clearly a syntype, though Blackwell mistakenly annotated it 'not a type' (even if the name has been lectotypified on the Sinclair material, the Hartweg is still a syntype); the third element on the sheet is *Pringle* 1724 (and not a type). At K is a duplicate of the *Hartweg* 99 syntype ex herb. Bentham, which Blackwell also mistakenly annotated 'not a type' in 1966.

Bouvardia tolucana Hook. & Arn., Bot. Beechey Voy. 9: 427. 1840. (RUBIACEAE).
Type: 'Toluca. *Andrieux, Pl. Mexic. exsicc. n.* 332'.
Not found at E.
Type at K: a sheet ex herb. Hooker (K000173706) with Andrieux's field ticket to which Hooker has added the epithet and reference – it was annotated 'holotype' by W.H. Blackwell in 1966 and published by him as 'type' (with a duplicate at W) in Ann. Missouri Bot. Gard. (55: 23. 1968).
= **Bouvardia ternifolia** (Cav.) Schlecht.

Bouvardia xylosteoides Hook. & Arn., Bot. Beechey Voy. 9: 428. 1840. (RUBIACEAE).
Type: 'On slightly elevated mountains about Mitlam, Province of Oaxaca. *Andrieux, Pl. Mexic. exsicc. n.* 333'.
Not found at E.

A sheet at K, ex herb. Hooker, bears what appear to be two duplicates of a single collection, though there is confusion over the numbering. The upper one is certainly a type as Andrieux's field label has been annotated with the epithet and reference by Hooker who also changed the number from 335 to 333; the lower specimen (ex herb. Gay) has the number '335' unchanged. For some unknown reason 'A.A.B.' (in 1935) annotated the upper specimen 'the number should be, apparently, 335', with which W.H. Blackwell concurred in 1966, but when the latter published this as 'type' (citing duplicates at G and 'F, fragment ex G-Deless.') in Ann. Missouri Bot. Gard. (55: 12. 1968) the number was cited as 333.

Bridelia collina (Roxb.) Hook. & Arn., Bot. Beechey Voy. 5: 211. 1836. (PHYLLANTHACEAE). [China].
Basionym cited: 'Cluytia collina. *Roxb. Cor.* 2. t. 169 [1802]; *Fl. Ind.* 3. *p.* 732. [1832]'.
≡ ***Cleistanthus collinus*** (Roxb.) Benth.

Bridelia diversifolia (Roxb.) Hook. & Arn., Bot. Beechey Voy. 5: 211. 1836. (PHYLLANTHACEAE). [China].
Basionym cited: 'Cluytia diversifolia. *Roxb. Fl. Ind.* 3. *p.* 731. [1832]'.
≡ ***Cleistanthus diversifolius*** (Roxb.) Müll. Arg.

Bridelia loureiroi Hook. & Arn., Bot. Beechey Voy. 5: 211. 1836 (as '*Loureiri*'), *nom. illeg.* ('Cluytia monoica. *Lour. Coch.* 2. *p.* 784' cited as synonym). (PHYLLANTHACEAE).
Cited material: '[specimen] received, about ten years ago, in Sir Wm. J. Hooker's first packet from [China, from] Mr. Millett'.
At E: a sheet ex herb. Arnott (E00369203), annotated by him 'Bridelia Loureirii H & A. Canton, China [per] Dr Hooker'.
At K: the top left-hand specimen on a sheet ex herb. Hooker annotated by him 'China, Mr. Millett' (on the sheet are two other unrelated collections, one from Java)
Note. To the K sheet is pinned a ticket annotated by Arnott with the name and the note 'this I got from you more than 10 years ago: it was in the first packet you ever got from China – we then supposed it a Phyllanthus'.
Note. The name is typified by the material on which the Loureiro name was based.
= ***Bridelia tomentosa*** Blume

Bridelia oblongifolia (Roxb.) Hook. & Arn., Bot. Beechey Voy. 5: 212. 1836. (PHYLLANTHACEAE).
Basionym cited: 'Cl[uytia]. oblongifolia. *Roxb. Fl. Ind.* 3. *p.* 730. [1832]'.
≡ ***Cleistanthus oblongifolius*** (Roxb.) Müll. Arg.

Alphabetical list of new taxa

Bridelia patula (Roxb.) Hook. & Arn., Bot. Beechey Voy. 5: 212. 1836. (PHYLLANTHACEAE).
Basionym cited: 'Cluytia patula. *Roxb. Cor.* 2. t. 170 [1802]; *Fl. Ind.* 3. *p.* 733. [1832]'.
≡ **Cleistanthus patulus** (Roxb.) Müll. Arg.

"*Bridelia stipularis* (L.) Hook. & Arn.", Bot. Beechey Voy. 5: 211. 1836. (PHYLLANTHACEAE).
Basionym cited: 'Cluytia stipularis. *Linn.* [Mant. Pl. 127. 1767]'.
In Govaerts *et al.* (World Checklist Euphorb. 1: 296, 371. 2000) the name *Bridelia stipularis* was attributed solely to Hooker & Arnott and said to be illegitimate. However, Hooker & Arnott were explicitly making a new combination and clearly did not know that Blume had already done so in 1826. Hooker & Arnott's is therefore merely a superfluous combination of **Bridelia stipularis** (L.) Blume, and cannot be a synonym of *Cleistanthus stipularis* (Kuntze) Müll. Arg. as stated by Govaerts *et al.*

Brizopyrum douglasii (Nees) Hook. & Arn., Bot. Beechey Voy. 9: 404. 1840. (GRAMINEAE). [California].
Basionym cited: 'Poa Douglasii**.** *Nees v. Esenb. in Tayl. Ann. of Nat. Hist. v.* I. *p.* 284. [1838]'.
≡ **Poa douglasii** Nees

Brizopyrum spicatum (L.) Hook. & Arn., Bot. Beechey Voy. 9: 403. 1840. (GRAMINEAE). [California].
Basionym cited: 'Uniola spicata, Lin. [Sp. Pl. 1: 71. 1751]'.
≡ **Distichlis spicata** (L.) Greene

Bromus carinatus Hook. & Arn., Bot. Beechey Voy. 9: 403. 1840. (GRAMINEAE).
Original material: California, Douglas.
  At E: a sheet ex herb. Arnott (E00064818), annotated by him with the name and 'California, [per] Hooker' is probably original material.
  At K: a sheet ex herb. Hooker, annotated by him on the sheet with the name, reference, and 'California, Douglas'.

Brongniartia glabrata Hook. & Arn., Bot. Beechey Voy. 6: 288. 1838. (LEGUMINOSAE).
Original material: Tepic, Mexico, Lay & Collie.
  At E: a sheet ex herb. Arnott (E00369038), annotated by him with the name and 'Mexico, Beechey'.
  At K: a sheet (K000297125) ex herb. Hooker annotated by him with the name, reference, and 'Mexico, Beechey'.

Brunellia quadrilocularis Hook. & Arn., Bot. Beechey Voy. 6: 282. 1838. (Generic placement queried). (?RUTACEAE).
Original material: [Tepic], Mexico, Lay & Collie.

At E: a sheet (E00369035), annotated by Arnott with the name and 'Acapulco, Beechey' – this is one of the sheets given to E by GL in 1902 with a printed 'Herb. Walker Arnott' label. There is a discrepancy over the locality, but 'Acapulco' could simply have been omitted from the protologue, leading to the assumption that it came from Tepic.

None found at K.

Note. In his monograph of Brunelliaceae (Fl. Neotropica 2: 177. 1970) José Cuatrecasas, who had not seen a specimen, wrote 'From the description it can be stated that this plant does not belong to the Brunelliaceae. It might well be a member of the Rutaceae'.

Brunellia sandwicensis Gaud. ex Hook. & Arn., Bot. Beechey Voy. 2: 80. 1832. (?RUTACEAE).
Original material: 'Oahu', Sandwich Islands, Lay & Collie.

None found at E or K, but at E is a specimen ex herb. Arnott, assigned to the same genus, which just might be of relevance: it is annotated 'Brunellia' by Arnott, 'among Beechey's Bonin collection, but more likely from the Sandwich islands'.

This was excluded from Brunelliaceae by José Cuatrecasas (Fl. Neotropica 2: 177. 1970), but without original material it is impossible to know where it should be placed.

Bryonia attenuata Hook. & Arn., Bot. Beechey Voy. 9: 424. 1840. (CUCURBITACEAE).
Original material: Tepic, Mexico, Lay & Collie; 'Acapulco', Mexico, Sinclair.

At E: a sheet ex herb. Arnott (E00307060) with a ticket bearing the name 'Bryonia attenuata' in what is possibly Hooker's hand, to which Arnott has added 'H & A, Bot. Beech. Voy. Suppl. Acapulco, (Dr Sinclair)'.

At K: two sheets, both ex herb. Hooker; one (K000424034) is annotated by him with the name and 'Acapulco, Sinclair', the other (K000424035) has a ticket with the name and 'Acapulco, Sinclair'.

Note. When better material became available, Hooker & Arnott were able to place this species more accurately as to genus, and give it a meaningful epithet, citing their earlier 'Anguria? dubia' (see above).

≡ ***Cayaponia attenuata*** (Hook. & Arn.) Cogn.

Buchnera densiflora Hook. & Arn., Bot. Beechey Voy. 5: 203. 1836. (Generic placement queried). (OROBANCHACEAE).
Original material: 'Canton; *Mr. Millett*'.

At E: a sheet ex herb. Arnott (E00369177), annotated by him with the

Alphabetical list of new taxa

name and 'Canton – China' (and later, also by Arnott, 'B. stricta Benth.') is almost certainly a Millett duplicate sent by Hooker to Arnott, and therefore original material.
  None found at K.
= ***Buchnera cruciata*** D. Don

Buddleja curviflora Hook. & Arn., Bot. Beechey Voy. 6: 267. 1838. (SCROPHULARIACEAE).
Original material: 'Loo Choo', Lay & Collie.
  None found at E or K.
Note. Sometimes sunk under *B. japonica* Hemsl., but that is a later epithet.

Bulbostylis rigida Hook. & Arn., Bot. Beechey Voy. 7: 297. 1838 (as '*Bolbostylis*'). (COMPOSITAE).
Original material: 'Tepic', Mexico, Lay & Collie.
  None found at E.
  At K: a sheet (K000486516) ex herb. Hooker annotated by him with the name might, just possibly, be original material – it bears two specimens and Hooker has deleted the words 'California, Douglas' and replaced them with 'Mexico' (though giving no collector).
= ***Brickellia lanata*** (DC.) A. Gray

Cacalia cirsiifolia Hook. & Arn., Bot. Beechey Voy. 10: 436. 1841. (COMPOSITAE).
Original material: 'Between San Blas and Tepic', Mexico, Sinclair.
  None found at E.
  Lectotype at K: a sheet (K000504234) ex herb. Hooker annotated by him with the name and 'Tepic, Sinclair' – though not so annotated this is doubtless the specimen intended as lectotype (cited as 'type') by R. McVaugh (Fl. Novo-Galiciana 12: 641. 1984).
Note. Sometimes placed in the genus *Odontotrichum* as *O. pringlei* (S. Watson) Rydb.
= ***Psacalium pringlei*** (S. Watson) H. Rob. & Brettell

Cacalia denticulata Hook. & Arn., Bot. Beechey Voy. 1: 29. 1830. (Generic placement queried). (COMPOSITAE).
Original material: 'Conception', Chili, Lay & Collie.
  None found at E or K.
= ***Senecio yegua*** (Colla) Cabrera

Cacalia sessilifolia Hook. & Arn., Bot. Beechey Voy. 10: 436. 1841. (COMPOSITAE).
Original material: 'Between San Blas and Tepic', Mexico, Sinclair.
  At E: a sheet ex herb. Arnott (E00369145), annotated by him with the

name, reference, and 'San Blas to Tepic, Dr Sinclair. Does this not belong with Perdiceae' – this is an isolectotype (see below).

At K: a sheet (K000504164) ex herb. Hooker annotated by him 'Cacalia n. sp. 1 section 1 subsect.', bearing a ticket annotated by Bentham with the name, reference, a short description, and 'Tepic, Sinclair'. This sheet is not annotated by R. McVaugh who cited a specimen 'between San Blas and Tepic, Sinclair, K!' as type both of this and of *Senecio beecheyanus* Schultz-Bip. (Fl. Novo-Galiciana 12: 704. 1984). Such a specimen cannot now be found, unless it be the Hooker sheet described above and that McVaugh took the locality details from the protologue rather than quoting the wording on the sheet – it is therefore probably either the lectotype or an isolectotype.
Note. Sometimes placed in the genus *Pericalia* as *P. sessilifolia* (Hook. & Arn.) Rydb.
≡ **Roldana sessilifolia** (Hook. & Arn.) H. Rob. & Brettell

Caelestina petiolata Hook. & Arn., Bot. Beechey Voy. 10: 433. 1841. (COMPOSITAE).
Original material: 'Realejo', Mexico [now Nicaragua], Sinclair.

A sheet at E, ex herb. Arnott (E00369108), annotated by him 'Caelestina ageratoides. San Blas to Tepic, Dr Sinclair' is possibly original material. Despite the discrepancy over the locality, no other species of *Caelestina* collected by Sinclair is listed in this work and the 'ageratoides' on the sheet might be an indication of its section, rather than a specific epithet, as in the protologue the name was given as 'Caelestina *petiolata* (n. sp. Sect. Ageratoides)'.

Lectotype at K: a sheet (K000488636) ex herb. Hooker with a ticket annotated by Bentham with the name and 'Realejo, Dr Sinclair' – this is annotated 'holotype' by D.J.N. Hind and was lectotypified (cited as 'holotype') by M.F. Robinson in Ann. Missouri Bot. Gard. (58: 74. 1971).
≡ **Ageratum petiolatum** (Hook. & Arn.) Hemsl.

Caesalpinia millettii Hook. & Arn., Bot. Beechey Voy. 4: 182. 1833. (LEGUMINOSAE).
Original material: Chiefly ... about Macao, Lay & Collie (specimen 'destitute of leaves'); 'specimens sent long ago [from China] by Mr. Millett'.

At E: a sheet ex herb. Arnott (E00369039), annotated by him with the name and 'Canton, China, [per] Dr Hooker'.

None found at K.

Calandrinia tenella Hook. & Arn., Bot. Beechey Voy. 1: 24. 1830. (PORTULACACEAE)
Original material: 'Valparaiso', Chili, Lay & Collie.

At E: a sheet ex herb. Arnott, bears two specimens, both annotated by him with the name – the right-hand one (E00094915) labelled 'Valparaiso – Beechey' is original material; that on the left, *Mathews* 241 (E00033164), is

Alphabetical list of new taxa 59

not, though it was mistakenly annotated 'isotype' by Iris Edith Perotta in 1982 – it is not known if this typification has been published.

None found at K.

= ***Calandrinia compressa*** Schrad. ex DC.

Callicarpa nudiflora Hook. & Arn., Bot. Beechey Voy. 5: 206, t. 46. 1836. (LABIATAE).
Original material: 'Canton, *Mr. Millett* [s.n.]. Lappas island; *Rev. G.H. Vachell, n. 263*'.

At E, three sheets. One ex herb. R.K. Greville (E00369187), with a printed Vachell label annotated 'The Peninsula July 20 – Aug 30: [1830]' and on the sheet, in Greville's hand '[per] Prof. Henslow. no. 263'. The other two sheets are ex herb. Arnott: one (E00369188) is annotated by him with the name and 'Canton – [per] Dr Hooker, calyx glabrous!' and is doubtless a duplicate of the Millett material; the second (E00369189) bears the printed Vachell label with the same annotations as on the Greville sheet, but is also annotated by Arnott '263 Callicarpa nudiflora' – on the sheet itself Arnott has later added the name 'C. Reevesii Wall. L. n. 1830 Schauer in DC'. There appears to be a discrepancy in the locality of the Vachell specimens between protologue and label.

Two sheets at K, ex herb. Hooker, might be original material, but appear to have been mounted at a later date, and are not annotated by Hooker with the Hooker & Arnott name. One is annotated by Hooker 'Callicarpa cana? China, Millett', to which someone else has later added in pencil 'Reevesii – non Wall., nudiflora H. et Arn.'. The second sheet annotated with these names bears three specimens: the two right-hand ones are possibly original material, the upper one being labelled by Hooker 'China, Mr Millett', but they differ from the material on the first sheet (the left-hand specimen is an unrelated Gaudichaud collection).

Callicarpa parvifolia Hook. & Arn., Bot. Beechey Voy. 7: 305. 1838. (LABIATAE).
Original material: published as from Tepic, Mexico – actually from Bonin, Lay & Collie.

Isolectotype at E: a sheet ex herb. Arnott (E00369190), annotated by him with the name and 'Mexico, Beechey'.

Types at K, two sheets. One ex herb. Hooker with a ticket annotated by Bentham with the name and 'Mexico, Beechey', annotated 'type' by H.N. Moldenke in 1930/1, and lectotypified (cited as 'type', with 'fragment' at N) by him in Fed. Rep. 40: 47. 1936. The second, ex herb. Bentham (given him by Hooker in 1845), bearing a ticket annotated by Bentham with the name and 'Mexico, Beechey', annotated 'iso[lecto]type' by H.N. Moldenke in 1930/1.

Callicarpa subpubescens Hook. & Arn., Bot. Beechey Voy. 7: 305. 1838. (LABIATAE).
Original material: published as from Tepic, Mexico – actually from Bonin, as realised by Maximowicz (Bull. Acad. Sci. St Petersburg 32: 77. 1887), Lay & Collie.
 At E: a sheet ex herb. Arnott (E00369191), annotated by him with the name and 'Mexico, Beechey'.
 At K: a sheeet ex herb. Hooker, annotated by him 'Bonin' may be original material, though lacking the name or collector – it bears a ticket illegibly annotated, possibly by Arnott, 'Callicarp. purpurea ... Roxb. Fl. Ind. ... Bonin'. Two specimens ex herb. Bentham, both with tickets annotated by him with the name and 'Mexico, Beechey', are certainly original material – someone (possibly Bentham) has crossed out Mexico and substituted 'Bonin'.

Calliglossa Hook. & Arn., Bot. Beechey Voy. 8: 357. 1839. (COMPOSITAE).
= ***Layia*** Hook. & Arn. ex DC.

Calliglossa douglasii Hook. & Arn., Bot. Beechey Voy. 8: 356. 1839. (COMPOSITAE). [California].
This was proposed as a new name for 'Oxyura chrysanthemoides [sensu Lindl.] Bot. Reg. t. 1850 (quaod tabulam) [and four other references]', i.e., non DC.
Hooker & Arnott provided only a diagnostic description (against *Oxyura*, *Hartmannia* and *Madaraglossa*) of their new genus, and the species should be typified on the Lindley plate, or material on which that was based (presumably Douglas Californian material grown in the garden of the Horticultural Society of London). However, it seems that they were splitting hairs, and theirs is not now regarded as distinct from Candolle's plant.
≡ ***Layia chrysanthemoides*** (DC.) A. Gray

Calochortus tolmiei Hook. & Arn., Bot. Beechey Voy. 9: 398. 1840. (LILIACEAE).
Original material: 'Banks of the Walamet river', Tolmie.
 None found at E.
 Lectotype at K: a partial sheet ex herb. Hooker annotated by him 'Wallamet, Tolmie', and also by him 'β' which probably refers to its location on the original sheet when it was referred to a variety of *C. elegans*. This sheet was published as 'type' by M. Ownbey (Ann. Missouri Bot. Gard. 27: 412. 1940) (also on the remounted sheet is *Howell* 301, which is not a type).

Calochortus uniflorus Hook. & Arn., Bot. Beechey Voy. 9: 398, t. 94. 1840. (LILIACEAE).
Original material: California, Douglas.
 Probable isolectotypes at E. One ex herb. Arnott (E00369226), annotated by him with the name and 'California, [per] Hooker'. The other, ex herb. R.K.

Greville (E00369227), was clearly distributed before the determinations were made, but is almost certainly part of the original collection: it is annotated 'Calochortus. California. Douglas – Hort. Soc. Lond.'.

Isoloectotypes at K, two sheets. One ex herb. Hooker with two collections – the upper is the type, annotated by him 'California n. sp.', to which he has added in pencil the name and reference (the other collection, *Coulter 735*, is not a type). The second sheet is ex herb. Bentham and also bears two collections. To the two upper specimens on the right-hand side refers a printed Horticultural Society label 'Nova California, Douglas 1833' annotated by Bentham with the name and reference – these are types (the other, *Greene s.n.*, is not).

Note. M. Ownbey (Ann. Missouri Bot. Gard. 27: 429. 1940), cited the 'type' as at G and NY, but the K and E material is isolectotype.

Calotheca stricta Hook. & Arn., Bot. Beechey Voy. 2: 50. 1832. (GRAMINEAE).
Original material: 'Conception', Chili, Lay & Collie.
    None found at E or K.
Note. Sometimes (as at K) placed in *Briza* as *B. subaristatum* Lam.
= ***Chascolytrum subaristatum*** (Lam.) Desv.

Calycanthus occidentalis Hook. & Arn., Bot. Beechey Voy. 8: 340, t. 84. 1839. (CALYCANTHACEAE).
Original material: California, Douglas.
    None found at E.
    At K, two sheets: one ex herb. Hooker annotated by him with the name, reference, and the note 'stems very fragrant. Calycantheae. California, Douglas'; the second ex herb. Bentham with a printed 'California, Douglas 1833' label annotated by Bentham with the name (attached to the sheet is a fine drawing annotated 'Calycanthus macrophyllus').

Calystegia subacaulis Hook. & Arn., Bot. Beechey Voy. 8: 363. 1839. (CONVOLVULACEAE).
Original material: California, Douglas.
    At E: a sheet ex herb. Arnott (E00288019), annotated by him with the name and 'California. D[avid] D[ouglas] per Hooker'.
    At K: a remounted partial sheet ex herb. Hooker, annotated by him 'California, Douglas', and bearing a ticket annotated with the name by ?Arnott.

Canavalia multiflora (Hook. & Arn.) Hook. & Arn., Bot. Beechey Voy. 9: 416. 1840. (LEGUMINOSAE). [Mexico].
Basionym cited: 'Neurocarpum multiflorum *Hook. & Arn. supra* [i.e., Bot. Beechey Voy.] *p.* 286'.
= ***Canavalia villosa*** Benth.

Canavalia pubescens Hook. & Arn., Bot. Beechey Voy. 2: 81. 1832. (LEGUMINOSAE).
Original material: 'Oneeheow', Sandwich Islands, Lay & Collie.
   None found at E.
   Lectotype at K: a sheet ex herb. Hooker, bearing a ticket annotated by Arnott with the name and 'Oneeheow, B[eechey]' – it was annotated 'lectotype' by J.D. Sauer in 1962, and published as such by him in Brittonia (16: 175. 1965), also citing an iso[lecto]type at G.

Canthium lucidum Hook. & Arn., Bot. Beechey Voy. 2: 65. 1832. (RUBIACEAE).
Original material: 'Society Islands', Lay & Collie.
   Isolectotype at E: a sheet ex herb. Arnott (E00369095), annotated by him with the name and 'Gambiers isld., Beechey'. Steudel (perhaps because he took Hooker & Arnott's to be a homonym of *C. lucidum* R. Br., *nom. nud.*) renamed this *C. beecheyi* Steudel (Nom. Bot., ed. 2, 1: 275. 1840).
   Lectotype at K: a sheet ex herb. Hooker annotated by him with the name, and in another hand 'Gambier Isls. Beechey', to which is attached a drawing possibly by Arnott – this has not been annotated by S.L. Welsh, but must be the one intended as lectotype (cited as 'holotype'), published by him in Fl. Societensis 249. 1998.
= ***Psydrax odorata*** (G. Forst.) A.C. Sm. & S. Darwin

Cardamine tenuirostris Hook. & Arn., Bot. Beechey Voy. 1: 6. 1830. (CRUCIFERAE).
Original material: 'Conception', Chili, Lay & Collie.
   None found at E.
   At K: the upper collection (K000485001) on a sheet ex herb. Hooker annotated by him with the name and reference 'Pl. of Beechey's Voy' (the lower specimen on this sheet, a Bridges collection, is not original material; neither are two collections (Bridges, *Lechler* 299) on another sheet bearing this name).

Carex bispicata Hook. & Arn., Bot. Beechey Voy. 3: 118, t. 28. 1832. (CYPERACEAE).
Original material: Avatschka Bay, Kamtschatka, Lay & Collie.
   At E: a sheet ex herb. Arnott (E00369233), annotated by him with the name and 'Kamtschatka, Beechey'.
   At K: a sheet ex herb. Hooker, bearing a ticket annotated by Arnott 'Avatska Bay Kamtschatka, Beechey' to which possibly Arnott has added the name in pencil.
= ***Carex longirostrata*** C.A. Mey. var. ***longirostrata***

Carex boottiana Hook. & Arn., Bot. Beechey Voy. 6: 273. 1838. (CYPERACEAE).
Original material: 'Bonin', Lay & Collie.

Alphabetical list of new taxa 63

None found at E.

At K: a sheet ex herb. Hooker annotated by him on the sheet with the name (to which he has later added '(non Benth.)' and 'C. Bongardi Boott') and the collecting details 'Bonin, Beechey'; it bears a ticket with the name and a long description in Arnott's hand.

Carex gmelinii Hook. & Arn., Bot. Beechey Voy. 3: 118, 131, t. 27. 1832 (as '*Gmelini*'). (CYPERACEAE).
Original material: Avatschka Bay, Kamtschatka; Kotzebue's Sound & American coast of Behring's Strait, from lat. 67° to 71°, Lay & Collie.

At E: a sheet ex herb. Arnott, bearing two specimens, both annotated by him with the name. One (E00021630) has the details 'Kotzebue Sound, Beechey', the other (E00021629) 'Avatshka Bay, Kamschatka, Beechey'. These are both original material, although the description is on p. 118, referring to the Kamtschatka specimen, there is a cross reference to this on p. 131 (referring to the Kotzebue Sound specimen) and the two were published simultaneously.

At K: a sheet ex herb. Hooker, annotated by him with the name and bearing three collections: the central one is annotated by Hooker 'Kotzebue's Sound, Beechey', the right hand one 'Kamtsatka, Beechey' – it also bears tickets with annotations by Francis Boott and C.B. Clarke (the left hand collection, *Tolmie* s.n., is not original material).

Carex hebecarpa Hook. & Arn., Bot. Beechey Voy. 2: 50. 1832, *nom. illeg.*, non C.A. Mey., 1831. (CYPERACEAE).
Original material: 'Conception', Chili, Lay & Collie.

None found at E.

At K: a sheet ex herb. Francis Boott with two collections. The left-hand one (K000584742) is the original material – it is annotated 'C. Beecheyana Boott, C. hebecarpa Hooker (non Meyer), C. hookeri Kunth (non Dewey). Chili, Capt. Beechey from Hooker!' (the other specimen, *Gay* s.n., is not original material).
≡ *Carex hookeri* Kunth

Carica peltata Hook. & Arn., Bot. Beechey Voy. 9: 425, t. 98. 1840. (CARICACEAE).
Original material: 'Realejo', Mexico [now Nicaragua], Sinclair.

At E: a sheet ex herb. Arnott (E00369081), bearing a label annotated with the name by ?Hooker, to which Arnott has added 'H & A, Bot. Beech. voy. Supp. Realejo Dr Sinclair'.

At K: a sheet ex herb. Hooker annotated by him with the name and 'Realejo, Sinclair' – this was annotated 'holotype' by V.M. Badillo in 1968, but it is not known if this typification has been published.
= *Carica papaya* L.

Casearia impunctata Hook. & Arn., Bot. Beechey Voy. 2: 61. 1832. (SALICACEAE).
Type: 'only one specimen', 'Society Islands', Lay & Collie.
   Not found at E or K.

Cassia gaudichaudii Hook. & Arn., Bot. Beechey Voy. 2: 81. 1832 (as '*Gaudichaudi*'). (LEGUMINOSAE).
Original material: Sandwich Islands, Lay & Collie.
   At E: two sheets ex herb. Arnott, each bearing a single specimen, one with pods (E00369045), one without (E00369046), both annotated by Arnott with the name and 'Oahu, Beechey'.
   At K: a sheet ex herb. Hooker bearing two specimens and a ticket annotated by Arnott 'Cassia Gaudichaudi H & A near [C.] Dispar (DC. 65). Oahu, Beechey'.
≡ **Senna gaudichaudii** (Hook. & Arn.) H.S. Irwin & Barneby

Cassia punctulata Hook. & Arn., Bot. Beechey Voy. 9: 420. 1840. (LEGUMINOSAE).
Original material: 'Tepic', Mexico, Sinclair.
   None found at E.
   At K: a sheet (K000478170) ex herb. Hooker with a ticket annotated by him with the name and 'Tepic', though no collector is given, is probably the original material – it was annotated 'isotype' by R. Barneby in 1974, but this appears not to have been published.
   A sheet (K000478171) ex herb. Bentham, with a ticket annotated by him with the name, was annotatated 'holotype' by Barneby in 1974, while at the same time determining it as *C. pauciflora* Kunth. This, however, was wrong – although the specimen is from Tepic it was collected by George Barclay and is <u>not</u> original material of *C. punctulata*, being part of the later H.M.S. *Sulphur* material worked on by Bentham, who identified it as *C. pauciflora* under which he sunk Hooker & Arnott's *C. punctulata*. Irwin & Barnaby fortunately appear not to have published this erroneous typification and in their publication (Mem. New York Bot. Gard. 35: 661, 904. 1982) maintained *Chamaecrista punctulata*, but sunk *Cassia pauciflora* under *Chamaecrista hispidula* (Vahl) H.S. Irwin & Barneby.
≡ **Chamaecrista punctulata** (Hook. & Arn.) H.S. Irwin & Barneby

Castilleja affinis Hook. & Arn., Bot. Beechey Voy. 4: 154. 1833. (OROBANCHACEAE).
Original material: San Francisco (or Monterey Bay), California, Lay & Collie.
   At E: a sheet ex herb. Arnott, annotated by him with the name and 'California, Beechey', bears three specimens, the central and right-hand ones (E00270109) were annotated as 'isotype' by M. Egger in 2009. The left-hand specimen (E00369178) was determined by Egger as *C. foliolosa* Hook. &

Alphabetical list of new taxa

Arn., and annotated 'presumably part of type gathering' (i.e., of *C. foliolosa*); however, this seems unwarranted as the specimen differs from the 'holotype' of that species (see below) in habit and leaf length.

At K: a sheet ex herb. Hooker with two collections – the left-hand one (K000195496) annotated 'Beechey' on the sheet by Hooker, and bearing a ticket annotated with the name and 'California' in an unknown hand is original material – it was annotated 'holotype' by J.M. Egger in 2005/6, but it is not known if this typification has been published (the other specimen, *Menzies* s.n., 'N.W.C.' is not original material, and was determined as *C. miniata* Hook. by Egger).

Castilleja ambigua Hook. & Arn., Bot. Beechey Voy. 4: 154. 1833. (OROBANCHACEAE).
Original material: San Francisco (or Monterey Bay), California, Lay & Collie.

Lectotype at E: a sheet ex herb. Arnott (E00267683), annotated by him with the name and 'California, Beechey', and later (also by Arnott) 'Orthocarpus densiflorus Benth.' – this was lectotypified (cited as 'holotype') by T.I. Chuang & L.R. Heckard (Syst. Bot. 16: 655. 1991).

Type at K: a remounted, partial sheet ex herb. Hooker (K000195556), annotated by Hooker 'Beechey', bearing a ticket annotated with the name and 'California' in an unknown hand – this was annotated 'iso[lecto]type' by L. Heckard in 1990, and published as such by Chuang & Hekcard (1991).

Castilleja foliolosa Hook. & Arn., Bot. Beechey Voy. 4: 154. 1833. (OROBANCHACEAE).
Original material: San Francisco (or Monterey Bay), California, Lay & Collie.

At E: a sheet ex herb. Arnott (E00272458), annotated by him with the name and 'California, Beechey' – this was annotated 'isotype' by M. Egger in 2005/8, but it is not known if this has been published. Another sheet from Arnott's herbarium bears the two Douglas specimens described, but not named, in the California Supplement (p. 380. 1839): these are annotated 'Castilleja foliolosa, forma secunda. California, D[avid] D[ouglas] per Hooker', and 'Castilleja foliolosa, forma tertia. California, D[avid] D[ouglas] per Hooker', but have no type status.

At K: a sheet ex herb. Hooker bearing three collections. The upper left-hand specimens (K000195531) annotated on the sheet by Hooker 'Beechey', associated with a ticket annotated with the name and 'California' in an unknown hand, are original material – these were annotated 'holotype' by J.M. Egger in 2005/6, but it is not known if this has been published (the other specimens: one certainly, the other possibly, a Douglas collection, are not original material).

Castilleja laciniata Hook. & Arn., Bot. Beechey Voy. 1: 40. 1830. (OROBANCHACEAE).
Original material: 'Conception', Chili, Lay & Collie.

None found at E or K. The specimen annotated with this name by Arnott at E is a later collection, *Cuming* 327; a duplicate of this at K was mistakenly annotated 'syntype' by J.M. Egger in 2005/6.

Castilleja latifolia Hook. & Arn., Bot. Beechey Voy. 4: 154. 1833. (OROBANCHACEAE).
Original material: San Francisco (or Monterey Bay), California, Mr. Collie.

At E: a sheet ex herb. Arnott (E00270107), annotated by him with the name and 'California, Beechey', and (presumably later, but also by Arnott) '*Castilleja macrocarpa* Benth., Benth in DC Prod.' – this was annotated 'isotype' by M. Egger in 2009/10.

At K: a sheet ex herb. Hooker bearing four collections. The top right-hand one (K000195503), annotated on the sheet by Hooker 'Beechey', associated with a ticket annotated with the name and 'California' in an unknown hand, is original material – it was annotated 'holotype' by J.M. Egger in 2005/6, but it is not known if this has been published (the other collections, *Coulter* 618, 1620, *Menzies* s.n., are not original material).

Caucalis microcarpa Hook. & Arn., Bot. Beechey Voy. 8: 348. 1839. (UMBELLIFERAE).
Original material: California, Douglas.

At E: a sheet ex herb. Arnott (E00000117), annotated by him with the name and 'California. D[avid] D[ouglas] per Hooker'.

At K, two sheets: one ex herb. Hooker, annotated by him with the name and 'California, Douglas'; one ex herb. Bentham, with a printed 'California, Douglas 1833' label, annotated by Bentham with the name and reference 'Torr. & Gr. Fl. N. Am. 1. 636. [1840]'.

≡ ***Yabea microcarpa*** (Hook. & Arn.) Koso-Pol.

Ceanothus cuneatus (Hook.) Nutt. "[var.] α *rufescens* Hook. & Arn.", Bot. Beechey Voy. 7: 329. 1838. (RHAMNACEAE).
As the basionym *Rhamnus cuneatus* Hook. is cited as a synonym here, then, under Art. 26, this variety is not validly published. The correct name is var. *cuneatus*, and the type is that of Hooker's *R. cuneatus*, which is a Douglas specimen from NW America, 'near the sources of the Multnonmak River'.

Type of *R. cuneatus* at K, the central (non-flowering) specimen on a sheet ex herb. Hooker annotated by him 'Ceanothus cuneatus α' – attached is a field ticket with the locality details and a description in Douglas's hand (for the left-hand specimen see var. β below; the right-hand specimen is a non-type, Coulter, collection).

Alphabetical list of new taxa 67

Ceanothus cuneatus (Hook.) Nutt. [var.] β *cinerascens* Hook. & Arn., Bot. Beechey Voy. 7: 329. 1838. (RHAMNACEAE).
Original material: California, Douglas.
  None found at E.
  At K: the left-hand specimen on a sheet ex herb. Hooker annotated by him 'β Douglas, California' (for other specimens see under "var. α rufescens" above).
Note. This is provided here as a varietal name for *C. cuneatus* sensu Nutt., non (Hook.) Nutt.

Ceanothus incanus Torr. & A. Gray [var.] β *minor* Hook. & Arn., Bot. Beechey Voy. 7: 328. 1838. (RHAMNACEAE).
Original material: California, Douglas.
  None found at E.
  A sheet at K, ex herb. Hooker annotated by him with the name and 'California, Douglas', bears three specimens: the central one, annotated by Hooker 'β', is the original material.
Note. In a letter attached to this sheet, written by Robert Sutherland in 1978, it is stated that the outer specimens are hybrids and that the central specimen (i.e., var. β) = *C. sorediatus*. If this is correct and if *C. sorediatus* is treated as a variety of *C. oliganthus*, then '*minor*' is the earliest epithet at varietal rank, though *C. sorediatus* has been maintained by recent Californian authors.
= **Ceanothus sorediatus** Hook. & Arn.

Ceanothus integerrimus Hook. & Arn., Bot. Beechey Voy. 7: 329. 1838. (RHAMNACEAE).
Original material: California, Douglas.
  None found at E.
  At K, two sheets: one ex herb. Hooker annotated by him 'California, Douglas' and on a ticket with two drawings with the name – this was annotated 'holotype' by N.C. Coile in 1988, but it is not known if this was published as a lectotypification; the second sheet is ex herb. Bentham, with a printed 'California, Douglas 1833' label, annotated on the sheet by Bentham with the name and reference (the sheet also bears a Hartweg specimen, which is not original material).

Ceanothus sorediatus Hook. & Arn., Bot. Beechey Voy. 7: 328. 1838. (RHAMNACEAE).
Original material: California, Douglas.
  None found at E.
  At K, two relevant sheets: the left-hand specimen on a sheet ex herb. Hooker annotated by him with the name and 'Douglas, California' to which is attached a ticket with drawings is original material (the right-hand, Lobb collection, is not); the left-hand specimen on a sheet ex herb. Bentham with a printed 'California, Douglas 1833' label, annotated on the sheet by Bentham

with the name and reference (also on the sheet are collections of Frémont and of Parry that are not original material).
Note. This has sometimes been treated as *C. oliganthus* Nutt. var. *sorediatus* (Hook. & Arn.) Hoover, but if treated at varietal rank, then according to a note on the type (see above) [*C. incanus*] var. *minor* would be the earliest available epithet at varietal rank – Hoover's combination dating from 1966 (Leafl. W. Botany 10: 349).

Cephaelis fragrans Hook. & Arn., Bot. Beechey Voy. 2: 64, t. 13. 1832. (Generic placement queried). (RUBIACEAE).
Original material: 'Elizabeth Island', Mr. Collie.
    None found at E.
    At K: a sheet ex herb. Hooker (K000297701) annotated by him with the name and 'Elizabeth isld.', to which is attached a pencil drawing possibly by Arnott.
≡ ***Ixora fragrans*** (Hook. & Arn.) A. Gray

Cerasus ilicifolius Nutt. ex Hook. & Arn., Bot. Beechey Voy. 8: 340, t. 83. 1839. (ROSACEAE). (FIGS 10, 11).
Original material: California, Douglas; N California, Nuttall.
    A sheet at E, ex herb. Arnott (E00369052), annotated by him 'Cerasus ilicifolius Nutt., California' is most probably original material.
    A sheet at K, ex herb. Hooker annotated by him 'Cerasus ilicifolius Nutt.', bears two collections – the one annotated by Hooker 'California, Douglas' beside which is a drawing of a flower annotated with the name by Hooker (and a reference to Beechey voyage in a later hand) is certainly original material. The other collection has a field ticket in Nuttall's hand 'Cerasus ilicifolius, N. Calif.'; Hooker & Arnott clearly saw this specimen as they took their name from it, even although there is no specific reference to this material in the protologue, it also constitutes original material. A second sheet ex herb. Hooker has a duplicate of the Douglas collection, which is also original material (and two Coulter collections that are not).
≡ ***Prunus ilicifolius*** (Nutt. ex Hook. & Arn.) Walp.

Cercocarpus parvifolius Nutt. ex Hook. & Arn., Bot. Beechey Voy. 8: 337. 1839 (as '*parvifolia*'). (ROSACEAE).
Original material: California, Douglas; Platte River, Nuttall.
    A specimen at E, distributed from Arnott's herbarium, bears a ticket annotated '194. Cercocarpus parvifolius. Nutt.' – without further details it is not safe to assume this to be original material, though it might.
    At K: a sheet ex herb. Hooker, bearing a single specimen with a ticket in Nuttall's hand 'Cercocarpus parvifolius, Platte', beside which Hooker has written 'Nuttall', is original material.
Note. Here (unlike the case of *Lupinus truncatus*, where the whole description is attributed to Nuttall), Hooker & Arnott attribute the name alone to Nuttall.

Three sources are cited, but none was published by this date: 'Nutt. in Herb. Hook. – Torr. et Gr. Fl. ined. [published 1840] – Hook. Ic. Pl. t. 323 [published 1841]'. Two other Nuttall manuscript names are mentioned in the note following the protologue, but neither of these has a validating description, so are not validly published here.
Note. Sometimes placed under *C. montanus* Raf.

Chaenactis achilleifolia Hook. & Arn., Bot. Beechey Voy. 8: 354. 1839 (as '*achilleaefolia*'). (COMPOSITAE).
Type: 'Dry plains in the Snake Country [Idaho]. [John McLeod] *Mr Tolmie*'.
   Not found at E.
   Type at K: a sheet ex herb. Hooker annotated by him with the name and 'Snake Country, Tolmie' – presumably the specimen cited by A. Cronquist (Intermountain Flora 5: 116. 1994) as 'holotype at K!' (also on the sheet is *Geyer* 142, which is not a type).
= ***Chaenactis douglasii*** (Hook.) Hook. & Arn.

Chaenactis douglasii (Hook.) Hook. & Arn., Bot. Beechey Voy. 8: 354. 1839. (COMPOSITAE). [California].
Basionym cited: '*Hymenopappus Douglasii*, Hook. Flor. Bor. Am. I. p. 316. [1833]'.

Chaenactis stevioides Hook. & Arn., Bot. Beechey Voy. 8: 353. 1839. (COMPOSITAE).
Original material: 'Snake Country [Idaho]. [John McLeod per] *Mr Tolmie*'.
   At E: a sheet (E00369140) with a label annotated by Arnott with the name and 'Snake Country'. This is a sheet distributed from Arnott's herbarium from GL to E in 1902, bearing a printed 'Herb. Walker Arnott' label.
   A sheet at K ex herb. Hooker apparently bearing two collections, both apparently original material – one (consisting of 3 specimens) is annotated by Hooker with the name and 'Snake Country, Tolmie'; the other (consisting of 2 specimens) is associated with a ticket annotated in an unknown hand with the name and 'Snake Country, Tolmie'. A. Cronquist (Intermountain Flora 5: 119. 1994) cited 'holotype at K!', but clarification of this typification is clearly required.

Chaetogastra ferruginea Hook. & Arn., Bot. Beechey Voy. 9: 423. 1840. (Generic placement queried). (MELASTOMATACEAE).
Original material: 'Realejo', [Nicaragua], Sinclair.
   At E: a sheet ex herb. Arnott (E00285746), bearing a label annotated with the name by ?Hooker, to which Arnott has added 'H & A, Bot. Beech. voy. Supp. Realejo (Dr Sinclair)'.
   At K: a sheet ex herb. Hooker bearing a ticket annotated by Arnott with the name and 'Realejo, Dr Sinclair', and also a ticket with drawings possibly by Arnott.
= ***Tibouchina longifolia*** (Vahl) Baill.

Chaetymenia Hook. & Arn., Bot. Beechey Voy. 7: 298. 1838. (COMPOSITAE).

Chaetymenia peduncularis Hook. & Arn., Bot. Beechey Voy. 7: 298, t. 62. 1838. (COMPOSITAE).
Original material: 'Talisco', Mexico, Lay & Collie.
   None found at E.
   At K: a sheet ex herb. Hooker (K000502207), annotated by Hooker with the name, reference and 'Talisco, Beechey', bearing a ticket with drawings possibly by Arnott.

Chenopodium vachellii Hook. & Arn., Bot. Beechey Voy. 6: 269. 1838. (AMARANTHACEAE).
Proposed here as a name for material Hooker & Arnott had previously referred, with a query, to 'Chenopodium acutifolium Kit.': the original material therefore includes the specimen cited under that name, '*Vachell n.* 112', and material from 'Loo Choo [Lay & Collie]'.
   At E: a sheet ex herb. Arnott (E00369198), bearing three specimens, annotated by Arnott with the name and 'Canton', it also has a printed Vachell label annotated with the locality 'The Peninsula', July 20 – Aug 30 1830, 112 'Chenopdium acutifolium H & A in Bot. Beech. Voy. (non auct.)'.
   At K: two sheets, both ex herb. Hooker. One has a printed Vachell ticket with the number '112', originally annotated 'Chenopodium patulum', on which Arnott has replaced the epithet with 'acutifolium?'. The other sheet has two specimens, the lower one, annotated by Hooker 'Chenop. Vachellii. Loo Choo' is original material (the other collection, *Karelin & Kiriloff* 1908, is not).
= ***Chenopodium acuminatum*** Willd.

Chiococca odorata Hook. & Arn., Bot. Beechey Voy. 2: 65. 1832. (RUBIACEAE).
Original material: 'Elizabeth Island', Lay & Collie.
   None found at E.
   At K: a sheet (K000213802) ex herb. Hooker, annotated 'Elizabeth Isld., Beechey' and by Hooker with the name 'Chiococca obtusifolia', which someone, possibly Arnott, has crossed out and replaced in pencil with 'odorata Hook. et Arn.' (on the same sheet is *Mathews* 130, which is not original material).
Note. Although 'Coffaea odorata. "Forst. Prodr. 1. n. 94"?' is cited, this synonymy is queried; furthermore the name is attributed to Hooker & Arnott in the index, so it should be treated as a new name (rather than as a new combination as has sometimes been done, e.g., S.L. Welsh (Fl. Societensis 249. 1998), and, more recently, by Nicolson & Fosberg (Forst. Bot. Second Cook Exped. 608. 2004).
= ***Cyclophyllum barbatum*** (G. Forst.) N. Hallé & J. Florence

Alphabetical list of new taxa

Chlamysperma arenarioides Hook. & Arn., Bot. Beechey Voy. 7: 300, t. 64. 1838. (COMPOSITAE).
Original material: Tepic, Mexico, Lay & Collie.
   At E: a sheet ex herb. Arnott (E00369141), annotated by him with the name, reference, and 'Mexico, Beechey'.
   At K: a sheet ex herb. Hooker annotated by him with the name, reference, and 'Talisco, Beechey', to which is attached a ticket of drawings possibly by Arnott, is probably original material – despite the discrepancy over the locality. Note. J.L. Strother (Fl. Chiapas 5: 52. 1999) commented 'TYPE: no specimen cited; the plate is diagnostic' – this is not true, the specimens are cited 'generically' in the introductory material to each section, and in this case there are original specimens at E and K, so there is no need to choose the plate as a lectotype.
= **Galeana pratensis** (Kunth) Rydb.

["*Chryseis californica* (Cham.) Hook. & Arn.", Bot. Beechey Voy. 7: 319. 1838. (PAPAVERACEAE).
Despite some rather garbled wording, Hooker & Arnott thought that they were making a new combination here for *Eschscholzia californica* Cham., and at the same time sinking under this *E. crocea* Benth., regarding the taxon then in cultivation under the name *E. californica*, introduced by David Douglas, as a different taxon. However, they failed to validly publish the provisional name "*Chryseis douglasii*" – the wording 'If, then, the species be really distinct' does not fully accept the species, and it is not included in the index. In fact the combination *C. californica* had been made the previous year by Lindley (Bot. Reg. 23 t. 1948. 1837): although Chamisso was not cited, neither was the place of publication, the combination is validly published (*Chryseis* was coined as a new name for *Eschscholzia* on the grounds that the latter was what would now be called a homonym of [Willdenow's] *Elsholtzia* (Labiatae), which he considered to have been mis-spelt and to have been commemorating a different member of the same family. In fact Lindley's *Chryseis* itself was an illegitimate homonym, non Cassini 1817)].

Chrysopsis scabra Hook. & Arn., Bot. Beechey Voy. 10: 434. 1841, *nom. illeg.*, non Ell., 1823. (Generic placement queried). (COMPOSITAE).
Original material: 'Between San Blas and Tepic', Mexico, Sinclair.
   At E: a sheet ex herb. Arnott (E00369139), annotated by him with the name, reference, and 'San Blas to Tepic, Dr Sinclair', to which he later added the name 'Oxypappus scaber Benth – Walpers Repert. VI. p. 178'.
   At K, despite a slight discrepancy over locality, are two sheets that are probably original material. On a sheet ex herb. Hooker, the right-hand specimen (K000502282) with a ticket annotated by Bentham 'Oxypappus scaber gen. n. Chrysopsis? scaber Hook. et Arn. Bot Beech. 434. Tepic, Dr Sinclair'. A duplicate of this, the left-hand specimen (K000502279) on a sheet

ex herb. Bentham, with a ticket annotated by him 'Oxypappus scaber Benth. Bot. Sulph. 118. Tepic, Sinclair'.
= ***Oxypappus seemannii*** (Schultz-Bip.) S.F. Blake

Cissus cantoniensis Hook. & Arn., Bot. Beechey Voy. 4: 175. 1833. (Generic placement queried). (VITACEAE).
Original material: Chiefly ... about Macao, China, Lay & Collie.
    At E: the upper specimen (E00369033) on a sheet ex herb. Arnott, annotated by him with the name and 'China, Beechey' (the lower specimen, E00369034, *Vachell* 262 is not mentioned in the protologue, so is not original material).
    None found at K.
≡ ***Ampelopsis cantoniensis*** (Hook. & Arn.) K. Koch

Citharexylum cyanocarpum Hook. & Arn., Bot. Beechey Voy. 2: 58, t. 11. 1832 (as '*Citharexylon*'). (VERBENACEAE).
Original material: 'Valparaiso', Chili, Lay & Collie; material from Cruckshanks, Mathews, Bridges (by implication from Chili), and from Mrs Graham and Bertero from Juan Fernandez, the latter under the MS name *Poppigia cyanocarpa*.
    At E: a sheet ex herb. Arnott with three specimens – the ticket of *Mathews* 236 (E00369183) is annotated by Arnott with the name 'Citharexylon cyanocarpa Hook. & Arn.', the other specimens are *Bridges* 123 (E00369184) and *Cuming* 625 (E00369185) – of these, the first two are original material.
    At K: no Beechey material, but a sheet bears two remounted partial sheets ex herb. Hooker, both of which are possible original material. The left-hand (K000487129) is *Bridges* 123, with a ticket annotated (not by Hooker or Arnott) with the name and the collecting details 'Amyan machos Quebradas Valpso. & Quittote, Bridges 1832'; the right-hand one (K000487128) is annotated by Hooker with the name, reference, and collector 'Bridges' (but no number). Another remounted, partial sheet ex herb. Hooker has a specimen of *Mathews* 236 and is also original material – it was annotated by H.N. Moldenke in 1936 as 'isotype' of *Rhaphithamnus cyanocarpus* var. *pallidus*. A sheet ex herb. Bentham annotated by him 'Duranta cyanea Lindl., Valparaiso; Bridges 1830' is also annotated 'isotype' of *R. cyanocarpus* var. *pallidus* by Moldenke, but is probably original material of *C. cyanocarpum*.
Note. Although in the note after the description Hooker & Arnott stated that the Bertero name was unpublished, they cited the reference 'Poppigia cyanocarpa. *Bert. in Bull. des Sc. Nat.* 1830. Oct. 109'; according to H.N. Moldenke (Fedd. Rep. 42: 69. 1937) it was not published there, so the new name is attributable to Hooker & Arnott.
= ***Rhaphithamnus spinosus*** (Juss.) Moldenke

Alphabetical list of new taxa 73

Clematis acapulcensis Hook. & Arn., Bot. Beechey Voy. 9: 410. 1840. (RANUNCULACEAE).
Original material: 'Acapulco'. Mexico, Sinclair.

At E: a sheet ex herb. Arnott (E00369004), annotated by him with the name and 'Acapulco, Beechey'. (As with all these specimens, while they were transmitted 'at the request of Captain Beechey', they were not collected by him).

At K: one sheet (K000220103) ex herb. Hooker bearing a ticket annotated with the name and 'Acapulco'; the other is the upper specimen (K000220101) on a sheet ex herb. Bentham, given him by Hooker in 1842, annotated with the name, reference, and 'Acapulco, Sinclair' (the lower specimen 'Clem. Caracasana DC., Mexico, Beechey' is not original material).

Clerodendrum castaneifolium Hook. & Arn., Bot. Beechey Voy. 5: 205. 1836. (LABIATAE).
Original material: 'Canton; *Mr. Millett*'.

At E, a sheet ex herb. Arnott (E00369192), annotated by him with the name and 'Canton, ([per] Dr Hooker)' is probably original material.

No certain original material at K – in a type cover labelled with the name is a sheet ex herb. Hooker, annotated by him 'Cler. lividum, Bot. Reg. 945. China, Millett'. Lacking the Hooker & Arnott name, and simply because of the collector and locality, there is no reason to think this a type of *C. castaneifolium*; nor does it appear to be a type of *C. lividum*, described by Lindley from cultivated material originating from China.
= ***Clerodendrum fortunatum*** L.

Cleyera millettii Hook. & Arn., Bot. Beechey Voy. 4: 171, t. 33. 1833. (PENTAPHYLACACEAE).
Original material: China, Mr. Millet.

At E: a sheet ex herb. Arnott (E00306439), annotated by him with the name and 'China, D Millett'. Also on the sheet is a ticket (possibly part of a letter) annotated by Hooker: 'I call this Cleyera Millettiana Can you refer it to anything described [from] China. You may keep this' and by Arnott 'is it not C. ochnacea DC. excluding of course DC's β & Wallich's species, which have nothing to do with it'.

At K: a sheet ex herb. Hooker annotated by him with the name and 'China, Millett', to which is attached a pencil drawing annotated by ?Arnott.
≡ ***Adinandra millettii*** (Hook. & Arn.) Hance

Cocculus diantherus Hook. & Arn., Bot. Beechey Voy. 4: 167. 1833. (Generic placement queried). (MENISPERMACEAE).
Original material: Chiefly ... about Macao, China, Lay & Collie. Also material 'from Lappas Island, from Mr. Millett and from Mr. Vachell'.

At E: no Beechey material, but a sheet ex herb. Arnott, annotated by him 'Cocculus hexagynus Colebr., Mennispermum hexagynum Roxb., Cocculus diantherus H & A. Canton – [per] Dr Hooker', which is most probably a duplicate of one of the Millett specimens.

At K, a sheet (K000644680) ex herb. Hooker annotated by him with the name and reference 'Bot. of Beech. Voy.'

= ***Cocculus orbiculatus*** (L.) DC.

Coffea chamissonis Hook. & Arn., Bot. Beechey Voy. 2: 86. 1832. (RUBIACEAE). Original material: Sandwich Islands, Lay & Collie.

At E: a sheet ex herb. Arnott (E00369096), bearing a flowering and a fruiting specimen, annotated by Arnott with the name and 'Oahu, Beechey'.

At K: a sheet ex herb. Hooker with a ticket annotated by ?Arnott with the name and 'Oahu, Beechey'.

= ***Psychotria kaduana*** (Cham. & Schltdl.) Fosberg

Collomia cavanillesii Hook. & Arn., Bot. Beechey Voy. 1: 37. 1830. (POLEMONIACEAE).
Cited material: 'Conception', Chili, Lay & Collie.
A new name for 'Phlox linearis Cav. Ic. v. 6. p. 17. t. 527', the epithet not being transferrable, preoccupied by *Collomia linearis* Nutt. This name should therefore be typified on the Cavanilles material (though the Beechey specimens from Conception might also be considered relevant in typification of the Hooker & Arnott name).

Of these none at E or K. The only specimens at E bearing the name in Arnott's hand, on two sheets, are later collections (*Bridges* 146 and *Cuming* 221, 549).

At K are duplicates of these later collections (and also *Bridges* 611) ex herb. Hooker.

= ***Collomia biflora*** (Ruiz & Pavon) Brand

Collomia nudicaulis Hook. & Arn., Bot. Beechey Voy. 8: 368. 1839. (POLEMONIACEAE).
Type: 'Green River, Snake Country [Wyoming]. [John McLeod per] *Mr Tolmie*'.

Type at E, a sheet ex herb. Arnott (E00369163), annotated by him with the name and 'Snake Country N.W. C[alifornia]. Tolmie'.

Two type sheets at K. One ex herb. Hooker annotated by him with the name, bearing two collections – the lower (six specimens) represent the type, annotated by Hooker '33 Tolmie. Snake Country, California' – this is presumably the material cited as 'holotype' by Cronquist *et al.* (Intermountain Flora 4: 139. 1984) (the upper collection, *C.L. Anderson* s.n., is not a type). A sheet ex herb. Bentham, bearing three collections, the upper, annotated with the name and reference by Bentham, is annotated 'ex herb. Hooker' and is almost certainly a duplicate of the type (the other collections, *Parry* 235, *Cusick* 2366, are not types).

Alphabetical list of new taxa 75

Note. Sometimes placed in *Gymnosteris* as *G. nudicaulis* (Hook. & Arn.) Greene.

Connarus juglandifolius Hook. & Arn., Bot. Beechey Voy. 4: 179. 1833. (Generic placement queried). (ANACARDIACEAE).
Type: ['the only specimen', in young fruit; chiefly ... about Macao, China, Lay & Collie].
   Not found at E.
   At K, a sheet ex herb. Hooker annotated by him with the name and 'China, Beechey'.
= **Rhus succedanea** L.

Connarus microphyllus Hook. & Arn., Bot. Beechey Voy. 4: 179. 1833, *nom. illeg.* ('Aegiceras minus Gaertn. Fruct. 1. t. 46' cited as a synonym). (CONNARACEAE).
Although Hooker & Arnott cited no particular specimens, from the format of the work their description must have been based on Lay & Collie Chinese material, of which there is none at E or K. Material seen by them, while having no type status, is of interest and becomes relevant in the typification of Planchon's *Rourea microphylla* (based on the Hooker & Arnott name, but due to its illegitimate status, to be taken as a new name rather than a new combination).
   At E is a specimen ex herb. Arnott, annotated by him with the name and 'Canton, [per] Dr Hooker', which is probably a Millett collection.
   At K are two sheets ex herb. Hooker in a type cover. On one of these are three collections: none is annotated with the name either by Hooker or Arnott, but attached are two drawings with notes by Arnott and one of the specimens is annotated by Hooker 'Millett, China' (the other collections are not relevant – Fortune, and an anonymous one from Hong Kong). The second sheet, annotated with the name 'Connarus mimosoides Vahl' by Hooker, also bears three collections – one is annotated by Hooker 'Canton, Millett', one '"Myrtus?". China, Lindley', an anonymous collection from Hong Kong is annotated by Arnott with the names 'Rourea microphyllus Planch.' and 'Connarus microphylla H & A' – these collections are probably original material of *Rourea microphylla* Planch.
≡ **Rourea microphylla** Planch.

Connarus roxburghii Hook. & Arn., Bot. Beechey Voy. 4: 179. 1833, *nom. illeg.* (Cnestis monadelpha Roxb., Fl. Ind. 2: 454. 1832, cited as a synonym). (CONNARACEAE).
Cited specimen: 'Macao. *Mr. Millett*'.
This material, while having no type status for Hooker & Arnott's name, becomes relevant in the typification of Planchon's *Rourea millettii*, a replacement for it. Of this there is none at E, but at K are two sheets in a type cover, both ex

herb. Hooker, one annotated in his hand 'China, Millett' (though not with the name *C. roxburghii*), which can probably be taken as the type of Planchon's name. (The other sheet, annotated by Hooker with the name *C. roxburghii* and 'China, Beechey', probably cannot, as it was not mentioned in Hooker & Arnott's description).
= **Rourea minor** (Gaertn.) Leenh.

Convolvulus densiflorus Hook. & Arn., Bot. Beechey Voy. 7: 303. 1838. (CONVOLVULACEAE).
Original material: Tepic, Mexico, Lay & Collie.
   At E: a sheet ex herb. Arnott (E00369173) annotated by him 'Ipomoea densiflorus H & A. Mexico, Beechey'.
   None found at K.
= **Merremia umbellata** (L.) Hall. f.

Convolvulus filifolius Hook. & Arn., Bot. Beechey Voy. 1: 35. 1830. (Generic placement queried). (CONVOLVULACEAE).
Original material: 'Coquimbo', Chili, Lay & Collie; 'specimens from Mr. Cruckshanks'.
   None found at E or K.
Note. According to Index Kewensis this ≡ *Ipomoea cruckshanksii* Choisy. This was coined as a replacement name for the Cruckshanks material cited by Hooker & Arnott, though Choisy (1845) misquoted their name as 'Conv.? linifoilus'; Choisy's name was superfluous, and by modern rules illegitimate, and G. Don had already (1837/8) transferred Hooker & Arnott's epithet to the genus *Ipomoea*. Current status uncertain and not treated in Zuloaga *et al.* (2: 1940. 2008).
≡ ***Ipomoea filifolia*** (Hook. & Arn.) G. Don

Cordia decandra Hook. & Arn., Bot. Beechey Voy. 1: 38, t. 10. 1830. (BORAGINACEAE).
Original material: 'Coquimbo', Chili, Lay & Collie; material collected by Cruckshanks and Macrae is also mentioned.
   None at E, the only sheet bearing this name in Arnott's hand is a later collection, *Bridges* 1297.
   At K, a sheet ex herb. Hooker – the bottom right-hand specimen (K000584787) is annotated by him with the name and 'Beechey's Voy.'; the other original material mentioned in the protologue is mounted on the same sheet – on the left-hand side are specimens and a drawing annotated by Hooker 'Valparaiso, Macrae' (K000583374), at top right a specimen annotated by Hooker 'No. 42, Chili, Mr Cruickshanks' (K000583375).

Alphabetical list of new taxa 77

Corrigiola deltoidea Hook. & Arn., Bot. Beechey Voy. 1: 24. 1830. (PORTULACACEAE).
Original material: 'Conception', Chili, Lay & Collie.
  At E: a sheet ex herb. Arnott, bears three specimens – the top right-hand one (E00369013), though it bears the name in Arnott's hand, is a later collection (*Cuming* 577) and is not original material; the top left-hand specimen (E00369014) is original material, annotated by Arnott with the name and 'Conception, Beechey', as might perhaps be the bottom one (E00369015), labelled 'Conception, [per] Dr Hooker.'
  None found at K.
= ***Calandrinia monandra*** (Ruiz & Pavon) DC.

Cristaria pinnatifida Hook. & Arn., Bot. Beechey Voy. 1: 12. 1830. (Generic placement queried). (MALVACEAE).
Type: a single, indifferent, specimen, from 'Coquimbo', Chili, Lay & Collie.
  Not found at E.
  Type at K: a sheet (K000528373) ex herb. Hooker annotated by him with the name, reference, and 'Coquimbo, Beechey'. M. Muñoz-Schick (Bol. Mus. Nac. Hist. Nat. Chile 45: 70. 1995), who saw a photo of this specimen, made the following tentative identification:
?= ***Cristaria aspera*** Gay

Crotalaria acapulcensis Hook. & Arn., Bot. Beechey Voy. 9: 414. 1840 (as '*Acapulcencis*'). (LEGUMINOSAE).
Original material: 'Acapulco', Mexico, Sinclair.
  At E: a sheet ex herb. Arnott (E00296005), bearing a label annotated with the name by ?Hooker, to which Arnott has added 'H & A, in Bot. Beech. Voy. Supp. Acapulco' and 'Dr Sinclair'.
  At K there are two sheets in a type cover: one (K000119947), ex herb. Hooker, bears a ticket annotated by him with the name and 'Acapulco' (but no collector) – this might, perhaps, be original material. The second sheet, ex herb. Bentham, is not original material – it is not annotated with the name and, though collected at Acapulco on the *Sulphur* voyage, is of the later material collected by R.B. Hinds and worked on by Bentham.

Crotalaria longirostrata Hook. & Arn., Bot. Beechey Voy. 6: 285. 1838. (LEGUMINOSAE).
Original material: 'Talisco', Mexico, Lay & Collie.
  At E: a sheet (E00296006), one of those given to E by GL in 1902 with a printed 'Herb. Walker Arnott' label, annotated by Arnott with the name and 'Talisco, Beechey'. (Two other sheets of this species ex herb. Arnott, collected at Acapulco by Dr Sinclair, referred to in the Mexico supplement (p. 414. 1840), are not original material).
  At K: a sheet (K000295690) ex herb. Hooker, annotated by him with the

name and 'Mexico. Talisco, Beechey'. (The later, Sinclair, collections from Acapulco in the type cover are not original material of *C. longirostrata*).

Crotalaria tepicana Hook. & Arn., Bot. Beechey Voy. 9: 414. 1840. (LEGUMINOSAE).
Original material: 'Tepic', Mexico, Sinclair.
 At E: a sheet ex herb. Arnott (E00285997), bearing a label annotated with the name by ?Hooker, to which Arnott has added 'H & A, in Bot. Beech. Voy. Supp. Tepic' and 'Dr Sinclair'.
 At K: a sheet ex herb. Bentham (K000295704) bearing a ticket annotated by Bentham with the name and 'Tepic, Dr Sinclair'.
 A sheet at K, ex herb. Hooker, annotated by him with the name, has the collecting details 'Tepic, Beechey' (it bears five specimens, apparently representing a single collection but to which two barcodes, K000295699, K000295700, have been attached) – this (the whole sheet?) was annotated 'holotype' by D.R. Windler in 1980, but Hooker & Arnott made no reference to Beechey material in the protologue so this is not original material. R. McVaugh (Fl. Nova-Galiciana 5: 388. 1987) also made a mistake (the collector is wrong), when he designated the type as 'Tepic, *Barclay*, K! [herb. Hook., MICH neg. 616], lectotype'.
= ***Crotalaria pumila*** Ortega

Crotalaria vachellii Hook. & Arn., Bot. Beechey Voy. 4: 180. 1833. (LEGUMINOSAE).
Original material: Chiefly ... about Macao, China, Lay & Collie. The authors noted 'exceedingly common at Canton', which, with the epithet chosen, suggests that they had additional material on which to base the description beyond the Beechey material, but none of this is specified.
 No Beechey sheet at E, but one ex herb. Arnott (E00369040) is annotated by him 'Crotalaria vatchellii [sic] H & A. Canton – [per] Dr Hooker', and later 'but is C. elliptica Roxb. Wall. L. n. 5438' – this is probably a Millett or Vachell collection and possibly original material.
 In the type cover at K are four sheets. Of these the most likely to be original material is one ex herb. Bentham (K000633843) annotated by him 'C. elliptica Roxb. – Benth. Lond. Journ. 2. 580, Crotalaria Vachellii Hook. et. Arn. Bot. of Beech. Voy. 180, Macao 1832 [per] Henslow 1834'. A sheet of Wall. Cat. no. 5433 is certainly not original material, and little more likely to be so are the two sheets (K000633841, K000633842) ex herb. Hooker, annotated by him 'Crot. variegata Wall. China, Millett' and in a later hand 'C. vachellii H & A'.
= ***Crotalaria uncinella*** Lam.

Crusea parviflora Hook. & Arn., Bot. Beechey Voy. 9: 430, t. 99C. 1840. (RUBIACEAE).
Original material: 'Acapulco', Mexico, Sinclair.

Alphabetical list of new taxa

At E: a sheet ex herb. Arnott (E00369097), annotated by him 'Crusea parviflora H & A. Bot. Beech. voy supp. Realejo, Dr Sinclair' is probably original material. As no specimen of this species was mentioned from Realejo in the Mexican 'Supplement', it seems likely (given Arnott's citation of the name and reference) that the locality on the sheet is a slip of the pen.

Types at K, two sheets. The one ex herb. Hooker (K000470237) bearing a ticket annotated by ?Arnott with the name and 'Acapulco, Sinclair' is presumably that intended as lectotype (cited as 'holotype') by W.R. Anderson in Mem. New York Bot. Gard. (22(4): 68. 1972), though it was not annotated by him as such. There is, however, another sheet (K000470238), ex herb. Bentham (given him by Hooker in 1843), annotated with the same name and details by Bentham, which is therefore an isolectotype.

Crusea subulata Hook. & Arn., Bot. Beechey Voy. 9: 431. 1840. (RUBIACEAE). Original material: 'Between San Blas and Tepic', Mexico, Sinclair.

Isolectotype at E: a sheet ex herb. Arnott (E00265953), bearing a label annotated with the name by ?Hooker, to which Arnott has added 'H & A. Bot. Beech. voy. Supp. San Blas to Tepic, Dr Sinclair'.

At K: a sheet ex herb. Bentham bearing two specimens (K000470240, and K000470239, the latter a remounted addition to the sheet) both with tickets annotated by Bentham with the name and 'San Blas – Tepic, Sinclair' – the sheet was determined by W.R. Anderson as *C. parviflora* in 1971, but when he published a lectotypification of *C. subulata* (citing 'Type: Sinclair (K! holotype)' in Mem. New York Bot. Gard. (22(4): 68. 1972) he did not specify which specimen he intended.

= ***Crusea parviflora*** Hook. & Arn.

Cuphea barbigera Hook. & Arn., Bot. Beechey Voy. 7: 289. 1838. (LYTHRACEAE).
Original material: 'Talisco', Mexico, Lay & Collie.

None at E: a Hartweg sheet, ex herb. Arnott, annotated by him 'Cuphea barbigera H & A, [C.] Llavea Benth. – non Llav. & Lex. Haltenango, Mexico, Hartweg No. 25' is not original material.

Likewise there is no Beechey material at K; though in a type cover is a sheet with a ticket in Arnott's hand – this is a Sinclair collection, later described in the Mexico Supplement. This sheet is not annotated by S.A. Graham, but is doubtless the Sinclair collection incorrectly cited by her as 'holotype' in Syst. Bot. Monog. (20: 94. 1988).

= ***Cuphea llavea*** Lex.

Cuphea bracteata Hook. & Arn., Bot. Beechey Voy. 7: 289. 1838, *nom. illeg.*, non Lag. (LYTHRACEAE).
Original material: 'Talisco', Mexico, Lay & Collie.

None found at E.

A sheet (K000532907) at K ex herb. Hooker is annotated by him with the name and details 'Tepic & Talisco, Sinclair & Beechey' clearly referring to more than one locality and collector – this sheet is not annotated by S.A. Graham, but was cited by her as a 'holotype' in Syst. Bot. Monog. (20: 105. 1988). One element has been removed from the sheet, and it is likely that what is left is the Beechey collection and therefore the original material. The reason for this assumption is that there is a duplicate at K ex herb. Bentham (given him by Hooker in 1843) with a ticket annotated by Bentham with the name and 'Talisco, Beechey', which must be original material. Clearly lectotypification and annotation of the sheets is required to resolve this matter.

Note. Although 'C. bracteata. *Lag.*?' was cited in the protologue due to the expression of doubt over its synonymy, and as the name was attributed to Hooker & Arnott in the index, it should be taken as an independent name, validated by their description and based on Beechey material. This, of course, means that it is an illegitimate later homonym as treated by Standley (1924) who renamed it *Parsonsia arnottiana* (*C. arnottiana* (Standl.) R.C. Foster). S.A. Graham (Syst. Bot. Monog. 20: 105. 1988) also treated it as an independent name for which she cited a 'holotype' – see above.

= **Cuphea lobophora** Koehne var. ***occidentalis*** S.A. Graham

Cuphea floribunda Hook. & Arn., Bot. Beechey Voy. 7: 289. 1838, *nom. illeg.*, non Lehm., 1831 (LYTHRACEAE).
Original material: 'Talisco and Tepic', Mexico, Lay & Collie.

At E, two sheets may be original material: one ex herb. Arnott (E00369072), annotated by him with the name and 'Mexico'; the other (E00369073) a duplicate, mounted much later, bearing a ticket annotated by Arnott 'Cuphea floribunda H & A. Mexico. Dupl.' and with a long description in Latin and English.

None at K. In a type cover is a sheet (K000532941) ex herb. Hooker bearing two specimens, but no reference to Beechey: the right-hand one is annotated by Hooker 'C. Llava β. Tepic, Sinclair'. The sheet bears a ticket annotated by ?Bentham 'Cuphea floribunda Hook. et Arn., C. hookeriana Walpers. San Blas to Tepic, Dr Sinclair', which might, perhaps, refer only to the left-hand specimen. In 1990 S.A. Graham attached a lectotype label also, perhaps, referring to the left-hand specimen (or perhaps to both) – she published this as a lectotypfication of *C. hookeriana* Walp. in Syst. Bot. Monog. (53: 57. 1998), but this is incorrect. Walpers's name was a replacement for Hooker & Arnott's illegitimate one and must therefore be based on Beechey material.

≡ **Cuphea hookeriana** Walp.

Cuphea tenella Hook. & Arn., Bot. Beechey Voy. 7: 289. 1838. (LYTHRACEAE).
Original material: Tepic, Mexico, Lay & Collie.

At E, two sheets: one ex herb. Arnott (E00369074), annotated by him with the name and 'Mexico, Beechey'. The other (E00369075) a duplicate,

Alphabetical list of new taxa 81

mounted much later, bearing a ticket annotated by Arnott 'Cuphea tenella H & A. Mexico. Dupl.'.

At K, two sheets: one (K000532884) ex herb. Hooker annotated by him with the name and 'Tepic, Beechey'; a duplicate ex herb. Bentham (given him by Hooker in 1843), with a ticket annotated by Bentham with the name and 'Tepic, Beechey'.

= ***Cuphea mimuloides*** Cham. & Schltdl.

Cupia mollissima Hook. & Arn., Bot. Beechey Voy. 4: 192. 1833. (RUBIACEAE). Original material: [China], specimens 'from Professor Lindley, and the late Dr. Livingstone'.

None found at E.

At K: the upper specimen on a sheet ex herb. Hooker annotated by him with the name and 'China, Lindley' (the lower specimen, 'China, Millett' is probably not original material).

≡ ***Tarenna mollissima*** (Hook. & Arn.) B.L. Rob.

Cuscuta californica Hook. & Arn., Bot. Beechey Voy. 8: 364. 1839. (CONVOLVULACEAE).
Original material: California, Douglas.

At E: a sheet ex herb. Arnott (E00369174), annotated by him with the name and 'California. D[avid] D[ouglas] per Hooker'.

At K, two sheets. One ex herb. Hooker with three collections, the left-hand one (K000195749), annotated by Hooker 'California, Douglas', beside which is mounted a ticket with drawings annotated with the name by Hooker is original material (the other collections, *Nuttall* s.n., *Asa Gray* s.n., are not). The other sheet, ex herb. Bentham, bears four collections – the top left-hand one (K000195754), with a printed 'California, Douglas 1833' label, though not annotated with the name by Bentham, is original material.

Cuscuta millettii Hook. & Arn., Bot. Beechey Voy. 5: 201. 1836. (CONVOLVULACEAE).
Original material: 'Canton [China]; *Mr. Millett*'.

At E: a sheet ex herb. Arnott (E00369175), annotated by him with the name and 'Canton, Mr Millett'.

None found at K.

Note. The name 'Grammica aphylla. *Lour. Fl. Coch.* 1. p. 212?' is cited, but as the synonymy is queried, this does not make Hooker & Arnott's name superfluous.

= ***Cuscuta australis*** R. Br.

Cyanostremma Benth. ex Hook. & Arn., Bot. Beechey Voy. 9: 415. 1840. (LEGUMINOSAE).
Hooker & Arnott did not publish a formal description of the genus, but the

English description under the species has been taken as a validating specific-generic description
= ***Calopogonium*** Desv.

Cyanostremma caeruleum (Benth.) Benth. ex Hook. & Arn., Bot. Beechey Voy. 9: 415. 1840. (LEGUMINOSAE). [Mexico].
Basionym cited 'Stenolobium caeruleum, *Benth. in Ann. Mus. Vind.* 2. *p.* 125 *et in Tayl. Ann. Nat. Hist.* 2. *p.* 436 [first published in Comentat. Legum. Gen. 61. 1837]'.
≡ ***Calopogonium caeruleum*** (Benth.) Hemsl.

Cynanchum birostratum Hook. & Arn., Bot. Beechey Voy. 1: 35. 1830. (APOCYNACEAE [ASCLEPIADACEAE]).
Original material: 'Conception', Chili, Lay & Collie; 'it has been sent us from Valparaiso also, by Mr. Cruckshanks and Mr. Bridges'.

G.H. Rua in Parodiana (5: 396. 1989) stated that the Beechey specimen at G (though lacking the locality) could probably be treated as 'holotype', which counts as a lectotypification. At E, the sheet ex herb. Arnott annotated with Hooker & Arnott's later combination 'Tweedia birostrata' bears two specimens, the right hand one is annotated by Arnott 'Conception, ([per] Dr Hooker)', which Rua interpreted as an isotype, but is possibly a Bridges or Macrae collection and therefore original material. When Hooker and Arnott made the new combination *Tweedia birostrata* (J. Bot. 1: 291. 1834) they cited additional specimens (*Bridges* 160 – the second specimen on the Arnott sheet; *Cuming* 520, of which a specimen at E ex herb. R.K. Greville), but these cannot be considered original material of *C. birostratum*.

At K no Beechey material, but there are two sheets ex herb. Hooker annotated by him with the name. One of these bears two collections: *Bridges* 160 (K000196845) and *Cruickshanks* 17 (K000196844), which are original material; the second sheet also has two collections: 'Hort. Soc. Lond. 1826' (K000196842), and one with no details (K000196843) – these are probably not original material.
≡ ***Tweedia birostrata*** (Hook. & Arn.) Hook. & Arn.

Cynoglossum paniculatum Hook. & Arn., Bot. Beechey Voy. 1: 37. 1830. (BORAGINACEAE).
Original material: 'Conception', Chili, Lay & Collie; specimens from Murillo Bay, Peru, sent by Mr. Macrae to the Horticultural Society.

None at E, the only specimen with the name in Arnott's hand being a specimen from Valparaiso, *Mathews* 230.

At K: a sheet ex herb. Hooker annotated by him with the name and reference bearing three collections – the right-hand one (K000573727) is annotated by Hooker 'Conception, Beechey'; the central specimen (K000573726) is the Macrae specimen from 'Murillo Bay, Peru' (the other specimen, *Germain* s.n., is not original material).

Alphabetical list of new taxa

Cynoglossum penicillatum Hook. & Arn., Bot. Beechey Voy. 8: 371. 1839. (BORAGINACEAE).
Original material: California, Douglas.
 At E: a sheet ex herb. Arnott (E00369165), annotated by him with the name and 'California, D[avid] D[ouglas] per Hooker--' (and later, also by Arnott, 'Pectocarya penicillata Alph DC') – this was annotated by Barbara Veno in 1982 but she failed to notice its type status.
 At K: a sheet ex herb. Hooker bears two collections, the lower one is annotated by Hooker with the name and 'California, Douglas' (the two upper collections, *Anon* 576, though bearing a ticket annotated with the name by Arnott, are not original material – they belong to a different species, determined as *P. anisocarpa* Veno by B. Veno in 1979). A sheet at K ex herb. Bentham bears two collections (and formerly another that has been removed) – the upper one, with a printed 'California, Douglas 1833' label annotated by Bentham with the name and the reference 'DC. Prod. 10 p. 120' is original material (the lower specimen, *Pringle* s.n., is not).
≡ ***Pectocarya penicillata*** (Hook. & Arn.) A. DC.

Cyperus caricifolius Hook. & Arn., Bot. Beechey Voy. 3: 99, 1832. (CYPERACEAE).
Type: Sandwich Islands, Lay & Collie.
 Not found at E.
 At K: a sheet ex herb. Hooker annotated by him 'Beechey', bearing a ticket annotated by Arnott with the name, and 'Oahu & Oneehow, B[eechey]'.
= ***Cyperus javanicus*** Houtt.

Cyperus multiceps Hook. & Arn., Bot. Beechey Voy. 3: 100. 1832. (CYPERACEAE).
Type: 'one specimen', Sandwich Islands, Lay & Collie.
 Not found at E.
 At K: a sheet ex herb. Hooker, bearing a ticket annotated by Arnott with the name and 'Oahu, Beechey'.
= ***Cyperus odoratus*** L.

Cyperus prescottianus Hook. & Arn., Bot. Beechey Voy. 3: 100. 1832. (CYPERACEAE).
Type: 'one specimen', Sandwich Islands, Lay & Collie.
 Not found at E.
 At K: a sheet ex herb. Hooker bearing two collections – the one with a ticket annotated by Arnott with the name and 'Oahu, Beechey' is the type (the other, a Barclay collection, is not).
= ***Cyperus odoratus*** L.

Cyperus trachysanthos Hook. & Arn., Bot. Beechey Voy. 3: 99. 1832. (CYPERACEAE).
Original material: Sandwich Islands, Lay & Collie.
    None found at E.
    At K: a sheet ex herb. Hooker annotated by him on the sheet 'Beechey', and bearing a ticket annotated by Arnott with the name and 'Oahu, B[eechey]'.

Cyrtandra menziesii Hook. & Arn., Bot. Beechey Voy. 2: 91. 1832. (GESNERIACEAE).
Original material: Sandwich Islands, Mr. Menzies.
    None found at E.
    At K: a sheet ex herb. Hooker, annotated by him with the name and 'Sandwh. Isles. A.M.'.

Dalea argyrostachys Hook. & Arn., Bot. Beechey Voy. 6: 285. 1838. (LEGUMINOSAE).
Original material: Tepic, Mexico, Lay & Collie.
    None found at E.
    Lectotype at K: a sheet (K000081930) ex herb. Hooker, annotated by him with the name and 'Talisco, Beechey' – although not annotated by R. Barneby it was lectotypified (cited as 'holotype') by him in Mem. New York Bot. Gard. (27: 497. 1977).
≡ ***Dalea versicolor*** Zucc. subsp. ***argyrostachys*** (Hook. & Arn.) Barneby var. ***argyrostachys***

Dalea crenulata Hook. & Arn., Bot. Beechey Voy. 6: 285. 1838. (LEGUMINOSAE).
Original material: 'Talisco', Mexico, Lay & Collie.
    Isolectotypes at E: two sheets (E00285915, E00285916), both given to E by GL in 1902, with 'Herb. Walker Arnott' labels, both annotated by Arnott with the name, and 'Talisco, Beechey'.
    Lectotype at K: a sheet ex herb. Hooker (K000082135) annotated by him with the name and 'Talisco, Mexico, Beechey' – although not annotated as such by R. Barneby it is doubtless the sheet lectotypified (cited as 'holotype') by him in Mem. New York Bot. Gard. (27: 116. 1977). A sheet (K000082136) ex herb. Hooker annotated by him 'Mexico, Beechey' is likely to be a duplicate and therefore an isolectotype.
≡ ***Marina crenulata*** (Hook. & Arn.) Barneby var. ***crenulata***

Dalea elata Hook. & Arn., Bot. Beechey Voy. 9: 416. 1840. (LEGUMINOSAE).
Original material: 'Acapulco', Mexico, Sinclair.
    At E: a sheet ex herb. Arnott (E00369041), bearing a label annotated with the name by ?Hooker, to which Arnott has added 'H & A. Bot. Beech. voy. Supp. Acapulco, (Dr Sinclair)'.

Alphabetical list of new taxa

At K, two sheets: one (K000082200) ex herb. Hooker bearing a ticket annotated by Arnott 'D. elata H & A. Acapulco, n. sp.'; the second a sheet ex herb. Bentham with a ticket annotated by him with the name and 'Acapulco, Sinclair'.

Dalea gracilis Hook. & Arn., Bot. Beechey Voy. 6: 286. 1838, *nom. illeg.*, non Kunth 1819. (LEGUMINOSAE).
Original material: Tepic, Mexico, Lay & Collie.
   None found at E.
   At K: a sheet ex herb. Hooker (K000082134), annotated by him 'Dalea. Mexico, Beechey' to which possibly he has later added in pencil 'gracilis H & A' – though not annotated by R. Barneby this is doubtless the sheet lectotypified (cited as 'holotype') by him in Mem. New York Bot. Gard. (27: 126. 1977). (The other sheets in the type cover – including Galeotti and Sinclair collections are not original material of the Hooker & Arnott name).
= ***Marina diffusa*** (Moric.) Barneby var. ***diffusa***

Delphinium sarcophyllum Hook. & Arn., Bot. Beechey Voy. 7: 317. 1838. (RANUNCULACEAE).
Original material: California, Douglas.
   Although 'D. nudicaule. Torr. et Gray' is cited as a synonym at the end of the description, in the note following Hooker & Arnott stated that while Douglas collected *D. nudicaule* [and there is a specimen at E], their *D. sarcophyllum* did 'not quite accord with' Torrey & Gray's, which means that *D. sarcophyllum* is not a superfluous name (though, in fact, they are now treated as synonymous). The identity of the two appears later to have been realised by Arnott, as there is a sheet at E (E00071241), probably mounted and annotated at a later date, with Arnott's annotations 'Delphinium nudicaule Torr. & Gr. "D. sarcophyllum". California, [per] Hooker'; this is probably original material of the latter name.
   At K is a sheet ex herb. Hooker annotated 'Delph. peltatum Hook. [ined.]. California, Douglas. D. sarcophyllum an D. nudicaule Torr. & Gr.', which might be original material of *D. sarcophyllum*.
= ***Delphinium nudicaule*** Torr. & A. Gray

Desmodium heterophyllum Hook. & Arn., Bot. Beechey Voy. 9: 417. 1840, *nom. illeg.*, non (Willd.) DC., 1825. (LEGUMINOSAE).
Type: 'Realejo ... the solitary specimen', [Nicaragua], Sinclair.
   Type at E, a sheet ex herb. Arnott (E00369043), bearing a label annotated with the name by ?Hooker, to which Arnott has added 'H & A. Bot. Beech. voy. Supp. Realejo, (Dr Sinclair)'.
   No type material at K.
?= ***Desmodium*** sp.

Desmodium podocarpum Hook. & Arn., Bot. Beechey Voy. 9: 417, t. 96. 1840, *nom. illeg.*, non DC., 1825. (LEGUMINOSAE).
Original material: 'Acapulco', Mexico, Sinclair.

At E: a sheet ex herb. Arnott (E00369042), bearing a label annotated with the name by ?Hooker, to which Arnott has added 'H & A. Bot. Beech. voy. Supp. Acapulco, (Dr Sinclair)'.

At K: a sheet (K000081855) ex herb. Hooker annotated by him with the name and 'Acapulco, Sinclair'. A second sheet (K000081854) ex herb. Hooker bears a ticket annotated by ?Arnott with the name and 'Acapulco, Beechey' – it is conceivable that the collector's name is a mistake, in which case this might also be original material (though a Barclay specimen from Acapulco ex herb. Bentham is certainly not).

Note. Although D. Dietrich (Syn. Pl. 4: 1151. 1847) did not mention the earlier Candollean name, it is clear that by citing the Hooker & Arnott reference, and naming the plant after Hooker, that he was providing a replacement name, for which the Sinclair material is also the type.
≡ ***Desmodium hookerianum*** D. Dietr.

Desmodium purpureum Hook. & Arn., Bot. Beechey Voy. 2: 62. 1832. (LEGUMINOSAE).
Original material: 'Society Islands', Lay & Collie; a Roxburgh specimen 'in Herb. nostr.' under the name *Hedysarum purpureum* [Roxb., nom. nud.]; a specimen from the Island of St Vincent. Illustrations in J. Burman's Thesaurus Zeylanicus (t. 53 f. 2), and N.L. Burman's Flora Indica (t. 55, f. 2) only 'appear to be the same', so should not be regarded as original material (this expression of doubt also means that their name not a superfluous one for N.L. Burman's *Hedysarum siliquosum*).

At E: a sheet ex herb. Arnott (E00369044), annotated by him 'Desmodium purpureum. Hedysarum purpureum Roxb. Gambiers island. Beechey' is original material – it was determined as *D. heterocarpon* (L.) DC. var. *strigosum* by F.R. Fosberg in 1982.

No original material found at K.
= ***Desmodium heterocarpon*** (L.) DC.

Dianella sandwicensis Hook. & Arn., Bot. Beechey Voy. 3: 97. 1832. (HEMEROCALLIDACEAE).
Original material: Sandwich Islands, Lay & Collie.

At E, two sheets. Both ex herb. Arnott (E00369228, E00369229), annotated by him with the name and 'Oahu, Beechey', to the latter of which is pinned a ticket with a description in Arnott's hand.

At K, two sheets. One (K000644331) annotated on the sheet by Hooker with the name and 'Oahu, Beechey'. The other (K000644332) bears a ticket annotated by Arnott with the name and 'Oahu, Beechey'.

Alphabetical list of new taxa 87

Dielytra chrysantha Hook. & Arn., Bot. Beechey Voy. 7: 320, t. 73. 1838. (PAPAVERACEAE).
Original material: California, Douglas.
　None found at E.
　At K, two sheets: one ex herb. Hooker annotated by him 'Dielytra (aurea Hook.). California, Douglas. D. chrysantha' – this was annotated 'holotype' by K.R. Stern in 1966, but it is not known if this typification has been published; the second sheet is ex herb. Bentham, with a printed 'California, Douglas 1833' label annotated by Bentham with the name and reference.
≡ *Dicentra chrysantha* (Hook. & Arn.) Walp.

Diodia barbigera Hook. & Arn., Bot. Beechey Voy. 7: 295. 1838. (RUBIACEAE).
Original material: 'Talisco', Mexico, Lay & Collie.
　None found at E or K.

Dioscorea gracilis Hook. & Arn., Bot. Beechey Voy. 1: 48. 1830. (DIOSCOREACEAE).
Original material: 'Valparaiso', Chili, Lay & Collie.
　None found at E.
　At K: a sheet ex herb. Hooker bears 4 specimens representing 2 collections. The original material probably comprises the two left-hand ones (K000099296), between which Hooker has written the name and details 'Chili, Beechey'. With the two right-hand ones (K000099295) is associated a ticket annotated with the collecting number '299' and the details 'Dioscorea humilis Bert. Valp[araiso]. Chili Septr'; this is a Mathews collection, and is not original material, though was cited as 'type' by L.E. Navas Bustamente & G. Erba (Revista Univ.-Univ. Catolica Chile 53: 49. 1969) – (they had seen only a photograph, from which they misread the number as '199').
≡ *Dioscorea humifusa* Poepp. var. *gracilis* (Hook. & Arn.) L.E. Navas

Dioscorea obtusifolia Hook. & Arn., Bot. Beechey Voy. 1: 48. 1830. (DIOSCOREACEAE).
Original material: 'Island of Quiriguina, near Conception', Chili, Lay & Collie.
　None found at E (the only specimen bearing this name in Arnott's hand is a later collection, *Mathews* 299).
　At K: a sheet ex herb. Hooker bears three collections, the original material is that at bottom right, annotated by Hooker with the name and 'Chili, Beechey' – it was annotated 'holotype' in an illegible hand in 1994 and is probably that to which the barcode K000099290 refers (the other collections, *Bridges* 685, *Anon s.n.*, are not original material).
Note. L.E. Navas Bustamente & G. Erba (Revista Univ.-Univ. Catolica Chile 53: 49. 1969) treated this as a synonym of *D. humifusa* var. *gracilis*, but cited no type; in Zuloaga *et al.* (1: 407. 2008) it is maintained as a distinct species.

Diplandra Hook. & Arn., Bot. Beechey Voy. 7: 291. 1838. (ONAGRACEAE).
= ***Lopezia*** Cav.

Diplandra lopezioides Hook. & Arn., Bot. Beechey Voy. 7: 292, t. 60. 1838. (ONAGRACEAE).
Original material: Tepic, Mexico, Lay & Collie.
   At E: a sheet ex herb. Arnott (E00369076), annotated by him with the name and 'Mexico' is probably original material. A second sheet from Arnott's herbarium, collected by Dr Sinclair and bearing a ticket with the name in what is possibly Hooker's hand, is referred to in the Mexico Supplement (p. 422. 1840).
   Lectotype at K: two sheets. One (K000533319) ex herb. Hooker annotated by him with the name and 'Mexico, Beechey', to which is attached a ticket with a detailed description by Arnott – though not annotated by Plitmann *et al.*, this is doubtless the specimen cited as type by them in Ann. Missouri Bot. Gard. (60: 500. 1973). The other specimen is a duplicate ex herb. Bentham (given him by Hooker in 1843), bearing a ticket annotated by Bentham with the name and 'Tepic, Beechey', and therefore an isolectotype.
≡ ***Lopezia lopezioides*** (Hook. & Arn.) Plitmann, P.H. Raven & Breedlove

Diplopappus occidentalis Hook. & Arn., Bot. Beechey Voy. 8: 350. 1839. (Generic placement queried). (COMPOSITAE).
Original material: California, Douglas.
   None found at E.
   At K: the right-hand specimen on a sheet (with two collections) ex herb. Hooker annotated by him 'California, Douglas' – beside it is a drawing of two florets annotated with the name by ?Arnott (the left-hand specimen, *Orcutt 329*, is not original material).
Note: Torrey and Gray transferred this to *Erigeron* in 1841, giving it the name *E. douglasii* as there was already an *E. occidentale* Nutt., 1840.
= ***Erigeron foliosus*** Nutt.

Diplopappus villosus (Pursh) Hook. & Arn., Bot. Beechey Voy. 4: 147. 1833. (COMPOSITAE). [California].
Basionym cited: 'Amellus villosa Pursh. [Fl. Amer. Sept. (Pursh) 2: 564. 1814]'.
Note. This combination has commonly (e.g. Semple, Brittonia 42: 226. 1990, with a discussion on typification) been attributed to Hook., Fl. Bor. Amer. 2: 22. 1834.
≡ ***Heterotheca villosa*** (Pursh) Shinners

Distasis concinna Hook. & Arn., Bot. Beechey Voy. 8: 350. 1839. (Generic placement queried). (COMPOSITAE).
Type: 'Snake River, below the Salmon Falls, Snake Country [Idaho]. [John McLeod per] *Mr. Tolmie*'.

Alphabetical list of new taxa

Type at E: a sheet ex herb. Arnott (E00369118), annotated by him with the name and 'Snake river below the Salmon falls, N. California – Tolmie' – this was effectively designated lectotype (cited as 'holotype') by G.L. Nesom in Sida (10: 164. 1983), and was annotated 'holotype' by him in 1985.

A sheet at K ex herb. Hooker annotated with this name (but probably not by Hooker) apparently bearing three collections – the (isolecto)types are two on the right-hand side to which refers a ticket annotated 'Erigeron concinnum Torr. & Gray. Snake Country, Tolmie' (the upper central specimen annotated by Hooker 'Snake Country, Douglas', and the five Torrey specimens bottom left, are not types).
≡ ***Erigeron concinnus*** (Hook. & Arn.) Torr. & A. Gray

Drosera loureiroi Hook. & Arn., Bot. Beechey Voy. 4: 167, t. 31. 1833 (as '*Loureirii*'). (DROSERACEAE).
Original material: Chiefly … about Macao, Lay & Collie.
This should be taken as the recognition as a distinct species of *D. rotundifolia* [sensu] Lour. Cochin. v. 1 p. 233' [i.e. non L.], and a Chinese specimen included by Candolle under his *D. burmannii*: 'D. burmannii DC Prodr. v. 1. p. 318 (quoad specimen Chinense)'. The Loureiro and Candolle material might also be considered as 'original', but as it is unlikely that Hooker & Arnott saw this, it makes sense to choose the type from the Beechey material.

At E: a sheet ex herb. Arnott (E00369065), annotated by him 'Drosera Loureirii H & A, [D.] rotundifolia Lour. non Lin. China – Beechey' (on the same sheet is also a Luzon specimen, *Cuming* 857, E00369066).

At K: a sheet ex herb. Hooker annotated by him 'Dr. Loureirii H & A, v. Bot. of Beech. Voy. see Lour. p. 883 [sic]', the specimen at top left is annotated by Hooker 'China, Beechey' and there are several other later collections on the sheet.
= ***Drosera spatulata*** Labill.

Dubautia laxa Hook. & Arn., Bot. Beechey Voy. 2: 87. 1832. (COMPOSITAE).
Original material: Sandwich Islands, Lay & Collie.

At E: a sheet ex herb. Arnott (E00369136), annotated by him with the name and 'Oahu, Beechey' and, probably later, with the reference 'DC. [Prod.] v. p. 681. n. 2'.

G.D. Carr (Allertonia 4: 66. 1985) stated that this was lectotypified by E.E. Sherff (Bull. Bishop Mus. 135. 1935) on a specimen at K, but this cannot now be found; Carr also cited a duplicate at G.

Ecdysanthera Hook. & Arn., Bot. Beechey Voy. 5: 198. 1836. (APOCYNACEAE).
= ***Urceola*** Roxb.

Ecdysanthera rosea Hook. & Arn., Bot. Beechey Voy. 5: 198, t. 42. 1836. (APOCYNACEAE).
Original material: 'Canton, Macao, and the adjacent islands. *Messrs. Lay and Collie* [s.n.], *Mr. Millett* [s.n.], *and Rev. G.H. Vachell*. (No. 144)'.

At E, three sheets. One ex herb. Edinburgh University (E00284959), a duplicate of *Vachell* 144 is an isolectotype (see below). The other two are ex herb. Arnott, annotated by him with the name: one of these (E00369159) is annotated by Arnott 'China, Beechey', the other (E00369160) 'Canton, ([per] Dr Hooker)' is almost certainly a duplicate of the Millett specimen.

At K, two sheets (though no Beechey material): both annotated with the name by Hooker. One has the printed Vachell label and was annotated 'lectotype' by D.J. Middleton in 1995, and published as such by him in Novon (4: 151. 1994). The second is annotated by Hooker 'China, Millett'.
≡ ***Urceola rosea*** (Hook. & Arn.) D.J. Middleton

Echites pubescens Hook. & Arn., Bot. Beechey Voy. 1: 34. 1830, *nom. illeg.*, non Willd. ex Roem. & Schult., 1819. (APOCYNACEAE).
Original material: 'Conception', Chili, Lay & Collie.
　　None found at E.
　　At K: a sheet ex herb. Hooker (K000582919) annotated by him with the name and 'Conception, Beechey'; it bears a ticket with drawings possibly by Arnott.
= ***Elytropus chilensis*** (A. DC.) Müll. Arg.

Elaeocarpus bifidus Hook. & Arn., Bot. Beechey Voy. 3: 110, t. 24. 1832. (ELAEOCARPACEAE).
Original material: 'Oahu', Sandwich Islands, Lay & Collie.
　　At E, two sheets ex herb. Arnott (E00369016, E00369017), both annotated by him with the name and 'Oahu, Beechey'.
　　At K, two sheets, both ex herb. Hooker, annotated by him with the name, reference and 'Oahu' – one has two attached pencil drawings.

Elaeocarpus photiniifolius Hook. & Arn., Bot. Beechey Voy. 6: 259, t. 53. 1838 (as '*photiniaefolius*'). (ELAEOCARPACEAE).
Original material: 'Bonin', Lay & Collie.
　　At E, a sheet ex herb. Arnott (E00369018), annotated by him 'Elaeocarpus photiniaefolius H & A. In both the Bonin and Mexican collections – Beechey'.
　　At K, a sheet ex herb. Hooker, annotated by him with the name and 'Bonin, Beechey'.
Note. On p. 279 it is explained that 'the majority of the specimens [of this species] collected in the expedition were placed along with the Mexican plants ... not doubting ... this took place through inadvertancy. It may, however, have been cultivated in some garden in Mexico'. The latter seems extremely unlikely and the type locality was doubtless Bonin, whence there are recent collections.

Emmenanthus Hook. & Arn., Bot. Beechey Voy. 5: 217. 1836. (IXONANTHACEAE).
Note. Not to be confused with *Emmenanthe* Bentham, 1835 (HYDROPHYLLACEAE).
= ***Ixonanthes*** Jack

Alphabetical list of new taxa

Emmenanthus chinensis Hook. & Arn., Bot. Beechey Voy. 5: 217. 1836. (IXONANTHACEAE).
Original material: 'Canton; *Messrs. Lay and Collie*'.

At E: a sheet ex herb. Arnott (E00369019), annotated by him with the name and 'China, Beechey' to which is attached a ticket with Arnott's MS of the description as printed. The sheet was annotated 'holotype' by R. Kool in 1979 – it is not known if this typification has been published.

None found at K.

Note. Hooker & Arnott were unable to place this genus in a family and left it 'at the end of the Dicotyledons'. It was subsequently placed in Linaceae, before coming to rest in Ixonanthaceae (initially treated as a distinct Chinese species *Ixonanthes chinensis* (Hook. & Arn.) Champ., later as a synonym of the SE Asian *I. reticulata*).

= ***Ixonanthes reticulata*** Jack

Eragrostis millettii Hook. & Arn., Bot. Beechey Voy. 6: 252. 1838. (GRAMINEAE).
Original material: 'Circa Macao, et insulis vicinis; *Millett* [s.n.]; *G.H. Vachell, n. 54*'.

At E, two sheets ex herb Arnott. The first bears two specimens – one (E00369236) annotated by Arnott 'Eragrostis Millettii H & A. Canton, [per] Dr Hooker', which is doubtless a Millett specimen; the other (E00369237) annotated by Arnott '"Eragrostis Brownii" (not ... [Kunth?)] Macao; Revd. Mr Vachell, n. 54; per Prof. Henslow'. The second sheet (E00369238) bears another Millett duplicate annotated by Arnott 'Eragrostis millettii H & A. Canton; [per] Dr Hooker'.

None found at K.

Note. This species is not treated in Fl. China. The specimens exactly match those identified by William Munro, E. Hackel and E.D. Merrill as *E. pilosissima* Link. However, that species is given in Fl. China 22: 474, 2006, for 'mountain slopes', whereas all the specimens at E are from coastal localities.

= ***Eragrostis pilosissima*** Link

Erigeron multiflorus Hook. & Arn., Bot. Beechey Voy. 2: 87. 1832. (COMPOSITAE).
Type: 'one specimen', Sandwich Islands, Lay & Collie.

Not found at E.

Type at K: a sheet ex herb. Hooker bearing a ticket annotated by Arnott with the name and 'Oahu, Capt. Beechey'. It was annotated by S. Sundberg in 1986 'Apparently an authentic specimen, but this species lectotypified by another specimen by Jones (1984)'. In fact this is the specimen cited as 'holotype' of *E. multiflorus* by A.G. Jones (Brittonia 34: 465. 1984) though his citation (mixed up with that of *Aster sandwicensis* (A. Gray)

Hieron.) is confusing and so it is not surprising that it was misunderstood by Sundberg.
= *Aster subulatus* Michx. var. ***parviflorus*** (Nees) Sundberg

Erigeron pauciflorus Hook. & Arn., Bot. Beechey Voy. 2: 87. 1832. (COMPOSITAE).
Original material: Sandwich Islands, Lay & Collie; 'we have it also from Mr. Macrae' – it seems doubtful if this was used in the description, but it might also be considered original material.

At E: a sheet ex herb. Arnott (E00369149) bearing the locality 'Oahu' and the name 'Erigeron pauciflorum H & A' which has been crossed out by Arnott, and the name '[E.] canadense var. Less.' substituted – also the reference 'DC. [Prod.] v. p. 284. n. 2 (which is E. pauciflorus Hook. & Arn.)'.

At K: a sheet ex herb. Hooker annotated by him 'E. lepidotus Less. Beechey', bearing a ticket annotated by Arnott with the name, the details 'Oahu, B[eechey]', and the note 'I suspect Lessing confused this with E. canadense' – this is annotated 'holotype' doubtless by T.K. Lowrey who cited it as such in Allertonia (4: 254. 1986). Also at K are sheets ex herb. Bentham and ex herb. Hooker of the 1825 Macrae collection from 'Woahoo'.
= ***Tetramolopium lepidotum*** (Less.) Sherff

Erigeron spiculosus Hook. & Arn., Bot. Beechey Voy. 1: 32. 1830 (as '*spiculosum*'). (COMPOSITAE).
Original material: 'Valparaiso', Chili, Lay & Collie; a Bridges collection is also mentioned and may have been used in making the description.

At E: the right-hand specimen (E00247234) on a sheet ex herb. Arnott annotated by him 'Erigeron spiculosum H & A in Beechey (ex parte). Valparaiso (Beechey)' (the other specimen, *Cuming* 387 (E00247233), is not original material).

At K there is no Beechey material, but there are two sheets ex herb. Hooker annotated with the name by Arnott: on one (K000221844), the left-hand specimen is *Bridges* 184, which might be original material (the right-hand specimen, *Cuming* 430, is not); the other sheet (K000221842) has a field ticket for *Bridges* 186 and a ticket with a note by Arnott – and might also be original material.
≡ ***Conyza spiculosa*** (Hook. & Arn.) Zardini

Erigeron velutipes Hook. & Arn., Bot. Beechey Voy. 10: 434. 1841. (COMPOSITAE).
Original material: 'Between San Blas and Tepic', Mexico, Sinclair.

At E: a sheet ex herb. Arnott (E00369117), annotated by him with the name, reference, and 'San Blas to Tepic, Dr Sinclair, infr. Hartweg No. 113'.

At K: a sheet ex herb. Hooker bearing two collections. One (K000221783) is associated with a field ticket annotated in pencil 'Erigeron near Hartweg no. 113, 5283' to which ?Arnott has added the epithet 'velutipes H & A' and Bentham the locality 'Tepic, Dr Sinclair' and is certainly original material. To this has been added part of a sheet (K000221782) ex herb. Bentham (given him by Hooker in 1844) with a ticket annotated by Bentham with the name and 'Tepic, Sinclair' – presumably also original material.

Eriocaulon cantoniensis Hook. & Arn., Bot. Beechey Voy. 5: 219. 1836. (ERIOCAULACEAE).
Original material: Chiefly ... about Macao, China, Lay & Collie; material 'from the neighbourhood of Macao from Mr. Millett, and Mr. Vachell, "j"' is also mentioned.
   None found at E.
   At K: a sheet ex herb. Hooker, annotated by him on the sheet 'China, Beechey', and bearing a ticket annotated with the name in what is possibly Arnott's hand.
= *Eriocaulon sexangulare* L.

Erodium macrophyllum Hook. & Arn., Bot. Beechey Voy. 7: 327. 1838. (GERANIACEAE).
Original material: California, Douglas.
   None found at E.
   At K, two sheets: one ex herb. Hooker, annotated by him with the name and 'California, Douglas'; the other ex herb. Bentham annotated by him on the sheet with the name and reference – the original material is the right-hand specimen with a printed 'California, Douglas 1833' label (the other, a Hartweg collection, is not).

Eryngium beecheyanum Hook. & Arn., Bot. Beechey Voy. 7: 294. 1838. (UMBELLIFERAE).
Original material: 'Talisco', Mexico, Lay & Collie.
   None found at E.
   At K: the right-hand specimen (K000529758) on a sheet ex herb. Hooker annotated by W.B. Hemsley 'type', and 'Beechey' – beneath the single specimen is a ticket with the name and a description in Arnott's hand; it is not known if this typification has been published (the left-hand collection, which has been cut from another sheet, and remounted is a Barclay specimen from Tepic, and not original material).

Eryngium tenue Hook. & Arn., Bot. Beechey Voy. 7: 293. 1838, *nom. illeg.*, non Lam., 1797. (UMBELLIFERAE).
Original material: 'Talisco', Mexico, Lay & Collie.
   None found at E or K.
= *Eryngium beecheyanum* Hook. & Arn.

Erysimum glaberrimum Hook. & Arn., Bot. Beechey Voy. 7: 323. 1838. (Generic placement queried). (CRUCIFERAE).
Type: 'Snake Country. Confluence of Reed's River with the Snake River [Oregon/Idaho border]. (John McLeod per] *Tolmie*)'.
 Not found at E.
 At K, a sheet ex herb. Bentham annotated by Bentham 'Sisymbrium linifolium Nutt., Erysimum glaberrimum H & A. Snake Country, [ex] Herb. Hooker'. The sheet from Hooker's herbarium cannot be found at K.
= **Schoenocrambe linifolia** (Nutt.) Greene

Erythraea centaurioides (Roxb.) Hook. & Arn., Bot. Beechey Voy. 6: 266. 1838. (GENTIANACEAE). [Loo Choo].
Basionym cited: 'Chironia centaurioides. *Roxb. Fl. Ind.* [1: 584. 1832]'.
≡ **Centaurium centaurioides** (Roxb.) R. Rao & Hemadri

Erythraea macrantha Hook. & Arn., Bot. Beechey Voy. 10: 438. 1841. (GENTIANACEAE).
The identification of the types and correct application of names of this species, and the only named variety described under it, by Hooker & Arnott is uncertain due to some exceptionally confusing wording, and further work is required to confirm the following interpretation. The Beechey material was from two localities, Tepic and Talisco, which on p. 302 was queried as all belonging to Grisebach's undescribed "E. Mexicana". With additional material from [San Blas to] Tepic collected by Dr Sinclair, they realised that the Beechey material belonged to two species – that from Talisco they referred (on p. 439) to *E. texensis* Griseb.; that from Tepic to two varieties of a new species *E. macrantha*. They did not name the 'typical' variety of *E. macrantha* or even assign it to 'α', though from the description of the leaves (linear, 3-nerved) this appears to be the broad-leaved (sic) state to which (on p. 439) they referred the Beechey Tepic material. They named and described a var. β major, (with even narrower leaves), based on the Sinclair San Blas to Tepic, material. Examination of the specimens at E and K adds to the confusion, not least as Bentham created a notional (unpublished) new variety "α latifolia" and (almost certainly mistakenly – see above) misapplied this to some (but not all!) of the Beechey Talisco specimens. Further confusion arises from the annotations (both typifcations and identifications) of C.E. Broome, which seem not to have been published. The following is the best that can be done with what is probably an irresolvable muddle.

Specimens referred by Hooker and Arnott on p. 439 to 'E. texensis Griseb.' (initially identified on p. 302 as 'Erythraea mexicana Griseb. ms').
Specimens collected at Talisco, by Lay & Collie.
 At E: the lower specimens on a sheet ex herb. Arnott (E00369247), annotated by him 'Erythraea mexicana Griseb: Talisco, Beechey' – these were

identified as 'perhaps an aberrant form of Centaurium madrense (Hemsl.) Robins.' by C.R. Broome in 1987.

At K, three sheets. (1) ex herb. Hooker (K000438624), annotated by Bentham as 'Erythraea macrantha α latifolia', as 'holotype' of *E. macrantha* (erroneously) by R.F. Martin in 1939, and as 'holotype' of the (unpublished) "var. latifolia" by C.R. Broome in 1975. (2) a partial, remounted, sheet ex herb. Hooker, annotated by him 'Talisco, Beechey, an E. Texensis', annotated by Bentham 'Erythraea Texensisis Griseb?', and identified as *C. madrense* by C.R. Broome in 1974. (3) a partial, remounted, sheet ex herb. Bentham, annotated by him 'Erythraea macrantha α latifolia. Talisco, Beechey', annotated 'isotype' of *E. macrantha* (erroneously) by J. Ewan in 1947, and as 'isotype' of the (unpublished) "var. latifolia" by C.R. Broome in 1975.

Erythraea macrantha Hook. & Arn. [var. *macrantha*], Bot. Beechey Voy. 10: 438. 1841. (GENTIANACEAE).
Original material: Tepic, Mexico, Lay & Collie.

At E: the top left-hand specimen on a sheet ex herb. Arnott (E00369245), annotated by him 'Erythraea mexicana Griseb? Tepic, Beechey' – this was identified as *Centaurium quitense* by C.R. Broome in 1987 (she made no comment on its type status).

No Beechey material from Tepic can be found at K.
?= ***Centaurium quitense*** (Kunth) B.L. Rob.

Erythraea macrantha [var.] β *major* Hook. & Arn., Bot. Beechey Voy. 10: 438. 1841. (GENTIANACEAE).
Original material: 'Between San Blas and Tepic', Mexico, Sinclair.

None found at E.

At K: the left-hand specimen (K000438602) on a sheet ex herb Hooker, with a ticket annotated by Bentham 'Gyrandra speciosa, Erythraea macrantha β major Hook. et Arn. San Blas – Tepic, Sinclair'. This was correctly annotated in 1939 as the 'type' of β *major* by R.F. Martin (who redetermined it as *Centaurium speciosum* (Benth.) Druce), and in 1974 as 'holotype' of the variety by C.R. Broome (who redetermined it as *C. tenuifolium*).
?= ***Centaurium tenuifolium*** (M. Martens & Galeotti) B.L. Rob.

"*Erythraea mexicana* Griseb. ex. Hook. & Arn.", Bot. Beechey Voy. 7: 302. 1838. (GENTIANACEAE). [Mexico].
This name is not validly published, though it was accepted in Index Kewensis. Hooker & Arnott were so unsure of it that 'we dare not venture upon offering a character', i.e. did not dare describe it – they took Grisebach's MS name from a specimen in their herbarium, and stated that there were 'two varieties, if not two distinct though closely allied species' among their 'imperfect specimens' – these they treated later (see above).

Eugenia temu Hook. & Arn., Bot. Beechey Voy. 2: 56. 1832. (MYRTACEAE).
Original material: 'probably at Valparaiso [in 1828]', Chili, Lay & Collie. Cruckshanks and Bridges material is also mentioned.
　　None found at E or K. The only sheet with this name in Hooker's hand at K is a later collection (*Cuming* 100).
= ***Myrceugenia exsucca*** (DC.) O. Berg

Eupatorium lasioneuron Hook. & Arn., Bot. Beechey Voy. 7: 297. 1838. (COMPOSITAE).
Original material: 'Talisco', Mexico, Lay & Collie.
　　None found at E.
　　At K: a sheet (K000500175) ex herb. Hooker, annotated by him with the name and 'Mexico, Beechey' – this sheet was annotated 'holotype' by H. Robinson in 1991 but it is not known if this typification has been published.
≡ ***Ageratina lasioneura*** (Hook. & Arn.) R.M. King & H. Rob.

Eupatorium nigrescens Hook. & Arn., Bot. Beechey Voy. 7: 297. 1838. (COMPOSITAE).
Original material: Tepic, Mexico, Lay & Collie.
　　None found at E.
　　At K: a sheet (K000486854) ex herb. Hooker annotated by him with the name and 'Mexico, Beechey'.
= ***Chromolaena collina*** (DC.) R.M. King & H. Rob.

Eupatorium ovalifolium Hook. & Arn., Bot. Beechey Voy. 7: 297. 1838. (COMPOSITAE).
Original material: Tepic, Mexico, Lay & Collie.
　　None found at E.
　　At K: a sheet (K000486848) ex herb. Hooker annotated by him with the name and 'Mexico, Beechey'.
= ***Chromolaena glaberrima*** (DC.) R.M. King & H. Rob.

Eupatorium reticulatum Hook. & Arn., Bot. Beechey Voy. 1: 29. 1830, *nom. illeg.*, non Desv., 1825. (COMPOSITAE).
Original material: 'Valparaiso', Chili, Lay & Collie.
　　At E: a sheet ex herb. Arnott bearing three specimens. The left-hand specimen (E00249942) is original material, annotated by Arnott 'Valparaiso, (Beechey)', at the bottom left-hand corner is the synonymy 'Eupatorium Salvia Colla. DC. V. p. 157. n. 108. [E.] reticulatum H & A (non Desv.)' showing that Arnott later realised they had not only coined a homonym, but that the plant had an earlier name (the other two specimens, *Bridges* 192 and *Cuming* 650, though also from Valparaiso, are not original material).
　　None at K: those in the type covers being later collections (one cover has *Cuming*, *Gillies*, and *King*, material, the other *Macrae*, and *Moseley*). At K is

Alphabetical list of new taxa

a photograph of a supposed isotype at New York Botanic Garden, but this is dubious as all that is visible on the photo is a ticket with the word 'Chile' – a word below this (just possibly 'Hooker') has been chopped off – and on the typed label the collectors' names Lay and Collie are queried.
= *Aristeguietia salvia* (Colla) R.M. King & H. Rob.

Euphorbia bifida Hook. & Arn., Bot. Beechey Voy. 5: 213. 1836. (EUPHORBIACEAE).
Type: 'Peninsula of China; *Rev. G.H. Vachell, n.* 240'.
Not found at E.
At K: the lower specimen (of two) on a sheet ex herb. Hooker, with a printed Vachell label annotated with the number '240', and by Arnott with the name.

Euphorbia clusiifolia Hook. & Arn., Bot. Beechey Voy. 2: 95. 1832 (as '*clusiaefolia*'). (EUPHORBIACEAE).
Original material: 'Oahu', Sandwich Islands, Lay & Collie.
At E: a sheet ex herb. Arnott (E00369204), annotated by him with the name and 'Oahu, Beechey' – this was annotated 'type' by R. Melville in 1960.
At K: a sheet ex herb. Hooker with a single specimen, attached is a ticket annotated by Arnott with the name and 'Oahu, Beechey'.

Euphorbia lathryrus L. [var.] β *minor* Hook. & Arn., Bot. Beechey Voy. 44. 1830 (as '*Lathyris*'). (EUPHORBIACEAE).
Original material: 'Conception', Chili, Lay & Collie.
None found at E.
At K: a sheet ex herb. Hooker with three collections – the right-hand one, though not annotated with this name, is almost certainly original material and is annotated by Hooker with the collection details 'Chili, Beechey'.
Note. Doubtless an introduction to Chile (perhaps only a casual one), and not treated in Zuloaga *et al.* (2: 2050. 2008).
= *Euphorbia lathyrus* L.

Euphorbia multiformis Gaud. ex Hook. & Arn., Bot. Beechey Voy. 2: 95. 1832. (EUPHORBIACEAE).
Original material: 'Oahu', Sandwich Islands, Lay & Collie.
At E: a sheet ex herb. Arnott (E00369205), annotated by him 'Euphorbia multiformis Gaud? Oahu – Beechey'.
At K: a sheet ex herb. Hooker bearing a ticket annotated by Arnott 'Euphorbia multiformis Gaud. Oahu, Beechey' – this has been annotated as 'type' by E.E. Sherff, and as 'holotype' by D.L. Koutnik.
Note. Hooker & Arnott cited the name as being taken from 'Gaud. in Freyc. Voy p. 100? [1827]'. In that work Gaudin gave no diagnostic description,

merely citing the name as an example of a species the appearance of which varied greatly with habitat – it is therefore a *nomen nudum*, and the name is to be typified solely on Beechey material.

Euphorbia myrtifolia Hook. & Arn., Bot. Beechey Voy. 2: 95. 1832, *nom. illeg.*, non (L.) Lam., 1788. (EUPHORBIACEAE).
Original material: 'Oahu', Sandwich Islands, Lay & Collie.

At E: a sheet ex herb. Arnott (E00369206), annotated by him with the name and 'Oahu, Beechey' – it was annotated 'holotype' of *Chamaesyce arnottiana* (Endl.) Deg. & Deg. by D.L. Koutnik in 1982, and had earlier been annotated as the type of *E. myrtifolia* by R. Melville in 1960.

At K: a sheet ex herb. Hooker, bearing a ticket annotated by Arnott with the name and 'Oahu, Beechey'. It bears two specimens, which belong to different taxa – E.E. Sherff appears to have drawn a pencil line linking the right-hand specimen with the Arnott annotations (and therefore identifying it as the original material) and which he determined as *E. hookeri* Steud. (the left-hand specimen he determined as 'E. multiformis var. microphylla Boiss.')

Note. In 1836 Endlicher provided the replacement name *E. arnottiana* for this; in 1840 Steudel coined a second replacement name, *E. hookeri*, also based entirely on Hooker & Arnott's homonym and therefore illegitimate.

≡ ***Euphorbia arnottiana*** Endl.

Euphorbia ramosissima Hook. & Arn., Bot. Beechey Voy. 2: 69. 1832, *nom. illeg.*, non Loisel., 1827. (EUPHORBIACEAE).
Original material: 'Elizabeth Island', Lay & Collie.

None found at E. The Arnott sheet has apparently gone missing – at K, however, is a photograph of it taken when it was 'in Herb. Glasgow' – it was annotated by Arnott 'Elizabeth Island, Beechey', and annotated as 'type' by R. Melville in 1960 (also on the sheet was *Mathews* 118, not original material).

At K: a sheet ex herb. Hooker annotated by him with the name and 'Elizabeth Island, Beechey'.

= ***Euphorbia sparrmanni*** Boiss.

Euphorbia rotundifolia Hook. & Arn., Bot. Beechey Voy. 1: 44. 1830, *nom. illeg.*, non Loisel., 1809. (EUPHORBIACEAE).
Original material: 'Conception', Chili, Lay & Collie.

None found at E.

At K: a remounted partial sheet ex herb. Hooker (K000254042), annotated by Hooker with the name and 'Chili, Beechey'.

Note. Boissier provided a new name for this homonym (but also included other material):

≡ ***Euphorbia engelmannii*** Boiss.

Alphabetical list of new taxa

Euphorbia strigosa Hook. & Arn., Bot. Beechey Voy. 7: 310. 1838. (EUPHORBIACEAE).
Original material: Tepic, Mexico, Lay & Collie.
  At E: a sheet ex herb. Arnott (E00369207), annotated by him with the name and 'Mexico, Beechey. Segments of involucre lacerated but no glands'. There are also two other specimens of this species ex herb. Arnott – these are from Realejo, are not annotated by him with the name, and are not original material.
  None found at K.

Euphorbia vachellii Hook. & Arn., Bot. Beechey Voy. 5: 213. 1836. (EUPHORBIACEAE).
Type: 'Macao; *Rev. G.H. Vachell, n.* 241'.
  Two sheets at E. One ex herb. R.K. Greville (E00369208), bears a printed Vachell label annotated 'Lappas Island 17 July [1830]', and is annotated on the sheet by Greville '[per] Prof. Henslow. no. 241'. The other sheet is ex herb. Arnott (E00369209), annotated by him with the name and 'Canton, Vachell no. 241'. The type locality is most likely to be Lappas Island, as noted by hand on the Vachell label.
  At K: a sheet ex herb. Hooker bears two specimens, the left-hand one is a type, with a printed Vachell label annotated with the number '241', annotated by Arnott with the name.
= **Euphorbia bifida** Hook & Arn.

Eutoca aretioides Hook. & Arn. [var.] α [*aretioides*], Bot. Beechey Voy. 8: 374. 1839. (Generic placement queried). (BORAGINACEAE).
Type: 'Between Burnt and Malheur Rivers [Oregon]. [John McLeod per] *Mr Tolmie*'.
  Not found at E.
  A sheet at K ex herb. Hooker is annotated with the name and the reference 'Ic. Plant. t. 355' by Hooker. It bears three collections and a sheet of drawings by Hooker – the specimens annotated 'Snake Country, California. Tolmie' are in the centre and on the right-hand side: three branched plants, and two tiny ones – the former, though not so annotated, must be the types of var. α – cited as 'holotype' by Cronquist *et al.* (Intermountain Flora 4: 196. 1984) (for the latter see below) (the other collections, *Fendler* 643, *Coulter* 463, are not types).
  Note. In this case the [var.] α is without doubt the 'typical' variety, to which the whole of the species description refers; the [var.] β being given a short, separate description, and a varietal epithet.
≡ **Nama aretioides** (Hook. & Arn.) Brand

Eutoca aretioides [var.] β *perpusilla* Hook. & Arn., Bot. Beechey Voy. 8: 374. 1839. (Generic placement queried). (BORAGINACEAE).
Type: 'Burnt River, Snake Country [Oregon]. [John McLeod per] *Mr Tolmie*'.

Not found at E.

Two tiny specimens on the Hooker sheet described under var. α must be the types of var. *perpusilla*, though they are not so annotated.

= **Nama aretioides** (Hook. & Arn.) Brand

Eutoca lutea Hook. & Arn., Bot. Beechey Voy. 8: 373. 1839. (Generic placement queried). (BORAGINACEAE).
Type: 'Snake Fort, Snake Country [Oregon/Idaho border]. [John McLeod per] *Mr Tolmie*'.

Type at E: a sheet ex herb. Arnott (E00369166), annotated by him with the name and 'Snake Country, N.W. C[alifornia]. Tolmie, per Hooker', and later (also by Arnott) 'Miltitzia lutea DC.'.

Cronquist *et al.* (Intermountain Flora 4: 176. 1984) cited 'holotype at K!', but no such specimen can be found.

Note. Sometimes placed in *Phacelia* as *P. lutea* (Hook. & Arn.) J.T. Howell.

≡ **Emmenanthe lutea** (Hook. & Arn.) A. Gray

Fabiana lanuginosa Hook. & Arn., Bot. Beechey Voy. 1: 35. 1830. (SOLANACEAE).
Original material: 'Coquimbo', Chili, Lay & Collie.

At E: a sheet ex herb. Arnott bears three specimens, the top right-hand one (E00369176), annotated by Arnott with the name and 'Coquimbo (Beechey)', is original material. (The other two specimens, *Cuming* 893 (E00130934), *Bridges* 1330 [cited in protologue as 1336] (E00130935), are isosyntypes of *Dolia vermiculata* Lindl.).

No type material found at K.

Note. A. Mesa (Fl. Neotrop. Monog. 26: 99. 1981) placed *D. vermiculata* and *F. lanuginosa* under *Nolana sedifolia*, but had not seen the type of the latter.

= **Nolana sedifolia** Poepp. subsp. **sedifolia**

Fabiana viscosa Hook. & Arn., Bot. Beechey Voy. 1: 36. 1830. (SOLANACEAE).
Type: 'Near Barasca in Chili ... *Mr. Cruckshanks*'.

Type at E: a sheet ex herb. Arnott (E00089282), annotated by him with the name and 'Barasca in Chili, Mr Cruckshanks per Dr Hooker'. G.E. Barboza & A.T. Hunziker (Kuntziana 22: 122. 1993) stated 'estudiamos un represente de la colección tipo (GL)', which, perhaps, counts as a lectotypification.

Type at K: a sheet ex herb. Hooker bearing three collections – the upper two specimens (K000585270) are types, labelled by Hooker on the sheet 'June 1826', and associated with a field ticket annotated, presumably by Cruckshanks, 'Pichanella (Fabiana?) South of Barasca' and a ticket with a drawing annotated by Hooker with the name and reference (the other collections, *Pearce* s.n., *Harvey* s.n., are not types).

Alphabetical list of new taxa 101

Fedia laxa Hook. & Arn., Bot. Beechey Voy. 1: 28. 1830. (VALERIANACEAE).
Original material: 'Conception', Chili, Lay & Collie.

None found at E or K.

Note. Not treated by O.E. Borsini in his monograph of South American Valerianaceae (Lilloa 32: 375–476. 1966), so its identity is uncertain; presumably a *Valerianella* (of which four species listed in Zuloaga *et al.*, 3: 3101. 2008) – perhaps a European introduction.

Ferula caruifolia Hook. & Arn., Bot. Beechey Voy. 8: 348. 1839. (UMBELLIFERAE).
Original material: California, Douglas.

None found at E.

At K, three sheets. On one ex herb. Hooker, annotated by him with the name, and bearing three collections, the right-hand specimen annotated by Hooker 'California, Douglas' is original material (the other collections, of Nuttall and Coulter, are not). The other two sheets are both ex herb. Bentham and bear printed 'California, Douglas 1833' labels annotated by Bentham with the name and a reference to 'Torr. & Gr. Fl. N. Am. 1: 628. [1840]' (on one is also mounted *Brewer* 1128, not original material).

≡ ***Lomatium caruifolium*** (Hook. & Arn.) Coult. & Rose

Ferula macrocarpa Hook. & Arn., Bot. Beechey Voy. 8: 348. 1839. (UMBELLIFERAE).
Original material: California, Douglas.

None found at E (though there is a duplicate of the specimen Hooker & Arnott treated under the name 'Ferula foeniculacea Nutt.', which was later annotated by Arnott 'est Peucedanum macrocarpum Nutt. [ex] Torr. & Gray'. The Torrey & Gray name is later (1840) and should presumably be treated as a new combination based on Hooker & Arnott's, though it has sometimes been taken to be the basionym of *Lomatium macrocarpum*.

At K, two sheets. One ex herb. Hooker, annotated by him with the name and 'California, Douglas'; one ex herb. Bentham, with a printed 'California, Douglas 1833' label annotated with the name by Bentham.

≡ ***Lomatium macrocarpum*** (Hook. & Arn.) Coult. & Rose

Ferula parvifolia Hook. & Arn., Bot. Beechey Voy. 8: 348. 1839. (UMBELLIFERAE).
Original material: California, Douglas.

None found at E.

At K, two sheets. On a sheet ex herb. Hooker, annotated by him with the name, bearing two collections, the right-hand specimen annotated by him 'California, Douglas' is orignal material (the left-hand specimen, *Coulter* 222, is not). A sheet ex herb. Bentham, with a printed 'California, Douglas 1833'

label, annotated by Bentham with the name and a reference to 'Torr. & Gr. Fl. N. Am. 1: 628. [1840]'.
≡ ***Lomatium parvifolium*** (Hook. & Arn.) Jepson

Ficus beecheyana Hook. & Arn., Bot. Beechey Voy. 6: 271. 1838. (MORACEAE).
Original material: 'Loo Choo', Lay & Collie.

At E: a sheet (E00369214), annotated by Arnott with the name and 'Loo Choo, Beechey', and later, also by Arnott, 'Miq. p. 437 n. 103', must be original material. This is one of the sheets given to E by GL in 1902 (prior to the sheets being trimmed); it has a printed 'Herb. Walker Arnott' label and was annotated by E.J.H. Corner in 1955 as 'Ficus erecta Thunb. var. sieboldiana Miq. (not <u>beecheyana</u> as usually understood)'. Corner cannot have appreciated the type status of this specimen; his determination suggesting that the name at that time had been misapplied, and (from his annotation on the Kew sheet – see below) that the collection must have been a mixed gathering.

At K: a sheet, ex herb. Hooker, is annotated on the sheet by Hooker with the name and 'Loo Choo' (but no collector's name), and also bears a ticket annotated 'Ficus Beecheyana H & A' by F.A.W. Miquel. This must also be original material and was determined by Corner in 1958 as *F. erecta* var. *beecheyana* (Hook. & Arn.) King.
= ***Ficus erecta*** Thunb.

Ficus lancifolia Hook. & Arn., Bot. Beechey Voy. 7: 310. 1838, *nom. illeg.*, non Moench, 1794. (MORACEAE).
Original material: Tepic, Mexico, Lay & Collie.

None found at E.

Lectotype at K: a sheet ex herb. Hooker (K000442847) with a ticket annotated by Bentham with the name, reference, and 'Mexico, Beechey'; it also bears a slip annotated by F.A.W. Miquel with the name 'Urostigma lancifolia Miq.'. This sheet was annotated as 'holotype' by C.C. Berg in 1997, and was cited by him and G.P. Dewolf (under *F. pertusa*) in Fl. Suriname (5(1): 257. 1975).
Note. Though *F. lancifolia* Moench (Meth. 347. 1794) was illegitimate when published (*F. indica* L. cited as a synonym in its protologue), Hooker & Arnott's name is still an illegitimate homonym.
= ***Ficus pertusa*** L. f.

Ficus pyriformis Hook. & Arn., Bot. Beechey Voy. 5: 216. 1836. (MORACEAE).
Original material: [not stated – but from the footnote on p. 201 not Beechey material, but a specimen in herb. Hooker or Arnott – apparently (see below) a Millett collection from Canton].

At E: a sheet (E00369212) annotated by Arnott with the name and 'Cant[on]. China, ([per] Dr Hooker)', and later, also by Arnott, 'F. Millettii

Alphabetical list of new taxa 103

Miq. n. 106'. This is one of the sheets given to E by GL in 1902 (prior to the sheets being trimmed); it has a printed 'Herb. Walker Arnott' label.

At K: a remounted partial sheet, ex herb. Hooker, annotated by Hooker with the name and 'China, Millett', it also bears a slip annotated by F.A.W. Miquel 'Ficus Millettii Miq.', and was annotated 'type of F. millettii Miq.' by E.J.H. Corner in 1957 (mounted with *Carles* 191, not original material).

Note. It is not clear why Miquel renamed this species.

Ficus setosa Hook. & Arn., Bot. Beechey Voy. 5: 216, t. 49. 1836. (MORACEAE).
Original material: [not stated – but from the footnote on p. 201 it should not be Beechey material, but a specimen in herb. Hooker or Arnott. However, from the material at E & K (see below), it appears that there was both Beechey and later material].

At E: a sheet (E00369213) annotated by Arnott initially with 'Ficus hispida Th.? "Celtis?' which he crossed out and replaced with 'Ficus setosa Bot. Beechey: voy. t. 49. Canton, [per] Dr Hooker'; later still Arnott added 'est F. hirta Vahl Enum. fide Miq. n. 133': from the annotation this is likely to be original material, but, given the Hooker source, it is probably a Millett specimen. This is one of the sheets given to E by GL in 1902 (prior to the sheets being trimmed); it has a printed 'Herb. Walker Arnott' label, and was determined as *F. hirta* by E.J.H. Corner in 1956.

At K: a sheet ex herb. Hooker annotated by him 'F. setosa H. & A', and also 'Ficus hispida?? Thunb? at non F. oppositifolia Roxb. China, Beechey'. This appears to be original material and was determined as *F. hirta* by E.J.H. Corner in 1958 (on the lower part of the sheet is a Hong Kong specimen, which is not original material).

= **Ficus hirta** Vahl

Fimbristylis affinis Hook. & Arn., Bot. Beechey Voy. 2: 72. 1832, *nom. illeg.*, non C. Presl, 1830. (CYPERACEAE).
Original material: 'Society Islands', Lay & Collie.

None found at E.

At K: a sheet ex herb. Hooker bearing a ticket annotated by Arnott with the name and 'Coral Island, Beechey' (determined as *F. diphylla* Vahl by C.B. Clarke in 1888).

= **Fimbristylis dichotoma** (L.) Vahl

Fraxinus dipetala Hook. & Arn., Bot. Beechey Voy. 8: 362, t. 87. 1839 (as '*Ornus dipelta*'). (OLEACEAE).
Original material: California, Douglas.

None found at E.

At K, two sheets: one ex herb. Hooker, annotated by him 'Ornus dipetala H. & A. Fraxinus. California, Douglas', to which is attached a ticket with drawings; a duplicate of this ex herb. Bentham, with a printed 'California,

Douglas 1833' label, annotated with the name (as published) by Bentham. (Also in the type cover is a sheet of fruiting material, ex herb. Bentham, with a printed 'California, Douglas 1833' label but as fruits were neither described in the protologue nor illustrated, this cannot be original material).

Galinsoga resinosa Hook. & Arn., Bot. Beechey Voy. 1: 32. 1830. (Generic placement in '*Galinsogea*' queried). (COMPOSITAE).
Original material: 'Coquimbo', Chili, Lay & Collie; material collected by Bridges at Viña de la Mar near Valparaiso is also mentioned – it is not certain that it was used in making the description, but might also represent original material.
  At E: the central specimen (E00301764) on a sheet ex herb. Arnott, annotated by him with the name and 'Coquimbo, (Beechey)', is original material (the other specimens on the sheet, *Cuming* 71, *Gillies* 53, are not).
  None found at K.
≡ **Gutierrezia resinosa** (Hook. & Arn.) S.F. Blake

Galium californicum Hook. & Arn., Bot. Beechey Voy. 8: 349. 1839. (RUBIACEAE).
Original material: California, Douglas; possibly also 'imperfect specimens ... collected ... by Mr Menzies'.
  At E: a sheet ex herb. Arnott (E00369098), annotated by him with the name and 'California, D[avid] D[ouglas] per Hooker'.
  At K: the top left-hand specimen on a sheet ex herb. Hooker annotated by him with the name and 'California, Douglas', and, possibly, the specimens annotated by Hooker 'N.W.C. Am. A. M[enzies]' (the other collections on the sheet, *Coulter* 196 and *Nuttall* s.n., are not original material). The left-hand specimen on a sheet ex herb. Bentham with a printed 'California, Douglas 1833' annotated by Bentham with the name, and reference 'Torr. & Gr. Fl. N. Am. 2. 20. [1841]' is also original material (but not the other collection on the sheet).

Gaura decorticans Hook. & Arn., Bot. Beechey Voy. 8: 343. 1839. (ONAGRACEAE).
Original material: California, Douglas.
  None at E.
  Lectotype at K: the three right-hand specimens on a sheet bearing two collections ex herb. Hooker – these are annotated with the name and 'California, Douglas' and probably to them also belongs a field ticket annotated with the name, number '151' and 'Gaura decorticans Spach. Dougl.' – though not annotated by P.H. Raven, this is doubtless the material cited by him as type in Contrib. U.S. Nat. Herb. (37: 358. 1969) (with 'iso[lecto]types' at BM, GH, NY).
≡ **Camissonia boothii** (Douglas) P.H. Raven subsp. **decorticans** (Hook. & Arn.) P.H. Raven

Alphabetical list of new taxa

Gilia squarrosa (Eschsch.) Hook. & Arn., Bot. Beechey Voy. 4: 151. 1833. (POLEMONIACEAE). [California].
Basionym cited: 'Hoitzia squarrosa. *Eschscholtz, in Mem. Acad. Imp. St. Petersb. v.* 10, (anno 1826) *p.* 283 [*recte* 282]'.
≡ **Navarretia squarrosa** (Eschsch.) Hook. & Arn.

Glochidion molle Hook. & Arn., Bot. Beechey Voy. 5: 210. 1836, *nom. illeg.*, non Blume, 1826. (PHYLLANTHACEAE).
Original material: '[a] few specimens [from China] … which we owe to Mr. Millett'.
  At E: a sheet ex herb. Arnott (E00369210), annotated by him with the name and 'Canton, ([per] Dr Hooker)'.
  None found at K.
Note. Hooker and Arnott cited 'Phyllanthus obscurus *Willd.*?' but the query prevents their name from being superfluous; it was, in any case, an illegitimate later homonym.
= **Glochidion zeylanicum** (Gaertn.) A. Juss. var. **talbotii** (Hook. f.) Haines

Glochidion sinicum (Gaertn.) Hook. & Arn., Bot. Beechey Voy. 5: 210. 1836. (PHYLLANTHACEAE).
Basionym cited: 'Bradleia Sinica. *Gaertn.* [Fruct. Sem. Pl. 2: 127. 1791]'
= **Glochidion puberum** (L.) Hutch.

Gnaphalium citrinum Hook. & Arn., Bot. Beechey Voy. 1: 31. 1830. (COMPOSITAE).
Original material: 'Conception', Chili, Lay & Collie.
  At E, although there is a discrepancy over the locality, the right-hand specimen (E00369120) on a sheet ex herb. Arnott, annotated by him with the name and 'Valparaiso, (Beechey)' may be original material (the other two collections, *Mathews* 279, *Cuming* 446, are not).
  No Beechey material found at K.
= **Gnaphalium cheiranthifolium** Lam.

Gnaphalium filaginoides Hook. & Arn., Bot. Beechey Voy. 8: 359. 1839. (Generic placement queried). (COMPOSITAE).
Original material: California, Douglas.
  None found at E.
  At K: the central specimen on a sheet ex herb. Hooker bearing three collections – it is annotated by Hooker with the name, reference and 'California, Douglas', beside it is a ticket with drawings, and it was annotated 'syntype (?)' by J.D. Morefield in 1991 (despite also being annotated 'syntype (?)' by Morefield the left-hand specimen, a Nuttall collection, is not original material; neither is the right-hand specimen, *Coulter* 352).
= **Filago californica** Nutt.

Gnaphalium sprengelii Hook. & Arn., Bot. Beechey Voy. 4: 150. 1833, *nom. illeg.* (COMPOSITAE). [California].
Proposed here as a replacement name for *G. chilense* Spreng., on the grounds that the plant came from California, not Chile.
= **Gnaphalium stramineum** Kunth

Gnaphalium ulophyllum Hook. & Arn., Bot. Beechey Voy. 1: 31. 1830. (COMPOSITAE).
Original material: 'Valparaiso [Chili] ... Mr. Bridges'.
At E: a sheet ex herb. Arnott bearing three specimens. The middle one (E00369123), given to Arnott by Hooker, is probably original material – though it lacks a collector's name it could well be a Bridges specimen and is annotated by Arnott with the name and 'Valparaiso, [per] Dr Hooker'. The left-hand specimen (E00369125) is annotated by Arnott 'Valparaiso, Bridges 229', but not with the name, and is also original material (the right-hand specimen, *Cuming* 334, is not). Arnott later realised the identity of the plant as the sheet is also annotated by him 'G. cymatoides Kunze – DC. n. 19'.
At K, two sheets. One ex herb. Hooker bears three specimens of which the left-hand one (K000500321), with a field ticket '229 ... Playa chncha Valpso. Bridges 1832' is original material (the others, *Anon* s.n., *Cuming* 334, are not). The other sheet, ex herb. Bentham, has three specimens, the middle one, with a printed 'Chile Bridges' label annotated with the name and number '229' is original material (the other specimens, *Cuming* 334, and an earlier *Bridges* collection, are not).
= **Gnaphalium cymatoides** Kunze ex DC.

Grayia Hook. & Arn., Bot. Beechey Voy. 9: 387. 1840. (AMARANTHACEAE).

Grayia polygonoides Hook. & Arn., Bot. Beechey Voy. 9: 388. 1840, *nom. illeg.* ('Chenopodium? spinosum Hook. Flor. Bor. Am. II p. 127' cited as a synonym). (AMARANTHACEAE).
The earlier name was based on 'extremely young and imperfect specimens collected by Mr Douglas during his first journey in North West America', cited again here as 'Interior of California, Nov. 1826; *Mr. Douglas*'. However, additional material from 'Snake country; [John McLeod per] *Mr. Tolmie*' allowed Hooker & Arnott to realise that a new genus was required, and, as usual, they used a new epithet. The type of *G. polygonoides* (and therefore also of the genus *Grayia*), nonetheless, has to be the inadequate Doulgas material.
At E is a duplicate of the Tolmie specimen in Arnott's herbarium initially annotated by Arnott 'Grayia. Snake country, N.W. Am. Tolmie, per Hooker' to which Arnott later, and curiously, added 'spinosa H & A' – this is not type material.
At K: a sheet ex herb. Hooker bears five specimens (a further one has been removed), representing three collections, but it is not clear to which the

three field tickets refer. The two similar left-hand ones and the upper central one are probably the Nuttall 'R[ocky] Mts' collections and not types. To the right-hand (and the one that has been removed) probably probably belongs the ticket annotated by Hooker with the name 'Chenop? spinosum' and the details 'Genus novum imperfect. In the interior of California Nov. 1826. D. D[ouglas]', which is the type (K000179029). The sheet was annotated 'holotype' by H. Flores in 2001 without making it clear to which specimen this referred (the third collection, bottom centre, *Geyer* 64, is not a type).
≡ **Grayia spinosa** (Hook.) Moq.

Grindelia hirsutula Hook. & Arn., Bot. Beechey Voy. 4: 147. 1833. (COMPOSITAE).
Original material: San Francisco (or Monterey Bay), California, Lay & Collie.

Lectotype at E: a sheet ex herb. Arnott (E00369114) bearing two specimens, annotated by Arnott with the name and 'California, Beechey' – it was annotated 'holotype' by M.A. Lane in 1993, and lectotypified (cited as 'holotype') by him in Novon 2: 261.1992.

Isolectotype at K: a sheet ex herb. Hooker bears three specimens of two collections – it is perhaps the central one (K000250075) that is the type, associated with the ticket annotated by Arnott with the name and 'California, Beechey' – it was annotated 'isotype' by M.A. Lane in 1993 (the other collections, *Douglas* s.n., California, are not types).

Grindelia humilis Hook. & Arn., Bot. Beechey Voy. 4: 147. 1833. (COMPOSITAE).
Type: a single specimen, San Francisco (or Monterey Bay), California, Lay & Collie.

Not found at E.

Lectotype at K: a sheet (K000250077) ex herb. Hooker annotated by him with the name and 'California, Beechey' – this was annotated as 'isotype' by M.A. Lane in 1993 and published by him as such in Novon (2: 216. 1992) – this can be taken as a lectotypification. In this work Lane stated 'holotype, E not seen', doubtless an assumption based on the impression given in TL2 that the top set of Beechey specimens is at E (GL): as in this example this is not always the case, and Arnott may not have kept a specimen.
= **Grindelia hirsutula** Hook. & Arn.

Grumilea reevesii (Wall.) Hook. & Arn., Bot. Beechey Voy. 5: 193. 1836. (RUBIACEAE). [China].
Basionym cited: 'Psychotria Reevesii. *Wall. in Roxb. et Wall. Fl. Ind. v.* 2. *p.* 164. [1824]'.
Although having no type status it is worth noting that there are two sheets at E from Arnott's herbarium annotated with Hooker & Arnott's combination. One sheet bears two collections, one annotated 'Grumilea Reevesii H & A, Psychotria Reevesii Wall. China, Beechey', the other 'Canton, ([per] Dr

Hooker)', the latter is probably a Millett collection. The second sheet is referrred to on p. 265, and is annotated by Arnott 'Grumilea Reevesii H & A, Psychotria mariana Bartl. Loo Choo, Beechey'.
Note. A.P. Davis *et al.* (Bot. J. Linn. Soc. 135: 35–42. 2001) in a discussion of the nomenclature and taxonomy of *Psychotria asiatica* concluded that *P. reevesii* (type: Wall. Cat. No. 8330, holo K-W) was probably synonymous.
= **Psychotria asiatica** L.

Gymnocoronis latifolia Hook. & Arn., Bot. Beechey Voy. 7: 296. 1838. (COMPOSITAE).
Original material: 'Talisco', Mexico, Lay & Collie.
  None found at E.
  At K: the upper specimen (K000486492) on a sheet ex herb. Hooker annotated by him with the name and 'Talisco, Mexico, Beechey' (the lower specimen is not original material).

Haplopappus ericoides (Less.) Hook. & Arn., Bot. Beechey Voy. 4: 146. 1833 (as '*Aplopappus*'). (COMPOSITAE). [California].
Basionym cited: 'Diplopappus ericoides *Less. in Linn[aea] v. 6. p.* 117. [1831]'
≡ **Ericameria ericoides** (Less.) Jepson

Haplopappus squarrosus Hook. & Arn., Bot. Beechey Voy. 4: 146. 1833 (as '*Aplopappus*'). (COMPOSITAE).
Original material: San Francisco (or Monterey Bay), California, Lay & Collie.
  None found at E.
  At K: the right-hand specimen on a sheet ex herb. Hooker annotated by him with the name and 'California, Beechey'; though not annotated by W.D. Clark it must be the specimen intended as lectotype (cited as holotype) in Madroño (26: 122. 1979) (the left-hand, Douglas specimen, is not original material).
≡ **Hazardia squarrosa** (Hook. & Arn.) Greene

Hartmannia pungens Hook. & Arn., Bot. Beechey Voy. 8: 357. 1839. (Generic placement queried). (COMPOSITAE).
Original material: California, Douglas.
  None found at E.
  At K, two sheets. One ex herb. Hooker, annotated by him with the name, a reference to 'Ic. Pl. t. 334 [1841]', and 'California, Douglas' – this was annotated 'type' by D.D. Keck in 1937, but it is not known if this has been published. A sheet ex herb. Bentham, annotated by him with the name, bearing three collections – the left-hand one, with a printed 'Nova California, Douglas 1833, Herb. Hort. Soc. Lond.' label and the field number '66' is original material.
≡ **Hemizonia pungens** (Hook. & Arn.) Torr. & A. Gray

Alphabetical list of new taxa

Hebeclinium tepicanum Hook. & Arn., Bot. Beechey Voy. 10: 434. 1841. (COMPOSITAE).
Original material: 'Between San Blas and Tepic', Mexico, Sinclair.
  None found at E.
  At K, two sheets: one (K000486739) ex herb. Hooker bearing a ticket annotated by Bentham with the name and 'Tepic, Dr Sinclair'; the second ex herb. Bentham (given him by Hooker in 1844) annotated by Bentham with the name, reference, and 'Tepic, Sinclair'.
= **Critonia hebebotrya** DC.

Hedyotis macrostemon Hook. & Arn., Bot. Beechey Voy. 4: 192. 1833. (RUBIACEAE).
Original material: Chiefly ... about Macao, China, Lay & Collie – 'only in fruit'; 'beautiful flowering specimens from Mr. Millett'.
  A sheet at E, ex herb. Arnott, bears four specimens – the one at top right (E00369099) is clearly annotated (by Arnott) 'Lappas island. Vachell, per Prof. Henslow, No. 104' and is not original material; the bottom right-hand one (E00369100), annotated by Arnott with the name and 'Canton, [per] Dr Hooker', is probably a Millett specimen and therefore original material (the upper left-hand specimen might belong to either collection, and the lower left-hand one possibly to a third that lacks data).
  At K the lowest collection (two specimens), annotated 'China, Beechey', on a sheet ex herb. Hooker annotated with the name (the other collections, *Henry* 8711, *Vachell* 104, are not original material). A second sheet, ex herb. Hooker, not bearing the name in his hand, but annotated by him 'China, Millett' is also original material.
= **Oldenlandia hedyotidea** (DC.) Hand.-Mazz.

Hedyotis uncinella Hook. & Arn., Bot. Beechey Voy. 4: 192. 1833. (RUBIACEAE).
Original material: China, material from Mr. Millett.
  At E: a sheet ex herb. Arnott (E00369101), annotated by him with the name and 'Canton, [per] Dr Hooker', with a later pencil addition by Arnott 'an var. H. centaliphora [sic, cephalophora] Br. W[allich] L[ist]. n. 842' is probably original material.
  At K: a sheet ex herb. Hooker annotated by him 'China, Millett', and with the name written by ?Bentham.

Hedyotis vachellii Hook. & Arn., Bot. Beechey Voy. 5: 194. 1836. (RUBIACEAE).
Type: '*Vachell n.* 105', China.
  A sheet at E, ex herb. Arnott, bears three specimens representing two collections: the two left-hand ones (E00220479) are types, annotated by Arnott 'Hedyotis vachellii H & A. Vachell No 105. Canton, ([per] Dr Hooker)'. The

right-hand specimen (E00220480) is annotated by Arnott 'Knoxia hedyotoides H & A. China, Beechey': this name was not published, and the specimen is not discussed under *H. vachellii*, with which Arnott clearly regarded it as conspecific by time he compiled this sheet.

No type material found at K.

≡ ***Oldenlandia vachellii*** (Hook. & Arn.) Kuntze

Helenium pubescens Hook. & Arn., Bot. Beechey Voy. 4: 149. 1833, *nom. illeg.*, non Ait., 1789. (COMPOSITAE).

Cited material at E: a sheet annotated by Arnott 'Helenium pubescens H & A an Ait.? Cephalophor. decurrens Less. in Linnaea v 6. p. 517– DC. V. p. 663. n. 8. California (Beechey) receptaculum globosum', to which Arnott has later added 'Helenium puberulum DC'.

Cited material at K: a sheet ex herb. Hooker annotated by him 'Helenium pubescens Ait? & Hook. & Arn. Cephalophora decurrens Less. in Linn. v. 6 p. 517. California, Beechey'.

Note. Although 'Helenium pubescens. *Ait.?*' [Hort. Kew. 3: 227. 1789] is cited in synonymy the expression of doubt, and the fact that Hooker & Arnott attributed this name to themselves in the index, establishes that they published a new name. However, this is not a new species based on Beechey material, but a new name for 'Cephalophora decurrens. *Lessing in Linnaea, v. 6. p. 517*', also cited as a synonym (a new epithet being used due to the change of genus). In publishing *C. decurrens*, Lessing also cited 'Helenium pubescens Ait.' followed by a query, precluding his name being treated as superfluous and illegitimate (Art. 52 Note 1). *H. pubescens* Hook. & Arn. is, of course, an illegitimate later homonym of *H. pubescens* Ait. (J. McN.).

= ***Helenium puberulum*** DC.

Helianthus glutinosus Hook. & Arn., Bot. Beechey Voy. 1: 32. 1830. (COMPOSITAE).

Original material: 'Valparaiso', Chili, Lay & Collie; 'Mr Bridges ... has furnished us with fine specimens'.

No Beechey material at E. A sheet ex herb. Arnott annotated by him with this name (and the names 'Helianthus thurifer Mol.' and 'Flourensia thurifera DC.') bears two collections, the left-hand specimen (E00322560) has the number 234 on a small paper square showing it to be a Bridges collection and therefore original material (the right-hand one, *Cuming* 631, is not). M.O. Dillon in Fieldiana (16 (n.s.): 30. 1984) cited 'TYPE: Chile, Valparaiso, *T. Bridges* s.n. (holotype, GL, not seen)', while not the most satisfactory citation, this can be taken as a lectotypification.

No Beechey type material at K, but there is a sheet ex herb. Hooker with the Bridges material – this is the left-hand specimen on a sheet annotated by Hooker 'Valparaiso, Bridges', beside which is a field ticket written by Bridges

Alphabetical list of new taxa 111

to which Hooker has added 'H. glutinosum H & A, thurifera Mol.' (the right-hand specimen is a Macrae specimen, also from Valparaiso but not original material).
= ***Flourensia thurifera*** (Molina) DC.

Heliotropium anomalum Hook. & Arn., Bot. Beechey Voy. 2: 66. 1832. (Generic placement queried). (BORAGINACEAE).
Original material: 'Whitsunday Island', Lay & Collie.
  None found at E.
  At K: a sheet ex herb. Hooker with three collections – the lower two specimens, associated with a ticket annotated by Arnott with the name and 'Whitsunday Island. Beechey', and a ticket with drawings possibly by Hooker, are original material (the other collections, by Wilkes, and Barclay, are not).

Heliotropium stenophyllum Hook. & Arn., Bot. Beechey Voy. 1: 38. 1830. (BORAGINACEAE).
Original material: 'Coquimbo', Chili, Lay & Collie.
  None found at E: the only sheet bearing the name in Arnott's hand bears three later collections (*Gillies* s.n., *Bridges* 235, *Cuming* 377).
  None found at K.

Helosciadium californicum Hook. & Arn., Bot. Beechey Voy. 3: 142. 1832. (Generic placement queried). (UMBELLIFERAE).
Original material: San Francisco (or Monterey Bay), California, Lay & Collie.
  At E: a sheet ex herb. R.K. Greville (E00369083), annotated 'California. Captn. Beechey's Voyage. From Hooker. 1832'.
  At K: the left-hand specimen on a sheet ex herb. Hooker annotated by him with the name and 'California, Beechey' (the two right-hand, Scouler, specimens are not original material).
= ***Oenanthe sarmentosa*** J. Presl

Hemizonia filipes Hook. & Arn., Bot. Beechey Voy. 8: 356. 1839. (COMPOSITAE).
Original material: California, Douglas.
  At E: a sheet (E00369138) with a label annotated by Arnott with the name and 'California', is probably original material. It is a sheet sent from GL to E in 1902, bearing a printed 'Herb. Walker Arnott' label.
  At K: a sheet ex herb. Hooker, annotated by him 'California, Douglas', bearing a ticket with drawings annotated with the name by ?Arnott, and with the reference in another hand. A sheet ex herb. Bentham is probably a duplicate, and also original material, annotated by Bentham with the name and number '70', with a printed 'California, Douglas 1833' label.
≡ ***Holozonia filipes*** (Hook. & Arn.) Greene

Hemizonia multicaulis Hook. & Arn., Bot. Beechey Voy. 8: 355. 1839. (COMPOSITAE).
Original material: California, Douglas.

At E: a sheet (E00369137) with a label annotated by Arnott with the name and 'California' is probably original material. It is a sheet sent from GL to E in 1902, bearing a printed 'Herb. Walker Arnott' label.

At K: a sheet ex herb. Hooker, annotated by him with the name and 'California, Douglas', bearing a ticket with drawings – it was annotated 'holotype' in 1980 by B.D. Tanowitz, who determined it as *H. congesta* DC. (other authors, however, have maintained Hooker & Arnott's species).

Hemizonia sericea Hook. & Arn., Bot. Beechey Voy. 8: 356. 1839. (COMPOSITAE).
Original material: California, Douglas.
None found at E or K.
= ***Hemizonia congesta*** DC. subsp. ***luzulifolia*** (DC.) Babc. & H.M. Hall

Hendecandra crotonoides Hook. & Arn., Bot. Beechey Voy. 9: 389. 1840, *nom. illeg.* (EUPHORBIACEAE).
Hooker and Arnott here cited 'Astrogyne crotonoides Benth.', Pl. Hartweg. No. 83, but that name was not actually published until 1841. Hooker & Arnott, however, (as did Bentham) also cited the earlier synonym *Croton gracilis* Kunth, rendering their name superfluous. Despite coining a new name and making a description, doubtless based on the Hartweg collection (of which none at E or K), the Hooker & Arnott name is to be typified on the material on which Kunth's name was based.
≡ ***Croton gracilis*** Kunth

Hermesia mexicana Hook. & Arn., Bot. Beechey Voy. 7: 309. 1838. (Generic placement queried). (EUPHORBIACEAE).
Original material: Tepic, Mexico, Lay & Collie.
None found at E.
At K, two sheets. A sheet ex herb. Hooker (K000600500) with two specimens, bearing a ticket annotated with the name in Hooker's hand, and a description in Arnott's; also attached is a ticket annotated by Bentham with the name and 'Mexico, Beechey'. The second sheet (K000600499), ex herb. Bentham (given him by Hooker in 1845), has a ticket annotated by Bentham with the name and 'Mexico, Beechey'.
≡ ***Bernardia mexicana*** (Hook. & Arn.) Müll. Arg.

Heterocentron Hook. & Arn., Bot. Beechey Voy. 7: 290. 1838. (MELASTOMATACEAE).

Alphabetical list of new taxa

Heterocentron mexicana Hook. & Arn., Bot. Beechey Voy. 7: 290. 1838. (MELASTOMATACEAE).
Original material: Tepic, Mexico, Lay & Collie.

At E: a sheet ex herb. Arnott (E00285694), annotated by him with the name and 'Mexico, Beechey', with an attached ticket bearing Arnott's MS description – it was annotated 'holotype' by T. Whiffin in 1972 but it is not known if this has been published. A second sheet from Arnott's herbarium is that referred to in the Mexico Supplement (p. 423. 1840) collected by Dr Sinclair, bearing a ticket with the name in what is probably Hooker's hand, to which Arnott has added 'San Blas to Tepic. Bot. Beech. Voy. Supp. Dr Sinclair', but this is not original material.

None at K (only the later Sinclair collection).

Heteropteris tomentosa Hook. & Arn., Bot. Beechey Voy. 6: 281. 1838, *nom. illeg.* (MALPIGHIACEAE).
Original material: Tepic, Mexico, Lay & Collie.

At E: a sheet ex herb. Arnott (E00197522), annotated by him 'Bannesteria tomentosa? Schl., Heteropteris tomentosa H & A (non Ad. Juss.). Acapulco, Beechey' and later, also by Arnott 'Heteropteris Beecheyana Ad. Juss. n. 221'.

None found at K.

Note. Although three synonyms are cited: 'Bannisteria tomentosa. Schlecht. in Linn. 11. p. 244? – B. paniculata. Fl. Mex. et De Cand. Prod. 1. p. 591? – Heterotropis brachiata. H.B.K. et De Cand. Prod. 1. p. 591?' – as each is queried, Hooker & Arnott's is a new species, based on Beechey material, rather than a new combination based on the first, or a superfluous name for either of the others. However, it is an illegitimate homonym of *Heteropteris tomentosa* A. Juss. (in St. Hil., Fl. Bras. Merid. 3: 31. 1833), which was renamed *H. beecheyana* A. Juss. (1843), of which this material is also the type.

= ***Heteropteris brachiata*** (L.) DC.

Heuchera hispida Hook. & Arn., Bot. Beechey Voy. 8: 347. 1839, *nom. illeg.*, non Pursh, 1814. (SAXIFRAGACEAE).
Original material: California, Douglas.

At E: a sheet ex herb. Arnott (E00369061), annotated by him with the name and 'California' is very probably original material.

At K: a sheet ex herb. Hooker annotated by him with the name and 'California, Douglas', to which is attached a ticket with pencil drawings probably by Hooker. Two sheets ex herb. Bentham, with printed 'California, Douglas 1833' labels, may also be original material, but are not annotated with the name.

= ***Heuchera pilossisima*** Fisch. & C.A. Mey.

Hisutsua serrata Hook. & Arn., Bot. Beechey Voy. 6: 265. 1838. (Generic placement queried). (COMPOSITAE).
Original material: 'Loo Choo', Lay & Collie.
    At E: a sheet ex herb. Arnott (E00369116) with two specimens, annotated by him with the name and 'Loo Choo, Beechey'.
    At K: the bottom left-hand specimen on a sheet ex herb. Hooker bearing four collections – it is annotated with the name and 'Loochoo, Beechey' (the other collections, of Fortune, are not original material).
= ***Kalimeris indicus*** (L.) Schultz-Bip.

Hoitzia amplectens Hook. & Arn., Bot. Beechey Voy. 10: 441. 1841. (POLEMONIACEAE).
Original material: 'Between San Blas and Tepic', Mexico, Sinclair.
    None found at E.
    At K, two sheets. One ex herb. Hooker (K000614085) with a ticket annotated by Bentham with the name and 'Between San Blas and Tepic, Dr Sinclair' – this was annotated 'holotype' by A. Day in 1989. The other sheet is ex herb. Bentham, given him by Hooker in 1842 – it bears a ticket annotated by Bentham with the name (and also 'Loeselia amplectans Benth. in DC. Prod. 9. 320') and the collecting details 'San Blas to Tepic, Sinclair'.
= ***Loeselia involucrata*** G. Don.

Hoitzia elata Hook. & Arn., Bot. Beechey Voy. 10: 441. 1841. (POLEMONIACEAE).
Original material: 'Near the city of Mexico. *Bates, in Herb. nostr.* [presumably Hooker's]'.
    None found at E or K.
= ***Loeselia glandulosa*** (Cav.) G. Don

Hoitzia lupulina Hook. & Arn., Bot. Beechey Voy. 10: 441. 1841. (POLEMONIACEAE).
Original material: Realejo [now Nicaragua] and Acapulco, Mexico, Sinclair.
    None found at E.
    At K: a sheet ex herb. Hooker bears two specimens, the left-hand one, annotated by Bentham with the name and 'Realejo and Acapulco, Dr Sinclair', is original material (the right-hand specimen, *Seemann* 1507, is not).
= ***Loeselia involucrata*** G. Don

Holarrhena affinis Hook. & Arn., Bot. Beechey Voy. 5: 198. 1836. (APOCYNACEAE).
Original material: Chiefly … about Macao, China, Lay & Collie.
    None found at E or K.
≡ ***Anodendron affine*** (Hook. & Arn.) Druce

Alphabetical list of new taxa 115

Horkelia grandis Hook. & Arn., Bot. Beechey Voy. 8: 339. 1839. (ROSACEAE).
Original material: California, Douglas.
   None found at E or K.
= **Horkelia californica** Cham. & Schltdl.

Horkelia parviflora Nutt. ex Hook. & Arn., Bot. Beechey Voy. 8: 338. 1839. (ROSACEAE).
Original material: 'Mountains of California', [Nuttall].
   None found at E.
   At K: the two right-hand specimens on a sheet ex herb. Hooker with tickets in Nuttall's hand 'Horkelia parviflora, R. Mts., N. California', beside which Hooker has written 'Nuttall' (the third, Bolander collection, is not original material).
≡ **Horkelia fusca** Lindl. subsp. ***parviflora*** (Nutt. ex Hook. & Arn.) Keck

Hosackia tomentosa Hook. & Arn., Bot. Beechey Voy. 3: 137. 1832. (LEGUMINOSAE).
Type: San Francisco (or Monterey Bay), California, Lay & Collie.
   A sheet ex herb. Arnott at E, annotated by him with the name and 'California, [per] Hooker' cannot be a type, as the description stated that in the Beechey collection was only a single, fruiting specimen, whereas this one has flowers. It was clearly sent by Hooker to Arnott, and is doubtless a later (possibly a Douglas) collection.
   No Beechey material at K – in the type cover are only later collections (including Douglas ones), which, although annotated with the name both by Bentham, and by Hooker cannot be type material.
= **Lotus eriophorus** Greene

Hypochaeris apargioides Hook. & Arn., Bot. Beechey Voy. 1: 28. 1830. (COMPOSITAE).
Original material: 'Conception', Chili, Lay & Collie.
   At E: a sheet ex herb. Arnott (E00208144), annotated by him with the name, reference, and 'Conception (Beechey)' – to this sheet Arnott has added two later names 'Seriola apargioides β H & A' and 'Achyrephorus apargioides DC. VII. 94. n. 14'. The former refers to Hooker & Arnott's later treatment in Comp. Bot. Mag. (1: 31. 1835), in which they accepted Lessing's transfer to *Seriola* and treated, but did not name, the Beechey material as a variety (β) with hispid stems; the Candollean name was published in 1838.
   No Beechey material found at K.

Ilex anomala Hook. & Arn., Bot. Beechey Voy. 3: 111. 1832. (Generic placement queried). (AQUIFOLIACEAE).
Original material: 'Oahu', Sandwich Islands, Lay & Collie.
   At E, two sheets, both ex herb. Arnott: one (E00369026) with two specimens annotated by Arnott with the name and 'Oahu, Beechey'; the other

(E00369027) with a single specimen with the same details in Arnott's hand, but the additional name 'Bryonia [sic, recte Byronia] Endl.', presumably a later addition by Arnott.

At K: a sheet ex herb. Hooker annotated by him with the name, reference, and 'Oahu', to which is attached a ticket with drawings possibly by Arnott.

Ilex pubescens Hook. & Arn., Bot. Beechey Voy. 4: 176, t. 35. 1833. (AQUIFOLIACEAE).
Original material: Chiefly … about Macao, China, Lay & Collie.

At E: a sheet ex herb. Arnott (E00369028), bearing a male and a female branch, annotated by him with the name and 'China, Beechey'.

At K: a sheet ex herb. Hooker to which is attached a ticket with drawings, annotated by Arnott with the name and 'China, Beechey'.

Indigofera torulosa Hook. & Arn., Bot. Beechey Voy. 6: 286. 1838, *nom. illeg.*, non E. Mey., 1836. (LEGUMINOSAE).
Original material: Tepic, Mexico, Lay & Collie.

None found at E.

At K: a sheet (K000500734) ex herb. Hooker, annotated by him with the name and 'Mexico, Beechey'.
= ***Indigofera constricta*** Rydb.

Inga dimidiata Hook. & Arn., Bot. Beechey Voy. 4: 181. 1833. (LEGUMINOSAE).
Original material: Chiefly … about Macao, China, Lay & Collie; 'also sent us by Mr. Millett'.

At E: a sheet ex herb. Arnott (E00369047), annotated by him with the name and 'China, Beechey', and also by Arnott with a later identification 'Pithecolobium clypearia Benth in [?Lg] B III p 209'.

At K: on a sheet ex herb. Hooker annotated by him with the name is material of both parts of the original material, the upper is annotated 'China, Millett', the lower 'China, Beechey'.
= ***Archidendron clypearia*** (Jack) I.C. Nielsen subsp. ***clypearia***

Inga guatemalensis Hook. & Arn., Bot. Beechey Voy. 9: 419. 1840. (Generic placement queried). (LEGUMINOSAE).
Original material: 'Realejo', [Nicaragua], Sinclair.

None found at E.

At K: a sheet (K000082081) ex herb. Hooker, annotated by him 'Realejo, Sinclair', though not with the name; it bears a ticket annotated by Bentham 'Mimosa Guatemalensis (Inga H. et A.)' and is original material. This has been annotated 'holotype', but it is not known if this typification has been published. (Also in the type cover are two Barclay collections from Tepic, but these are later collections from the *Sulphur* voyage, worked on by Bentham, who transferred the species to *Mimosa*, but not original material of the Hooker & Arnot name).

Alphabetical list of new taxa

≡ ***Mimosa guatemalensis*** (Hook. & Arn.) Benth.

Inga patens Hook. & Arn., Bot. Beechey Voy. 9: 419. 1840. (Generic placement queried). (LEGUMINOSAE).
Original material: 'Realejo', [Nicaragua], Sinclair.
   None found at E.
   Lectotype at K: a sheet (K000503065) ex herb. Hooker annotated by him with the name and 'Realejo, Sinclair' – it is annotated 'holotype' doubtless by J.P.M. Brenan, who lectotypified it (cited as 'holotype') in Kew Bull. (41: 80. 1986).
≡ ***Adenopodia patens*** (Hook. & Arn.) J. Dixon ex Brenan

[*Iris beecheyana* Herb., in Hook. & Arn., Bot. Beechey Voy. 9: 395. 1840. (IRIDACEAE).
Original material: San Francisco (or Monterey Bay), California, Lay & Collie. The protologue of this species and ensuing note by Herbert published in the California Supplement (and therefore the typification) is confusing. Hooker & Arnott had earlier in the same work (p. 160. 1833) identified two Beechey collections from California as *I. humilis* and *I. sibirica*. The confusion arose when Hooker & Arnott wrote the Supplement, using information supplied by William Herbert. From Herbert's note on p. 396 he clearly intended his *I. beecheyana* to be based entirely on the Beechey specimens earlier identified as *I. humilis*. A sheet of this at K, ex herb. Hooker, is annotated by Hooker on the sheet 'Beechey' and bears a ticket annotated possibly by Arnott 'Iris humilis California' – it bears Herbert's name by neither, but has been annotated in a later hand (perhaps N.E. Brown) 'Iris Beecheyana Herbert ... Type!' and was cited as such by W.R. Dykes (Genus Iris 90. 1913), which counts as a lectotypification – this was clearly what Herbert intended, and Dykes reduced the species to *I. douglasiana*.
In the protologue of *I. beecheyana*, however, Hooker & Arnott also added reference to 'I sibirica [sensu] Hook. et Arn. supra, p. 160', based on Beechey collections under this name. From Herbert's note on p. 396, and his annotations on the specimens, this is clearly not what he intended, but this material nevertheless also has to be considered as among the syntypes of *I. beecheyana*. There is a specimen of this at E (E00369223) annotated by Arnott 'Iris sibirica. California, Beechey', and also by him 'an I. longipetala Herb?', and another at K, ex herb. Hooker, annotated by Herbert 'I believe it is I. longipetala mihi'. Given the doubt this should not be taken as a syntype of *I. longipetala* Herb. (see below), and as Dykes has lectotypified I. *beecheyana* on the 'humilis' element, the *longipetala* element can be excluded from *I. beecheyana*.
= ***Iris douglasiana*** Herb.]

[***Iris douglasiana*** Herb., in Hook. & Arn., Bot. Beechey Voy. 9: 395. 1840. (IRIDACEAE).
Original material: California, Douglas.

This species comprises the two following named varieties, neither of which can be taken as a 'var. *douglasiana*'. The sheet of original material ex herb. Hooker bears a ticket in Herbert's hand with a long description under the name 'Iris Douglasiana Herbert' – it bears a specimen of each variety].

[*Iris douglasiana* var. *bracteata* Herb., in Hook. & Arn., Bot. Beechey Voy. 9: 395. 1840. (IRIDACEAE).
Original material: California, Douglas.
  None found at E.
  At K: the left-hand specimen on a sheet ex herb. Hooker, with a ticket annotated by Herbert 'Iris Douglasiana v[ar.] 1 …'.
= **Iris douglasiana** Herb.]

[*Iris douglasiana* var. *nuda* Herb., in Hook. & Arn., Bot. Beechey Voy. 9: 395. 1840. (IRIDACEAE).
Original material: California, Douglas.
  None found at E.
  At K: the right-hand specimen on a sheet ex herb. Hooker, with a ticket annotated by Herbert 'Iris Douglasiana W. H[erbert] v[ar.] 2 …', and by Hooker 'California, Douglas'.
= **Iris douglasiana** Herb.]

[**Iris longipetala** Herb., in Hook. & Arn., Bot. Beechey Voy. 9: 395. 1840. (IRIDACEAE).
Original material: California, Douglas.
  At E: a (badly insect damaged) sheet ex herb. Arnott (E00369225), annotated by him 'Iris longipetala Herb. … California – D[avid] D[ouglas] per Hooker'
  At K, two sheets. One ex herb. Hooker bearing a ticket annotated by Hooker 'California, Douglas', and by Herbert annotated with the name and a short description. The second sheet, ex herb. Bentham, bears two specimens – the right-hand one has a printed Horticultural Society label 'Nova California. Douglas, 1833'].

[*Iris tolmieana* Herb., in Hook. & Arn., Bot. Beechey Voy. 9: 396. 1840. (IRIDACEAE).
Original material: 'Prope fluvium Walamet in Fl[umen] Columbiam ex parte meridionali tendentem legit *Tolmie*'.
Published here as a new name and rank for '*I. haematophylla* var. *Valametiana* [sic, recte *Valametica*] Herb. in Hook. Flor. Nor. Am. II. p. 206. [1839].'
  Isolectotype at E: a sheet ex herb. Arnott (E00369224), annotated by him 'Iris haematophylla Fisch. var. Wallamatica N.W. Am., at river Wallamat Tolmie per Hooker' and 'an I. Tolmiaeana'.
  Lectotype at K: a sheet ex herb. Hooker bearing two attached tickets annotated by Herbert: on the upper of these is the locality 'N.W. America

Alphabetical list of new taxa 119

river Wallamet. Tolmie' and Herbert's first thought that it was 'Iris sanguinea otherwise called haematophylla'; the lower ticket has the name 'Iris haematophylla var. Valametica' in Herbert's hand, to which someone (?Hooker) has later added 'I. Tolmieana Herb.'. This sheet was cited as type by W.R. Dykes (Genus Iris 90. 1913).
= ***Iris missouriensis*** Nutt.]

Isopyrum occidentale Hook. & Arn., Bot. Beechey Voy. 7: 316. 1838. (RANUNCULACEAE).
Original material: California, Douglas.
At E: a sheet ex herb. Arnott (E00369005), annotated by Arnott '"Isopyrum occidentale Hook. mst." California, [per] Dr Hooker'.
No original material found at K.

Itea chinensis Hook. & Arn., Bot. Beechey Voy. 4: 189, t. 39. 1833. (ITEACEAE).
Original material: Chiefly ... about Macao, China, Lay & Collie.
At E: a sheet (E00369058), bearing a branch with inflorescence and leaves, and two detached leaves is probably original material. It has two attached tickets – one with a predominantly English description, the other with the name 'Itea chinesnsis' and a Latin description, all in Arnott's hand. It has been remounted at an early date and has a 'Herb. Walker Arnott' printed label, but does not have the 'Beechey, China' annotation, which was probably written on the original sheet.
None found at K.

Jaegeria pedunculata Hook. & Arn., Bot. Beechey Voy. 7: 299. 1838. (COMPOSITAE).
Original material: 'Talisco', Mexico, Lay & Collie.
None found at E.
Lectotype at K: the lower right-hand specimen on a sheet ex herb. Hooker bearing three collections; it is annotated by Hooker with the name and 'Talisco, Beechey' and was cited as 'type' by A.M. Torres (Brittonia 20: 62. 1968) (the other collections, *Palmer* 427, 1899, are not original material).

Juncus menziesii R. Br. [var.] β *californicus* Hook. & Arn., Bot. Beechey Voy. 9: 402. 1840. (JUNCACEAE).
Original material: California, Douglas.
At E: a sheet ex herb. Arnott (E00369231), annotated by him 'Juncus menziesii β. California. D[avid] D[ouglas] per Hooker'.
None found at K.
Note. J. Kirschner (Sp. Plant. Juncaceae 2: 55. 2002) referred to a non-existent specimen and mistook the collector when he cited 'T: [California], *Lay & A. Collie*; syn: K, *n.v.*'.
= ***Juncus longistylis*** Torr.

Kadua centranthoides Hook. & Arn., Bot. Beechey Voy. 2: 85. 1832. (RUBIACEAE).
Original material: Sandwich Islands, Mr Macrae.
  None found at E.
  At K, two sheets. One ex herb. Hooker, annotated with the name by Arnott, and by Hooker with the details 'Volcano, Owhyhee. Hort. Soc.' (bearing another collection that is not original material). The second sheet is ex herb. Bentham and not annotated with the name, but bears the printed label 'Ins. Owhyhee, ad montem ignivomem, Macrae, Junio, 1825. Herb. Hort. Soc. Lond.'

Kadua glomerata Hook. & Arn., Bot. Beechey Voy. 2: 85. 1832. (RUBIACEAE).
Original material: Sandwich Islands, Lay & Collie.
  None found at E.
  A sheet ex herb. Hooker bears a ticket annotated by Arnott with the name and 'Oahu, B[eechey]' – this probably refers to the right-hand specimen, which is therefore original material (the left-hand one was determined as *K. schlechtendaliana* by F.R. Fosberg).
= **Kadua centranthoides** Hook. & Arn.

Kadua smithii Hook. & Arn., Bot. Beechey Voy. 2:86. 1832, *nom. illeg.* (RUBIACEAE).
[Sandwich Islands].
Proposed as a replacement name for *Hedyotis coriacea* Sm.
≡ **Kadua coriacea** (Sm.) W.L. Wagner & Lorence

Kallstroemia maxima (L.) Hook. & Arn., Bot. Beechey Voy. 6: 282. 1838. (ZYGOPHYLLACEAE). [Mexico].
Basionym cited: 'Tribulus maximus. *Linn.* [Sp. Pl. 1: 386. 1753]'.
Note. In Index Kewensis this combination was attributed to Wight & Arnott (Prod. Fl. Penins. Ind. Or. 145. 1834), but the formal combination in the genus *Kallstroemia* was not formally made in that work. Index Kewensis also cited a new combination of *Ehrenbergia tribuloides* Mart., as being made in Wight & Arnott's *Prodromus*, but it was made neither there, nor in Bot. Beechey Voy. (where it is discussed).

Krameria cistoidea Hook. & Arn., Bot. Beechey Voy. 1: 8, t 5. 1830. (KRAMERIACEAE).
Original material: 'Coquimbo', Chili, Lay & Collie.
  None found at E.
  At K: the upper specimen (K000471018) on a sheet ex herb. Hooker annotated by him with the name, reference, and 'Coquimbo, Beechey' – it was annotated 'lectotype' by B.B. Simpson and this was published by him in Fl. Neotropica (49: 40. 1989) (the lower collection, *Bridges* 242, is not a type).

Alphabetical list of new taxa 121

Lantana lippioides Hook. & Arn., Bot. Beechey Voy. 7: 305. 1838, *nom. illeg.*, non Spreng., 1825. (VERBENACEAE).
Original material: 'Talisco and Acapulco', Mexico, Lay & Collie.
 At E: a sheet ex herb. Arnott (E00369186), annotated by him with the name and 'Mexico, Beechey'.
 None found at K.
?= ***Lippia*** sp.

Lathyrus decaphyllus Hook. [var.] β *minor* Hook. & Arn., Bot. Beechey Voy. 3: 138. 1832. (LEGUMINOSAE).
Original material: San Francisco (or Monterey Bay), California, Lay & Collie.
 None found at E or K.
?= ***Lathyrus venosus*** Muhl. ex Willd.

Lathyrus macraei Hook. & Arn., Bot. Beechey Voy. 1: 21. 1830. (LEGUMINOSAE).
Original material: 'Conception ... Mr. Macrae'; 'Valparaiso ... Mr. Bridges and Mr. Cruckshanks'.
 At E: a sheet ex herb. Arnott (E00249303), annotated by him 'Vicia nigricans H & A "Lathyrus Macraei"! in Beech. Voy. Valparaiso, Mr Cruckshanks per Dr Hooker'.
 At K are two Macrae collections, which, despite discrepancies over the localities, might, perhaps, be original material: one sheet (K000328155) ex herb. Hooker annotated by him with the name and 'Cordillera of Chili, Macrae'; the other (K000328156) ex herb. Bentham with a printed Hort. Soc. Lond. label 'Cumbre, Andium Claustrum, Chili, Macrae 1825'.
= ***Vicia nigricans*** Hook. & Arn.

Lathyrus pubescens Hook. & Arn., Bot. Beechey Voy. 1: 21. 1830. (LEGUMINOSAE).
Original material: 'Conception', Chili, Lay & Collie.
 None found at E or K; specimens at E ex herb. Arnott annotated by him with the name are later collections of Gillies, and Cuming.

Lathyrus sessilifolius Hook. & Arn., Bot. Beechey Voy. 1: 20. 1830, *nom. illeg.*, non (Sibth. & Sm.) Ten., 1826. (LEGUMINOSAE).
Original material: 'Conception', Chili, Lay & Collie.
 None found at E or K; specimens at E ex herb. Arnott annotated by him with the name are later collections of Bridges, Cuming, Mathews *et al*.
= ***Lathyrus magellanicus*** Lam.

Layia Hook. & Arn., Bot. Beechey Voy. 4: 182. 1833, *nom. rejec.* (LEGUMINOSAE).
The Leguminous genus *Layia* Hook. & Arn. [China] has been rejected in favour of *Layia* Hook. & Arn. ex DC. (COMPOSITAE) – see below.

"*Layia* Hook. & Arn.", Bot. Beechey Voy. 4: 148. 1833. (COMPOSITAE).
A provisional name, not validly published: the authors stated that 'If this were [emphasis added] to form a new genus, we would propose the name of LAYIA'. On p. 182 of the same work, synchronously published, Hooker & Arnott formally described the genus *Layia* in Leguminosae. Candolle (Prod. 7: 294. 1832) (presumably because he thought the single species in the leguminous genus should be referred to some other genus) took up and validated Hooker & Arnott's provisional usage in Compositae, and this name has been conserved over the name in Leguminosae.
= **Layia** Hook. & Arn. ex DC.

Layia douglasii Hook. & Arn., Bot. Beechey Voy. 8: 358. 1839. (COMPOSITAE). Type: 'On the gravelly islands of the river Columbia, between the "Narrows" and "Great Falls". *Douglas*'.
   Not found at E.
   At K a remounted partial sheet, presumably ex herb. Hooker, is the type – attached is a ticket with Douglas's original number and note as cited in the protologue – it was annotated 'type' by J. Clausen in 1936, but it is not known if this has been published.
= **Layia glandulosa** (Hook.) Hook. & Arn.

Layia emarginata Hook. & Arn., Bot. Beechey Voy. 4: 183, t. 38. 1833. (LEGUMINOSAE). (FIG. 2).
Original material: 'Captain Beechey's Collection [i.e., Chiefly … about Macao, Lay & Collie] … foliage and ripe fruit'; 'from Mr. Millett, specimens in flower'.
   At E: a sheet ex herb. Arnott (E00369048), annotated by him with the name and 'China, D Millett', with three attached notes: part of a letter in the hand of W.J. Hooker 'This flowering specimen from Millett is surely the same as Beechey's in fr. What do you think of it? I have sent a character to press but it is not too late to alter it'; another ticket in Hooker's hand 'Layia emarginata Arn. & Hook. if new …'; a ticket with a description in Arnott's hand.
   At K: a sheet ex herb. Hooker annotated by him with the name and reference, bears material of both parts of the original material: the upper, flowering specimen, is annotated 'China, Millett', the lower, fruiting one, 'China, Beechey' – also on the sheet is a ticket of drawings annotated by ?Hooker.
≡ **Ormosia emarginata** (Hook. & Arn.) Benth.

Layia glandulosa (Hook.) Hook. & Arn., Bot. Beechey Voy. 8: 358. 1839. (COMPOSITAE). [California].
Basionym cited: 'Blepharipappus glandulosus *Hook. Fl. Bor. Am. 1. p.* 316. [1833]'.

Alphabetical list of new taxa 123

Layia heterotricha (DC.) Hook. & Arn., Bot. Beechey Voy. 8: 358. 1839. (COMPOSITAE). [California].
Basionym cited: 'Madaraglossa heterotricha. *De Cand. Prod.* 5. *p.* 694. [1836]'.

Layia hieracioides (DC.) Hook. & Arn., Bot. Beechey Voy. 8: 358. 1839. (COMPOSITAE). [California].
Basionym cited: 'Madaraglossa hieracioides. *De Cand. Prod.* 5. *p.* 694 [1838]'.

Lepidium corymbosum Hook. & Arn., Bot. Beechey Voy. 7: 323. 1838. (CRUCIFERAE).
Type: 'Snake Country. American falls of Snake River [Idaho]. ([John McLeod per] *Tolmie*)'.
At E, a sheet ex herb. Arnott (E00369008), annotated by him with the name and 'Snake Country, N.W. America, Tolmie per Hooker'.
At K, two sheets: one ex herb. Hooker annotated by him with the name and 'Snake Country (Tolmie)' – this is presumably the one cited by N.H. Holmgren as 'holotype: K!' in Intermountain Flora (2B: 255. 2005). The other sheet ex herb. Bentham has a ticket annotated by Hooker with the name and locality (but no collector's name).
= ***Lepidium montanum*** Nutt.

Lepidium leiocarpum Hook. & Arn., Bot. Beechey Voy. 7: 324. 1838, *nom. illeg.*, non DC., 1821. (CRUCIFERAE).
Original material: California, Douglas.
None found at E.
At K: the top specimen on a sheet ex herb. Hooker with three colletions, it is annotated by Hooker with the name and 'California, Douglas' (the other collections, Coulter, Anon., are not original material); on the other sheet the bottom left-hand specimen, ex herb. A. Gray is original material, annotated 'California, Douglas' and with the name 'Lepidium nitidum Nutt.' in addition to Hooker & Arnott's (the other collections, Coulter, Hartweg, on the sheet are not original material).
= ***Lepidium nitidum*** Torr. & A. Gray

Leptodactylon Hook. & Arn., Bot. Beechey Voy. 8: 369. 1839. (POLEMONIACEAE).

Leptodactylon californicum Hook. & Arn., Bot. Beechey Voy. 8: 369, t. 89. 1839. (POLEMONIACEAE).
Original material: California, Douglas.
At E: a sheet ex herb. Arnott (E00369164), annotated by him with the name and 'California, Douglas', and later (also by Arnott) 'Gilia californica Benth. in DC. prod. n. 40'.
At K: the middle upper specimen on a sheet ex herb. Bentham, with a printed 'California, Douglas 1833' label that Bentham has annotated with

the name 'Gilia californica Benth. in DC. Prod. 9.316' (the other specimens, *Hooker & Gray* s.n., and a Nuttall specimen on part of a Hooker sheet, are not original material).
Note. In a note following the protologue, it is stated that '*Phlox Hookeri* Dougl. in Hook.' belongs to the same genus, but the combination is not formally made.

Leptopetalum Hook. & Arn., Bot. Beechey Voy. 7: 295. 1838. (RUBIACEAE).

Leptopetalum mexicanum Hook. & Arn., Bot. Beechey Voy. 7: 295, t. 61. 1838. (RUBIACEAE). (FIG. 1).
Original material: Bonin, but published as from Tepic, Mexico, Lay & Collie.
 At E: a sheet ex herb. Arnott (E00369102), annotated by him with the name and 'Mexico, Beechey', with an attached ticket with Arnott's MS description.
 At K: a sheet ex herb. Hooker annotated by him with the name and 'Mexico, Beechey', and a ticket with two drawings possibly by Arnott – the locality has been crossed out and replaced in a later hand with 'Bonin'.
Note. This is clearly one of the Loo Choo/Bonin specimens mistakenly labelled as from Mexico referred to on p. 275, but this one was not recognised as such by Hooker & Arnott (and hence given a misleading epithet).

Lespedeza striata (Thunb.) Hook. & Arn., Bot. Beechey Voy. 6: 262. 1838. (LEGUMINOSAE). [Bonin].
Basionym cited: 'Hedysarum striatum. *Thunb. Fl. Jap. p.* 291 [first published Syst. Veg., ed. 14, 675. 1784]'.

Leucas benthamiana Hook. & Arn., Bot. Beechey Voy. 5: 204. 1836. (LABIATAE).
Original material: 'Canton. *Mr. Millett.* Lappas island; *Rev. G.H. Vachell, n.* 172'.
 At E, two sheets. One ex herb. Arnott (E00369193), annotated by him with the name and 'Canton, China – an L. javanica Benth.? …[rest of annotation chopped off]', is almost certainly a Millett specimen given to Arnott by Hooker and probably original material. The other sheet (E00369194), ex herb. R.K. Greville, bears a printed Vachell label annotated with the date May 1829, the sheet itself is annotated by Greville 'Prof. Henslow. no. 172'.
 At K, in a type cover, are various sheets with the name *L. Benthamiana* or *L. mollissima* β *chinensis*. On one of these, ex herb. Bentham, the specimen in the top right-hand corner (given him by Lindley in 1834) is labelled by Bentham 'China, Vachell' and may be original material.
Note. 'Ballota pilosa. *Lour. Fl. Coch.* 2. *p.* 442?' is cited, but as this was queried it does not make Hooker & Arnott's name superfluous.
= **Leucas mollissima** Wall. ex Benth.

Alphabetical list of new taxa

Leucheria senecioides Hook. & Arn., Bot. Beechey Voy. 1: 28. 1830 (as '*Leucaeria*'; generic placement queried). (COMPOSITAE).
Original material: 'Conception', Chili, Lay & Collie.

At E: the left-hand specimen (E00249417) on a sheet ex herb. Arnott, annotated by him 'Leuchaeria senecioides H & A – β DC. Conception, Beechey'. The sheet must have been assembled later as the Candollean purple-flowered variety was not published until 1838 (Prodromus 7: 57), when Candolle realised this was conspecific with Hooker's earlier white-flowerd *Trixia senecioides* (Exotic Fl. 2, t. 101. 1824), a species based on Cruckshanks material and purely coincidentally sharing the same epithet with the later Hooker & Arnott species (the other two specimens on the sheet *Bridges* 495, *Mathews* 255, are not original material; the latter is annotated by Arnott with the unpublished name 'Leuceria pedunculosa H & A').

None found at K.

["*Linum oligophyllum*" –why this name should have been attributed to Hooker & Arnott, in Index Kewensis and elsewhere, is inexplicable. In Zuloaga *et al.* (Cat. Pl. Vas. Cono Sur 3: 2412. 2008) it was stated it to be an illegitimate homonym coined by Hooker & Arnott. Although they attributed the name to 'Schiede', in the cited reference Schiede correctly attributed the name to '[Roem. &] Schult. Syst. Veg. 6 p. 758 [1820]'), so there is no question of its being a homonym coincd by Hooker & Arnott].

Liparis revoluta Hook. & Arn., Bot. Beechey Voy. 2: 70, t. 16. 1832. (ORCHIDACEAE).
Original material: Society Islands, Lay & Collie.

At E: a sheet ex herb. Arnott (E00369222), annotated by him with the name and 'Tahiti – Beechey'.

At K: a sheet ex herb. Hooker annotated with the reference and collecting details 'Socy. Islds., Beechey', and bearing a ticket of drawings annotated with the name by Hooker.

Lipochaeta macrocephala Hook. & Arn., Bot. Beechey Voy. 10: 436. 1841. (COMPOSITAE).
Original material: 'Between San Blas and Tepic', Mexico, Sinclair.

None found at E.

At K: a sheet (K000487697) ex herb. Hooker bearing a ticket in Bentham's hand with the name and 'Acapulco, Sinclair'. Despite the discrepancy over locality this was annotated 'holotype' by K.M. Becker in 1976 and published as such (Mem. New York Bot. Gard. 31(2): 26. 1979). There is a duplicate of this at K, ex herb. Bentham (given him by Hooker in 1841) annotated with the same details by Bentham, and therfore an isolectotype. (Presumably either the locality was wrongly cited in the protologue, or Bentham made a mistake when he wrote the labels).

≡ ***Lasianthera macrocephala*** (Hook. & Arn.) K. Becker

Lithospermum chinense Hook. & Arn., Bot. Beechey Voy. 5: 202. 1836. (BORAGINACEAE).
Type: 'Macao [China]; *Rev. G.H. Vachell, n.* 286'.

Two type sheets at E. One ex herb. Arnott (E00369167), annotated by him with the name and 'Canton, Vachell no. 286'. Also a duplicate, ex herb. Edinburgh University (E00369168), with a printed Vachell label, to which the details 'About Macao, Oct – Nov [1830] 286' have been added by hand.

Not found at K.
= **Heliotropium strigosum** Willd.

Lithospermum circumscissum Hook. & Arn., Bot. Beechey Voy. 8: 370. 1839. (Generic placement queried). (BORAGINACEAE).
Type: 'Snake Fort, Snake Country [Oregon/Idaho border]. [John McLeod per] *Mr Tolmie*'.

Type at E, a sheet ex herb. Arnott (E00026028), annotated by him with the name and 'Snake Country, Tolmie per Hooker'.

Type at K, a sheet ex herb. Hooker bearing three collections – the types are the three central specimens annotated by Hooker '75. Snake Country, California. Tolmie', associated with a ticket of drawings by Hooker annotated by him with the name and locality – these were annotated 'type' by P.H. Raven in 1960, and it was cited by Cronquist *et al* in Intermountain Flora (4: 268. 1984) as 'holotype at K!' (the other collections, *Pringle* s.n., *Purpus* 5712, are not types).
≡ ***Cryptantha circumscissa*** (Hook. & Arn.) I.M. Johnston

Lobelia angulatodentata Hook. & Arn., Bot. Beechey Voy. 7: 301. 1838 (as '*angulato-dentata*'). (CAMPANULACEAE).
Original material: Tepic, Mexico, Lay & Collie.

At E: a sheet ex herb. Arnott (E00084456), annotated by him 'Tupa Lobelia angulatodentata H & A. Mexico, Beechey, near L. persicifolia Cav., stem herbaceous' – it was annotated 'isotype' by T.G. Lammers & M.J. Eakes in 1995

At K: the right-hand specimen (K000494277) on a sheet ex herb. Hooker, bearing a ticket annotated by Bentham with the name (and the later determination *L. laxiflora*) and 'Mexico, Beechey' – it was annotated 'holotype' by Lammers & Eakes in 1995 (mounted on the same sheet as the type of *L. lanceolata* – see below).
= **Lobelia laxiflora** Kunth subsp. ***laxiflora***

Lobelia arabidoides Hook. & Arn., Bot. Beechey Voy. 7: 301, t. 66. 1838. (CAMPANULACEAE).
Original material: Tepic, Mexico, Lay & Collie.

At E: a sheet ex herb. Arnott (E00084457), annotated by him with the name and 'Tepic, Beechey' – it was annotated 'isotype' by T.G. Lammers in 1995.

Alphabetical list of new taxa

At K: a sheet (K000494287) ex herb. Hooker bearing a ticket annotated by Bentham with the name and 'Mexico, Beechey' – it was annotated 'holotype' by T.J. Ayers in 1986.
= *Lobelia flexuosa* (C. Presl) A. DC. subsp. *flexuosa*

Lobelia carnosula Hook. & Arn., Bot. Beechey Voy. 8: 362. 1839. (CAMPANULACEAE).
Type: 'Blackfoot River, Snake Country [Idaho]. [John McLeod per] *Mr Tolmie*'.
Type at E, a sheet ex herb. Arnott (E00369152), annotated by him with the name and 'Snake Country, N.W.C. Tolmie per Hooker'.
Type at K: the lower specimen on a sheet ex herb. Hooker annotated by him with the name, and 'California, Snake Country. Tolmie' (the upper specimens, *Parry* 192, are not types).
Note. Cronquist *et al.* in Intermountain Flora (4: 520. 1984) cited 'type at NY!'.
≡ *Porterella carnosula* (Hook. & Arn.) Torr.

Lobelia cordifolia Hook. & Arn., Bot. Beechey Voy. 7: 301. 1838. (CAMPANULACEAE).
Original material: Tepic, Mexico, Lay & Collie.
At E: a sheet ex herb. Arnott (E00259112), annotated by him with the name and 'Mexico, Beechey' – it was annotated 'holotype' by T.J. Ayers in 1986.
At K: a sheet (K000494286) ex herb. Bentham (given him by Hooker in 1844), annotated by Bentham with the name and 'Mexico, Beechey' – it was annotated 'isotype' by T.J. Ayers in 1986.

Lobelia divaricata Hook. & Arn., Bot. Beechey Voy. 7: 301, t. 67. 1838. (CAMPANULACEAE).
Original material: 'Talisco', Mexico, Lay & Collie.
At E: a sheet ex herb. Arnott (E00369153), annotated by him with the name and 'Talisco, Beechey'.
At K: the most likely to be original material is a remounted partial sheet (K000494258) ex herb. Bentham (given him by Hooker in 1844) bearing a ticket annotated by Bentham with the name and 'Mexico, Beechey'. This is mounted on the same sheet as part of a dismembered sheet ex herb. Hooker, the upper eight specimens of which might also be original material (and annotated as 'type' by N.Y. Sandwith and R. McVaugh) (the lower two, *Coulter* 26, belong to a different species and are not original material).

Lobelia lanceolata Hook. & Arn., Bot. Beechey Voy. 7: 301. 1838. (CAMPANULACEAE).
Original material: Tepic, Mexico, Lay & Collie.

None found at E.

At K: the left-hand specimen (K000494278) on a sheet ex herb. Hooker, bearing a ticket annotated by Bentham with the name (and a later determination as *L. laxiflora*) and 'Mexico, Beechey' – it was annotated 'holotype' by T.G. Lammers and M.J. Eakes (mounted on the same sheet as the type of *L. angulatodentata* – see above).

= **Lobelia laxiflora** Kunth subsp. **laxiflora**

Lobelia macrostachys Hook. & Arn., Bot. Beechey Voy. 2: 88. 1832. (CAMPANULACEAE).

Original material: Sandwich Islands, Lay & Collie.

At E: a sheet ex herb. Arnott (E00239730), annotated by him with the name and 'Oahu, Beechey'.

≡ **Trematolobelia macrostachys** (Hook. & Arn.) Zahlbr. ex Rock

Lobelia ovalifolia Hook. & Arn., Bot. Beechey Voy. 7: 300. 1838. (CAMPANULACEAE).

Original material: Tepic, Mexico, Lay & Collie.

At E: a sheet ex herb. Arnott (E00084455), annotated by him with the name and 'Mexico, Beechey (near *L. mucronata*)' – this was annotated 'isotype' by T.G. Lammers & M.J. Eakes in 1995.

At K: the left-hand collection (K000494279) on a sheet ex herb. Hooker bearing two collections – it bears a ticket annotated by Bentham with the name (and a later determination, *L. laxiflora*), and 'Mexico, Beechey' – it was annotated 'holotype' by Lammers & Eakes in 1995 (the other specimen, *Anon 420*, is not original material).

= **Lobelia laxiflora** Kunth subsp. **laxiflora**

Lobelia polyphylla Hook. & Arn., Bot. Beechey Voy. 1: 33. 1830. (CAMPANULACEAE).

Original material: 'Valparaiso', Chili, Lay & Collie.

None found at E or K. The only sheet from Arnott's herbarium at E bearing this name is a Macrae collection. T.G. Lammers (Sida 19: 94. 2000) cited 'TYPE: CHILE. Valparaiso ... *Beechey. s.n.* (HOLOTYPE: K!)', but this specimen cannot be found.

Lonicera affinis Hook. & Arn., Bot. Beechey Voy. 6: 264. 1838. (CAPRIFOLIACEAE).

Original material: 'Loo Choo', Lay & Collie.

At E: a sheet ex herb. Arnott (E00369088), annotated by him with the name and 'Loo Choo, Beechey'.

At K: a sheet ex herb. Hooker annotated by him with the name and 'Loo Choo, Beechey'.

Lonicera subspicata Hook. & Arn., Bot. Beechey Voy. 8: 349. 1839. (Generic placement queried). (CAPRIFOLIACEAE).
Type: 'a solitary specimen', California, Douglas.
   Not found at E.
   At K, the left-hand specimen on a sheet ex herb. Hooker annotated by him 'Scroph^ae. Douglas, California' beneath which is a ticket with drawings possibly by Arnott (the other specimen, *Coulter* 201, is not a type). A sheet ex herb. Bentham with a printed 'California, Douglas 1833' annotated by Bentham with the name and reference to 'Torr. & Gr. Fl. N. Am. 2 p. 8 [1841]' may be a duplicate or part of Hooker's 'solitary specimen', in which case it would also be a type.

Lonicera telfairii Hook. & Arn., Bot. Beechey Voy. 4: 190. 1833. (CAPRIFOLIACEAE).
Original material: Chiefly ... about Macao, China, Lay & Collie; 'specimens sent from the Mauritius by Mr. Telfair to Dr. Hooker'.
   At E: a sheet ex herb. Arnott, bearing two specimens, both annotated by Arnott 'Lonicera Telfairii H & A': the left-hand one (E00369089) has the details 'China, Beechey', the right-hand (E00369090) 'Mauritius, [per] Dr Hooker'.
   At K: the right-hand specimen on a sheet ex herb. Hooker, annotated by him 'Maurit. Telfair (cultd?)' (the left-hand specimen, a Millett one from China, is not original material).
Note. This should be taken as the recognition as a distinct species of 'L. Periclymenum. [sensu] *Lour. Cochin. v.* 1. *p.* 185' [i.e., non L.].
= ***Lonicera confusa*** (Sweet) DC.

Loranthus cactorum Hook. & Arn., Bot. Beechey Voy. 1: 25. 1830. (LORANTHACEAE)
Original material: 'Coquimbo', Chili, Lay & Collie.
   None found at E or K.
Note. J. Kuijt (Syst. Bot. Monogr. 19: 15, 19. 1988) mistakenly cited a specimen at E as 'holotype'. This refers to a sheet ex herb. Arnott bearing two specimens: the upper is a Gillies specimen from the Andes of Mendoza, labelled by Gillies as 'Loranthus aphylla', to which Arnott has added the authority 'Miers'; the lower specimen is annotated by Arnott 'Loranthus aphyllus Miers. [L.] cactorum H & A, Cordillera of Chili Hb. Cuming no 259'. The latter is clearly a later collection than the Beechey material, and shows that Arnott came to realise that the plant had an earlier name.
= ***Tristerix aphyllus*** (Miers ex DC.) Barlow & Wiens

Lucuma ferruginea Hook. & Arn., Bot. Beechey Voy. 7: 302. 1838. (Generic placement queried). (SAPOTACEAE).
Original material: published as from Tepic, Mexico – actually from Bonin, Lay & Collie.
 At E: a sheet ex herb. Arnott (E00207247), annotated by him with the name and 'Mexico, Beechey'.
 None found at K.
Note. On distributional grounds this must be one of the Loo Choo/Bonin collections referred to on p. 267 mislabelled as from Mexico, though not spotted as such by Hooker & Arnott. It is even possible that it is part of the same Bonin collection described on p. 266 as *Sideroxylon ferrugineum*.
= **Pouteria obovata** (R. Br.) Baehni

Lupinus macrocarpus Hook. & Arn., Bot. Beechey Voy. 3: 138. 1832. (LEGUMINOSAE)
Original material: San Francisco (or Monterey Bay), California, Lay & Collie; also stated to have been 'found by Mr. Menzies', but no specific collection is mentioned.
 None found at E or K.
?= **Lupinus arboreus** Sims

[*Lupinus parviflorus* Nutt., in Hooker & Arnott, Bot. Beechey Voy. 7: 336. 1838. (LEGUMINOSAE).
Type material: Nuttall specimens.
The description (and not the name alone) is firmly attributed by Hooker & Arnott to Nuttall. The name therefore has to be typified by Nutall specimens, which are NOT cited here; the material cited by Hooker & Arnott ('Between Henry and Smith's Rivers. Snake Country [Wyoming]. ([John McLeod per] *Tolmie*)') is not the type of Nuttall's name and W.E. Harmon (Trans. Miss. Ac. Sci. 6: 162. 1972), cited the type as a Nuttall specimen from 'Columbia Plains' (PH, isotype GH).
 Of this 'additional' Tolmie material there is a sheet at E, ex herb. Arnott (E00369049), with a label annotated by ?Hooker 'L. parviflora Nutt.' and by Arnott 'Snake Country, N.W. Am. Tolmie per Hooker'. On a sheet ex herb. Hooker at K, the left-hand specimen is annotated 'Snake Country, California. Tolmie'; but the right-hand one might be a type as it has a ticket in Nuttall's hand annotated with the name, though the locality is 'R. Mts. Oregon' and it has (the unpublished) designation 'α'. A second sheet bears two further Nuttall collections, which might also be types].

[*Lupinus truncatus* Nutt., in Hooker & Arnott, Bot. Beechey Voy. 7: 336. 1838. (LEGUMINOSAE).
Type material: 'San Diego, N. California', Nuttall.
As with *L. parviflorus* the description (and not the name alone) is attributed to Nuttall.

Alphabetical list of new taxa 131

No type material found at E.

Types at K: two collections on a sheet ex herb. Hooker, with tickets annotated by Nuttall with the name and 'St Diego, N. Calif.' (the third, left-hand, collection is annotated by Hooker 'California, Douglas' and is not a type)].

Lysimachia glaucophylla Hook. & Arn., Bot. Beechey Voy. 7: 306, t. 68. 1838. (PRIMULACEAE).

Original material: published as from Tepic, Mexico – actually from Bonin, Lay & Collie.

None found at E.

At K: a sheet ex herb. Hooker annotated by him with the name and 'Mexico, Beechey'; to which is attached a ticket with drawings possibly by Arnott.

Note. J.D. Ray (Illinois Biol. Mem. 24: 107. 1956) explained that this was another of the confused 'Mexican' collections, as the plant is actually from Bonin.

= **Lysimachia mauritiana** Lam.

Lysimachia lineariloba Hook. & Arn., Bot. Beechey Voy. 6: 268. 1838. (PRIMULACEAE).

Original material: 'Loo Choo', Lay & Collie.

At E: a sheet ex herb. Arnott (E00369157), annotated by him with the name and 'Loo Choo. Beechey'.

At K: a sheet ex herb. Hooker annotated by him with the name and 'Loo Choo' (on the same sheet is a C. Wright collection, which is not original material).

Note. In the protologue it is stated that plate 56 is of this plant, but that plate depicts the fern *Woodwardia prolifer*.

= **Lysimachia mauritiana** Lam.

Macrorhynchus lessingii Hook. & Arn., Bot. Beechey Voy. 8: 361. 1839, *nom. illeg.* (COMPOSITAE). [California].

Hooker & Arnott intended to make a new combination based on their *Borkausia lessingii* (l.c. p. 145. 1833), but as that name was superfluous they effectively made a new name, rather than a new combination. However, this name is also superfluous and illegitimate, as *Troximon apargioides* Less. was again cited as a synonym.

≡ **Agoseris apargioides** (Less.) Greene

Malva malachroides Hook. & Arn., Bot. Beechey Voy. 7: 326. 1838. (MALVACEAE).

Original material: California, Douglas.

None found at E.

At K, two sheets: one ex herb. Hooker annotated by him 'California, Douglas'; a sheet ex herb. Bentham with a printed 'California, Douglas 1833' label annotated by Bentham with the name and reference.
≡ ***Sidalcea malachroides*** (Hook. & Arn.) A. Gray

Maurandya stricta Hook. & Arn., Bot. Beechey Voy. 8: 375. 1839 (as '*Maurandia*'; generic placement queried). (PLANTAGINACEAE).
Original material: California, Douglas.

At E: a sheet ex herb. Arnott (E00369180), annotated by him with the name and 'California, [per] Hooker' is probably original material.

At K: a sheet ex herb. Hooker annotated in pencil by ?Hooker with the name, and by Hooker in ink 'California, Douglas' – this is probably the specimen cited as 'holotype' (with an isotype at GH) by W.J. Elisens (Syst. Bot. Monog. 5: 84. 1985); it was again cited as 'holotype' by D.M. Thompson (Syst. Bot. Monog. 22: 109. 1988). A sheet ex herb. Bentham is also original material, it bears a printed 'California, Douglas 1833' label and the sheet is annotated by Bentham with the name and reference 'Benth. in DC Prod. 10. 296' – it was cited as 'isotype' by Thompson (1988).

Note. Sometimes placed in *Neogaerrhinum* as *N. strictum* (Hook. & Arn.) Rothm.
= ***Antirrhinum kelloggii*** Greene

Melampodium tenellum Hook. & Arn., Bot. Beechey Voy. 7: 299. 1838. (COMPOSITAE).
Original material: Tepic, Mexico, Lay & Collie.

At E: the top right-hand specimen (E00369127) on a sheet ex herb. Arnott, annotated by him 'Melampodium (Zarabellia) tenellum H & A. Mexico – Beechey' (on the same sheet is a Sinclair collection from Acapulco, which is not original material).

At K: the top left-hand specimen (K000502035) on a sheet ex herb. Hooker, annotated by him with the name and 'Mexico, Beechey' – it was annotated 'holotype' by T.F. Stuessy in 1969, but it is not known if this has been published (the other specimens on the sheet – Sinclair collections from Acapulco and Tepic – are not original material).

Melochia hispida Hook. & Arn., Bot. Beechey Voy. 2: 60. 1832. (MALVACEAE).
Type: 'a solitary and indifferent specimen', from 'Society Islands', Lay & Collie.
Not found at E or K.
Note. A. Goldberg (Contrib. U.S. Nat. Herb. 34(5): 353. 1967) commented 'the description is inadequate for a determination, and the type cannot be located'.

Memecylon nigrescens Hook. & Arn., Bot. Beechey Voy. 4: 186. 1833. (MELASTOMATACEAE).
Original material: Chiefly … about Macao, China, Lay & Collie.

Alphabetical list of new taxa   133

At E: a sheet ex herb. Arnott (E00369071), annotated by him 'Memecylon nigricans [sic] H & A. China, Beechey'.

At K: a sheet ex herb. Hooker annotated by him with the name and 'China, Beechey'.

[*Meoschium lodiculare* Nees, in Hook. & Arn., Bot. Beechey Voy. 6: 246. 1838. (GRAMINEAE).
Original material: 'In vicinia Macao urbis inque insulis adjectis; *Meyen; Millett; G.H. Vachell, n.* 47.b'. Another case where Hooker & Arnott were merely publishing a Nees name and description; the name is therefore attributable to Nees – as shown on a sheet of original material at E, which Arnott has annotated 'Meoschium lodiculare NE! Canton: Dr Hooker', doubtless a duplicate Millett specimen
= **Ischaemum barbatum** Retz.]

Metrosideros macropus Hook. & Arn., Bot. Beechey Voy. 2: 83. 1832. (MYRTACEAE).
Original material: Sandwich Islands, Lay & Collie; 'specimens collected by Mr. Macrae'.

At E: a sheet ex herb. Arnott (E00369067), bearing two specimens and one fragment, annotated by Arnott with the name and 'Oahu, Beechcy'.

At K: the lower specimen on a sheet ex herb. Hooker with a ticket annotated by ?Arnott with the name and 'Oahu, B[eechey]'. There are also four sheets of original Macrae material at K: two ex herb. Hooker both annotated with the name by ?Arnott, and by Hooker 'Wooahoo, Socy. [sic] Islands, Macrae'; two ex herb. Bentham, both distributed by Hort. Soc. London, one with a printed label 'Woahoo, Ins. Sandwich, Macrae, Maio, 1825'.

Metrosideros obovata Hook. & Arn., Bot. Beechey Voy. 2: 63, t. 12. 1832. (MYRTACEAE).
Original material: 'Gambier's Island', Lay & Collie.

At E: a sheet ex herb. Arnott (E00369068), annotated by him with the name and 'Pitcairn's Island – Beechey'.

At K: a sheet ex herb. Hooker, annotated by him with the name and 'Pitcairn's Isld., Beechey'.
Note. There is a discrepency in locality between that given in the protologue, and that on both the sheets of original material.

Mimulus nanus Hook. & Arn. [var.] α *pluriflorus* Hook. & Arn., Bot. Beechey Voy. 8: 378. 1839. (PHRYMACEAE).
Original material: [Snake Country (Idaho), (John McLeod per) Tolmie – not cited in the protologue, but see below]; 'Hook. Ic. Pl. ined.'.

In this case, unusually for Hooker & Arnott, the [var.] α was not taken by them as the typical variety, as the species description includes both the two varieties α and β which comprise the species. Although by current rules a notional 'var. *nanus*' was automatically created when the species name was published, this did not exist taxonomically until it was created by the first author who effectively 'typified' the name. Bentham did so when he described *Eunanus tolmiaei* (Benth. in A. DC. Prod. 10: 374. 1846) based on the α element. Under this name Bentham specifically included the type of *M. nanus* by citing 'M. nanus et [var. α] plurifolius Hook. et Arn.' – this not only typified the name and typical variety, but made his species superfluous, and by modern rules illegitimate.

Hooker & Arnott neglected to mention the locality and collector for this element (leaving the assumption that it must have been 'California, Douglas'). However, from the extant specimens (which were known to Bentham) the specimens with shorter corollas, matching the description, were actually a Tolmie collection. The case is even more confused as the annotations on the specimens of the two varieties on the Arnott sheet are (largely) reversed, as was realised and resolved by D.M. Thompson (Syst. Bot. Monog. 75: 68. 2005).

Isotype at E: the lower four specimens (E00279297) on a sheet ex herb. Arnott. These were later correctly annotated by Arnott with the name 'Eunanus Tolmiaei Benth – No. 2', but the initial name and collecting details 'Mimulus nanus α Snake Country Tolmie per Hooker' were wrongly placed by him against the upper specimens.

Holotype at K: the remounted upper part of a sheet ex herb. Hooker, annotated by him 'Snake Country, California Tolmie', annotated 'holotype' of *M. nanus* subsp. *nanus* by W.L. Ezell in 1986, and of *M. nanus* by D.M. Thompson in 1992 (an un-numbered Anderson collection is also mounted on the same sheet).
≡ ***Mimulus nanus*** Hook. & Arn. var. ***nanus***

Mimulus nanus [var.] β *subuniflorus* Hook. & Arn., Bot. Beechey Voy. 8: 378. 1839. (PHRYMACEAE).
Original material: [California, Douglas – not cited in the protologue, but see below]; 'Hook. Ic. Pl. ined,'.
See note above under var. *pluriflorus*.

Bentham described this variety as a distinct species, *Eunanus douglasii* (Benth. in A. DC. Prod. 10: 374. 1846). Here again the locality and collector was not mentioned in the protologue, but these are clear from the types that were known to Bentham. On the type sheet in Arnott's herbarium the specimens and labels of the two varieties are (largely) reversed.

Isotype at E (see D.M. Thompson, Syst. Bot. Monog. 75: 45. 2005): the upper nine specimens (E00279298) on a sheet ex herb. Arnott. These were later correctly annotated by Arnott with the name 'Eunanus Douglasii Benth. No. 3', but the initial name and collecting details 'Mimulus nanus β California D[avid] D[ouglas] per Hooker', were wrongly placed by him against the lower

Alphabetical list of new taxa 135

specimens. Other isotypes cited by Thompson at BM, CGE, GH, LE, NY, OXF).

Holotype at K: the remounted upper part of a sheet ex herb. Hooker, annotated by him 'Snake Country California (Douglas) Tolmie', annotated 'holotype' of β *subuniflorus* (and 'isotype' of *E. douglasii* Benth.) by D.M. Thompson in 1992, noting that the locality and collector are in error. Isotype at K, a sheet ex herb. Bentham from which part has been removed leaving two collections – the upper one has a printed 'California, Douglas 1833' label and is annotated by Bentham 'Eunanus Douglasii Benth. in DC. Prod. 10. 374', annotated 'isotype' of β *subuniflorus* (and 'holotype' of *E. douglasii* Benth.) by D.M. Thompson in 1992
≡ ***Mimulus douglasii*** (Benth.) A. Gray

Mitracarpus pallidus Hook. & Arn., Bot. Beechey Voy. 9: 430. 1840 (as '*Mitracarpum pallidum*'). (RUBIACEAE).
Original material: 'Realejo', Mexico [now Nicaragua], Sinclair.

At E: a sheet ex herb. Arnott (E00369103), bearing a label annotated with the name by ?Hooker, to which Arnott has added 'H & A Bot Beech. voy. Supp. Realejo, Dr Sinclair' – this was determined as *M. hirtus* by C.M. Taylor in 2003, but without noticing its type status.

At K: a sheet ex herb. Hooker (K000174516), bearing a ticket annotated by ?Arnott with the name and 'Realejo, Sinclair'.
= ***Mitracarpus hirtus*** (L.) DC.

Mulinum cuneatum Hook. & Arn., Bot. Beechey Voy. 1: 26. 1830. (UMBELLIFERAE).
Original material: 'Valparaiso', Chili, Lay & Collie. Specimens from Mr Cruckshanks are also referred to but these were sterile and were referred 'to *Mulinum* on account of its habit', these could also, perhaps be taken as original material.

At E: on a sheet ex herb. Arnott, two small specimens (E0022402) annotated 'Valparaiso. Mr Cruckshanks per Dr. Hooker' are probably original material (the other specimens on the sheet, *Bridges* 71, *Cuming* 633 and *Mathews* 253 are later collections and not original material, though the latter two are annotated with the name in Arnott's hand).

At K a sheet ex herb. Hooker has five collections: of these one (K000532301) annotatated by Hooker with the name and '"186" Chili, Cruckshanks' can be considered original material – it was annotated 'holotype' by J.C. Zech 1993, but this appears not to have been published (though doubtless included in his Ph.D. dissertation) and in the absence of Beechey material would be a suitable lectotype. (The other collections on the sheet, *Reed* s.n., *Bridges*, s.n., *Capt. King* s.n., *Mathews* 253, are not original material. There are two sheets in a type cover, both ex herb. Hooker: one with specimens of *Bridges* 71, the other with three collections *Gay* s.n., *Philippi* s.n., *Germain* s.n. – but none of this is original material).

Note. In the protologue *Fragosa spinosa* Ruiz & Pavon and *Azorella spinosa* Pers. are both queried as synonyms, but the Hooker & Arnott name is not superfluous.
= **Azorella spinosa** (Ruiz & Pavon) Pers.

Myginda scoparia Hook. & Arn., Bot. Beechey Voy. 6: 283. 1838 (as '*Mygindus*'). (CELASTRACEAE).
Original material: 'Acapulco', Mexico, Lay & Collie.

At E: a sheet ex herb. Arnott (E00369032), annotated by him 'Myginda scoparia H & A. Acapulco, Beechey, conf. M. uragoga var. foliis angustioribus Schl. in Lin. V. p. 603'.

None found at K. There is a sheet ex herb. Hooker to which is attached a ticket annotated by Arnott with the name, a brief description and the locality 'Acapulco' which clearly <u>does</u> belong with the type specimen – probably that retained in his own collection, but Hooker's annotation 'Mexico. W. Bates' appears to refer to the two specimens on the sheet, which are therefore not original material.

Note. Hooker & Arnott also cited a variety described, but not named, by Schlechtendal & Chamisso: 'Myginda Uragoga [Jacq.], var. foliis angustioribus. *Schlecht. in Linn[aea]* 5. *p.* 603', which was included within the number *Schiede & Deppe* 727. As Hooker & Arnott probably did not see this specimen (regardless of its un-named status and different rank) this should not be considered in the typification of *M. scoparia*.
≡ **Crossopetalum scoparium** (Hook. & Arn.) Kuntze

Myoporum euphrasioides Hook. & Arn., Bot. Beechey Voy. 2: 67. 1832. (Generic placement queried). (OROBANCHACEAE).
Original material: 'Whitsunday Island', Lay & Collie.

At E: a sheet ex herb. Arnott (E00369179), annotated possibly by him (the writing is atypical) with the name and 'Whitsunday Isld., Beechey'.

At K: a sheet ex herb. Hooker bearing a ticket annotated by Arnott with the name and 'Whitsunday Isd. Beechey'; also attached is a ticket with drawings possibly by Arnott.

Note. The authors noted that they knew of no 'genus to which ... [this singular plant] is decidedly referable'; it is now placed in a genus referred either to its own family or to Orobanchaceae.
≡ **Nesogenes euphrasioides** (Hook. & Arn.) A. DC.

Myosotis fulva Hook. & Arn., Bot. Beechey Voy. 1: 38. 1830. (BORAGINACEAE).
Original material: 'Conception', Chili, Lay & Collie; 'Near Valparaiso. *Mr. Bridges*'.

No certain original material found at E. There is no Beechey material, and a sheet with this name in Arnott's writing bears two collections neither of which have the details of the original material: one from Valparaiso is a Cuming collection (*Cuming* 707); the other though collected by Bridges (*Bridges* 309), has a different locality 'Questa de Chili Languen near Quillota'.

At K there is similarly no certainly original material – none from Beechey, and on a sheet ex herb. Hooker are duplicates of both the collections on the Arnott sheet: the left-hand one (K000573645) is *Cuming* 707; the others (K000573644) appear to be associated with the label for *Bridges* 309 with the same locality as on the Arnott sheet, labelled by Hooker as 'Eritrichium' to which has been added in a later hand, in pencil, 'fulvum Alph. DC., M. fulva'.

≡ ***Plagiobothrys fulvus*** (Hook. & Arn.) I.M. Johnston

Myosotis muricata Hook. & Arn., Bot. Beechey Voy. 8: 369. 1839. (BORAGINACEAE).
Original material: California, Douglas.

At E: a sheet ex herb. Arnott (E00369169), annotated by him with the name and 'California, [per] Hooker', and later (also by Arnott) 'Eritrichium muriculatum Alph. DC.' is probably original material.

At K, two sheets. One ex herb. Hooker bearing three collections, the sheet is annotated by Hooker 'Eritrichium', to which has been added in a later hand in pencil 'muricatum Alph. DC.' – the two right-hand specimens, annotated by Hooker 'California, Douglas', associated with a ticket with a drawing of a nutlet annotated with the name by Hooker are original material (the other collections, *Coulter* 523, *Gordon* s.n., are not). The second sheet is ex herb. Bentham and has a printed 'California, Douglas 1833' label and despite not being annotated with the name is almost certainly original material.

≡ ***Cryptantha muricata*** (Hook. & Arn.) Nelson & J.F. Macbr.

Myrsine ardisioides Hook. & Arn., Bot. Beechey Voy. 5: 197. 1836, *nom. illeg.*, non Kunth 1818. (Generic placement queried). (SABIACEAE).
Type: 'one specimen, destitute of both *corolla* and *stamens* [among the Beechey, China collection]'.
Not found at E or K.
Note. T.P.M. van de Water (Blumea 26: 44. 1980) did not treat this name, but L. Chen, when she described the no longer recognised *Sabia limoniacea* var. *ardisioides* (Sargentia 3: 59. 1943) stated that 'The varietal name *ardisioides* has been selected independently of Hooker & Arnott's use of it, but with the definite conviction that [the two taxa are the same]', (she did not cite a Beechey collection in her extensive list of specimens seen).

= ***Sabia limoniacea*** Wall. ex Hook. f. & Thomson

Navarretia atractyloides (Benth.) Hook. & Arn., Bot. Beechey Voy. 8: 368. 1839. (POLEMONIACEAE). [California].
Basionym cited: 'Ægochloa atractyloides. *Benth. l.c.*' [i.e., *Bot. Reg. sub folio* 1622. 1833].

Navarretia cotulifolia (Benth.) Hook. & Arn., Bot. Beechey Voy. 8: 368. 1839 (as '*cotulaefolia*'). (POLEMONIACEAE). [California].
Basionym cited: 'Ægochloa cotulaefolia. *Benth. l.c.*' [i.e., *Bot. Reg. sub folio* 1622. 1833].

Navarretia pubescens (Benth.) Hook. & Arn., Bot. Beechey Voy. 8: 368. 1839. (POLEMONIACEAE). [California].
Basionym cited: 'Ægochloa pubescens. *Benth. l.c.*' [i.e., *Bot. Reg. sub folio* 1622. 1833].

Navarretia squarrosa (Eschsch.) Hook. & Arn., Bot. Beechey Voy. 8: 368. 1839. (POLEMONIACEAE). [California].
Basionym cited: 'Hoitzia squarrosa. *Eschscholtz* (1826) [Mem. Acad. Imp. St. Petersb. 10: 282]'.

Nemophila menziesii Hook. & Arn., Bot. Beechey Voy. 4: 152. 1833. (BORAGINACEAE).
Original material: San Francisco (or Monterey Bay), California, Lay & Collie; specimens in Menzies's herbarium and those of this friends 'to whom he liberally communicated specimens', which clearly included Hooker (see below).
   None found at E.
   At K: a sheet ex herb. Hooker, annotated with the name by Hooker bears four collections, the specimen in the bottom left-hand corner annotated by Hooker 'California, Beechey' is certainly original material, but probably not the smaller five specimens to its right. Five specimens on the same sheet annotated 'California, Menzies' are those referred to in the protologue and were annotated 'type' by L. Constance in 1938, but it is not known if this typification has been published.
Note. Later, in the California Supplement (p. 372. 1839), Hooker & Arnott described but did not name two varieties α and β; a sheet at E bears specimens of both of these, annotated by Arnott 'Nemophila Menziesii α H & A. Snake Country, N.W.C[alifornia]. Tolmie per Hooker' and 'Nemophila Menziesii β H & A, N – insignis Dougl. California, D[avid] D[ouglas] per Hooker' (though of interest they have no type status).

Neurocarpum multiflorum Hook. & Arn., Bot. Beechey Voy. 6: 286. 1838. (LEGUMINOSAE).
Original material: Tepic, Mexico, Lay & Collie.
   At E: a sheet (E00296697) annotated by Arnott with the name and 'Mexico, Beechey'. This is one of the sheets distributed from GL to E in 1902, bearing a printed 'Herb. Walker Arnott' label – it was annotated '?type' by J. Sauer in 1970, but he had not seen this specimen when he published his monograph of the genus (Brittonia 16: 133. 1964).

Alphabetical list of new taxa 139

None found at K.
= ***Canavalia villosa*** Benth.

Nuttallia Torr. & A. Gray ex Hook. & Arn., Bot. Beechey Voy. 7: 336. 1838, *nom. illeg.*, non Raf., 1817. (ROSACEAE).
The earliest of several different uses of this generic name was by Rafinesque. Hooker & Arnott proposed the name as a subsitute for its use by 'De Candolle or Dick', on the grounds that the several species placed in genera of the same name by those authors had since been referred to (three) other genera. (The 'Dick' usage is obscure, but presumably refers to a MS name taken up in W.P.C. Barton's Fl. N. America 2: 74. 1822).
= ***Oemleria*** Rchb.

Nuttallia cerasiformis Torr. & A. Gray ex Hook. & Arn., Bot. Beechey Voy. 8: 337, t. 82. 1839. (ROSACEAE).
Original material: 'specimens gathered on the Columbia by Mr Douglas and Dr Scouler in 1825'; later specimens from the same country by Dr Gairdner and Mr Tolmie. California, Douglas. Columbia River, Nuttall.

None at E, despite the large number of collections on which this species was based.

Two sheets at K ex herb. Hooker. One has three collections, all of which are original material: two are annotated by Hooker 'California, Douglas', the third has a ticket in Nuttall's hand 'Nuttallia cerasiformis Torr., Oregon woods' beside which Hooker has written 'Nuttall'. The second sheet has two collections, both original material: one is annotated by Hooker 'Columbia R[iver], Scouler', the other is *Gairdner* 48, bearing a ticket in Gairdner's hand and annotated by Hooker 'Dr Gairdner'.
Note. Although Hooker & Arnott's generic name is illegitimate, the species is not.
≡ ***Oemleria cerasiformis*** (Hook. & Arn.) J.W. Landon

Oenothera alyssoides Hook. & Arn., Bot. Beechey Voy. 8: 340. 1839. (ONAGRACEAE).
Type: 'Pine Creek, Snake Country [Wyoming]. [John McLeod per] *Mr Tolmie*'.

A sheet at E, ex herb. Arnott, annotated by him 'Oenothera (Holostigma) alyssoides H & A. California, D[avid] D[ouglas]' is not a type.

A sheet at K, ex herb. Hooker, annotated by him with the name bears nine specimens and collecting details for two different collections – one of which 'Pine Creek, Snake Country, Tolmie' is clearly that of the type, though it is not clear with which specimens this belongs. The more precise details 'Tolmie 41, Snake Country' refer to the same 'Tolmie' collection (from the list in McKelvey 1955: 633, *Tolmie* 41 was, indeed, collected at Pine Creek). The other collection on the sheet is 'California, (Douglas)', doubtless the same as the E specimen. On the sheet the Douglas annotation runs into the 'Pine Creek'

Tolmie one, which caused P.H. Raven to misread it as referring to a single Douglas collection when cited by him as type in Contrib. U.S. Nat. Herb. (37: 363. 1969) ('isotype' at GH). This lectotypification requires to be clarified.
≡ *Camissonia boothii* (Douglas) P.H. Raven subsp. *alyssoides* (Hook. & Arn.) P.H. Raven

Oenothera graciliflora Hook. & Arn., Bot. Beechey Voy. 8: 341. 1839. (ONAGRACEAE).
Original material: California, Douglas.
Isolectotypes at E, two sheets: one ex herb. Arnott (E00369078), annotated by him 'Oenothera (Hol[ostigma]) graciliflora H & A. California, D[avid] D[ouglas]'; the other sheet ex herb. R.K. Greville (E00369079), annotated by him 'California. Douglas. H[orticultural] S[ociety of] L[ondon]'.
Lectotype at K. The upper six specimens on a sheet bearing three collections ex herb. Hooker, annotated by Hooker with the name, reference 'Ic. Pl.', and 'California, Douglas' are original material (the lower collections, *Coulter* 173, *Hartweg* 1732, are not); though not annotated by P.H. Raven, this is doubtless the material cited as type in Contrib. U.S. Nat. Herb. (37: 251. 1969) (with 'iso[lecto]types' at BM, GH, NY). The second sheet at K (and therefore also an 'iso[lecto]type') is a duplicate ex herb. Bentham with a printed 'California, Douglas 1833' label annotated with the name by Bentham, and below it with the reference 'Hook. Ic. t. 338'.
≡ *Camissonia graciliflora* (Hook. & Arn.) P.H. Raven

Oenothera heterophylla Nutt. ex Hook. & Arn., Bot. Beechey Voy. 8: 341. 1839, *nom. illeg.*, non Spach, 1835. (ONAGRACEAE).
Original material: California, [Nuttall].
None at E.
Isolectotype at K, the lowest specimen (horizontally mounted) on a sheet ex herb. Hooker, with a ticket annotated by Nuttall with the name and 'N. Calif.' beside which Hooker has written 'Nuttall'. The sheet bears five specimens of four collections, but it is not clear to which of the upper four specimens the three other field tickets refer – though the 'Coulter 158, California' might belong with the two outer specimens; the others are in Nuttall's hand – 'Oenothera bistorta St Diego, N. Calif.', and 'Oenothera asperifolia, N. California' and may well be the types of those species and have been related to the two cental specimens in an illegible French hand. P.H. Raven has not annotated this sheet, and in Contrib. U.S. Nat. Herb. (37: 267. 1969) he lectotypified the name *O. heterophylla* on a Nuttall specimen at BM ('Type: San Diego, San Diego Co., California, April – May 1836, *T. Nuttall* (BM)').
= *Camissonia bistorta* (Nutt. ex Torr. & A. Gray) P.H. Raven

Oenothera marginata Nutt. ex Hook. & Arn., Bot. Beechey Voy. 8: 342. 1839. (ONAGRACEAE).
Original material: 'Near the Blue Mountains, and about the Salmon Falls of the Snake River, Snake Country [Oregon & Idaho]. [John McLeod per] *Mr Tolmie*'.

Isolectotype at E: a sheet ex herb. Arnott (E00288170), annotated by him 'Oenothera (Euoenothera) marginata Nutt., California mountains, Tolmie' – annotated 'isolectotype' by W.L. Wagner in 1980.

Lectotype at K: a sheet ex herb. Hooker bearing four specimens of two collections – the top right-hand one is a Nuttall specimen, with a ticket in Nuttall's hand 'Oenothera marginata R[ocky] Mts' – although Hooker & Arnott took the epithet from this, as correctly annotated by W.L. Wagner, it is not a type. The other specimens are annotated by Hooker 'Snake Country Tolmie 45.6' and are annotated by Wagner 'lectotype', though when he published this (Mon. Syst. Bot. 12: 75. 1985) he added the extra locality detail 'Salmon Falls of Snake River' (this is not on the sheet, but is that given for *McLeod* 45 in McKelvey 1955: 633). (A second sheet in the type cover at K, ex herb. Hooker and annotated by him 'Oenothera caespitosa', bears a duplicate of the Nuttall collection of *O. marginata*, and a Tolmie specimen of *O. caespitosa* subsp. *caespitosa*, but neither of these is a type of *O. marginata*).

≡ **Oenothera caespitosa** Nutt. subsp. ***marginata*** (Nutt. ex Hook. & Arn.) Munz.

Orthocarpus tolmiei Hook. & Arn., Bot. Beechey Voy. 8: 379. 1839. (OROBANCHACEAE).
Type: 'Between Henry's and Smith's Rivers, Snake Country [Wyoming]. [John McLeod per] *Mr Tolmie*'.

Type at E, a sheet ex herb. Arnott (E00272544), annotated by him with the name and 'Snake Country, N.W. C[alifornia], Tolmie per Hooker' – it was annotated 'isotype' by M. Egger in 2005/8.

Two type sheets at K. The first is a remounted partial sheet ex herb. Hooker (K000097455) bearing four specimens – these are annotated by Hooker 'Snake Country, California, Tolmie', but the name was been removed with the lower part of the original sheet. This was annotated as 'type' by A. Eastwood in 1911, and as 'holotype' by T.I. Chuang & L.R. Heckard in 1982 and J.M. Egger in 2005/6, but it is not known if any of these typifications has been published. The second sheet is ex herb. Bentham, and bears two collections of which the right-hand one, with a ticket annotated with the name and 'Snake Country, California' in an unknown hand, is a type – this was also (!) annotated 'holotype' by L. Heckard (in 1982).

Osmorhiza chilense Hook. & Arn., Bot. Beechey Voy. 1: 26. 1830. (UMBELLIFERAE).
Original material: 'Conception', Chili, Lay & Collie.

None found at E or K. The two sheets at E annotated with the name by Arnott are later collections (*Cuming* 335, *Bridges* 768). At K is a duplicate of *Cuming* 335, which was cited by Constance & Shan (Univ. Calif. Publ. Bot. 23: 140. 1948) as 'cotype', but it has no type status unless chosen as a neotype.

Oxalis glomerata Hook. & Arn., Bot. Beechey Voy. 1: 13. 1830. (Generic placement queried). (OXALIDACEAE).
Original material: 'Coquimbo', Chili, Lay & Collie.
   At E: a sheet ex herb. Arnott (E00369024), annotated by him 'Oxalis tortuosa Lindl., O. glomerata H & A. Coquimbo – Beechey'.
   At K: a sheet ex herb. Hooker annotated by him with the name *O. tortuosa* Lindl. bears three collections – the top right-hand one is annotated by Hooker 'Beechey, Chili' and may be original material of *O. glomerata* (though not annotated with the name, by the time it was mounted it might have been realised to be synonymous with Lindley's species).
= **Oxalis tortuosa** Lindl.

Oxalis laxa Hook. & Arn., Bot. Beechey Voy. 1: 13. 1830. (OXALIDACEAE).
Original material: 'Conception', Chili, Lay & Collie.
   At E: the bottom left-hand specimen (E00369021) on a sheet ex herb. Arnott annotated by him with the name and 'Conception – Beechey' (also mounted on the sheet are specimens of *Cuming* 421 (E00369022) and *Mathews* 275 (E00369023), which are not original material).
   At K: the top right-hand specimen (K000531669) on a sheet ex herb. Hooker annotated by him 'Oxalis laxa α Hook. & Arn', this collection is annotated by Hooker 'Conception, Beechey' (the three other collections on the sheet, Philippi, Germain, Cuming, are not original material).

Panax ovatum Hook. & Arn., Bot. Beechey Voy. 2: 84. 1832. (Generic placement queried). (ARALIACEAE).
Type: 'neither flower nor fruit on the only specimen in the Collection, which was found in Oneeheow', Sandwich Islands, Lay & Collie.
   Type at E: a sheet ex herb. Arnott (E00369087), bearing a single leaf annotated by Arnott with the name and 'Oneeheow, Beechey (folia)', which must be part of the holotype.
   Type at K: a sheet ex herb. Hooker bearing a single, sterile specimen, annotated by Hooker with the name and 'Oneeheouw, Beechey' – it has been annotated (anonymously) 'holotype'.
Note. A.A. Heller (Minnesota Bot. Stud 1: 870. 1897) noted that 'Panax? ovatum of Hooker & Arnott may be distinct' from *Cheirodendron trigynum*, the species to which it has usually been referred.
= **Cheirodendron trigynum** (Gaud.) A. Heller

Alphabetical list of new taxa 143

Panax platyphyllum Hook. & Arn., Bot. Beechey Voy. 2: 84. 1832. (Generic placement queried). (ARALIACEAE).
Original material: 'Oahu', Sandwich Islands, Lay & Collie.
   At E: a sheet ex herb. Arnott (E00369086), bearing two specimens (one fertile, one sterile), annotated by Arnott with the name and 'Oahu, Beechey'.
   At K, two sheets both annotated by Hooker with the name and 'Oahu, Beechey'.
≡ ***Cheirodendron platyphyllum*** (Hook. & Arn.) Seem.

Panicum affine Hook. & Arn., Bot. Beechey Voy. 3: 100. 1832, *nom. illeg.*, non Poir., 1816. (GRAMINEAE).
Original material: Sandwich Islands, Lay & Collie.
   At E: a sheet ex herb. Arnott (E00369239) annotated by him in ink with the name and 'Oahu, Beechey', and in pencil, probably also by him, 'Isachne sandwicensis Arn. mst.' This is doubtless also a type of *P. colliei* Endl.
   At K: a sheet ex herb. Hooker bearing two collections and six specimens – it is not entirely clear to which of these the collecting details refer, though the right-hand specimen is certainly annotated by Hooker 'Beechey', and to this a ticket annotated by Arnott with the name and 'Oahu, B[eechey]' also belong (the second collection, *Douglas* 26, is not original material).
= ***Panicum pellitum*** Trin.

Panicum beecheyi Hook. & Arn., Bot. Beechey Voy. 3: 100. 1832. (GRAMINEAE).
Original material: Sandwich Islands, Lay & Collie.
   At E: a sheet ex herb. Arnott (E00369240), annotated by him with the name and 'Oneeheow, Beechey'.
   At K: a sheet ex herb. Hooker annotated by him on the sheet with the name and 'Oneeheow, Beechey'.

Panicum gossypinum Hook. & Arn., Bot. Beechey Voy. 3: 100. 1832. (GRAMINEAE).
Original material: Sandwich Islands, Lay & Collie.
   At E: a sheet ex herb. Arnott (E00369241), annotated by him with the name and 'Oahu, Beechey'.
   At K: a sheet ex herb. Hooker annotated by him on the sheet 'Beechey', and bearing a ticket annotated by Arnott with the name and 'Oahu, B[eechey]'.
Note. This has sometimes been taken as synonymous with *P. torridum* Gaud.
= ***Panicum pellitum*** Trin.

Panicum tenuifolium Hook. & Arn., Bot. Beechey Voy. 3: 101. 1832. (GRAMINEAE).
Original material: Sandwich Islands, Lay & Collie.

At E: a sheet ex herb. Arnott (E00369242), annotated by him with the name and 'Oahu, Beechey'.

At K: a sheet ex herb. Hooker annotated by him on the sheet 'Beechey', and bearing a ticket annotated by Arnott with the name and 'Oahu, B[eechey]'.

Paratropia cantoniensis Hook. & Arn., Bot. Beechey Voy. 4: 189. 1833. (ARALIACEAE).
Original material: [China] a single leaf from the Beechey collection; 'specimens … from Mr. Millett'.

At E: a sheet ex herb. Arnott, annotated by him 'Paratropia cantoniensis H & A, Aralia octophylla Lour. – var. Canton, [per] Dr Hooker', identified as *Schefflera heptaphylla* by D. Frodin in 1998.
Note. Hooker & Arnott cited 'Aralia octophylla var. Cantoniensis. *Lour. Cochin. v.* 1. *p.* 233', implying that they were making a new rank for a variety described by Loureiro. However, neither in this reference (Willdenow's edition of 1793), nor in the first edition, was any such formal variety described.
= ***Schefflera heptaphylla*** (L.) Frodin

Parsonsia helicandra Hook. & Arn., Bot. Beechey Voy. 5: 197. 1836. (Generic placement queried). (APOCYNACEAE).
Original material: Chiefly … about Macao, China, Lay & Collie.

None found at E or K.
Note. The name 'Apocynum reticulatum. Lour. Cochin. v. 1. p. 208?' was cited, but as the synonymy is queried, this does not make Hooker & Arnott's name superfluous. They also queried the generic placement, but the proposed name in a new genus "Helicandra" is merely provisional and not validly published: 'we think there are sufficient characters … in which case it may be named *Helicandra Sinensis*' (this name is not in the index, confirming that it was not fullly accepted by the authors).

No specimen was seen by D.J. Middleton when he revised the genus, but he accepted the synonymy as
= ***Parsonsia alboflavescens*** (Dennst.) Mabberley

"*Passiflora pannosa* Hook. & Arn.", Bot. Beechey Voy. 7: 293. 1840. (PASSIFLORACEAE).
In the protologue 'P. pannosa. Smith?' was cited as a synonym, but in the index the name was not attributed to Hooker & Arnott, suggesting that they did not intend to describe a new species based on Beechey material, and were merely querying the identification of their material.

Pavonia racemifera Hook. & Arn., Bot. Beechey Voy. 6: 277. 1838. (MALVACEAE).
Original material: Tepic, Mexico, Lay & Collie.

Alphabetical list of new taxa

Isolectotype at E: a sheet ex herb. Arnott (E00162411), annotated by him 'Pavonia (Cancellaria) racemifer H & A. Mexico, Beechey, cupr. "Malvaceae No. 1309 Ch. Schl. in Linnaea VI. p. 423 et Linn. XI. p. 370' – this was annotated 'isotype' by P.A. Fryxell in 1994.

Lectotype at K: a sheet (K000535310) ex herb. Hooker annotated by him 'Pavonia racemiflora [sic] H. & A.', and 'Mexico, Beechey' – though not annotated by P.A. Fryxell, this specimen was lectotypified (cited as 'holotype') by him in Syst. Bot. Monogr. 25: 333. 1988.

Note. This genus is sometimes sunk under *Hibiscus*.

= ***Pavonia pleurantha*** (DC.) Fryxell

Pectis diffusa Hook. & Arn., Bot. Beechey Voy. 7: 296. 1838. (COMPOSITAE). Original material: 'Talisco', Mexico, Lay & Collie.

None found at E.

At K: a sheet ex herb. Hooker has been cut up, one element removed and two parts remounted on separate sheets – these are both original material and were annotated 'isotype' by D.J. Keil in 1985: the former upper part of the sheet (K000504033) was annotated by Hooker with the name and 'Talisco, Beechey'; the former lower part (K000504034) was annotated by Hooker 'Talisco, Beechey'.

Pectis taliscana Hook. & Arn., Bot. Beechey Voy. 7: 296. 1838. (COMPOSITAE). Original material: 'Talisco', Mexico, Lay & Collie.

None found at E.

At K: the lower specimen (K000504012) on a sheet ex herb. Hooker, annotated by him with the name and 'Talisco, Beechey' – it was annotated 'holotype' by D.J. Keil in 1973 (the upper specimen, *Bates* s.n., is not original material).

= ***Pectis uniaristata*** DC.

Penstemon laricifolius Hook. & Arn., Bot. Beechey Voy. 8: 376. 1839 (as '*Pentstemon*'). (PLANTAGINACEAE).

Type: 'Snake Fort, Snake Country [Oregon/Idaho border]. [John McLeod per] *Mr Tolmie*'.

Type at E, a sheet ex herb. Arnott (E00369181), annotated by him with the name and 'Snake Country, N.W. C[alifornia]. Tolmie per Hooker'.

Type at K, a sheet ex herb. Hooker bearing three collections: the types are probably the central and top left specimens that appear to be associated with Hooker's annotation of the name and the details 'Snake Country. California, Tolmie' (the other collections, *Nuttall* s.n., *Geyer* 239, are not types).

Peperomia leptostachya Hook. & Arn., Bot. Beechey Voy. 2: 96. 1832. (PIPERACEAE).

Original material: Sandwich Islands, Lay & Collie.

None found at E.

Lectotype at K: a sheet ex herb. Hooker annotated by him 'Beechey', bearing a ticket annotated by Arnott with the name and 'Oahu, B[eechey]' – this was cited as 'Type' by T.G. Yuncker in Bull. Bishop Mus. (112: 57. 1933) and has since been determined by J. Florence (1996) as
= ***Peperomia blanda*** Kunth var. ***floribunda*** (Miq.) Hüber

Peperomia membranacea Hook. & Arn., Bot. Beechey Voy. 2: 96. 1832. (Generic placement queried). (PIPERACEAE).
Original material: Sandwich Islands, Lay & Collie.

None found at E.

Lectotype at K: a sheet ex herb. Hooker bearing a ticket annotated by Arnott with the name, and 'Oahu, Beechey' – this was cited as 'Type' by T.G. Yuncker in Bull. Bishop Mus. 112: 39. 1933.

"*Peperomia pallida* (Spreng.) Hook. & Arn.", Bot. Beechey Voy. 2: 96. 1832. (PIPERACEAE).
Hooker & Arnott believed they were making a new combination here based on 'Piper pallidum … *Spreng. Syst. Veg. v.* 1. *p.* 116', but this had already been made by A. Dietrich, so their name is an isonym.

Peperomia rhomboidea Hook. & Arn., Bot. Beechey Voy. 2: 70. 1832. (PIPERACEAE).
Original material: 'Society Islands', Lay & Collie.

None found at E.

At K: a remounted partial sheet ex herb. Hooker, bearing a ticket annotated by Arnott with the name and 'Coral isld.' – a recent hand has added 'Coral Isld. = Henderson I. (Pitcairn)', and the sheet was annotated 'type' by T. Düll in 1965.

Peperomia tetraphylla Hook. & Arn., Bot. Beechey Voy. 3: 97. 1832. (PIPERACEAE).
Original material: Sandwich Islands, Lay & Collie.

None found at E.

At K: a sheet ex herb. Hooker bearing six specimens, representing four different collections – the central two, associated with a ticket annotated by Arnott 'Peperomia heterophylla. Oahu, Beechey' – epithet crossed out and replaced in a later hand with 'tetraphylla', are original material, and were annotated 'holotype' by P.S. Green in 1989, (the other collections, Sellow from Brazil, Mrs Cunningham, 'Oahu, Barclay', are not original material).
Note. Although Hooker & Arnott cited 'Piper tetraphyllum. "*Forst. Prodr. n.* 25."? – P. reflexum. *Vahl. – Spreng. Syst. Veget. v.* 1. *p.* 121?'. As both names were queried, and they commented 'We are very doubtful of the synonyms', this should be treated as a new Hooker & Arnott name and neither a new

Alphabetical list of new taxa

combination (as, for example in Nicolson & Fosberg, Forst. Bot. Sec. Cook Exped. 556. 2004), nor superfluous.
= ***Peperomia reflexa*** (L.) A. Dietr.

[*Perotis longiflora* Nees, in Hook. & Arn., Bot. Beechey Voy. 6: 247. 1838. (GRAMINEAE).
Original material: 'Ad Macao et in vicinis insulis; *Millett*; *G.H. Vachell, n. 38*'.

At E: two sheets, one ex herb Arnott. bearing two collections, annotated by Arnott 'Perotis longiflora NE! 1. Canton, [per] Dr Hooker. 2. Macao. Revd. Mr. Vachell, n. 38, per Prof Henslow', the Canton specimens doubtless the Millett collection. The other sheet ex herb. Edinburgh University with a Vachell printed label, with the date May 1829, but no collection number, is doubtless a duplicate of no. 38.

At K: a sheet ex herb. Hooker, bearing six specimens representing four collections: at top left is a printed Vachell label with the number '38', which an unknown hand has marked '2' corresponding to two of the specimens annotated as types of *P. longiflora* (the other collections are *Wallich* 3787F; *Fortune* s.n. and *Meyen* s.n., the last being the type of *P. patula* Nees).
= ***Perotis rara*** R. Br.]

Petesia carnosa Hook. & Arn., Bot. Beechey Voy. 2: 64. 1832. (RUBIACEAE).
Original material: 'Society Islands', Lay & Collie.
None found at E or K.
= ***Bikkia tetrandra*** (L. f.) A. Rich.

Petesia coriacea Hook. & Arn., Bot. Beechey Voy. 2: 85. 1832. (Generic placement queried). (RUBIACEAE).
Original material: 'only ... in a very imperfect state', Sandwich Islands, Lay & Collie.
None found at E.
At K: a sheet ex herb. Hooker with a ticket annotated by Arnott with the name and 'Oahu, B[eechey]'.
= ***Kadua affinis*** Cham. & Schltdl.

Petesia terminalis Hook. & Arn., Bot. Beechey Voy. 2: 85. 1832. (Generic placement queried). (RUBIACEAE).
Original material: Sandwich Islands, Lay & Collie.
None found at E.
At K: a sheet ex herb. Hooker annotated by him with the name and 'Oahu, Beechey'.
= ***Kadua affinis*** Cham. & Schltdl.

Phaca leucophylla (Torr.) Hook. & Arn., Bot. Beechey Voy. 7: 333. (Dec) 1838. (LEGUMINOSAE). [California].
Basionym cited: 'Astragalus leucophyllus. Torr. et Gr. Fl. 1. p. 336 [Oct 1838]'.
≡ **Astragalus leucophyllus** Torr.

Phaca macrodon Hook. & Arn., Bot. Beechey Voy. 7: 333. 1838. (LEGUMINOSAE).
Original material: California, Douglas.
   None found at E.
   At K, two sheets: one ex herb. Hooker annotated by him with the name and 'California, Douglas', bearing a ticket with a drawing probably by Hooker; the left-hand specimen on a sheet ex herb. Bentham, with a printed 'California, Douglas 1833' label, annotated on the sheet by Bentham with the name and reference to 'Torr. & Gr. Fl. [N. Am.] 1. 694 [1840]'.
≡ **Astragalus macrodon** (Hook. & Arn.) A. Gray

"*Phacelia brunoniana* Gillies", in Hooker & Arnott, Bot. Beechey Voy. 8: 374. 1839. (BORAGINACEAE).
In a note under 'P. ramosissima Dougl. [ex Lehm.]', Hooker & Arnott wrote 'We have an allied species, or perhaps a mere variety, from Dr. Gillies, under the name of P. Brunoniana, collected on El Cerro del Diamante and Andes of Mendoza ...', for which they noted its distinction from *P. ramosissima*. However, as they did not accept the species (and it is not included in the index), it is not validly published. Alphonse De Candolle (Prodr. 9: 299. 1845) later published it as *P. ramosissima* [var.] β *Brunoniana*, citing 'Hook. et Arn. bot. Beech. p. 374. An varietas? an species'.
   There are two sheets at E, ex herb. Arnott, annotated by him with the name: the type of Candolle's variety is the top right-hand specimen (E00369170) on one of these with a ticket in Gillies's hand 'Phacelia Brunonia n sp. Gillies, Cerro del diamante & Andes of Mendoza, J. Gillies' (the other collections, *Gillies* 171, 172, are not types). The second sheet has two further, non-type, Gillies specimens from other localities, and was later annotated by Arnott 'Ph. ramosissima Benth. β Brunoniana DC.'.
= **Phacelia cumingii** (Benth.) A. Gray

Phalaris californica Hook. & Arn., Bot. Beechey Voy. 4: 161. 1833. (GRAMINEAE).
Original material: San Francisco (or Monterey Bay), California, Lay & Collie.
   At E: a sheet ex herb. Arnott (E00369243), annotated by him with the name and 'California, Beechey'.
   At K: a sheet ex herb. Hooker annotated by him on the sheet 'Beechey', bearing a ticket with the name in what is possibly Arnott's hand – it has been annotated 'lectotypus' by R.M. Boldini, but it is not known if this typification has been published.

Alphabetical list of new taxa 149

Phania dissecta Hook. & Arn., Bot. Beechey Voy. 10: 433. 1841. (Generic placement queried). (COMPOSITAE).
Original material: 'Acapulco', Mexico, Sinclair.

At E: a sheet ex herb. Arnott (E00369111), annotated by him with the name and 'Acapulco' – the words 'Beech voy.' have been deleted and replaced with 'Dr Sinclair', Arnott later added the name 'Eupatorium dissectum Benth.' A second sheet (E00369112) has the same details, and although 'Beechey' has not been replaced with 'Dr Sinclair', this must surely also be original material, as the species was not listed among the Beechey Mexican collections.

At K two sheets, both annotated by Bentham with the name and 'Acapulco, Dr Sinclair' – one ex herb. Hooker (K000500316), the other (K000500315) ex herb. Bentham (given him by Hooker in 1843).
≡ ***Hofmeisteria dissecta*** (Hook. & Arn.) R.M. King & H. Rob.

Phania urenifolia Hook. & Arn., Bot. Beechey Voy. 7: 297. 1838. (Generic placement queried). (COMPOSITAE).
Original material: Tepic, Mexico, Lay & Collie.

At E: a sheet ex herb. Arnott (E00369113), annotated by him with the name and 'Mexico, Beechey'.

At K: a sheet ex herb. Hooker (K000500313), annotated by him with the name and 'Mexico, Beechey'.
≡ ***Hofmeisteria urenifolia*** (Hook. & Arn.) Walp.

Phaseolus micranthus Hook. & Arn., Bot. Beechey Voy. 6: 287. 1838. (LEGUMINOSAE).
Original material: 'Talisco', Mexico, Lay & Collie.
   None found at E or K.

Photinia serrulata DC. [var.] β *prunifolia* Hook. & Arn., Bot. Beechey Voy. 4: 185. 1833. (ROSACEAE).
Original material: Chiefly … about Macao, China, Lay & Collie.

Isolectotype at E, a sheet ex herb. Arnott (E00369054), annotated by him 'Photinia serrulata β prunifolia H & A. China, Beechey'.

At K the 'type' sheets of 'P. prunifolia Lindl.' ex herb. Hooker have been much cut up and remounted. One (which must previously have formed the top part of a sheet) has a specimen annotated by Hooker 'China, Beechey', but Hooker's annotation of the name must have been removed with the lower part of the sheet – this is original material of Hooker & Arnott's variety, and though it is not annotated by J.-E. Vidal, must be the lectotype, cited by him as 'type' in Adansonia (5: 223. 1965).
≡ ***Photinia prunifolia*** (Hook. & Arn.) Lindl.

Photinia serrulata DC. [var.] δ *obovata* Hook. & Arn., Bot. Beechey Voy. 4: 185. 1833. (ROSACEAE).
Original material: 'China ... from the late Dr. Livingstone'.

At E: a sheet ex herb. Arnott (E00369053), annotated by him 'Photinia serrulata δ obovata H & A. China, [per] Dr H[ooker?]' is probably original material.

None found at K: there is a specimen ex herb. Hooker labelled by him 'Macao, Dr Livingstone' but the specimen does not match the description (the leaves being neither obovate nor emarginate) so cannot be original material – it is possible that an error has occured when the sheet was cut up and remounted, and that this data (which does belong to the type) has become associated with the wrong specimen.

This variety was not treated by Vidal or in the recent Flora of China.

Phyllanthus cinerascens Hook. & Arn., Bot. Beechey Voy. 5: 211. 1836. (PHYLLANTHACEAE).
Type: 'the only specimen we have seen, sent by Mr. Millett [from China], is very imperfect'.

Not found at E.

Type at K: a sheet ex herb. Hooker with two specimens, the right-hand one is the type, annotated by Hooker with the name and 'China, Millett' – attached is a ticket with a rough drawing (possibly by Arnott) and there are some beautiful pencil drawings on the sheet itself possibly by Hooker (the left-hand specimen, *Hance* s.n., is not a type).
= **Phyllanthus cochinchinensis** Spreng.

Phyllanthus distichus Hook. & Arn., Bot. Beechey Voy. 2: 95. 1832. (PHYLLANTHACEAE).
Original material: Sandwich Islands, Lay & Collie.

At E: a sheet ex herb. Arnott (E00369211), annotated by him with the name and 'Oahu, Beechey'.

At K, two sheets: both ex herb. Hooker, but clearly representing two different collections. One, annotated on the sheet by Hooker with the name and 'Oahu – Beechey', has smaller leaves. The specimen on the other sheet has larger leaves, and bears a ticket annotated by Arnott with the name and 'Oahu, B[eechey]'.

Pilea peploides (Gaud.) Hook. & Arn., Bot. Beechey Voy. 2: 96. 1832. (URTICACAE). [Sandwich Islands].
Basionym cited: 'Dubreulia peploides. *Gaud. in Freyc. Voy. p.* 495 [1830]'.

Piper begoniifolium Hook. & Arn., Bot. Beechey Voy. 7: 310. 1838 (as '*begoniaefolium*'). (PIPERACEAE).
Original material: Tepic, Mexico, Lay & Collie.

Alphabetical list of new taxa 151

   None found at E or K.
Note. This has sometimes been treated (e.g., 'Tropicos') as a combination based on *Zippelia begoniaefolium* Blume (1830), but this is unwarranted: a connection between a SE Asian and a Mexican plant is unlikely, and there is no reason to think that the same epithet was used anything other than coincidentally.

Piper ellipticum Hook. & Arn., Bot. Beechey Voy. 10: 443. 1841, *nom. illeg.*, non Lam., non Roem. & Schult. (PIPERACEAE).
Original material: 'Realejo', Mexico [now Nicaragua], Sinclair.
   At E: a sheet ex herb. Arnott (E00369201), annotated by him with the name, reference, and 'Realejo. Dr Sinclair'. The sheet is also annotated by Arnott with the name 'Artanthe Beecheyana Miq. p. 403' – this was a replacement name for Hooker & Arnott's homonym, based on the same type. The specimen was determined as *P. arboreum* subsp. *tuberculatum* by M.C. Tebbs in 1987.
   None found at K.
= ***Piper arboreum*** Aublet subsp. ***tuberculatum*** (Jacq.) Tebbs

Piper patens Hook. & Arn., Bot. Beechey Voy. 7: 310. 1838, *nom. illeg.*, non Opiz, 1828. (PIPERACEAE).
Original material: Tepic, Mexico, Lay & Collie.
   None found at E or K.
= ***Piper nervosum*** C. DC.

Piper scabrifolium Hook. & Arn., Bot. Beechey Voy. 7: 310. 1838. (PIPERACEAE).
Original material: Tepic, Mexico, Lay & Collie.
   None found at E or K.
?= ***Piper microstachyum*** Vahl

Pittosporum glabrum Hook. & Arn., Bot. Beechey Voy. 3: 110. 1832. (PITTOSPORACEAE).
Original material: Sandwich Islands, Lay & Collie.
   At E: a sheet ex herb. Arnott (E00369011) with two specimens (one fertile, one sterile), annotated by him with the name and 'Oahu, Beechey'.
   At K: a sheet ex herb. Hooker, annotated by him with the name and 'Oahu, Beechey', to which is attached a pencil drawing possibly by Arnott – this was annotated 'holotype' by J.E. Haas in 1976, but it is not known if this typification has been published.

Pittosporum pauciflorum Hook. & Arn., Bot. Beechey Voy. 4: 168, t. 32. 1833. (PITTOSPORACEAE).
Original material: Chiefly ... about Macao, China, Lay & Collie.

At E: a sheet ex herb. Arnott (E00369010), annotated by him with the name and 'China, Beechey'.

At K: a sheet ex herb. Hooker, annotated by him with the name, reference and 'China, Beechey'.

Plantago mollis Hook. & Arn., Bot. Beechey Voy. 1: 43. 1830. (PLANTAGINACEAE).
Original material: 'Conception', Chili, Lay & Collie; 'We have also received this from Mr. Bridges, from the mountains about Valparaiso'.

None found at E or K. A later, Gillies, specimen at K is labelled with the name both by Hooker and by Bentham, which allows interpretation of the name (which is not listed in Zuloaga *et al.*, 3: 2750. 2008).
= **Plantago patagonica** Jacq.

Polygala aparinoides Hook. & Arn., Bot. Beechey Voy. 6: 277. 1838. (POLYGALACEAE).
Original material: Tepic, Mexico, Lay & Collie.

At E: a sheet ex herb. Arnott (E00369012) bearing two specimens, annotated by him with the name, reference, and 'Mexico, Beechey'.

Despite a discrepancy over the locality, the right-hand specimen (K000478526) on a sheet at K, ex herb. Hooker, is probably original material – it is annotated by Hooker with the name and 'Talisco, Mexico. Beechey' (the other collection on the sheet, *Parry & Palmer* 391/2, is not original material).

Pomaderris zizyphoides (Spreng.) Hook. & Arn., Bot. Beechey Voy. 2: 61. 1832 (as '*ziziphoides*'). (RHAMNACEAE). ['Society Islands'].
Basionym cited: 'Rhamnus ziziphoides. *Spr.* [first published Diss. Biehler 15 n. 29. 1807]'.
≡ **Alphitonia zizyphoides** (Spreng.) A. Gray

Pontederia ovata Hook. & Arn., Bot. Beechey Voy. 5: 218. 1836, *nom. illeg.*, non L., 1753. (PONTEDERIACEAE).
Original material: 'Canton; *Mr. Millett*'.

Lectotype at E: a sheet ex herb. Arnott (E00369230), annotated by him 'Monochoria ovata Kth., Pontederia ovata H & A in Bot. Beechey Voy. Canton, Beechey', and bearing a ticket with Arnott's MS description. It is mounted on a smoother, bluer paper than Arnott's original Beechey specimens; the annotation with Kunth's 1843 combination and the darker ink suggest that the annotation by Arnott is later, and that 'Beechey' is simply a mistake. Furthermore the Beechey specimens are usually labelled 'China', those labelled 'Canton' usually being Millett collections sent to Arnott by Hooker. The sheet was annotated by C.D.K. Cook in 1987 'probably holotype of *M. ovata* (Hook. & Arn.) Kunth', which he published (with no query) in Davis & Hedge Festschrift (p. 162. 1989).

Alphabetical list of new taxa 153

None found at K.
= ***Monochoria vaginalis*** (Burm. f.) Kunth

Potentilla villosa Pallas [var.] β *gracilis* Hook. & Arn., Bot. Beechey Voy. 3: 113. 1832. (ROSACEAE).
Original material: Avatschka Bay, Kamtschatka, Lay & Collie.

At E: the lower collection (E00369055) on a sheet ex herb. Arnott, with a ticket annotated by him 'Potentilla villosa var. Kamtschatka, Beechey' – although it does not have the varietal epithet, this was the only form found in Kamchatka (the other collections, from North America (Unalashka, Dr. Fischer (E00369057), and Kotzebue's Sound [probably Beechey] (E00369056) are not original material).

At K: a specimen on a sheet ex herb. Hooker with a ticket annotated 'Potentilla villosa var. Avatscha Bay, Kamtshatka, Beechey' by ?Arnott – this is in a North American cover, as the other two collections on the sheet are from North America (one a Beechey collection from Kotzebue Sound).
= ***Potentilla*** sp.

Pothos loureiroi Hook. & Arn., Bot. Beechey Voy. 5: 220. 1836 (as '*Loureiri*'), *nom. illeg.* (ARACEAE).
The name 'Flagellaria repens. Lour. *Fl. Coch.* 1. *p.* 263' is cited, which renders Hooker & Arnott's superfluous and illegitimate. (Hooker & Arnott usually used a new epithet when transferring a species to a new genus).
Cited material: [none specified, but from the footnote on p. 201 not a Beechey specimen, and most likely a Millett or Vachell one].

At E: a sheet ex herb. Arnott (E00018677) is probably one of the specimens on which Hooker & Arnott's description was based, it is annotated by Arnott 'Pothos scandens, Flagellaria repens Lour. certe. Canton – China [per] Dr Hooker'. This is probably a Millett specimen sent by Hooker to Arnott; the smoother paper and darker writing than those on Arnott's Beechey sheets suggest a later date, by which time Arnott referred the material to *P. scandens*, and probably simply did not bother add their (superfluous) name to it.

At K: two sheets ex herb. Hooker annotated by him 'China, Mr. Millett', with the name added in pencil in a later hand.
≡ ***Pothos repens*** (Lour.) Druce

Pottsia Hook. & Arn., Bot. Beechey Voy. 5: 198. 1836. (APOCYNACEAE).

Pottsia cantonensis Hook. & Arn., Bot. Beechey Voy. 5: 199, t. 43. 1836. (APOCYNACEAE).
Original material: 'Canton; *Mr. Millett* [s.n.]'.

A sheet at E, ex herb. Arnott (E00369161), annotated by him with the name and 'Canton, [per] Dr Hooker', is almost certainly an isolectotype (see below).

Lectotype at K: a sheet ex herb. Hooker, annotated by him with the name and 'China, Millett', to which is attached a ticket with drawings; this was

annotated by D.J. Middleton in 2004 as 'holotype', and published as such by him in Fl. Malesiana (18: 345. 2007).
≡ ***Pottsia laxiflora*** (Blume) Kuntze

Prinos asprellus Hook. & Arn., Bot. Beechey Voy. 4: 176, t. 36. 1833. (AQUIFOLIACEAE).
Original material: Chiefly … about Macao, China, Lay & Collie.

At E, two sheets, both ex herb. Arnott: one (E00369028) has a male specimen, annotated by Arnott 'Prinos asprellus H & A, ♂. China, Beechey' (and also a specimen (E00369030) labelled 'Canton, [per] Dr Hooker' – probably a Vachell or Millett collection); the second sheet (E00369031) bears a female specimen annotated by Arnott 'Prinos asprellus ♀, H & A. China, Beechey'.

At K: a sheet ex herb. Hooker annotated by him with the name, reference and 'China, Beechey'.
≡ ***Ilex asprella*** (Hook. & Arn.) Champion ex Benth.

Prinos integra Hook. & Arn., Bot. Beechey Voy. 6: 261. 1838. (AQUIFOLIACEAE).
Original material: 'Bonin', Lay & Collie.

None found at E.

At K: the upper specimen on a sheet ex herb. Hooker annotated by him 'Bonin, Beechey'; it bears a ticket annotated by Arnott with the names 'Prinos integra H & A, Ilex asiatica L?, [I.] integra Thunb.', a description, and the locality 'Bonin' – it was determined by L.E.T. Loesener as *I. integra* 'var. c. *Beecheyi* Loes., var. nov.' (Nov. Act. Acad. Caes. Leop. 78: 273. 1901), and is original material of the variety.
Note. Two synonyms were cited by Hooker & Arnott, but both with queries: 'Ilex integra Thunb. Fl. Jap. p. 77? – I. asiatica. Linn. Sp. p. 710?'; furthermore, Hooker & Arnott, gave two characters in which their plant differed from Thunberg's, so this should be regarded as a new species based on the Beechey material, rather than a new combination of Thunberg's name, or a superfluous renaming of Linnaeus's.
≡ ***Ilex integra*** Thunb. var. ***beecheyi*** Loes.

Procris glabra Hook. & Arn., Bot. Beechey Voy. 2: 96. 1832. (URTICACEAE).
Original material: Sandwich Islands, Lay & Collie.

At E: a sheet ex herb. Arnott (E00369217), annotated by him with the name and 'Oahu, Beechey'.

At K: a sheet ex herb. Hooker bearing a ticket annotated by Arnott with the name and 'Oahu, Beechey'.
≡ ***Urera glabra*** (Hook. & Arn.) Wedd.

Procris sessilis (J.R. & G. Forst.) Hook. & Arn., Bot. Beechey Voy. 2: 70. 1832. (URTICACEAE). ['Society Islands'].
Basionym cited: 'Elatostema sessile. *Forst. Gen. p.* 106 [1775]'.
≡ ***Elatostema sessile*** J.R. & G. Forst.

Proustia ilicifolia Hook. & Arn., Bot. Beechey Voy. 1: 28. 1830. (COMPOSITAE).
Original material: 'Coquimbo', Chili, Lay & Collie.

No certainly original material found at E or K, and H.A. Fabris in his revision (Revista Mus. La Plata 11: 34. 1968) cited no type for this name. At K is a sheet ex herb. Hooker annotated by him 'Coquimbo, Proustia', but, with no epithet or collector, it is not safe to take it as original material as there is also a (later) Macrae collection from Coquimbo.

Psoralea strobilina Hook. & Arn., Bot. Beechey Voy. 7: 332, t. 80. 1838. (LEGUMINOSAE).
Original material: California, Douglas.

None found at E.

At K are two sheets of Douglas Californian original material: one ex herb. Hooker, annotated by him 'California, Douglas', to which is attached a ticket with drawings annotated with the name in Hooker's hand; a sheet ex herb. Bentham, with a printed 'California, Douglas 1833' label annotated by Bentham with the name and reference 'Torr. & Gr. Fl. [N. Am.] 1: 689 [1840]'. Both sheets were annotated 'isotype' by James Grimes in 1987 – it is not known if this typification has been published, and the name could also be typified on the material on which Lindley's name was based (see below).

Note. Coined here as the name of a new species incorporating the un-named and doubtful variety 'P. macrostachya, β ? *Torr. et Gray, Fl.* 1 *p.* 304' (the question mark here being not an indication of doubt on the part of Hooker & Arnott, but a quote from Torrey & Gray). Hooker & Arnott also included 'P. macrostachya [sensu] Lindl. Bot. Reg.', i.e., non DC. – the Candollean taxon being treated separately by Hooker & Arnott.

≡ **Hoita strobilina** (Hook. & Arn.) Rydb.

Psychotria scandens Hook. & Arn., Bot. Beechey Voy. 5: 193. 1836. (RUBIACEAE).
Original material: Chiefly … about Macao, China, Lay & Collie.

At E: a sheet ex herb. Arnott bears two specimens: the right-hand one (E00369104) labelled by Arnott 'China – Beechey' is original material; the left-hand one (E00369105) annotated by Arnott 'Psychotria scandens H & A, "P– serpens Hook. herb". Canton – [per] Dr Hooker', is probably a Millett specimen and not original material.

At K: the uppermost specimen on a sheet ex herb. Hooker annotated with the name and bearing three collections – the specimen is annotated 'China, Beechey' (the others, *Vachell* s.n., *Wykeham Perry* s.n., are not original material).

= **Psychotria serpens** L.

Pterochilus Hook. & Arn., Bot. Beechey Voy. 2: 71. 1832. (ORCHIDACEAE).
= **Crepidium** Blume

Pterochilus plantaginea Hook. & Arn., Bot. Beechey Voy. 2: 71, t. 17. 1832. (ORCHIDACEAE).
Type: 'One specimen alone', 'Society Islands', Lay & Collie.
   Not found at E.
   Type at K: a sheet ex herb. Hooker, annotated by Hooker with the name and locality 'Society islands', also annotated by him with the name 'Microstylis Rheedei Lindl.'; attached is a ticket with drawings, annotated with the Hooker & Arnott name by Hooker.
= **Crepidium resupinatum** (G. Forst.) Szlach.

Pyrrocoma menziesii Hook. & Arn., Bot. Beechey Voy. 8: 351. 1839. (COMPOSITAE).
Original material: California, Mr Menzies.
   None found at E.
   At K: a sheet ex herb. Hooker annotated in a later hand with the name and reference bears five specimens and details for two different collections, and it is not entirely clear to which specimen(s) the details '"California", A. M[enzies]' refer (the second, Nuttall collection, is not original material). Based on a photograph of the sheet (at GH and US) G.L. Nesom (Phytologia 70: 97. 1991) cited the Menzies specimen at K as type, but the sheet should be annotated to clarify this.
≡ **Isocoma menziesii** (Hook. & Arn.) G.L. Nesom

Quercus aristata Hook. & Arn., Bot. Beechey Voy. 10: 444. 1841. (FAGACEAE).
Original material: 'Between San Blas and Tepic', Mexico, Sinclair.
   At E: a sheet ex herb. Arnott (E00296137), annotated by him with the name and 'San Blas to Tepic, Dr Sinclair' – this was annotated 'isotype' by D.E. Breedlove in 1987.
   At K: a sheet (K000512917) ex herb. Bentham (given him by Hooker in 1845), bearing a ticket annotated by Bentham with the name and 'Tepic, Sinclair'.
Note. The Hooker sheet (which was presumably annotated 'holotype') cannot be found at K.

Quercus densiflora Hook. & Arn., Bot. Beechey Voy. 391. 1840. (FAGACEAE).
Original material: California, Douglas; 'Hook. Ic. Pl. ined.'
   None found at E.
   At K, two sheets. A sheet ex herb. Hooker bearing two collections, the upper (K000512263), annotated by Hooker on the sheet 'California, Douglas', and with a ticket annotated by Hooker with the name, reference, and 'Ic.Pl. tab.' is original material (the lower specimen, *Coulter* 663, is not). A sheet ex herb. Bentham, also bearing two collections, the upper, with a printed 'California, Douglas 1833' label, though not annotated with the name, is almost certainly original material (the lower specimen, a later collection, is

Alphabetical list of new taxa

not). The illustration was later published by Hooker (Ic. Pl. t. 380. 1841), but the original cannot be found in the Wing C illustrations collection.
≡ *Lithocarpus densiflorus* (Hook. & Arn.) Rehder

Quercus douglasii Hook. & Arn., Bot. Beechey Voy. 9: 391. 1840. (FAGACEAE). Original material: California, Douglas; 'Hook. Ic. Pl. ined.'

At E, two sheets of possibly original material. One ex herb. Arnott (E00369218), annotated by him with the name and 'California, Beechey'. This species was not collected by Beechey, and from the paper and the writing it seems possible that this is a specimen sent to Arnott by Hooker some time after the publication of this volume, and that Arnott may simply have mistaken the collector. The other sheet (E00369219) is ex herb. R.K. Greville, doubtless distributed before the determinations were made, annotated 'California, Douglas, Hort. Soc. London, Quercus' – as this was later identified by C.S. Sargent as *Q. douglasii*, it seems likely to be original material.

At K: neither the drawing, nor any original specimen, can be found, but the plates were later published by Hooker (Ic. Pl. tt. 82, 83. 1841).

Quinchamalium chilense Molina [var.] α *robustior* Hook. & Arn., Bot. Beechey Voy. 1: 44. 1830. (SANTALACEAE).
Original material: 'Conception', Chili, Lay & Collie.

At E: a sheet ex herb. Arnott bears two specimens annotated by Arnott '"Quinch. chilense"'. Conception, Beechey', which must be original material of var. *robustior* – these were annotated by E. Navas in 1959, but from the position of her determinavit slips it is impossible to be sure if she regarded the Beechey collection as *Q. bracteosum* Phil. or as *Q. chilense* (also on the sheet are three Cuming and a Mathews collection).

At K: two specimens centre- and lower-right (K000573543) on a sheet ex herb. Hooker annotated by Hooker 'α ... Conception, Beechey' – these were identified by E. Navas in 1959 as *Q. majus* Brongn. (also on the sheet is original material of the following variety, and collections of Darwin, Gillies and Bridges).
Note. Given the difference in identity of the material in Hooker's and Arnott's herbaria lectotypifcation is required, and both sheets must be considered.
?= *Quinchamalium majus* Brongn.

Quinchamalium chilense Molina [var.] β *gracilis* Hook. & Arn., Bot. Beechey Voy. 1: 44. 1830. (SANTALACEAE).
Original material: 'Valparaiso', Chili, Lay & Collie.

None found at E.

At K: on the sheet described above (also bearing collections by Darwin, Gillies, and Bridges), two slender specimens (K000573545) to the left of those of var. *robustior* are annotated by Hooker 'β H & A' – though lacking

the epithet, locality or collector, these must be the original material, and were annotated 'type' in 1959 by E. Navas, who determined them as *Q. gracile*.
= **Quinchamalium gracile** Brongn.

Ranunculus aquatilis L. var. *brachypus* Hook. & Arn., Bot. Beechey Voy. 7: 316. 1838. (RANUNCULACEAE).
Original material: California, Douglas.
   None found at E.
   At K: a sheet ex herb. Hooker annotated by him with the name and 'California, Douglas'.; the upper specimen on a sheet ex herb. Bentham, with a printed 'California, Douglas 1833' label and the ?field number '4' – though it does not bear the name in Bentham's hand it was later identified by W.P. Hiern as this variety, and is therefore almost certainly original material.
= **Ranunculus aquatilis** L. var. **capillaceus** (Thuill.) DC.

Ranunculus dissectus Hook. & Arn., Bot. Beechey Voy. 7: 316. 1838, *nom. illeg.*, non Bieb., 1819. (RANUNCULACEAE).
Original material: California, Douglas.
   None found at E.
   At K, two sheets: one ex herb. Hooker, annotated by him with the name and 'California, Douglas'; the other ex herb. Bentham, with a printed 'California, Douglas 1833' label annotated by Bentham with the name and reference.
= **Ranunculus californicus** Benth.

Ranunculus hebecarpus Hook. & Arn., Bot. Beechey Voy. 7: 316. 1838. (RANUNCULACEAE).
Original material: California, Douglas; 'R. parviflorus. γ. Torr. et Gr. Fl. I p. 25'.
   At E, two sheets: ex herb. Arnott (E00369006, E00369007), both annotated by Arnott 'Ranunculus hebecarpus Hook. California, [per] Dr Hooker', the second of these has the additional reference 'DC. n. 126^x'.
   At K: the upper specimen on a sheet ex herb. Hooker annotated by him 'R. hebecarpus Hook. R. parviflorus γ. Torr. et Gr. California, Douglas' (the lower specimen is not original material); the right-hand specimen on a sheet ex herb. Bentham with a printed 'California, Douglas 1833' label annotated by Bentham on the label with the Torrey & Gray name, and on the sheet with the Hooker & Arnott name and reference (the left-hand specimen is not original material).
Note. In this case (and that of *R. dissectus*) the name is attributed to Hooker alone, suggesting that he started to work on the Douglas collections on his own, before enlisting Arnott's help.

Ranunculus humilis Collie ex Hook. & Arn., Bot. Beechey Voy. 1: 4, t. 2. 1830, *nom illeg.*, non Pers., 1806. (RANUNCULACEAE).
Original material: 'Conception', Chili, Collie.

Alphabetical list of new taxa 159

At E: the upper specimen (E00070364) on a sheet ex herb. Arnott, annotated by him 'Ranunculus humilis Collie, Conception – Beechey' (the lower, E00070360, is a Tweedie specimen from Buenos Ayres).

At K: on a sheet ex herb. Hooker annotated by him 'R. humilis Collie, Hook. & Arn. in Beechey's Voy.', the two right-hand specimens (K000220238) are the original material, annotated 'Captn. Beechey' (the left-hand specimen, K000220237, is labelled 'Tweedie, B. Ayres').

Note. It should be noted that the Beechey material as labelled matches the plate, and that the material on both sheets was determined by Alicia Lourteig as *R. bonariensis* Poir. var. *trisepalus* (Gillies ex Hook. & Arn.) Lourt. (the Tweedie material as *R. hydrophilus* Gaud.). The simplest interpretation is that the Beechey specimens are correctly labelled and that *R. humilis* = **Ranunculus bonariensis** Poir. var. **trisepalus** (Gillies ex Hook. & Arn.) Lourteig.

However, Lourteig believed that the data on the two collections had been switched (on the grounds that *R. hydrophilus* did not occur at Buenos Aires, but that *R. bonariensis* var. *trisepalus* did). Such distributional evidence/opinion is not incontravertible, and when she published on the subject (Darwinia 9: 465, 520. 1951) she muddied the waters even further, citing *R. humilis* as a synonym both of *R. bonariensis* var. *trisepalus*, with a reference to Hooker & Arnott plate '2 … p.p.', and of *R. hydrophilus*, with a reference to Hooker & Arnott's plate '1 … p.p.'. This is nonsensical as plate 2 does not show a mixed collection, and plate 1 is *Anemone decapetala*.

Raphiolepis integerrima Hook. & Arn., Bot. Beechey Voy. 6: 263. 1838. (Generic placement queried). (ROSACEAE).
Original material: 'Bonin', Lay & Collie.
   None found at E.
   At K: a sheet ex herb. Hooker, annotated by him with the name, bears four specimens (representing possibly three collections) – the top left-hand specimen is annotated by Hooker 'Bonin in Loochoo, Beechey' and the right-hand central one 'Bonin, Beechey', which must both be original material. To a second sheet, ex herb. Hooker, is pinned part of a dissected sheet ex herb. Bentham, annotated by Bentham with the name and 'Loochoo? Beechey', this may also be original material.
= **Raphiolepis umbellata** (Thunb.) Makino

Rhus caustica (Molina) Hook. & Arn., Bot. Beechey Voy. 1: 15, t. 7. 1830. (Generic placement queried). (ANACARDIACEAE). [Chili].
Basionym cited: 'Laurus caustica. *Molina* [Sagg. Chile 176. 1782]'. The same authors later (Bot. Misc. 3: 175. 1833) transferred the epithet to the genus *Lithraea* Miers ex Hook. & Arn., where it has remained.
≡ **Lithraea caustica** (Molina) Hook. & Arn.

Rhus macrophylla Hook. & Arn., Bot. Beechey Voy. 9: 413. 1840. (ANACARDIACEAE).
Original material: 'Acapulco', Mexico, Sinclair.
   None found at E or K.

Rhynchosia mexicana Hook. & Arn., Bot. Beechey Voy. 6: 287. 1838. (LEGUMINOSAE).
Original material: Tepic, Mexico, Lay & Collie.
   Isolectotype at E: a sheet (E00369050) annotated by Arnott with the name and 'Mexico, Beechey'. This is one of the sheets given to E by GL in 1902, with a printed 'Herb. Walker Arnott' label.
   Lectotype at K: a sheet ex herb. Hooker annotated by him with the name and 'Mexico, Beechey' – it was annotated 'holotype' by J.W. Grear in 1976 and lectotypified (cited as 'holotype') by him in Mem. New York Bot. Gard. (31: 76. 1978).
= ***Rhynchosia minima*** (L.) DC.

Rhynchospora sclerioides Hook. & Arn., Bot. Beechey Voy. 3: 99. 1832. (CYPERACEAE).
Original material: Sandwich Islands, Lay & Collie.
   None found at E.
   At K: a sheet ex herb. Hooker bearing a ticket annotated by Arnott with the name and 'Oahu, Beechey'.

Ribes californicum Hook. & Arn., Bot. Beechey Voy. 8: 346. 1839. (GROSSULARIACEAE).
Original material: California, Douglas.
   At E: a sheet ex herb. Arnott (E00369063), annotated by him 'Ribes (Grossularia) californica [sic] H & A. California, [per] Hooker', is probably original material.
   At K, two sheets: one ex herb. Hooker, annotated by him with the name and 'California, Douglas' (it bears two other collections by E.L. Greene that are not original material); a sheet ex herb. Bentham, annotated by him with the name and reference 'Torr. et Gr. Fl. [N. Am.] 1.548 [1840]' with a printed 'California, Douglas 1833' label.

Ribes occidentale Hook. & Arn., Bot. Beechey Voy. 8: 346. 1839. (GROSSULARIACEAE).
Original material: California, Douglas.
   At E: a sheet ex herb. Arnott (E00369064), annotated by him 'Ribes (Grossularia) occidentalis [sic] H & A, California, [per] Hooker', is probably original material.
   At K, two sheets. One sheet ex herb. Hooker annotated by him with the name and reference bears three collections of which the right-hand one

Alphabetical list of new taxa 161

annotated by Hooker 'California, Douglas' is certainly original material (the other two are probably not: one has a field ticket '233 R. occidentale' to which Hooker has added 'California. (Douglas) Dr Coulter' – despite the ambiguity of the collector citation this is probably a Coulter collection, as is the third specimen with a field ticket '228 Ribes Menziesii'). The second sheet, ex herb. Bentham has a printed 'California, Douglas 1833' label annotated by Bentham with the name and reference.
= **Ribes menziesii** Pursh

Ribes subvestitum Hook. & Arn., Bot. Beechey Voy. 8: 346. 1839. (GROSSULARIACEAE).
Original material: California, Douglas.

At E: a sheet ex herb. Arnott (E00369062), annotated by him 'Ribes (Grossularia) subvestitum. California, D[avid] D[ouglas] per Hooker'.

At K, two sheets. The two left-hand specimens on a sheet ex herb. Hooker annotated by him with the name and 'California, Douglas' are original material (the right-hand specimen is also annotated by Hooker 'California, Douglas', and has a field ticket '236. R. subvestitum', but is not original material and belongs to a different taxon, determined as *R. menziesii* var. *hystrix* by Jepson in 1930). The two left-hand specimens on a sheet ex herb. Bentham agree with the left-hand specimens on the Hooker sheet, and have a printed 'California, Douglas 1833' label – the sheet is annotated by Bentham with the name and reference and these are also original material (the two right-hand specimens, a Jepson collection, are not).
= **Ribes menziesii** Pursh

Rottlera aurantiaca Hook. & Arn., Bot. Beechey Voy. 6: 270. 1838. (EUPHORBIACEAE).
Original material: 'Loo Choo', Lay & Collie.

None found at E.

At K: a sheet ex herb. Hooker bearing two collections. The right-hand one (K000185510), annotated on the sheet by Hooker with the name and locality 'Loochoo', but no collector's name, is original material (the left-hand specimen, *Henry* 7988, is not).
= **Mallotus philippensis** (Lam.) Müll. Arg.

Rourea oblongifolia Hook. & Arn., Bot. Beechey Voy. 6: 283. 1838. (Generic placement queried). (CONNARACEAE).
Original material: Tepic, Mexico, Lay & Collie.

None found at E.

E. Forero (Mem. New York Bot. Gard. 26: 51. 1976) cited as seen a 'presumed holotype' ('Guerrero, Acapulco, *Beechey s.n.*') at K, but no such specimen can now be found and in any case the locality is incorrect.
= **Rourea glabra** Kunth var. ***glabra***

Rubus velutinus Hook. & Arn., Bot. Beechey Voy. 3: 140. 1832. (ROSACEAE).
Original material: 'San Francisco', California, Lay & Collie.
    None found at E or K.
≡ **Rubus parviflorus** Nutt. var. **velutinus** (Hook. & Arn.) Greene

Rytidostylis Hook. & Arn., Bot. Beechey Voy. 9: 424. 1840. (CUCURBITACEAE).

Rytidostylis gracilis Hook. & Arn., Bot. Beechey Voy. 9: 425, t. 97A. 1840. (CUCURBITACEAE).
Original material: 'Realejo', Mexico [now Nicaragua], Sinclair.
    None found at E or K.

Salix speciosa Hook. & Arn., Bot. Beechey Voy. 3: 130. 1832, *nom. illeg.*, non Host, 1828. (SALICACEAE).
Original material: Kotzebue's Sound & American coast of Behring's Strait, from lat. 67° to 71°, Lay & Collie.
    At E: the right-hand specimen (E00369220) on a sheet ex herb. Arnott, annotated by him with the name and 'Kotzebue Sound, Beechey' is original material (the left-hand one, E00369221, from the Franklin Expedition, is not).
    None found at K.
= **Salix alaxensis** (Anders. ex DC.) Coville

Salpiglossis prostrata Hook. & Arn., Bot. Beechey Voy. 4: 153. 1833. (Generic placement queried). (SOLANACEAE).
Original material: San Francisco (or Monterey Bay), California, Lay & Collie.
    At E: a sheet ex herb. Arnott (E00019755), annotated by him with the name and 'California, Beechey' (to which he added in pencil 'videas species affinem Bonariensia, quae Lindernia montevidensis Spr.'); it also bears a ticket with the name 'Petunia parviflora' in the hand of C.G.D. Nees von Esenbeck (a determination confirmed by J.R. Steamann in 1996).
    At K: a sheet ex herb. Hooker, annotated by him on the sheet 'Beechey', bearing a ticket annotated with the name and 'California' in an unknown hand.
Note. At both E and K are the Douglas specimens referred to on p. 376 (1839), which 'may prove a distinct species'.
= **Petunia parviflora** Juss.

Salvia lasiocephala Hook. & Arn., Bot. Beechey Voy. 7: 306. 1838. (LABIATAE).
Original material: Tepic, Mexico, Lay & Collie.
    Isolectotype at E: a sheet ex herb. Arnott (E00259584), annotated by him with the name and 'Mexico, Beechey'. There are also two specimens from the later Sinclair collection, annotated with the name by Arnott – but these are not original material.
    Lectotype at K: a sheet ex herb. Hooker (K000247994) annotated by him with the name and bearing a ticket in ?Arnott's hand 'Salvia sp. n. Mexico,

Alphabetical list of new taxa 163

Capt. Beechey'. It was annotated 'lectotype' in 2007 by M.R. Garcia Pena giving the reference for this designation as Epling (Repert. Sp. Nov. Reg. Veg. Beih. 110: 145. 1938). (Pena annotated another sheet, K000247995, as 'probably an isotype', but it is not a type, being a later Sinclair collection).

Sanicula arctopoides Hook. & Arn., Bot. Beechey Voy. 3: 141. 1832. (UMBELLIFERAE).
Original material: San Francisco (or Monterey Bay), California, Lay & Collie. It is stated that this was 'First discovered ... by Mr Menzies', implying that Hooker & Arnott saw a Menzies specimen, which would also be original material.

None found at E: a sheet, ex herb. Arnott, annotated by him with the name 'California, D[avid] D[ouglas] per Hooker' is a later collection.

At K: the uppermost specimen (of three) on a sheet ex herb. Hooker annotated by him with the name and 'California, Beechey' marked 'drawn' (the other two, *Hartweg* 1744, *Douglas* s.n., are not original material).

Sanicula bipinnata Hook. & Arn., Bot. Beechey Voy. 8: 347. 1839. (UMBELLIFERAE).
Original material: California, Douglas.
None found at E.

At K, two sheets. One ex herb. Hooker annotated by him with the name bears two collections (three specimens); it is not clear to which of these the details 'California, Douglas' refer, though probably the lower two (the other collection, *Coulter* 208, is not original material). The second sheet is ex herb. Bentham – the right-hand specimen, with a printed 'California, Douglas 1833' label annotated with the name by Bentham is original material (the other, *Hartweg* 1749(231), is not).

Sanicula laciniata Hook. & Arn., Bot. Beechey Voy. 8: 347. 1839. (UMBELLIFERAE).
Original material: California, Douglas.

A sheet at E, ex herb. R.K. Greville (E00369084), though it does not bear this name, is most probably original material of this distinctive species (distributed before it was named): it is annotated by Greville 'Sanicula. California – Douglas – Hort. Soc. Lond. 1834'.

At K, two sheets. One, ex herb. Hooker, annotated by him with the name, bears two collections, the right-hand one, annotated 'California Douglas' by Hooker is original material (the left-hand one, *Bigelow* s.n., is not). The second sheet is ex herb. Bentham and also bears two collections: the right-hand one, with a printed 'California Douglas, 1833' label annotated with the name by Bentham, is original material (the left-hand specimen, *Hartweg* 1745(173), is not).

Sanicula menziesii Hook. & Arn., Bot. Beechey Voy. 3: 142. 1832. (UMBELLIFERAE).
Original material: San Francisco (or Monterey Bay), California, Lay & Collie. Under *S. arctopoides* it is stated that this species was 'First discovered … by Mr Menzies', implying that Hooker & Arnott had seen a specimen, which (together with the choice of epithet) suggests that such a specimen would also constitute original material.

None found at E. The only sheet ex herb. Arnott, annotated by him has two later collections: 'California, D[avid] D[ouglas] per Hooker' and a Scouler specimen from Columbia.

At K: a sheet ex herb. Hooker with three collections – the left-hand specimen beside which is a ticket annotated by ?Arnott with the name and 'California, Beechey', and a specimen annotated by Hooker with the name and 'N.W. Coast Am. Menzies' (the two 'California, Douglas' specimens on the sheet are not original material).
= **Sanicula crassicaulis** DC.

Sanicula nudicaulis Hook. & Arn., Bot. Beechey Voy. 8: 347. 1839. (UMBELLIFERAE).
Original material: California, Douglas.

At E: a sheet ex herb. Arnott (E00369085), annotated by him with the name and 'California, D[avid] D[ouglas] per Hooker'.

At K: a sheet ex herb. Hooker annotated by him with the name and 'California, Douglas'. A sheet ex herb. Bentham annotated by him with this name is not original material of *S. nudicaulis* and has clearly been mixed up as the specimen on it is *S. laciniata*.
= **Sanicula crassicaulis** DC.

Santalum paniculatum Hook. & Arn., Bot. Beechey Voy. 2: 94. 1832. (SANTALACEAE).
Original material: 'volcano of Owhyhee [Sandwich Islands], collected by Mr. Macrae'.

None found at E.

At K: three relevant sheets – that ex herb. Bentham is certainly original material, with a printed Horticultural Society label 'Ins. Owhyhee, ad montem ignivomem, Macrae Junio 1825', annotated on the sheet with the name by Bentham. A second sheet with a printed Macrae label, with the locality 'Woahoo, Ins. Sandwich' may also be original material, but mislabelled as to locality, as Skotsberg has noted on the sheet that *S. paniculatum* has never been found on Oahu. A third sheet, ex herb. Hooker, is annotated by Hooker 'Volcano, Owhyhee' (but with no collector) and in another hand with the name – at least some of the specimens on the sheet must belong with these details and be original material, but more than one collection may be represented on the sheet as it also bears a field ticket for *Diell* 103 from 'Oahu' (though

Alphabetical list of new taxa 165

Skotsberg has noted that this label must be misplaced – for the same reason as that given on the second sheet).

Sapindus drummondii Hook. & Arn., Bot. Beechey Voy. 6: 281. 1838. (SAPINDACEAE).
Under this name Hooker & Arnott described, but did not name, two varieties:

[var.] α, the typical one, based on 'Drummond Fl. Tex. [ined.] III. n. 54'

[var.] β, which they query as synonymous with 'Sapindus inaequalis. Schlecht. in Linn. 6. p. 419? (vix Lam.)', based on Beechey material from Mexico.

At E are sheets of both, ex herb. Arnott: of α, a sheet (E00369036) annotated by Arnott 'Sapindus saponaria? Texas III. n. 54. Drummond'. Arnott crossed out 'saponaria' and later wrote in pencil 'inaequalis Schl. – Linn. VI. p. 419?', and presumably later still, also in pencil 'S. marginatus Willd! certe'. Of β, a sheet (E00369035) annotated by Arnott 'Sapindus Drummondi β H&A, Bot. Beech. Voy. S. inaequalis Schl. in Linn. VI. p. 419. Mexico Beechey', and a later note 'Torrey & Gray refer the α (or Drummond plant) to S. marginatus Willd.'.

At K a sheet ex herb. Bentham bears two specimens, the lower is a duplicate of the Texan material [α] with a printed label 'Texas, Drummond, 1835, Third Collection, No 54' – the sheet is annotated by Bentham both with the Hooker & Arnott name and *S. marginatus* Willd. (the upper specimen is a Palmer collection). At K a sheet ex herb. Hooker has a duplicate of the Mexican material [β], annotated by Hooker 'Sapindus Drummondii H & A, Mexico Beechey'.

Note. As implied from the annotation on the Mexican sheet ex herb. Arnott, Torrey & Gray (Fl. N. Am. 1: 685. 1840) typified the species on the α element (while sinking it under *S. marginatus* Willd.) – they excluded the other element: 'not β, which is probably a different species'. L.D. Benson (Am. J. Bot. 30: 239. 1943), by citing the Drummond element and omitting any reference to the Mexican element, also took the former as the type when reducing it to **Sapindus saponaria** L. var. **drummondii** (Hook. & Arn.) L.D. Benson. (The Mexican element is probably only a form of the very variable *S. saponaria* L.)

Sapindus glabrescens Hook. & Arn., Bot. Beechey Voy. 6: 281. 1838. (MELIACEAE).
Original material: Tepic, Mexico, Lay & Collie.
    None found at E.
    At K: a sheet ex herb. Hooker annotated by him with the name and 'Mexico, Beechey' – this was lectotypified (cited as 'holotype') by T.D. Pennington (Fl. Neotrop. Monog. 28: 268. 1981).

Note. T.D. Pennington (pers. comm.) intends to recognise this as a subspecies of *Guarea glabra*.
= **Guarea glabra** Vahl

Sarcostemma bilobum Hook. & Arn., Bot. Beechey Voy. 10: 438. 1841. (APOCYNACEAE [ASCLEPIADACEAE]).
Original material: 'Acapulco', Mexico, Sinclair.
　None found at E.
　At K: a sheet ex herb. Hooker (K000196775) bearing a ticket annotated by Hooker with the name, and in another hand with 'Acapulco, Sinclair'. It is not annotated by R.W. Holm, but is presumably the sheet cited by him as type in Ann. Missouri Bot. Gard. (37: 517. 1950), where he mistakenly gave the 'collector' as 'Beechey'.
≡ **Funastrum bilobum** (Hook. & Arn.) J.F. Macbr.

Saxifraga cernua L. [var.] β *multiflora* Hook. & Arn., Bot. Beechey Voy. 3: 124. 1832. (SAXIFRAGACEAE).
Original material: Kotzebue's Sound & American coast of Behring's Strait, from lat. 67° to 71°, Lay & Collie.
　At E, two sheets. One ex herb. Arnott (E00369059), annotated by him 'Saxifraga cernua β, Kotzebue Sound (Beechey)'; the other (E00369060) ex herb. William Gourlie annotated 'Saxifraga cernua, Lin. β, Kotzebue Sound [per] Dr. W. Arnott'.
　At K: a possibly eighteenth-century sheet originally bearing only two small specimens, later incorporated into Hooker's herbarium, to which were added three Beechey specimens annotated (perhaps by W. Gourlie) 'S. cernua β – sed potius distincta species et S. sibirica, Kotzebue's Sound, Beechey' – these additions represent original material of the Hooker & Arnott variety and were determined as *S. sibirica* L. by A.E. Porsild in 1955.
= **Saxifraga sibirica** L.

Scaevola gaudichaudii Hook. & Arn., Bot. Beechey Voy. 2: 89. 1832 (as 'Gaudichaudi'). (GOODENIACEAE). [Sandwich Islands].
A replacement name for *S. montana* Gaud., an illegitimate later homonym of *S. montana* Labill.

Scaevola glabra Hook. & Arn., Bot. Beechey Voy. 2: 89. 1832. (GOODENIACEAE).
Original material: Sandwich Islands, Lay & Collie.
　At E: a sheet ex herb. Arnott (E00369150), annotated by him with the name and 'Oahu, Beechey'.
　At K: a sheet (K000229927) ex herb. Hooker annotated by him 'Beechey', bearing a ticket annotated by Arnott with the name and 'Oahu, B[eechey]'.

Alphabetical list of new taxa 167

Scaevola mollis Hook. & Arn., Bot. Beechey Voy. 2: 89. 1832. (GOODENIACEAE).
Original material: Sandwich Islands, Lay & Collie.
 At E: a sheet ex herb. Arnott (E00369151), annotated by him with the name and 'Oahu, Beechey'.
 At K: a sheet ex herb. Hooker annotated by him 'Beechey', bearing a ticket annotated by Arnott with the name and 'Ohau, B[eechey]'.

Scirpus longifolius Hook. & Arn., Bot. Beechey Voy. 2: 49. 1832. (CYPERACEAE).
Original material: 'Conception', Chili, Lay & Collie.
 None found at E or K.
= **Schoenoplectus pungens** (Vahl) Palla var. ***pungens***

Scleria neesiana Hook. & Arn., Bot. Beechey Voy. 5: 229. 1836. (CYPERACEAE). Original material: 'one specimen sent by Mr Millett' from 'Circa urbem Macao'; 'another, but imperfect one, in Prof. Henslow's collection', [by elimination] '*G.H. Vachell, n.* 66. (ex parte)'.
 None found at E.
 At K: the only relevant material is a remounted sheet annotated by J.D. Hooker '"Scleria Neesiana H. & A." "China, Beechey" (vix JDH)' – it cannot be said what Hooker was questioning – the identification, or the source of the specimen, but it might represent original material (it was identified as *S. scrobiculata* by C.B. Clarke in 1890).
= **Scleria scrobiculata** Nees & Meyen

Sedum uniflorum Hook. & Arn., Bot. Beechey Voy. 6: 263. 1838, *nom. illeg.*, non Raf., 1810. (CRASSULACEAE).
Original material: 'Loo Choo', Lay & Collie.
 None found at E.
 At K: a sheet ex herb. Hooker bears specimens from two sources, but apparently part of the same collection and original material: the upper is annotated by Hooker 'Loo Choo, Beechey'; the single specimen below has a ticket annotated by ?Arnott 'Sedum uniflorum H & A. Loo Choo'.
Note. A new name appears to be required for this species – it is filed under this name at K, and E.H. Walker in Fl. Okinawa & S Ryukyu Islands 507, 1976, treated it under Hooker & Arnott's name, despite giving the earlier homonym.

Semeiandra Hook. & Arn., Bot. Beechey Voy. 7: 291. 1838. (ONAGRACEAE).
= **Lopezia** Cav.

Semeiandra grandiflora Hook. & Arn., Bot. Beechey Voy. 7: 291, t. 59. 1838. (ONAGRACEAE).
Original material: Tepic, Mexico, Lay & Collie.
 At E: a sheet ex herb. Arnott (E00369077), annotated by him with the name and 'Mexico' is probably original material.

At K, three type sheets. Two ex herb. Hooker annotated by him with the name and 'Mexico, Beechey', one of which (K000533318), annotated 'figd.', is that on which Hooker's published drawing was based; neither sheet is annotated by Plitmann *et al.*, but one must be the Hooker sheet cited by them as 'type' (i.e., lectotype) in Ann. Missouri Bot. Gard. (60: 502. 1973); the third specimen, ex herb. Bentham, has a ticket annotated by Bentham with the name and 'Tepic, Beechey' and was cited by Plitmann *et al.* (l.c.) as 'iso[lecto]type'.
≡ **Lopezia semeiandra** Plitmann, P.H. Raven & Breedlove

Semeiandra grandiflora [var.] β *subhirsuta* Hook. & Arn., Bot. Beechey Voy. 9: 422. 1840. (ONAGRACEAE).
Original material: 'Between San Blas and Tepic', Mexico, Sinclair.
 At E: a sheet ex herb. Arnott (E00285578), bearing a ticket with the name 'Semeiandra grandiflora β' in what is probably Hooker's hand, to which Arnott has added 'San Blas & Tepic (Dr Sinclair) Bot. Beech. Voy. Suppl.'.
 None found at K.
= **Lopezia semeiandra** Plitmann, P.H. Raven & Breedlove

Senebiera mexicana Hook. & Arn., Bot. Beechey Voy. 6: 276. 1838. (CRUCIFERAE).
Original material: Tepic, Mexico, Lay & Collie.
 None found at E or K.
= **Lepidium virginicum** L.

Senecio arnicoides Hook. & Arn., Bot. Beechey Voy. 1: 32. 1830. (COMPOSITAE).
Original material: 'Conception', Chili, Lay & Collie.
 None found at E or K.

Senecio bipinnatifidus Hook. & Arn., Bot. Beechey Voy. 32. 1830. (COMPOSITAE).
Original material: 'Coquimbo', Chili, Lay & Collie.
 None found at E or K.
Note. A.L. Cabrera (Lilloa 15: 482. 1949) placed this among doubtful and imperfectly known species.

Senecio bridgesii Hook. & Arn., Bot. Beechey Voy. 2: 57. 1832. (COMPOSITAE).
Original material: 'Valparaiso', Chili, Lay & Collie; Bridges material from Valparaiso.
 At E: on a sheet ex herb. Arnott, a single specimen (E000251495 – mounted upside-down) annotated by him with the name and 'Valparaiso, Beechey' (on the same sheet are two specimens of *Cuming* 65, cited under *S. bridgesii* by Hooker & Arnott in J. Bot. 3: 335, 1841, and a specimen of *Gillies* 111 – but these are not original material).
 No Beechey material found at K; but several sheets ex herb. Hooker annotated by him with the name, bearing various collections, of which the

Alphabetical list of new taxa 169

Bridges ones from Valparaiso are original material (the others, including ones by Gillies, are not).

Senecio glabratus Hook. & Arn., Bot. Beechey Voy. 1: 32. 1830. (COMPOSITAE).
Original material: 'Conception', Chili, Lay & Collie.

None found at E or K. In a type cover at K are two sheets, ex herb. Hooker annotated by him with the name, but these are later collections – including Bridges (Valparaiso), McLean, and Edmonston – and are not original material.

Senecio nigrescens Hook. & Arn., Bot. Beechey Voy. 1: 32. 1830. (COMPOSITAE).
Original material: 'Conception', Chili, Lay & Collie.

None found at E.

At K: the lower specimen (K000527590) on a sheet ex herb. Hooker annotated by him with the name and 'Captn. Beechey' (the upper specimen is not original material).

Sesbania tomentosa Hook. & Arn., Bot. Beechey Voy. 6: 286. 1838. (LEGUMINOSAE).
Original material: 'Acapulco', Mexico, Lay & Collie.

None found at E or K.

Sicyos pachycarpus Hook. & Arn., Bot. Beechey Voy. 2: 83. 1832. (CUCURBITACEAE).
Type: 'volcanic rocks on Diamond Hill, in Oahu', Sandwich Islands, Collie.

Not found at E.

Type at K: what was originally a single sheet ex herb. Hooker bearing a ticket annotated by Arnott with the name and 'Oahu, B[eechey]' – this bore two specimens, which are now mounted on separate sheets.

In 1953 H. St John determined the two specimens as two different species, annotating the (former) top left-hand one as the 'lectotype' of *S. pachycarpus*, determining the other as *S. microcarpus* Mann. It is not known if he published this lectotypification (and these are now regarded as synonymous). In 1987 St John (Phytologia 63: 192) published a new species, *S. waimanaloensis* based on *Degener* 17416, making no mention of the Beechey specimen.

By contrast, in 1988, J.R. Telford annotated the (former) right-hand specimen as 'lectotype' of *S. pachycarpus* and determined the other specimen as *S. waimanaloensis*.

If St John had not, by then, published his lectotypification, then Telford was at liberty to choose as he did, but it is not known if his later choice of lectotype has been published, so there is still confusion as to the correct application of the name and identity of the two elements.

Sida grossulariifolia Hook. & Arn., Bot. Beechey Voy. 7: 326. 1838 (as '*grossulariaefolia*'). (MALVACEAE).
Type: 'Bamcoch [= Bannock] River, Snake Country [Idaho]. ([John McLeod per] *Tolmie*)'.
   Not found at E or K.
T.H. Kearney (Univ. California Pub. Bot. 19: 87. 1935) cited '*Type locality* – "Bamcoch River, Snake County" [The Bannock River, Power County, Idaho is probably meant]. Type specimen (Kew) collected by W.F. Tolmie' – but this does not necessarily mean that Kearney saw a specimen.
≡ ***Sphaeralcea grossulariifolia*** (Hook. & Arn.) Rydb.

Sideroxylon ferrugineum Hook. & Arn., Bot. Beechey Voy. 6: 266, t. 55. 1838. (SAPOTACEAE).
Original material: 'Bonin', Lay & Collie.
   At E: a sheet ex herb. Arnott (E00369158), annotated by him with the name and 'Bonin, Beechey'.
   None found at K.
= ***Pouteria obovata*** (R. Br.) Baehni

Sideroxylon wightianum Hook. & Arn., Bot. Beechey Voy. 5: 196, t. 41. 1836. (SAPOTACEAE)
Original material: 'Macao [China]; *Mr. Millett*'.
There is some confusion here, as Hooker & Arnott cited '*Wall. Cat. of E.I.P.* n. 4147' as the source of the name. However, this is mistaken as 4147 in the 'Wallich Catalogue' is 'Mimusops lucida Wall'. 'Sideroxylon Wightianum Wall.' is the name given for 'Hb. Wight' specimens under the number 4154, almost certainly referring to South Indian material. Both these names are *nomina nuda*, so have no significance nomenclaturally; because Hooker & Arnott specifically cited only the Millett Chinese material, it would appear that they did not intend to include the Wight specimens, but only the name (as a token of respect to Wight?). If the name were to be taken as 'Wall. ex Hook. & Arn.', the Wight material would presumably have to be explicitly excluded, but it seems more sensible to treat it as an independent Hooker & Arnott name based solely on the Chinese material, of which there is none at E.
   At K (in the type cover): a fragment of a sheet ex herb. Hooker annotated by him 'China, Millett', and bearing a ticket with pencil drawings of three floral details possibly in the hand of Arnott.

"*Silvaea* Hook. & Arn.", Bot. Beechey Voy. 5: 211. 1836. (EUPHORBIACEAE). This generic name is not validly published. From the wording 'It is probable that C[luytia] semperflorens, Roxb. Fl. Ind. 3. p. 730, from Silhet, must form a genus (SILVAEA, Hook. et Arn.) distinct from either', it was clearly not fully accepted by the authors, and it was not included in the index. The genus is given as a synonym of *Trigonostemon* Blume in Radcliffe-Smith (Gen. Euphorb. 308. 2001), but, as will be seen from the wording above, the combination "*S. semperflorens* (Roxb.) Hook. & Arn." cited by Radcliffe-Smith was not actually made by Hooker & Arnott.

Sinclairia Hook. & Arn., Bot. Beechey Voy. 10: 433. 1841. (COMPOSITAE).
= ***Liabum*** Adans.

Sinclairia discolor Hook. & Arn., Bot. Beechey Voy. 10: 433. 1841. (COMPOSITAE).
Original material: 'Realejo', Mexico [now Nicaragua], Sinclair.
   None found at E or K. R. McVaugh (Fl. Novo-Galiciana 12: 583. 1984) cited 'type (*Sinclair*, K!)', but this cannot now be found.
≡ ***Liabum discolor*** (Hook. & Arn.) Hemsl.

Sisyrhinchium sessiliflorum Hook. & Arn., Bot. Beechey Voy. 1: 47. 1830, *nom. illeg.*, non Poepp., 1829. (IRIDACEAE).
Original material: 'Conception', Chili, Lay & Collie.
   None found at E.
   At K: a sheet ex herb. Hooker, annotated by him with the name. This bears two flowering scapes, a rosette of leaves presumably belonging to one of these, and also a complete, small plant. The last seems to be associated with the details 'Valparaiso, Bridges' and is not original material. The extreme left of the sheet is annotated by Hooker 'Beechey (Tweedie)' – it is not clear what this means, but at least one of the flowering scapes must be original material. P. Goldblatt & M. Celis (Sida 21: 2111. 2005) cited the type as ' Conception, *Beechey s.n.* (probable HOLOTYPE: K!)', but have not annotated the sheet so as to fix the designation.
= ***Libertia sessiliflora*** (Poepp.) Skottsb.

Solanum refractum Hook. & Arn., Bot. Beechey Voy. 7: 304. 1838. (SOLANACEAE).
Original material: Tepic, Mexico, Lay & Collie.
   None found at E.
   At K: a sheet (K000195651) ex herb. Hooker, annotated by him with the name and the note 'I can find none like this', and by Bentham 'Mexico, Beechey'. It was annotated 'holotype' by M. Nee in 2005, but it is not known if this typification has been published.

Solanum sandwicense Hook. & Arn., Bot. Beechey Voy. 2: 92. 1832. (SOLANACEAE).
Original material: Sandwich Islands, Lay & Collie.
   At E: a sheet (E00243620) ex herb. Arnott, annotated by him with the name and 'Oahu, Beechey'.

At K, two sheets ex herb. Hooker. One is annotated on the sheet by Hooker with the name and 'Oahu, Beechey' and was annotated 'holotype' by H. St John in 1977, but it is not known if this typification has been published. The other sheet bears a ticket annotated with the name and 'Oahu, Beechey' by Arnott.

Sonchus californicus Hook. & Arn., Bot. Beechey Voy. 8: 361. 1839. (Generic placement queried). (COMPOSITAE).
Original material: California, Douglas.
   None found at E.
   At K: a sheet ex herb. Hooker bearing two collections, but not annotated with the name by Hooker – someone has added 'Hieracium? californicum DC', and there is a later annotation in a different hand '?type collection of Sonchus? californicus' – this refers to the left-hand specimen, annotated by Hooker 'California, Douglas' and it might well be original material (the other specimen, *Coulter* 246, is certainly not).
= ***Malacothrix saxatilis*** (Nutt.) Torr. & A. Gray

Spodiopogon aureus Hook. & Arn., Bot. Beechey Voy. 6: 273. 1838. (GRAMINEAE).
Original material: 'Loo Choo', Lay & Collie.
   At E: a sheet ex herb. Arnott (E00369244), annotated by him with the name and 'Loo Choo, Beechey'.
   At K: a partial, remounted sheet ex herb. Hooker, annotated by him on the sheet '(672) Loochoo, Beechey', and with a ticket annotated by Arnott with the name and 'Loochoo' (also attached is a sheet of fine drawings of dissections by C.E. Hubbard).
≡ ***Ischaemum aureum*** (Hook. & Arn.) Hack.

Spodiopogon ischaemoides Hook. & Arn., Bot. Beechey Voy. 6: 274. 1838. (GRAMINEAE).
Original material: 'Bonin', Lay & Collie.
   None found at E.
   At K: a sheet ex herb. Hooker annotated by him on the sheet 'Beechey', bearing two tickets in the hand of Arnott – one with the name and locality 'Bonin', the other with the name and a long description (it was identified as *I. sieboldii* Miq. by O. Stapf).
Note. The name 'Ischaemum minus Presl, in Kunth, En. 1. p. 514?' is cited as a synonym, but because this identity is queried, Hooker and Arnott's is not a superfluous name.
= ***Ischaemum sieboldii*** Miq.

"*Stachys biflora* Hook. & Arn.", Bot. Beechey Voy. 4: 155. 1833. (LABIATAE). This name is not validly published – although there is a Latin description based

Alphabetical list of new taxa 173

on a fragmentary specimen from California, it was not fully accepted by the authors ('This, if new, may be called ...') and it is not included in their index.

Stevia elliptica Hook. & Arn., Bot. Beechey Voy. 10: 434. 1841. (COMPOSITAE). Original material: 'Between San Blas and Tepic', Mexico, Sinclair.

At E: a sheet ex herb. Arnott (E00369109), annotated by him with the name and 'San Blas to Tepic, Dr Sinclair'.

At K: a sheet (K000488674) ex herb. Hooker bearing three specimens and two tickets, both annotated (one in Bentham's hand) with the name and 'San Blas to Tepic, Dr Sinclair' – this sheet was annotated 'holotype' by J.L. Grashoff in 1972 but this typification appears not to have been published.
= ***Stevia caracasana*** DC.

Stevia glandulosa Hook. & Arn., Bot. Beechey Voy. 7: 296. 1838. (COMPOSITAE). Original material: 'Talisco', Mexico, Lay & Collie.

At E: a sheet ex herb. Arnott (E00369110), annotated by him 'Stevia glandulosa H & A, monardaefolia Kunth? DC ...4?, Mexico, B[eechey]'. A second sheet annotated with the name by Arnott, is from later Sinclair material: it is not listed in the Mexico Supplement, and is not original material.

At K: a sheet (K000488696) ex herb. Hooker annotated by him with the name and 'Talisco, Beechey' – this sheet was annotated 'holotype' by J.L. Grashoff in 1972 but this typification appears not to have been published.

Strophanthus divaricatus (Lour.) Hook. & Arn., Bot. Beechey Voy. 5: 199. 1836. (APOCYNACEAE). [China].
Basionym cited: 'Pergularia divaricata. *Lour. Cochin. v.* 1. *p.* 210 [this is the second edition of 1793, first published p. 169, 1790]'.

Styrax suberifolius Hook. & Arn., Bot. Beechey Voy. 5: 196, t. 40. 1836. (STYRACACEAE).
Original material: Chiefly ... about Macao, China, Lay & Collie.

At E; a sheet (E00105499) ex herb. Arnott, annotated by him with the name and 'China, Beechey'.

None found at K: the sheet in a type cover, though bearing the name and a sheet of drawings in Hooker's hand, is not original material, being a Millett collection that is not mentioned in the protologue.

Syzygium buxifolium Hook. & Arn., Bot. Beechey Voy. 4: 187. 1833. (Generic placement queried). (MYRTACEAE).
Original material: Chiefly ... about Macao, China, Lay & Collie.

At E: the lower two specimens (E00369069) on a sheet ex herb. Arnott, annotated by him 'China – Beechey' (the upper specimen (E00369070) is annotated by Arnott with the name and 'Canton – [per] Dr Hooker' – it is probably a Millett collection and not original material).

At K: a sheet ex herb. Hooker annotated by him with the name and 'China, Beechey'.

Tabernaemontana mollis Hook. & Arn., Bot. Beechey Voy. 5: 199. 1836. (APOCYNACEAE).
Original material: Chiefly ... about Macao, China; Lay & Collie.
At E: a sheet ex herb. Arnott (E00369162), with two specimens, annotated by Arnott with the name and 'China, Beechey'.
None found at K.
= ***Tabernaemontana pandacaqui*** Poir.

Tagetes congesta Hook. & Arn., Bot. Beechey Voy. 7: 299. 1838. (COMPOSITAE).
Original material: Tepic, Mexico, Lay & Collie.
None found at E or K.
= ***Tagetes micrantha*** Cav.

Tellima heterophylla Hook. & Arn., Bot. Beechey Voy. 8: 346. 1839. (SAXIFRAGACEAE).
Original material: California, Douglas.
None found at E.
At K: two sheets in a type cover ex herb. Hooker both annotated by him with the name and 'California, Douglas'. One bears three specimens of a single collection and a drawing probably by Hooker – this is clearly original material though it was annotated 'paratype' by R.L. Taylor in 1962. The second sheet has two collections, one of which is similar to that on the first sheet, and are also original material; the other collection, to which the label *Coulter* 186 probably refers, was determined by R.L. Taylor as a hybrid with *Lithophragma affinis* – Taylor's comment that, because of the mixed nature of the sheet, it should not be considered a 'paratype' is unjustified.
≡ ***Lithophragma heterophyllum*** (Hook. & Arn.) Torr. & A. Gray

Tetradymia spinosa Hook. & Arn., Bot. Beechey Voy. 8: 360. 1839. (COMPOSITAE).
Type: 'Snake Country [Idaho]. [John McLeod per] *Mr Tolmie*'.
Isotype at E, a sheet ex herb. Arnott (E00369146), annotated by him with the name and 'Snake Country, Tolmie'.
Type at K is a sheet ex herb. Hooker annotated by him 'Tetradymia spinescens H & A, 64. Snake Country, California, Douglas' – the number confirms this as a 'Tolmie' collection, and the collector's name, like the mis-spelling of the epithet, is a *lapsus calami*. This was cited as 'holotype' by J.L. Strother (Brittonia 26: 195. 1974). (Also mounted on the sheet is *Gordon* 143, annotated with the same mis-spelt name, but this is certainly not a type).

Alphabetical list of new taxa

Tetranthera californica Hook. & Arn., Bot. Beechey Voy. 4: 159. 1833. (Generic placement queried). (LAURACEAE).
Original material: San Francisco (or Monterey Bay), California, Lay & Collie.
  At E: a sheet ex herb. Arnott (E00369202), annotated by him with the name and 'California, Beechey'. It also bears two tickets annotated by C.G.D. Nees von Esenbeck – one with a Latin description, the other with the name 'Oreodaphne (Umbellularia) californica N ab E', to which Arnott has added the reference 'NE. Syst. Laur. p. 462. n.60'.
  At K: a sheet ex herb. Hooker annotated by him 'Beechey', bearing a ticket annotated in an unknown hand with the name, and locality 'California' (another sheet in the type cover has Douglas, Nuttall and Coulter collections, but these are not original material of the Hooker & Arnott name).
≡ **Umbellularia californica** (Hook. & Arn.) Nutt.

Tetrapterys mexicana Hook. & Arn., Bot. Beechey Voy. 6: 281. 1838. (MALPIGHIACEAE).
Original material: 'Talisco', Mexico, Lay & Collie.
  At E: a sheet ex herb. Arnott (E00369020), annotated by him 'Tetrapterys mexicana H & A. Talisco, Beechey, Tetr. schiediana Schlr f. Ad. Juss n. 37'.
  At K, a sheet (K000427358) ex herb. Hooker, annotated by him with the name and 'Mexico, Beechey'.

Thermopsis macrophylla Hook. & Arn., Bot. Beechey Voy. 7: 329. 1838. (LEGUMINOSAE).
Original material: California, Douglas.
  None found at E.
  Two sheets at K: one (K000642382) ex herb. Hooker, annotated by him with the name and 'California, Douglas'; the other (K000642383) ex herb. Bentham with a printed 'California, Douglas 1833' label annotated by Bentham with the name and reference to 'Torr. & G. Fl. N. Am. 1. 690 [1840]'.

Tillaea erecta Hook. & Arn., Bot. Beechey Voy. 1: 24. 1830. (CRASSULACEAE).
Original material: 'Conception', Chili, Lay & Collie.
  None at E or K. Bywater & Wickens (Kew Bull. 39: 722. 1984) stated 'holotype not located'.
= **Crassula connata** (Ruiz & Pavon) A. Berger

Tithonia angustifolia Hook. & Arn., Bot. Beechey Voy. 10: 435. 1841. (COMPOSITAE).
Original material: 'Between San Blas and Tepic', Mexico, Sinclair; Lay & Collie material previously (l.c. p. 299) determined as *T. pachycephala* DC.
  At E: a sheet ex herb. Arnott (E00369134), annotated by him 'Tithonia angustifolia H & A, Bot. Beech. voy. T. pachycephala H & A (non DC). San Blas to Tepic, Dr. Sinclair'.

At K, three sheets. Two ex herb. Hooker: one annotated by him with both the Hooker & Arnott name and the misapplied Candollean one, the reference and 'Mexico, Beechey'; the other (K000487794) bearing two tickets, on which Hooker has crossed through the epithet of the original identification and replaced it with the new one, which Bentham has annotated 'Tepic, Sinclair'. A sheet ex herb. Bentham (given him by Hooker in 1844) bearing two collections of which the central specimen (K000487795) is original material, with a ticket annotated by Bentham with the name, reference, and 'Tepic, Sinclair'. None of these is annotated by S.F. Blake, but in Contrib. Gray Herb. (54: 58. 1918) he cited the type as 'Tepic, *Sinclair* (TYPE of *T. angustifolia*: K)'.
≡ **Viguiera angustifolia** (Hook. & Arn.) S.F. Blake

Toxocarpus wightianus Hook. & Arn., Bot. Beechey Voy. 5: 200. 1836. (APOCYNACEAE [ASCLEPIADACEAE]).
Original material: 'specimens received direct from China from Mr. Vachell and Mr. Millett'.

At E: a sheet ex herb. Arnott bearing a ticket annotated by him with the name and the details 'Canton, Vachell per Henslow no. 239'.

At K, two 'China, Millett' sheets. One has the name added in a later hand, but could be original material. The other is annotated by Hooker 'Perg?? rostrata nobis', and bears a ticket annotated 'an Periploca indica Burm. t. 83 Pergularia sinensis?' – although it has later been annotated 'Toxocarpus wightii vid. Beechey Voy.' this seems unlikely to be original material. A sheet with a Meyen collection, though annotated with the name in a contemporary hand, certainly cannot be original material.
Note. Hooker & Arnott cited 'Asclepias Curassavica. *Lour. Cochin.* v. 1. p. 211? (*non Linn.*)', but as this synonymy was queried, this does not make their name either a replacement name (i.e. 'sensu Lour., non L.'), or a superfluous one. They stated that their description was 'entirely derived' from the Vachell and Millett material, so this is the original material.

Trevirana parviflora Hook. & Arn., Bot. Beechey Voy. 7: 302. 1838 (as '*Trevirania*'). (PLANTAGINACEAE).
Original material: Tepic, Mexico, Lay & Collie.

At E: a sheet ex herb. Arnott (E00369182), annotated by him with the name and 'Mexico, Beechey'.
P.C. Standley & L.O. Williams (Fieldiana (Botany) 24(9): 406. 1973) realised the true identity of this plant, but cited no type material.

None found at K.
= **Stemodia peduncularis** Benth.

Tridax gaillardioides Hook. & Arn., Bot. Beechey Voy. 4: 148. 1833 (as '*galardioides*'). (Generic placement queried). (COMPOSITAE).
Original material: San Francisco (or Monterey Bay), California, Lay & Collie.

Alphabetical list of new taxa

None found at E.

At K: the lower specimen (K000251304) on a sheet ex herb. Hooker, annotated by him with the name 'Tridax galardioides Hook. & Arn.' and 'California, Beechey' – it was annotated 'Type specimen' by J. Clausen in 1936 (the upper specimen on the sheet, *Coulter* 315, is not original material). Note. There are problems over the spelling of the epithet as Hooker & Arnott used '*galardioides*'. When Candolle made the new combination in *Layia* he corrected the spelling of the epithet to '*gaillardioides*', which has been followed since. Hooker & Arnott probably formed the epithet from "*Galardia* Lamarck" (Encycl. 2: 590. 1788), but this was an orthographic variant of *Gaillardia* Foug. (Fougeroux himself spelt the name in two different ways, though not Lamarck's!). Later in the same work (p. 357. 1839) Hooker & Arnott evidently accepted that their epithet was based on a mis-spelling and altered it to follow Candolle. (J. McN.).

≡ ***Layia gaillardioides*** (Hook. & Arn.) DC.

Trifolium chilense Hook. & Arn., Bot. Beechey Voy. 1: 16. 1830. (LEGUMINOSAE).
Original material: 'Conception', Chili, Lay & Collie.

None found at E.

None found at K, though several sheets are incorrectly labelled 'type'. The sheet ex herb. Hooker annotated by him with the name has three collections, of which the right-hand one (K000500697), *Cuming* 115 from Conception, was incorrectly annotated 'holotype' by M.A. Vincent in 1996 (Zohary & Heller cited this as 'isotype' in Gen. Trifolium 535. 1984); the other collections on the sheet are by Tweedie, and Bridges. On a sheet ex herb. Bentham, the left-hand specimen (K000555228) is a duplicate of *Cuming* 115 and was incorrectly annotated 'isotype' by M.A. Vincent; the other collection on the sheet is by Lechler.

Trifolium dichotomum Hook. & Arn., Bot. Beechey Voy. 7: 330. 1838. (LEGUMINOSAE).
Original material: California, Douglas.

None found at E.

Lectotype at K: on a sheet ex herb. Hooker, annotated by him with the name, the right-hand collection annotated by Hooker 'California, Douglas' is original material (the other collections, Brewer, Coulter, are not) – this is not annotated as such, but is doubtless the collection lectotypified (cited as 'type', with an 'iso[lecto]type' at G) by Zohary & Heller (Gen. Trifolium 260. 1984); a sheet ex herb. Bentham, with a printed 'California, Douglas 1833' label, annotated by Bentham with the name and reference to 'Torr. & G. Fl. N. Am. 1. 690 [1840]' is also an isolectotype.

Trifolium grandiflorum Hook. & Arn., Bot. Beechey Voy. 1: 16. 1830, *nom. illeg.*, non Schreb., 1767. (LEGUMINOSAE).
Original material: 'Conception', Chili, Lay & Collie.
   None found at E or K.
= **Trifolium polymorphum** Poir.

Trifolium melananthum Hook. & Arn., Bot. Beechey Voy. 7: 331. 1838. (LEGUMINOSAE).
Original material: California, Douglas.
   None found at E.
   A sheet at K, ex herb. Hooker, with the name in his hand bears four specimens, but it is not clear to how many collections these belong: one of the two central ones was annotated by P.B. Kennedy in March 1911 'I take this to be the type of T. melananthum H & A' but there is nothing to indicate that this is a Douglas Californian collection – the only collector's name written on the sheet by Hooker is 'Gordon' but it is not clear to which (or all?) this refers. However, there is what is undoubtedly original material at K – the right-hand collection on a sheet ex herb. Bentham with a printed 'California, Douglas 1833' label, annotated by Bentham 'Trifolium variegatum β Torr. et Gr., T. melananthum Hook. et Arn.' (the other, Coulter, collection on the sheet is not original material).
= **Trifolium variegatum** Nutt. var. **variegatum**

Triumfetta paniculata Hook. & Arn., Bot. Beechey Voy. 6: 279. 1838. (MALVACEAE).
Original material: Tepic, Mexico, Lay & Collie.
   None at E.
   At K: a sheet ex herb. Hooker (K000381784), annotated by him with the name and 'Mexico, Beechey'; also with the two Linnaea references (see below) and some diagnostic details of the capsules.
Note. Hooker & Arnott also cited 'Triumfetta sp. *Schlecht.* in '*Linn[aea]* 6. p. 424, *et* 11. p. 376'. Although this refers to two collections [*Schiede & Deppe* 1316 and *Schiede* 375], it is by no means certain that Hooker & Arnott saw these, so they should not be considered part of the original material.

Trixis latifolia Hook. & Arn., Bot. Beechey Voy. 7: 300. 1838. (COMPOSITAE).
Original material: Tepic, Mexico, Lay & Collie.
   At E: a sheet ex herb. Arnott, annotated by him with the name and 'Mexico, Beechey, pappus certe biserialis, itaque nec Acourtia, nec Dumerilia'.
   In the Mexico Supplement (p. 437. 1840), based on a later collection, Hooker & Arnott referred this species to *Acourtia formosa* D. Don – at K is a specimen of this later collection (Tepic, *Sinclair* 765) ex herb. Hooker (K000504498) annotated by ?Arnott 'Acourtia formosa Don. Trixis latifolia H & A'.
= **Acourtia fruticosa** (LaLlave & Lex.) B.L. Turner

Alphabetical list of new taxa 179

Trixis obvallata Hook. & Arn., Bot. Beechey Voy. 7: 300, t. 65. 1838. (COMPOSITAE).
Original material: Tepic, Mexico, Lay & Collie.
 At E: a sheet ex herb. Arnott (E00369148), annotated by him with the name and 'Mexico, B[eechey]'.
 At K: a sheet (K000504465) bearing a ticket annotated by Bentham with the name, reference, and 'Acapulco, Beechey' – this was cited by C. Anderson (Mem. New York Bot. Gard. 22: 47. 1972) as 'holotype', but the sheet is not so annotated.
= ***Trixis michuacana*** Lex. var. ***longifolia*** (D. Don) C. Anderson

Trophis fruticosa (Roxb.) Hook. & Arn., Bot. Beechey Voy. 5: 215. 1836. (MORACEAE).
Basionym cited: 'Batis fruticosa. *Roxb. Fl. Ind. 3. p.* 763 [1832]'.
≡ ***Maclura fruticosa*** (Roxb.) Corner

Trophis scandens (Lour.) Hook. & Arn., Bot. Beechey Voy. 5: 214. 1836. (MORACEAE). [China].
Basionym cited: 'Caturus scandens. *Lour.* [Fl. Cochin.] 2. *p.* 751 [this reference is to the 1793 edition; it was first published on p. 612 of the 1790 edition]'.

Tulocarpus Hook. & Arn., Bot. Beechey Voy. 7: 298. 1838. (COMPOSITAE).
= ***Guardiola*** Cerv. ex Bonpl.

Tulocarpus mexicanus Hook. & Arn., Bot. Beechey Voy. 7: 299, t. 63. 1838. (COMPOSITAE).
Original material: Mexico, Lay & Collie.
 At E: a sheet ex herb. Arnott (E00369126), annotated by him with the name, reference, and 'Talisco – Mexico, Beechey'.
 At K: a sheet ex herb. Hooker (K000502060), annotated by him 'Talisco, Beechey' to which is attached a sheet of drawings annotated by Hooker 'Tulocarpus mexicanus H & A cum Ic.'. A second sheet (K000502059), bears another sheet of drawings annotated with the name, the sheet itself annotated by Hooker merely with the generic name – the specimens are larger than those on the first sheet and are therefore probably not original material.
Note. As no locality is given in the protologue, it would normally be taken as the 'default' locality Tepic; but as 'Talisco' is given on the material at E and K, this is presumably correct and Hooker & Arnott presumably merely omitted it by mistake.
≡ ***Guardiola tulocarpus*** A. Gray

Turritis lasiophylla Hook. & Arn., Bot. Beechey Voy. 7: 321. 1838. (Generic placement queried). (CRUCIFERAE).
Original material: California, Douglas.

A sheet of this species at E, ex herb. R.K. Greville (E00369009), does not bear the name and was doubtless distributed before the identification was made; however, it bears the details 'California – Douglas – Hort. Soc. Lon. 1834' and is almost certainly original material.

At K: the left-hand specimen on a sheet ex herb. Hooker annotated by him 'Turritis lasiophylla H. & Arn. (pet. angust.). California, Douglas' (the other, Brewer, specimen is not original material); a sheet ex herb. Bentham with a printed 'California, Douglas 1833' label annotated by Bentham with the name and reference.

Note. Hooker & Arnott were not the only ones to have difficulty placing this species and it has since been placed in no fewer than six other cruciferous genera!

≡ ***Caulanthus lasiophyllus*** (Hook. & Arn.) Payson

Tylophora ovata (Lindl.) Hook. & Arn., Bot. Beechey Voy. 5: 201. 1836. (APOCYNACEAE [ASCLEPIADACEAE]). [China].
Basionym cited: Diplolepis ovata Lindl., 'Hort. Soc. Trans. v. 2, p. 268, [1826]'.
Note. This combination has sometimes (e.g., Fl. China 16: 258. 1995) been attributed to Steudel, 1841.

Urtica affinis Hook. & Arn., Bot. Beechey Voy. 2: 69. 1832. (URTICACEAE).
Original material: 'Society Islands', Lay & Collie.

At E: a sheet ex herb. Arnott (E00279583), annotated by him with the name and 'Tahiti, Beechey' – it was annotated 'isotype' by J. Florence in 1993.

At K: the upper collection on a sheet ex herb. Hooker, annotated by him with the name and 'Coral Isles, Beechey' – it was annotated 'Lecto- of Urtica affinis H & A. Coral Isles = Tuamotu I. but is wrong, must be Society I., this plant don't occur on coral soil' by J. Florence in 1993, but it is not known if this typification has been published (the lower collection, *Barclay* s.n., is not original material).

= ***Laportea interrupta*** (L.) Chew

Urtica grandis Hook. & Arn., Bot. Beechey Voy. 2: 95. 1832. (URTICACEAE).
Original material: Sandwich Islands, Lay & Collie.

None found at E.

At K: a sheet ex herb. Hooker bearing a ticket annotated by Arnott with the name and 'Oahu, Beechey'.

≡ ***Boehmeria grandis*** (Hook. & Arn.) A. Heller

Urtica millettii Hook. & Arn., Bot. Beechey Voy. 5: 214. 1836. (URTICACEAE).
Type: 'one specimen, and that very imperfect ... sent by Mr. Millett [from China]'.

Not found at E or K.
Note. The identity of this plant is unknown, it was merely listed as a dubious species by Weddell, and Hemsley, and is not treated in the recent Flora of China.

Vaccinium ovatum Pursh [var.] β *angustifolium* Hook. & Arn., Bot. Beechey Voy. 8: 362. 1839. (ERICACEAE).
Original material: California, Douglas.

At E: a sheet ex herb. Arnott bearing two specimens (E00369156) annotated by Arnott 'Vaccinium ovalifolium. California, Beechey' – this is the material described on p. 144 under the name *V. ovatum*, where it looks superficially like a new Hooker & Arnott name, but is actually by Pursh. At the bottom right of the same sheet is a sterile specimen (E00369155) labelled by Arnott 'Vacc. ovatum β. California, D[ouglas]', which is a type of var. *angustifolium*.

None found at K.
= ***Vaccinium ovatum*** Pursh

"*Valeriana pterocarpa* Hook. & Arn.", Bot. Beechey Voy. 1: 28. 1830. (VALERIANACEAE).
This is not validly published, as it was only proposed by Hooker & Arnott as a provisional name, should the Beechey specimen 'prove distinct' from *Valeriana crispa* Ruiz & Pav.

Verbena salviifolia Hook. & Arn., Bot. Beechey Voy. 1: 42. 1830 (as '*salviaefolia*'). (VERBENACEAE).
Original material: 'Coquimbo', Chili, Lay & Collie.
None found at E.
At K: Arnott's MS description has been mistakenly attached to a sheet annotated 'Lippia cilensis Schauer' bearing specimens of *Lobb* 453 and a Gillies collection from Mendoza, which are not original material.
≡ ***Aloysia salviifolia*** (Hook. & Arn.) Moldenke

Verbesina hastulata Hook. & Arn., Bot. Beechey Voy. 2: 87. 1832. (COMPOSITAE).
Original material: 'Sandwich Islands', Lay & Collie.
None found at E.
At K: a sheet ex herb. Hooker, annotated by him with the name and 'Oahu, Beechey' – it was annotated 'holotype' by R.C. Gardner in 1976 but it is not known if this typification has been published.
= ***Lipochaeta lobata*** (Gaud.) DC.

Verbesina prostrata Hook. & Arn., Bot. Beechey Voy. 5: 195. 1836, *nom. illeg.*, non L., 1753. (COMPOSITAE).
Original material: Chiefly … about Macao, China, Lay & Collie; material is also mentioned 'from Mr. Millett and Mr. Vachell, (No. 208)' though it is not clear if it was used in the description.

At E: a sheet ex herb. Arnott (E00369129) annotated 'Verbesina prostrata H & A. Canton, [per] Dr Hooker. Wollastonia (DC!) prostrata closely allied to W. asperrima DC. p. 547. n. 2 also from Prof. Henslow – no. 208'. The change in generic name on this sheet perhaps explains the unusual creation of a homonym of a Linnaean name.

None found at K.
= ***Sphagneticola calendulacea*** (L.) Pruski

Verbesina succulenta Hook. & Arn., Bot. Beechey Voy. 2: 87. 1832. (COMPOSITAE).
Original material: 'among volcanic rocks on the shore of the island of Oneeheow', Sandwich Islands, Collie.

Despite a discrepancy in the locality, what appears to be original material at E is a sheet (E00369131) bearing the name and 'Oahu, Beechey' in Arnott's hand; he has (probably later) added the reference 'Lipochaeta succulenta DC. V. p. 611.n. 9'.

The same discrepancy occurs on the sheet at K, ex herb. Hooker, bearing a ticket annotated by Arnott 'Verbesina? succulenta. Oahu, B[eechey]', which was annotated 'holotype' by R.C. Gardner in 1976.
≡ ***Lipochaeta succulenta*** (Hook. & Arn.) DC.

Viburnum chinense Hook. & Arn., Bot. Beechey Voy. 4: 190. 1833. (Generic placement queried). (LABIATAE).
Original material: [China], 'from Mr. Millett'.

At E: a sheet ex herb. Arnott (E00369091), annotated by him '"Viburnum? sinense H & A – mst" Premna integrifolia. Canton – [per] Dr Hooker', which shows that by time this specimen was mounted Arnott had realised the mistake over the generic placement of this species.

None found at K.
= ***Premna serratifolia*** L.

Viburnum nervosum Hook. & Arn., Bot. Beechey Voy. 4: 190. 1833,
nom. illeg., non D. Don, 1825. (CAPRIFOLIACEAE).
Original material: Chiefly … about Macao, China, Lay & Collie.

At E: a sheet ex herb. Arnott (E00369092), annotated by him with the name and 'China, Beechey'.

None at K.
Note. It is surprising that Hooker & Arnott coined this homonym as they were careful about such matters, and *V. nervosum* D. Don is treated in Vol. 4 of Candolle's *Prodromus*, from which they quote. However, as no reference

Alphabetical list of new taxa

is made to Don, and the the two plants are clearly distinct (this one being evergreen), then it has to be taken as an independent name.
= ***Viburnum sempervirens*** K. Koch

Vicia linearifolia Hook. & Arn., Bot. Beechey Voy. 1: 20. 1830. (LEGUMINOSAE).
Original material: 'Conception', Chili, Lay & Collie.
   None found at E.
   At K: a sheet ex herb. Hooker annotated by him with the name and 'Conception, Beechey'.

Vicia nigricans Hook. & Arn., Bot. Beechey Voy. 1: 20. 1830. (LEGUMINOSAE).
Original material: 'Conception', Chili, Lay & Collie.
   None found at E. There are two sheets ex herb. Arnott, annotated by him with the name: one is a later collection (*Cuming* 697), the other a type of *Lathyrus macraei* Hook. & Arn., later redetermined by Arnott as *V. nigricans*.
   At K: the right-hand specimen on a sheet ex herb. Hooker annotated by him with the name and 'Conception, Beechey' (the left-hand, Bridges, collection is not original material).

Vicia parviflora Hook. & Arn., Bot. Beechey Voy. 1: 20. 1830, *nom. illeg.*, non Cav., 1801. (LEGUMINOSAE).
Original material: 'Conception', Chili, Lay & Collie.
   None found at E. Hooker & Arnott (Bot. Misc. 3: 197. 1833) later realised they had made a homonym and renamed this *V. micrantha* Hook. & Arn., citing an additional collection: Valparaiso, *Cuming* 725. Of this latter there are two duplicates at E – one ex herb. Arnott (which bears both names in Arnott's hand), the other ex herb. R.K. Greville.
   At K: the upper specimen on a sheet ex herb. Hooker annotated by him with the name and 'Conception, Beechey' – it has later been annotated by Bentham 'V. micrantha H. et Arn. in Bot. Misc.' (the other specimens, Darwin, Cuming, are not original material).
= ***Vicia linearifolia*** Hook. & Arn.

Viscum chilense Hook. & Arn., Bot. Beechey Voy. 1: 25. 1830, *nom. illeg.*, non Molina, 1810. (VISCACEAE).
Original material: 'Conception', Chili, Lay & Collie.
   None found at E or K.
Note. Not treated in the monograph of *Phoradendron* by J. Kuijt (Syst. Bot. Monogr. 66: 1–643. 2003), but perhaps
?= ***Phoradendron*** sp.

Vitex loureiroi Hook. & Arn., Bot. Beechey Voy. 5: 206, t. 48. 1836 (as '*Loureiri*'), *nom. illeg.* (LABIATAE).
Cited material: 'Canton; *Mr. Millett*'.

At E: two sheets, both ex herb. Arnott – one (E00369195) annotated by him 'Vitex Loureirii H & A ['V. negundo Lour. non Linn.' has been deleted] near V. leucoxylon Linn., Canton, [per] Dr Hooker'; the other (E00369196) annotated by Arnott 'Vitex Loureiri H & A. Canton, ([per] Dr Hooker)'.

No relevant Millett material found at K.

Note. The name 'Cornutia quinata. *Lour. Fl. Coch.* 2. *p.* 470' is cited, without a query, making Hooker & Arnott's superfluous and illegitimate. As usual when they transferred an existing species to a different genus they gave it a new epithet, by conventions operating at the time (later called the 'Kew Rule'). The name should be typified by the type of the Loureiro name.

≡ **Vitex quinata** (Lour.) F.N. Williams

Wedelia cordata Hook. & Arn., Bot. Beechey Voy. 10: 435. 1841. (COMPOSITAE).
Original material: 'Realejo', Mexico [now Nicaragua], Sinclair.

At E: a sheet ex herb. Arnott (E00369132), annotated by him with the name, reference, and 'Realejo, Dr Sinclair'.

W.G. D'Arcy (Phytologia 30: 6. 1975) cited 'Type: Nicaragua, Sinclair (K, not seen)', but as no such specimen can be found, its existence may have been an assumption.

≡ **Viguiera cordata** (Hook. & Arn.) D'Arcy

Wedelia populifolia Hook. & Arn., Bot. Beechey Voy. 10: 435. 1841. (COMPOSITAE).
Original material: 'Realejo', Mexico [now Nicaragua], Sinclair.

None found at E.

Lectotype at K: a sheet (K000502052) ex herb. Hooker bearing a ticket annotated by Arnott with the name and 'Realejo, Sinclair' – although not annotated by T.F. Stuessy, it was cited by him as 'type' in Fieldiana (36: 37. 1973).

= **Baltimora recta** L.

Wedelia strigosa Hook. & Arn., Bot. Beechey Voy. 10: 435. 1841. (COMPOSITAE).
Original material: 'Acapulco', Mexico, Sinclair.

Isolectotype at E: a sheet ex herb. Arnott (E00369130), annotated by him with the name and 'Acapulco, Sinclair'.

Lectotype at K: a sheet ex herb. Hooker (K000487617) bears a ticket annotated by ?Arnott with the name and 'Acapulco', and a ticket annotated with the name by Bentham. On it are three specimens – the left- and right-hand ones are annotated 'lectotype' by J.L. Strother and this typification was published in Syst. Bot. Monogr. (33: 44. 1991) (the central specimen is not a type and was determined by Strother as *W. acapulcensis* Kunth).

Alphabetical list of new taxa 185

Wedelia subflexuosa Hook. & Arn., Bot. Beechey Voy. 10: 435. 1841. (COMPOSITAE).
Original material: 'Realejo', Mexico [now Nicaragua], Sinclair.
At E: a sheet ex herb. Arnott (E00369133), annotated by him with the name, reference, and 'Realejo, Dr. Sinclair, near W. frutescens: stem probably climbing and shrubby at the base'.
None found at K.
= ***Viguiera cordata*** (Hook. & Arn.) D'Arcy

Wigandia californica Hook. & Arn., Bot. Beechey Voy. 8: 364, t. 88. 1839. (Generic placement queried). (BORAGINACEAE).
Original material: California, Douglas.
None found at E.
At K, two sheets. One ex herb. Hooker, annotated with the name and reference in a later hand – the left-hand specimen, annotated by Hooker 'California, Douglas' associated with two tickets of drawings one of which is annotated with the name by Hooker is original material (the right-hand specimen, *Anon* 1864, is not). The other sheet, ex herb. Bentham, bears three collections, the top left-hand one is original material, with a printed 'California, Douglas 1833' label annotated by Bentham 'Eriodyction glutinosum Benth. Bot. Sulph. 36', beneath which Bentham has written 'Wigandia Californica Hook. et Arn. Bot. of Beechey t. 88' on the sheet (the other two collections, *Hooker & Gray* s.n., are not original material).
≡ ***Eriodyction californicum*** (Hook. & Arn.) Torr.

Wollastonia prostrata Hook. & Arn., Bot. Beechey Voy. 6: 265. 1838. (COMPOSITAE). [Loo Choo].
Coined as a new name for 'Verbesina prostrata. H. et A. supra, p. 547 [sic, recte 195]', presumably having realised that they had created a homonym. As the 'basionym' was illegitimate *W. prostrata* should be treated as a new name, rather than a new combination (though based on the same type – for which see above).
At K is a specimen of the additional material cited when creating this new name, a sheet ex herb. Hooker annotated by him with the name *Wollastonia prostrata* and locality 'Loochoo'.
= ***Sphagneticola calendulacea*** (L.) Pruski

Zuccagnia angulata Hook. & Arn., Bot. Beechey Voy. 1: 22. 1830. (Generic placement queried). (LEGUMINOSAE).
Original material: 'Coquimbo', Chili, Lay & Collie.
None found at E.
At K: the top left-hand specimen on a sheet ex herb. Hooker annotated by him with the name and 'Beechey, Coquimbo' (the other collections, *Cuming* 902, *Reed* 53, are not original material).
≡ ***Caesalpinia angulata*** (Hook. & Arn.) Baill.

GYMNOSPERMS

Juniperus taxifolia Hook. & Arn., Bot. Beechey Voy. 6: 271. 1838. (CUPRESSACEAE).
Original material: 'Bonin', Lay & Collie.
The name 'J. virginica. *Thunb. Fl. Jap. p.* 264' is cited as a synonym, which would initially appear to make this name superfluous and illegitimate. But evidently Hooker & Arnott considered Thunberg to have mis-spelt and misapplied an earlier name, as is clear from Thunberg's mis-spelling of the Linnaean name *J. virginiana*, and that what they were doing was providing a new name for *J. virginiana* sensu Thunb., non L. The name *J. taxifolia* has been widely used for a distinct species, e.g. by Farjon (Mon. Cupress. 388. 2005), without noting the nomenclatural problem, and Farjon (l.c., p. 258) referred '*J. virginica* Thunb.' to *J. chinensis* var. *chinensis*. Given this, the name should be typified on the specimens from which Hooker & Arnott made their description.

None found at E.

At K: a sheet ex herb. Hooker (K000089847) annotated on the sheet by Hooker with the name and 'Bonin' – annotated 'holotype' by A. Farjon in 1999.

Juniperus thunbergii Hook. & Arn., Bot. Beechey Voy. 6: 271. 1838. (CUPRESSACEAE).
Original material: 'Loo Choo', Lay & Collie.
The synonym 'J. Barbadensis. [sensu] *Thunb. Fl. Jap. p.* 264, [i.e. non L.]' is cited as a synonym. But here the situation is clearer than in *J. taxifolia*, as Thunberg spelt the Linnaean name correctly, and Hooker & Arnott were clearly establishing a new species for what they considered to be Thunberg's misapplication of a Linnaean name (which Farjon referred to *J. chinensis* var. *chinensis*). Hence it makes sense to typify their name on the specimens from which they made their description (of which none can be found at E or K) rather than on Thunberg material.
= ***Juniperus chinensis*** L. var. ***chinensis***

Pinus sinclairii Hook. & Arn., Bot. Beechey Voy. 9: 392, t. 93. 1840. (PINACEAE).
Original material: 'hills from Monterrey to Carmelo and to Punto Pinos. *Dr Sinclair* of H.M.S. Sulphur'.

None found at E.

At K: a sheet ex herb. Hooker (K000287566) bearing two specimens (and a packet of unrelated material) – it is annotated on the sheet by Hooker 'Dr Sinclair'; and in another hand (which might be copied from the protolgue, rather than original data) – 'Covers the hills from Monterey …'. The sheet was annotated 'holotype' by A. Farjon in 2006.
= ***Pinus radiata*** D. Don var. ***radiata***

4.2 CRYPTOGAMS

Note. Beechey specimens were not searched for at K.

Pteridophytes
Antrophyum plantagineum (Cav.) Kaulf. [var.] β *lessonii* (Bory) Hook. & Arn., Bot. Beechey Voy. 2: 74. 1832 (as '*Lessoni*'). (VITTARIACEAE). ['Society Islands'].
Basionym cited 'A[ntrophyum] Lessoni. *Bory in Duperrey Voy. p.* 255. *t.* 28. *f.* 2. [1828]'.
= ***Antrophyum plantagineum*** (Cav.) Kaulf.

Aspidium molle Sw. [var.] γ *paucisorum* Hook. & Arn., Bot. Beechey Voy. 6: 256. 1838. (DRYOPTERIDACEAE).
Original material: not entirely clear, especially bearing in mind the footnote on p. 201, but presumably including 'several specimens [?Chinese] gathered by Messrs. Lay and Collie ... [and] a Chinese specimen in our herbarium from Prof. Lindley'.
   None found at E.
?= ***Dryopteris parasitica*** (L.) Kuntze

Aspidium subintegerrimum Hook. & Arn., Bot. Beechey Voy. 2: 52. 1832. (DRYOPTERIDACEAE).
Original material: 'Conception', Chili, Lay & Collie.
   None found at E.
Note. The combination in *Polystichum* was first made by R. Rodríguez Rios (Gayana 44: 48. 1987), who lectotypified the name citing '*Typus*: "Conception, Chile" (BM, Fototypus!)'. It was 'remade' two years later by D.S. Barrington (Ann. Missouri Bot. Garden 76: 373. 1989), who cited 'holotype, K' (though without explicitly stating that he had seen such a specimen).
≡ ***Polystichum subintegerrimum*** (Hook. & Arn.) R. Rodr.

Asplenium acuminatum Hook. & Arn., Bot. Beechey Voy. 3: 106. 1832. (ASPLENIACEAE).
Original material: Sandwich Islands, Lay & Collie.
   At E: a sheet (E00348215) ex herb. Arnott, annotated by him with the name and 'Oahu – Beechey'.

Asplenium diplazioides Hook. & Arn., Bot. Beechey Voy. 3: 107. 1832. (WOODSIACEAE).
Original material: Sandwich Islands, Lay & Collie.
   At E: two sheets (E00348211, E00348211) ex herb. Arnott annotated by him with the name and 'Oahu, Beechey'; one sheet (E00348210) ex herb.

Trinity College Glasgow, annotated by William Gourlie with the name and 'Oahu, [per] Dr Walker Arnott'.
≡ **Diplazium arnottii** Brack.

Asplenium subalatum Hook. & Arn., Bot. Beechey Voy. 7: 312, t. 71. 1838. (ASPLENIACEAE).
Original material: Tepic, Mexico, Lay & Collie.
    None found at E.
= **Asplenium formosum** Willd.

Cheilanthes dissecta Hook. & Arn., Bot. Beechey Voy. 2: 75. 1832. (DENNSTAEDTIACEAE).
Original material: Society Islands, Lay & Collie.
    At E: a sheet (E00348216) ex herb. Arnott annotated by him with the name and 'Tahiti, Beechey'.
= **Hypolepis tenuifolia** (G. Forst.) Bernh.

Davallia macraeana Hook. & Arn., Bot. Beechey Voy. 3: 108. 1832. (LINDSAEACEAE).
Original material: Sandwich Islands, Lay & Collie.
    At E: a sheet (E00348218) ex herb. Arnott, annotated by him with the name and 'Oahu, Beechey' (and also later determinations by Arnott as *Odontolma Hookeri* J. Sm., and *Davallia Boryana* Presl).
≡ **Lindsaea repens** (Bory) Thw. var. **macraeana** (Hook. & Arn.) C. Chr.

Hymenophyllum lanceolatum Hook. & Arn., Bot. Beechey Voy. 3: 109. 1832. (HYMENOPHYLLACEAE).
Original material: Sandwich Islands, Lay & Collie.
    At E, two sheets: one ex herb. Arnott bearing two specimens, the lower (E00348230) is original material, annotated by Arnott with the name and 'Oahu, Beechey' (the upper specimen 'Islands of the Pacific [per] Sir W. Hooker' is not original material); a remounted sheet (E00348190), bearing a ticket annotated by Arnott with the name and 'Oahu, B[eechey]'.
Note. Sometimes placed in the genus *Sphaerocionium* as *S. lanceolatum* (Hook. & Arn.) Copel.

Hymenophyllum obtusum Hook. & Arn., Bot. Beechey Voy. 3: 109. 1832. (HYMENOPHYLLACEAE).
Original material: Sandwich Islands, Lay & Collie.
    At E, two sheets: one (E00348231) ex herb. Arnott, annotated by him with the name and 'Oahu, Beechey'; a remounted sheet (E00348189), bearing a ticket annotated by Arnott with the name and 'Oahu, B[eechey]'.
Note. Sometimes placed in the genus *Sphaerocionium* as *S. obtusum* (Hook. & Arn.) Copel.

Alphabetical list of new taxa

Lindsaea variabilis Hook. & Arn., Bot. Beechey Voy. 6: 257, t. 52. 1838. (LINDSAEACEAE).
Original material: 'Macao [China]; *Millett*'.
 At E: a sheet (E00348232) ex herb. Arnott, annotated by him with the name and 'Canton: Beechey [i.e., Lay & Collie]', and, later, with the synonyms 'Schizoloma heterophylla J. Sm.' and 'Lindsaea heterophylla Dry.' is possibly original material, despite the discrepancy over the locality and collector between the sheet and the protologue.
= **Schizoloma heterophyllum** (Dryand.) J. Sm.

Lomaria longifolia Hook. & Arn., Bot. Beechey Voy. 6: 257. 1838, *nom. illeg.*, non Kaulf., 1824.
Original material: [not stated, but from the footnote on p. 201, not Beechey material, but a specimen in herb. Hooker or Arnott, possibly Millett or Vachell material from Canton].
 None found at E.

Lycopodium phyllanthum Hook. & Arn., Bot. Beechey Voy. 3: 102. 1832. (LYCOPODIACEAE).
Original material: Sandwich Islands, Lay & Collie.
 None found at E.
≡ **Huperzia phyllantha** (Hook. & Arn.) Holub

Nephrodium apiifolium Hook. & Arn., Bot. Beechey Voy. 3: 105. 1832 (as '*apifolium*'). (TECTARIACEAE).
Original material: Sandwich Islands, Lay & Collie.
 None found at E.
Note. Two names are cited in synonymy under this name: 'Aspidium apifolium? Schkuhr, Fil. t. 56. b', and 'Aspidium sinuatum. [sensu] Gaud. in Freyc. Voy. p. 343 (non Labill.)'. The name is clearly not a superfluous one for the latter. The expression of doubt over the former means that it cannot be taken as a new combination based on the Schkuhr name. Despite Hooker & Arnott's statement, after discussing differences in colour, that 'in all other respects, it seems entirely to accord with the plant, whence we have been induced to adopt that name', the name is attributed to Hooker & Arnott in the index and should be accepted as a new species, which could be typified either on Beechey or Gaudichaud material.
= **Tectaria gaudichaudii** (Mett.) Maxon

Nephrodium dubrueilianum (Gaud.) Hook. & Arn., Bot. Beechey Voy. 3: 105. 1832. (THELYPTERIDACEAE). [Sandwich Islands].
Basionym cited: 'Polystichum Dubrueilianum. *Gaud. in Freyc. Voy. p.* 333. *t.* 9 [1830]'.

Note. Although *Aspidium cyatheoides* Kaulf. is also cited it is with a query, so does not render the new combination superfluous.
= **Christella cyatheoides** (Kaulf.) Holttum

Nephrodium squamigerum Hook. & Arn., Bot. Beechey Voy. 3: 106. 1832. (DRYOPTERIDACEAE).
Original material: Sandwich Islands, Lay & Collie.
　At E: a sheet (E00348213) ex herb. Arnott, annotated by him with the name and 'Oahu – Beechey'.
≡ **Ctenitis squamigera** (Hook. & Arn.) Copel.

Niphobolus macrocarpus Hook. & Arn., Bot. Beechey Voy. 2: 74, t. 18. 1832. (POLYPODIACEAE).
Original material: 'Society Islands', Lay & Collie.
　At E: a sheet (E00348214) ex herb. Arnott, annotated by him with the name and 'Tahiti – Beechey'.
= **Cyclophorus angustatus** (Sw.) Desv.

Notholaena pilosa Hook. & Arn., Bot. Beechey Voy. 2: 74. 1832 (as '*Notochlaena*'). (SINOPTERIDACEAE).
Original material: Society Islands, Lay & Collie.
　At E: a sheet ex herb. Arnott bears two collections, annotated by him with the name – the lower one (E00348192), annotated by Arnott 'Tahiti, Beechey' is original material (the upper, *Mathews* 23, is not). At E is a sheet ex herb. Menzies annotated 'Otaheite, Mr Collie', and by Menzies only with the generic name – this has much broader pinnules than the Arnott specimen, and is probably not original material.
= **Notholaena hirsuta** (Poir.) Desv.

Ophioglossum tuberosum Hook. & Arn., Bot. Beechey Voy. 2: 53. 1832. (OPHIOGLOSSACEAE).
Original material: 'Conception', Chili, Lay & Collie.
　At E: a sheet ex herb. Arnott (E00348194), annotated by him with the name and 'an var. O. bulbosi?', and the locality 'Conception, Beechey'.
= **Ophioglossum crotalophoroides** Walter

Polypodium adenophorus Hook. & Arn., Bot. Beechey Voy. 3: 104, t. 22. 1832, *nom. illeg.* (*Adenophorus pinnatifidus* Gaud. cited as synonym). (POLYPODIACEAE).
Cited material: Sandwich Islands, Lay & Collie.
　At E: a sheet (E00348223) ex herb. Arnott, annotated by him with the name and 'Oahu – Beechey'.
≡ **Adenophorus pinnatifidus** Gaud.

Alphabetical list of new taxa

Polypodium crinale Hook. & Arn., Bot. Beechey Voy. 3: 105. 1832. (DRYOPTERIDACEAE).
Original material: Sandwich Islands, Lay & Collie.
  At E: a sheet (E00348220) ex herb. Arnott, annotated by him with the name and 'Oahu, Beechey'.
≡ **Dryopteris crinalis** (Hook. & Arn.) C. Chr.

Polypodium intermedium Hook. & Arn., Bot. Beechey Voy. 9: 405. 1840, *nom. illeg.*, non Colla, 1836. (POLYPODIACEAE).
Original material: 'San Francisco', California, Sinclair.
  None found at E.
= **Polypodium californicum** Kaulf.

Polypodium polycarpon Hook. & Arn., Bot. Beechey Voy. 3: 104. 1832. (THELYPTERIDACEAE).
Original material: Sandwich Islands, Lay & Collie.
  None found at E.
= **Pneumatopteris sandwicensis** (Brack.) Holttum

Polypodium sandwicense Hook. & Arn., Bot. Beechey Voy. 3: 104. 1832. (DRYOPTERIDACEAE).
Original material: Sandwich Islands, Lay & Collie.
  At E: a sheet (E00348221) ex herb. Arnott, annotated by him with the name and 'Oahu, Beechey'.
≡ **Dryopteris sandwicensis** (Hook. & Arn.) C. Chr.

Polypodium setigerum Hook. & Arn., Bot. Beechey Voy. 3: 103, t. 21A. 1832. (GRAMMITIDACEAE).
Original material: Sandwich Islands, Lay & Collie.
  At E: a sheet (E00348222) ex herb. Arnott, annotated by him with the name and 'Oahu – Beechey'.
= **Grammitis hookeri** (Brack.) Copel.

Polypodium subtriphyllum Hook. & Arn., Bot. Beechey Voy. 6: 256, t. 50. 1838. (TECTARIACEAE).
Original material: 'Macao [China]; *Vachell*'.
  None found at E.
≡ **Tectaria subtriphylla** (Hook. & Arn.) Copel.

Polypodium unidentatum Hook. & Arn., Bot. Beechey Voy. 3: 105. 1832. (DRYOPTERIDACEAE).
Original material: Sandwich Islands, Lay & Collie.
  At E: a sheet (E00348219) ex herb. Arnott, annotated by him with the name and 'Oahu – Beechey'.

≡ ***Dryopteris unidentata*** (Hook. & Arn.) C. Chr.

Sadleria pallida Hook. & Arn., Bot. Beechey Voy. 2: 75. 1832. (BLECHNACEAE).
Original material: as from Society Islands, Lay & Collie – actually from Hawaii, see below.

Lectotype at E: the lower specimen (E00268453) on a sheet ex herb. Arnott annotated by him with the name, originally annotated by Arnott 'Oahu, Beechey', which he has later crossed out and replaced with 'Tahiti'. This was apparently incorrect – the specimen was annotated 'lectotype' by D.D. Palmer and when he published this (Pacific Science 51: 298. 1997) he gave the locality as 'Oahu'. (The upper specimen (E00348191) is annotated 'Oahu, Beechey', it has been re-determined as *S. cyatheoides* Kaulf. and is not a type).

Woodwardia prolifera Hook. & Arn., Bot. Beechey Voy. 6: 275, t. 56 [as 'LVII']. 1838. (BLECHNACEAE).
Original material: 'Loo Choo', Lay & Collie.

At E: a sheet ex herb. Arnott (E00290161), annotated by him with the name and 'Loochoo, Beechey'.
Note. Although the name '*W. orientalis?* Sw, Syn. Fil. p. 117 *et* 315' is cited, it is queried and the authors explicitly state that 'it can scarcely be the *W. orientalis* of Swartz', so this is not a superfluous name.
= ***Woodwardia orientalis*** Sw.

ALGAE (PHAEOPHYTA)
Dictyota spinulosa Hook. & Arn., Bot. Beechey Voy. 6: 275. 1838.
Original material: 'Loo Choo', Lay & Collie.
None found at E.
Note. O. De Clerck (Op. Bot. Belgica 13: 177. 2003) cited 'lectotype: TCD s.n.' – however he incorrectly attributed the name to 'Harvey in Hooker & Arnott' (as did de Toni in Syllog. Algarum 3: 270. 1895). There is nothing in the protologue, or anywhere else in the book, to say that W.H. Harvey had any involvement in the work (which is not to say that he did not), and the name is to be attributed to Hooker & Arnott, as it was in the index.

ALGAE (CHLOROPHYTA)
Mycinema flava Hook. & Arn., Bot. Beechey Voy. 2: 54. 1832. (Generic placement queried).
Original material: 'Conception; on the dead leaves of *Quadria heterophylla*', Chili, Lay & Collie.
None found at E.
≡ ***Trentopohlia flava*** (Hook. & Arn.) De Toni

Alphabetical list of new taxa

BRYOPHYTES

Hypnum fuscescens Hook. & Arn., Bot. Beechey Voy. 2: 76, t. 19. 1832. (HYPNACEAE).
Original material: Society Islands, Lay & Collie.
 At E: a sheet from Arnott's herbarium annotated by him 'Hypnum fuscescens H. & Arn. in Bot. Beech. Voy. t. 19 Tahiti (Beechey)'; there is also a duplicate with a slip on the packet labelled in Arnott's hand 'Hyp. fuscescens H & A. Tahiti, Beechey'.
= ***Vesicularia inflectens*** (Brid.) C. Muell.

[*Hypnum laricinum* Wilson, in Hooker & Arnott, Bot. Beechey Voy. 3: 120. 1832, *nom. illeg.*, non Hook., 1818. (HELODIACEAE).
Original material: Avatschka Bay, Kamtschatka, Lay & Collie; specimens in Hooker/Arnott's herbarium labelled 'H. abietinum *Sw.* ... non *Hedw.*'; fruiting material from Cheshire.
 At E: a packet with a label annotated in Arnott's hand 'Hyp. laricinum H & A, in Bot. Beech. Voy. Avatschka bay, Kamtschatka (Beechey)'.
Note. This name has sometimes been taken to have been published by Wilson in 1833, but it was published here (i.e., the previous year) by Hooker & Arnott, though credited by them to Wilson.
= ***Helodium blandowii*** (Web. & Mohr) Warnst.].

Hypnum sandvicense Hook. & Arn., Bot. Beechey Voy. 3: 109. 1832. (HYPNACEAE).
Original material: Sandwich Islands, Lay & Collie.
 At E: a sheet annotated by Arnott 'Hypnum sandwichense [sic] H & A. Oahu, Beechey'.
≡ ***Ectropothecium sandvicense*** (Hook. & Arn.) Mitt.

Jungermannia conchifolia Hook. & Arn., Bot. Beechey Voy. 3: 110, t. 23. 1832. (PLEUROZIACEAE).
Original material: Sandwich Islands, Lay & Collie.
 None found at E.
Note. B.M. Thiers (Bryologist 96: 526. 1993) lectotypified this name, citing 'holotype' at BM, with iso[lecto]types at FH, H, NY, PC.
≡ ***Pleurozia conchifolia*** (Hook. & Arn.) Aust. var. ***conchifolia***

Leptostomum splachnoideum Hook. & Arn., Bot. Beechey Voy. 2: 53. 1832. (Generic placement queried). (LEPTOSTOMATACEAE).
Original material: 'Conception', Chili, Lay & Collie.
 At E: a sheet annotated by Arnott 'Leptostomum splachnoideum H & A. Conception – Beechey. Schu. Supp. 4. t. 305'.

Neckera californica Hook. & Arn., Bot. Beechey Voy. 4: 162. 1833. (LEPTODONTACEAE).
Original material: San Francisco (or Monterey Bay), California, Lay & Collie.
 At E: a packet ex herb. G.J. Lyon, with a ticket annotated by Lyon 'H. 2119 Neckera californica. California, Beechy. G.J. Lyon 1846'.
≡ ***Alsia californica*** (Hook. & Arn.) Sull.

Polytrichum canaliculatum Hook. & Arn., Bot. Beechey Voy. 2: 54. 1832. (POLYTRICHACEAE).
Original material: 'Conception', Chili, Lay & Collie.
 At E: a (tiny) packet with a ticket annotated by Arnott 'Polytrichum canaliculatum H & A, Schwaegr. Supp. 4. t. 324. Conception, Beechey'.
≡ ***Oligotrichum canaliculatum*** (Hook. & Arn.) Mitt.

FUNGI (ASCOMYCOTA)
Dothidea granulosa Hook. & Arn., Bot. Beechey Voy. 2: 54. 1832.
Original material: 'Valparaiso; on the lower side of the leaves of *Eugenia Temu*', Chili, Lay & Collie.
 At E: a sheet with two leaves in a packet labelled in a Continental hand 'Dothidea granulata Tribus II. Erumpentes in Systema friesii. Capt. Beechey'.
Note. This name has sometimes been attributed to Klotzsch in Gay Fl. Chil. 7: 450. 1850.
≡ ***Polystomella granulosa*** (Hook & Arn.) Theiss. & Syd.

LICHENS
Collema turneri Hook. & Arn., Bot. Beechey Voy. 2: 77. 1832.
Original material: Society Islands, Lay & Collie.
 At E: a packet bearing a label in Arnott's hand 'Collema Turneri H & A. Tahiti, Beechey'.
≡ ***Leptogium phyllocarpum*** var. ***turneri*** (Hook. & Arn.) Zahlbr.

Parmelia calicarpa Hook. & Arn., Bot. Beechey Voy. 2: 77. 1832.
Original material: Society Islands, Lay & Collie.
 At E: a packet annotated by Arnott 'Parmelia calicarpa H & A. Taiti, Beechey'.
= ***Leptogium*** sp.

APPENDIX I

Collectors of new taxa described by Hooker & Arnott in *The Botany of Captain Beechey's Voyage*

In addition to the major collections of Lay & Collie, Millett, Vachell, Douglas, Sinclair and McLeod described in the Introduction, the *Botany* treats smaller amounts of material from a number of other collectors. From North America: T. Nuttall, J. Scouler, M. Gairdner, T. Drummond; from Mexico: G. Andrieux, W. Bates, C.T. Hartweg; from China: Dr J. Livingstone; from the Pacific: J. Macrae, A. Menzies; from Chile: A. Cruckshanks, T. Bridges, J. Gillies; from Mauritius: C. Telfair.

Andrieux, G. (fl. 1834)
Almost nothing is known of Andrieux, who collected in Mexico in the States of Oaxaca, Puebla and Mexico. He sent sets of specimens to W.J. Hooker and J. Gay (both now at K) and to Benjamin Delessert (now at G).

Bates, W. (fl. ?1830s)
Nothing is known about this collector, whose Mexican collections are in Hooker's herbarium (K) and also at Cambridge (CGE).

Bridges, Thomas (1807–1865)
Bridges was the son-in-law of Hugh Cuming the noted collector of plants and shells. Some of Bridges's Chilean collections are described in the *Botany of Captain Beechey's Voyage* (he also collected in Peru, Bolivia and California).

Collie, Alexander (1793–1835)
See Introduction.

Cruckshanks, Alexander (fl. 1820s to 1850s)
Little is known of Cruckshanks (sometimes spelled 'Cruickshanks'), a correspondent of Hooker, who worked in Chile and Peru.

Douglas, David (1799–1834)
See Introduction.

Drummond, Thomas (c. 1790–1835)
Scottish horticulturist and important North American collector. While naturalist on one of the Franklin expeditions he met Douglas in Saskatchewan in 1827, and they travelled home together from Douglas's second expedition. Drummond comes into the *Botany of Captain Beechey's Voyage* only incidentally, under *Sapindus drummondii*, through its connection with a related Mexican taxon. This was from Drummond's last expedition made for the Glasgow Botanic Garden, on which he collected extensively in Texas before travelling to Cuba (where he met his death).

Gairdner, Dr Meredith (1800–37)
Pupil of Hooker and Hudson's Bay Company surgeon; a friend of David Douglas, who collected in the Columbia River region. His specimens were mostly described in Hooker's *Flora Boreali-Americana*, and he comes into the *Botany of Captain Beechey's Voyage* only because *Atenia gairdneri* was also collected in California.

Gillies, Dr John (1792–1834)
Orcadian naval surgeon, who collected extensively in Chile and Argentina. After five years at Mendoza, he returned, due to ill health, to Edinburgh where he worked on his collections and wrote for the *Encyclopaedia Britannica*. His somewhat prickly disposition led to difficulties with both Hooker and Arnott. Despite this they published extensively on Gillies's extremely rich botanical collections (that in the *Botany of Captain Beechey's Voyage* is more or less incidental) and there are important sets of specimens in both Hooker's and Arnott's herbaria, though those at E have been generally overlooked. See Dawe (1988) for further details on the life of this little-known but interesting man.

Hartweg, Carl Theodor (1812–1871)
German plant collector and horticulturist who collected for the Horticultural Society of London in Mexico 1836–9; these collections were published by Bentham as *Plantas Hartwegianas* (1839–57), but one was used in the description of *Bouvardia scabra* in the *Botany of Captain Beechey's Voyage*. (Hartweg's later collections for the Horticultural Society were from California, Guatemala, Ecuador, Peru, Jamaica and Madeira).

Lay, George Tradescant (1799–1845)
See Introduction.

Livingstone, Dr John (?–1829)
East India Company surgeon who worked in China. Two species (*Photinia serrulata*, *Cupania mollissima*) described in the *Botany of Captain Beechey's Voyage* were based partly on his material.

Appendix I

Macrae, James (?–1830)
Horticulturist and plant collector who died in Ceylon, where he was superintendent of botanic gardens. Collected for the Horticultural Society of London in Chile, Peru, Brazil, and the Galapagos and Sandwich Islands. Macrae specimens from Chile and Hawaii are mentioned in the discussions of several species in the *Botany of Captain Beechey's Voyage*, and were certainly used in the descriptions of *Lathyrus macraei*, *Metrosideros macropus* and *Kadua centranthoides*.

McLeod, John (fl. 1821–1842)
See Introduction.

Menzies, Archibald (1754–1842)
Scottish naval surgeon who started out as a gardener at RBGE (to which he later left his herbarium), under John Hope. Most famously he was surgeon-naturalist on Vancouver's circumnavigation on H.M.S. *Discovery*, 1791–4. Specimens collected in California and Hawaii on this voyage were used in the *Botany of Captain Beechey's Voyage* as the basis of descriptions of *Pyrrrocoma menziesii*, *Cyrtandra menziesii* and *Achyranthes velutina*; others were mentioned in the discussions of several other taxa.

Millett, Charles (fl. 1820s, 1830s)
See Introduction.

Nuttall, Thomas (1786–1859)
Born in Yorkshire, Nuttall went to America in 1808; from 1822 to 1834 he was Professor of Botany at Harvard, before returning to Britain in 1842. He travelled extensively in the US 1811–34, and made important collections of which Hooker had many duplicates (with MS names): some were used in the *Botany of Captain Beechey's Voyage* and published first there, though were being worked on simultaneously in America by Torrey and Gray.

Scouler, Dr John (1804–1871)
Scottish botanist and surgeon, a medical pupil of Hooker's at Glasgow. He was surgeon-naturalist on an expedition to the Columbia River in 1824/5; collections from this expedition were used in the Beechey work. (In 1825 he was surgeon on the *William and Ann*, the ship that took Douglas to his second American expedition. Scouler later became Professor of Natural History at the Glasgow College of Science & Technology, and Professor of Geology, Botany & Zoology to the Royal Dublin Society).

Sinclair, Dr Andrew (1794–1861)
Paisley-born naval surgeon, who graduated MD from Edinburgh in 1818. Surgeon on H.M.S. *Sulphur* 1835–9 under Beechey then Belcher. After this

he was appointed to a convict ship and botanised with J.D. Hooker in New Zealand in 1841, where he returned as private secretary to Robert Fitzroy in 1843, becoming Colonial Secretary there 1844–56. He retired to Britain, but in 1858 returned to New Zealand to collect plants, where he was drowned in 1861.

Telfair, Charles (1778–1833)
Irish-born surgeon who was Supervisor of the Mauritius Botanic Garden 1826–9, whence he sent specimens to Hooker. One such, along with Lay & Collie material from China, was used when describing *Lonicera telfairii*.

Tolmie, Dr William Fraser (1812–1886)
A Scottish medical pupil of Hooker's at Glasgow, who went to Fort Vancouver (Washington State, on the Columbia River opposite Portland) as medical officer in 1832, where he met Douglas. Most of Tolmie's collections were described by Hooker in *Flora Boreali-Americana*, and those attributed to him in the 'California Supplement' of the Beechey work were nearly all collected by John McLeod (see above); however *Calochortus tolmiei* described in this work was collected by Tolmie on the Wallamet River.

Vachell, the Rev. George Harvey (1799–?)
See Introduction.

APPENDIX II
Details of collecting localities

The co-ordinates given below are taken from 'Google Earth', and are intended only as <u>approximate</u> locations, the precise collecting localities being unknown. The dates are taken from Beechey's 'Narrative', which seem likely to be more accurate than the slightly different ones he gave Hooker (KDC 44 f. 19), published by Hooker & Arnott (pp i–ii).

Acapulco, Guerrero State, Mexico. 16°51'N, 99°53'W. Lay/Collie, 12 – 18 iii 1828; Sinclair, i 1838.

Awtaschka [= Avacha] Bay, see Petropaulski.

Bonin (Archbishop's) Islands = Ogasawara Gunto, Japan. Lay/Collie, 9 – 16 vi 1827.
Peel Island = Chichijima 27°04'N, 142°12'E.

Bow Island = Hao or Haorangi Island, French Polynesia. 18°05'S, 140°57'W. Lay/Collie, 14 – 20 ii 1826.

Conception = Concepción, Concepción Province, Chile. 36°50'S, 73°00'W. Lay/Collie, 8 – 20 x 1825.

Coquimbo, Elqui Province, Chile. 29°59'S, 71°20'W. Lay/Collie, 23 v – 3 vi 1828.

Ducie's Island, Pitcairn Islands. 24°40'S, 124°47'W. Lay/Collie, 28 xi 1825.

Easter Island. 27°07'S, 109°22'W. Lay/Collie, 16 xi 1825.

Elizabeth Island = Henderson Island, Pitcairn Islands. 24°20'S, 128°20'W. Lay/Collie, 3 xii 1825.

Gambier Islands = Iles Gambier or Mangareva Group, French Polynesia. 23°09'S, 134°58'W. Lay/Collie, 29 xii 1825 – 13 i 1826.

Appendix II

Great (= Celilo) Falls of the Columbia, Oregon. 45°38'N, 120°58'W. D. Douglas.

Kotzebue Sound, Alaska (from a base on Chamisso Island, 66°13'N, 161°49'W, excursions were made, both summers, northwards up the coast as far as Point Barrow); Collie, 25 vii – 14 x 1826; Lay/Collie, 4 viii – 5 x 1827.

Loo-Choo = Ryu Kyu Islands, Japan (the *Blossom* anchored at 'Napa-kiang' = Naha, Okinawa. 26°13'N, 127°40'W). Lay/Collie, 17–26 v 1827.

Macao = Macau, Macau Special Administrative Region, China. 22°10'N, 113°33'E.
Lay/Collie, 11 – 30 iv 1827.

Monterey, Monterey County, California. 36°36'N, 121°53'W. Collie 12 – 14 xi 1826, 1 – 5 i 1827; Lay/Collie, 29 x – 17 xi 1827.

Otaheite = Tahiti, Society Islands, French Polynesia. 17°38'S, 149°27'W. Lay/Collie, 18 iii – 26 iv 1826.

Petropaulski = Petrapavlovsk-Kamchatsky, Kamchatka Krai, Russia. 53°03'N, 158°36'E. Collie, 28 vi – 5 vii 1826; Lay/Collie, 3–18 vii 1827.

Pitcairn Island. 25°04'S, 130°04'W. Lay/Collie, 4 – 21 xii 1825.

[El] Realejo, Chinandega Department, Nicaragua. 12°32'N, 87°10'W. Sinclair, ii 1838.

San Blas, Nayarit State, Mexico. 21°32'N, 105°17'W. Lay/Collie, 20 xii 1827 – 8 iii 1828. Sinclair, xii 1837.

San Francisco, California. 37°48'N, 122°29'W. Collie, 7 xi – 28 xii 1826; Lay/Collie 18 xi – 3 xii 1827.

Sandwich Islands = Hawaii
Oahu. 21°16'N, 157°49'W. Lay/Collie, 20 – 31 v 1826; Lay/Collie, 26 i – 1 iii 1827.
Oneeheow = Ni'ihau. 21°54'N, 160°10'W. Collie, 1 – 2 vi 1826.

'Snake Country' – used generally, presumably refers to the plains of the Snake River, southern Idaho. John McLeod. Summer 1837.
The following more specific localities are also used (the co-ordinates are very approximate):
American Falls, Snake River, Idaho. 42°46'N, 112°50'W.

Appendix II

'Bamcoch' = Bannock River, Idaho. 42°39'N, 112°36'W.
Blackfoot River, Idaho. 43°10'N, 112°19'W.
Blue Mountains, Oregon. 45°06'N, 118°12'W.
Burnt River, Oregon. 44°30'N, 118°05'W.
between Burnt and Malheur Rivers, Oregon. 44°13'N, 117°31'W.
Green River (+ Pine Creek), Wyoming. 42°45'N, 110°01'W.
between Henry's and Smith's Rivers, Wyoming. 42°04'N, 110°31'W.
Salmon Falls, Idaho. 42°45'N, 114°52'W.
Snake Fort (near confluence of Reed's [= Boisé] River with Snake River), Oregon/Idaho. 43°48'N, 117°01'W.

'Talisco' = Xalisco, Nayarit State, Mexico, a town 6.4 km SW of Tepic. 21°30'N, 104°54'W. Lay/Collie, xii 1827.

Tepic, Nayarit State, Mexico. 21°30'N, 104°54'W. Lay/Collie, xii 1827. Sinclair, xii 1837.

Valparaiso, Chile. 33°02'S, 71°36'W. Lay/Collie, 27 – 29 x 1825; 29 iv – 20 v 1828.

Walamet = Willamette River, Oregon. 44°41'N, 122°58'W. W.F. Tolmie. Date unknown.

Whitsunday Island = Pinaki, Tuamotu group, French Polynesia. 19°23'S, 138°40'W. Lay/Collie, 23 i 1826.

APPENDIX III

Original drawings by W.J. Hooker for *The Botany of Captain Beechey's Voyage*

Of the hundred drawings, 21 have been located during the research for this project: 19 at Kew, two at Edinburgh. Those at Kew are not a random selection (nine out of ten from part 4, but none from part 5 or any from parts 8 to 10), suggesting that most of them never were in Hooker's collection. The single fern drawing is annotated 'Ex Bibl. R.T. Lowe', and the two at Edinburgh are from the collection of Hugh Cleghorn (at Edinburgh there are also copies made from the engravings by his Indian artists of the sedge plates 27 (split into two) and 28). It would therefore appear that the drawings were not all given back to Hooker by the Admiralty (except perhaps those of part 4), and, as they had paid for them, there was no reason why they should. It is possible that the Admiralty, as they had with some of the specimens presented some of the drawings 'to private individuals'. On the other hand, Cleghorn is known to have bought botanical plates from William Pamplin, so it is possible that the original drawings somehow got into the London book trade, and that Hooker only subsequently acquired ones in which he was particularly interested. Being modest, uncoloured, works, their appeal would have been strictly limited and it seems doubtful if more have survived and await discovery in other collections. Enquiries at the Natural History Museum have proved negative, though this (or rather the British Museum, before the natural history collections were separated) seemed a likely place to which the Admiralty might have given material.

The drawings are of great delicacy (FIG. 10), in pencil, with pinkish-sepia wash added by Hooker to show the engraver, Joseph Swan, where he was to add shading, which he did by means of parallel engraved lines (FIG. 11). Hooker also used this technique in the drawings he made for his *Flora Boreali-Americana* and the *Botanical Miscellany*. In this case Hooker has also added a pencil 'box' around most drawings, and annotated two with notes on how the drawing was to be positioned with respect to the caption. Unusually the engravings are in the same orientation as the original drawings (rather than reversed) – suggesting that some sort of transfer paper was used to trace the drawing and reverse it onto the plate prior to engraving.

CATALOGUE

Plate 6. *Monnina linearifolia* Ruiz & Pavon
Hooker annotations: Tab. VI. 1. 2. 3. 4. 5. 6. 7. 8. Monnina linearifolia. R. & P.
Pencil with sepia wash. 190 x 252 mm. Royal Botanic Gardens Kew blind stamp.
Note. The habit drawing is on a separate sheet (shaped and trimmed) stuck onto a larger sheet bearing the dissections (the latter has a J WHATMAN TURKEY MILL 1823 watermark).
Published in Part 1, 1830.
Royal Botanic Gardens, Kew.

Plate 9. *Adesmia microphylla* Hooker & Arnott
Hooker annotations: Captn. Beechey [in pencil]. Adesmia microphylla. 1. 2. 3. 4. 5. 6. 7. Tab. IX.
Pencil with sepia wash. 202 x 254 mm. Royal Botanic Gardens Kew blind stamp.
Published in Part 1, 1830.
Royal Botanic Gardens, Kew.

Plate 11. *Citharexylon cyanocarpum* Hooker & Arnott
Hooker annotations: Tab. XI. 1. 2. 3. 4. 5. 6. 7. Citharexylon cyanocarpum. W.J.H. del.
Pencil with sepia wash. 215 x 250 mm. Royal Botanic Gardens Kew blind stamp.
Published in Part 2, 1832.
Royal Botanic Gardens, Kew.

Plate 12. *Metrosideros obovata* Hooker & Arnott
Hooker annotations: Tab. XII. 1. 2. 3. 4. 5. Metrosideros obovata.
Pencil with sepia wash. 217 x 245 mm. Royal Botanic Gardens Kew blind stamp.
Published in Part 2, 1832.
Royal Botanic Gardens, Kew.

Plate 14. *Chiococca barbata* G. Forster
Hooker annotations: Tab. XIV. Chiococca barbata. 1. 2. 3. 4. 5. 6.
Pencil with sepia wash. 198 x 258 mm. Royal Botanic Gardens Kew blind stamp.
Published in Part 2, 1832.
Royal Botanic Gardens, Kew.

Plate 18. *Niphobolus macrocarpus* Hooker & Arnott
Hooker annotations: Tab. XVIII. Niphobolus macrocarpus. 1. 2.

Appendix III

Pencil with sepia wash. 192 x 252 mm. Royal Botanic Gardens Kew blind stamp.
NB. Later pencil annotation 'Ex Bibl. R. T. Lowe'.
Published in Part 2, 1832.
Royal Botanic Gardens, Kew.

Plate 29 (bis). *Tofieldia coccinea* Richardson
Hooker annotations: Beechey. A little higher on the plate [in pencil]. Tab. XXIX (bis). 1. 2. 3. 4. 5. 6. 7. 8. Tofieldia coccinea. Rich.
Pencil with sepia wash. 225 x 255 mm. Royal Botanic Gardens Kew blind stamp.
Published in Part 3, 1832.
Royal Botanic Gardens, Kew.

Plate 30. *Adenostoma fasciculatum* Hooker & Arnott
Hooker annotations: Beechey [pencil]. Tab. XXX. 1. 2. 3. 4. 5. 6. 7. 8. 9. Adenostoma fasciculata.
Pencil with sepia wash. 204 x 251 mm. Royal Botanic Gardens Kew blind stamp.
Published in Part 3, 1832.
Royal Botanic Gardens, Kew.

Plate 31. *Drosera loureiroi* Hooker & Arnott
Hooker annotations: Beechey. 31. Tab. XXXI. 1. 2. 3. 4. 4. Drosera Loureirii.
Pencil with sepia wash. 205 x 261 mm. Royal Botanic Gardens Kew blind stamp.
Published in Part 4, 1833.
Royal Botanic Gardens, Kew.

Plate 32. *Pittosporum pauciflorum* Hooker & Arnott
Hooker annotations: Beechey. Tab. XXXII. 1. Pittosporum pauciflorum.
Pencil with sepia wash. 205 x 256 mm. Royal Botanic Gardens Kew blind stamp.
Published in Part 4, 1833.
Royal Botanic Gardens, Kew.

Plate 33. *Cleyera millettii* Hooker & Arnott
Hooker annotations: Cleyera Millettiana. Tab XXXIII. 1. 2. 3. 4.
Pencil with sepia wash. 208 x 240 mm. Royal Botanic Gardens Kew blind stamp.
Published in Part 4, 1833.
Royal Botanic Gardens, Kew.

Plate 34. *Aglaia odorata* Loureiro
Hooker annotations: Beechey. Aglaia odorata. Place a little higher in the plate, & there will be room for the name at the bottom. Tab XXXIV. 1. 3. 2.
Pencil with sepia wash. 178 x 229 mm. Royal Botanic Gardens Kew blind stamp.
Published in Part 4, 1833.
Royal Botanic Gardens, Kew.

Plate 35. *Ilex pubescens* Hooker & Arnott
Hooker annotations: Ilex pubescens. Tab XXXV. 1. 3. 4. 2.
Pencil with sepia wash. 204 x 259 mm. Royal Botanic Gardens Kew blind stamp.
Published in Part 4, 1833.
Royal Botanic Gardens, Kew.

Plate 36. *Prinos asprellus* Hooker & Arnott
Hooker annotations: Prinos asprellus. Tab XXXVI.
Pencil with sepia wash. 204 x 248 mm. Royal Botanic Gardens Kew blind stamp.
Published in Part 4, 1833.
Royal Botanic Gardens, Kew.

Plate 37. *Berchemia lineata* De Candolle
Hooker annotations: Berchemia lineata. Tab XXXVII. 1. 2. 3. Berchemia lineata.
Pencil with sepia wash. 200 x 254 mm. Royal Botanic Gardens Kew blind stamp.
Published in Part 4, 1833.
Royal Botanic Gardens, Kew.

Plate 38. *Layia emarginata* Hooker & Arnott
Hooker annotations: Tab. XXXVIII. 1. 2. 3. 4. 5. Layia emarginata.
Pencil with sepia wash. 193 x 243 mm. Royal Botanic Gardens Kew blind stamp.
Published in Part 4, 1833.
Royal Botanic Gardens, Kew.

Plate 39. *Itea chinensis* Hooker & Arnott
Hooker annotations: Beechey [pencil]. Itea Chinensis. Tab XXXIX. 1. 2. 3. 4. Itea Chinensis.
Pencil with sepia wash. 211 x 257 mm. Royal Botanic Gardens Kew blind stamp.
Published in Part 4, 1833.
Royal Botanic Gardens, Kew.

Appendix III

Plate 53. *Elaeocarpus photiniifolius* Hooker & Arnott
Hooker annotations: LI[II]. Elaeocarpus photiniaefolius.
Cleghorn annotations: Hook. & Arn. Beech. Voy. t. LIII.
Pencil with sepia wash. 162 x 245 mm.
Published in Part 6, 1838.
Royal Botanic Garden, Edinburgh.

Plate 58. *Rhynchosia grandiflora* Schlechtendal & Chamisso
Hooker annotations: LVIII. Tab. 1. 2. 3. Rhynchosia grandiflora.
Pencil with sepia wash. 207 x 243 mm. Royal Botanic Gardens Kew blind stamp.
Published in Part 6, 1838.
Royal Botanic Gardens, Kew.

Plate 59. *Semeiandra grandiflora* Hooker & Arnott
Hooker annotations: Tab. LIX. 1. 2. 3. Semeiandra grandiflora.
Pencil with sepia wash. 219 x 248 mm. Royal Botanic Gardens Kew blind stamp.
Published in Part 7, 1838.
Royal Botanic Gardens, Kew.

Plate 83. *Cerasus ilicifolius* Nuttall ex Hooker & Arnott (FIG. 10)
Hooker annotations: Tab. LXXXIII. 1. Cerasus ilicifolius.
Cleghorn annotations: Hook. & Arnott. Beech. Voy.
Pencil with sepia wash. 163 x 243 mm.
Published in Part 9, 1840.
Royal Botanic Garden, Edinburgh.

APPENDIX IV

Taxa for which no original material has been found at Edinburgh or Kew

A. Lay and Collie material

Abutilon albidum (Mexico)
Arbutus furiens (Chile)
Arbutus punctata (Chile)
Aster tomentellus (California)
Baccharis rigida (Chile)
Brunellia sandwicensis (Sandwich Islands)
Buddleja curviflora (Loo Choo)
Cacalia denticulata (Chile)
Calotheca stricta (Chile)
Casearia impunctata (Society Islands)
Castilleja laciniata (Chile)
Convolvulus filifolius (Chile)
Diodia barbigera (Mexico)
Eryngium tenue (Mexico)
Eugenia temu (Chile)
Fedia laxa (Chile)
Heliotropium stenophyllum (Chile)
Lathyrus decaphyllus var. *minor* (California)
Lathyrus pubescens (Chile)
Lathyrus sessilifolius (Chile)
Lobelia polyphylla (Chile)
Loranthus cactorum (Chile)
Lupinus macrocarpus (California)
Melochia hispida (Society Islands)
Myrsine ardisioides (China)
Osmorhiza chilense (Chile)
Parsonsia helicandra (China)
Petesia carnosa (Society Islands)
Phaseolus micranthus (Mexico)

Piper begoniifolium (Mexico)
Piper patens (Mexico)
Piper scabrifolium (Mexico)
Plantago mollis (Chile)
Rourea oblongifolia (Mexico)
Rubus velutinus (California)
Scirpus longifolius (Chile)
Senebiera mexicana (Mexico)
Senecio arnicoides (Chile)
Senecio bipinnatifidus (Chile)
Senecio glabratus (Chile)
Sesbania tomentosa (Mexico)
Tagetes congesta (Mexico)
Tillaea erecta (Chile)
Trifolium chilense (Chile)
Trifolium grandiflorum (Chile)
Viscum chilense (Chile)

B. Other collectors

Arundinella glabra (China). Vachell.
Arundo henslowiana (China). Vachell.
Bahia gracilis (Idaho). McLeod/Tolmie.
Hemizonia sericea (California). Douglas.
Hoitzia elata (Mexico). Bates.
Horkelia grandis (California). Douglas.
Rhus macrophylla (Mexico). Sinclair.
Rytidostylis gracilis (Nicaragua). Sinclair.
Sida grossulariifolia (Idaho). McLeod/Tolmie.
Sinclairia discolor (Nicaragua). Sinclair.
Urtica millettii (China). Millett.

Acknowledgements

As with the author's previous 'Nomenclator', which dealt primarily with Robert Wight but also involved George Walker-Arnott in a typically modest role as co-author, my greatest debt in compiling the present work is to John McNeill. He has, as always, been more than generous in sharing his unparalleled nomenclatural expertise and in unscrambling nomenclatural knots – some particularly complex ones are accompanied by his initials; for all others the author takes sole responsibility (*caveat lector*).

Sally Rae kindly looked for, and found, most of the fern types among material recently donated by the University of Glasgow (GL) and currently being incorporated into the Edinburgh herbarium (E).

Alan Elliott for electronic wizardry in making the map.

Gwen Chessell for an interesting conversation about her hero Alexander Collie.

Curators of the Natural History Museum, London and the Royal Botanic Gardens, Kew, for facilities while looking for Beecheyana.

Michele Losse and Hannah Jenkinson of the Kew archives for making printouts of the Beechey correspondence. Ann Marshall for providing a copy of Stafleu's dates of publication as given in his facsimile edition.

Marie Long and Doug Mitchell of the LuEsther T. Mertz Library, New York Botanical Garden, for information on their three(!) copies of the *Botany*, one of which consists of the first four parts unbound; and on J.H. Barnhart's invaluable annotations of publication dates.

For sending images of specimens currently on loan from E: Bruce G. Baldwin, John L. Clark, Andrew S. Doran, Peter Fritsch, Jens Klackenberg, David McClelland and Debra Trock.

References

Manuscripts

Letters in the Director's Correspondence at the Royal Botanic Gardens, Kew are cited as 'KDC' followed by volume and folio number.

Printed works

Beechey, F.W. (1831). *Narrative of a Voyage to the Pacific and Beering's Strait* ... 2 vols. London: Henry Colburn & Richard Bentley.

Bretschneider, E. (1898). *History of European Botanical Discoveries in China*. London: Sampson Low, Marston & Company.

Chessell, G. (2008). *Alexander Collie: Colonial Surgeon, Naturalist and Explorer*. Crawley: University of Western Australia Press.

Dawe, O. (1988). *Piedras de Afilar: the Unfulfilled Dream of a 19th-century Scottish Botanist in South America*. Haddington: Charles Skilton Ltd.

Desmond. R. (1994). *Dictionary of British and Irish Botanists and Horticulturists*, ed. 2. London: Taylor & Francis, and The Natural History Museum.

Fleming, F. (1999). *Barrow's Boys* [paperback edition]. London: Granta Books.

Gough, B.M. (1973). *To the Pacific and Arctic with Beechey: the journal of Lieutenant George Peard of H.M.S. 'Blossom' 1825 – 1828*. Cambridge: for the Hakluyt Society by Cambridge University Press.

Gray, A. (1840). Notices of European herbaria, particularly those most interesting to the North American botanist. *American Journal of Science* 40: 1–18.

Harvey, A.G. (1947). *Douglas of the Fir: a biography of David Douglas botanist*. Cambridge, Massachusetts: Harvard University Press.

Hemsley, W. Botting (1886–8). *Biologia Centrali-Americana ... Botany. Vol. IV*. London: For the editors (F.D. Godman & O. Salvin) by R.H. Porter and Dulau & Co.

Hooker, W.J. (1836). A brief memoir of the life of Mr. David Douglas, with extracts from his letters. *Companion to the Botanical Magazine* 2: 79–182.

Jackson, B.D. (1893). Bibliographical notes. II. – 'Botany of Beechey's Voyage' ... *Journal of Botany British & Foreign* 31: 297–9.

Knobloch, I.W. (1983). A Preliminary Verified List of Plant Collectors in Mexico, forming *Phytologia Memoirs VI*. Plainfield: H.N. & A.L Moldenke.

Lambert, A. (2004). Beechey, Frederick William (1796–1856) in *Oxford Dictionary of National Biography* 4: 802–3. Oxford: O.U.P.

Lincoln, A. (1969a). The Beechey expedition visits San Francisco. *Pacific Discovery* 22(1): 1–8.

Lincoln, A. (1969b). The natural history of the Beechey expedition. *Pacific Discovery* 22(4): 1– 8.

McKelvey, S.D. (1955). *Botanical Exploration of the Trans-Mississippi West 1790–1850*. Jamaica Plain: Arnold Arboretum.

Miller, H.S. (1970). The herbarium of Aylmer Bourke Lambert. *Taxon* 19: 489–656.

Mitchell, A.L. & House, S. (1999). *David Douglas: Explorer and Botanist*. London: Aurum Press Ltd.

Richardson, J. *et al.* (1839). *The Zoology of Captain Beechey's Voyage*. London: Henry G. Bohn.

Rickett, H.W. (1945). [Dates of publication for *The Botany of Captain Beechey's Voyage*] *North American Flora* 28B: 337. New York: New York Botanical Garden.

Stafleu, F.A. (1965). Facsimile edition of *The Botany of Captain Beechey's Voyage*. Weinheim: J. Cramer.

Stafleu, F.A. & Cowan, R.S. (1979). *Taxonomic Literature. Ed 2. Vol II: H–Le*. Utrecht: Bohn, Scheltema & Holkema & The Hague: W. Junk.

Turrill, W.B. (1920). Botanical exploration in Chile and Argentina. *Kew Bulletin 1920*: 57–66.

Zuloaga, F.O., Morrone, O. & Belgrano, M.J. (eds) (2008). *Catálogo de las Plantas Vasculares del Cono Sur*. Vols 1–3. St Louis: Missouri Botanical Garden.

Index of Scientific Names

Accepted names are in ***bold***; Hooker & Arnott names that are not currently accepted, and species mentioned only incidentally, are in *italics*.

Abutilon
  albidum Hook. & Arn., 35, 209
  albidum (Willd.) Sweet, 35
Acacia
  "*caven* (Molina) Hook. & Arn.", 36
  caven (Molina) Molina, 36
  "*cavenia* Hook. & Arn.", 35
Achyranthes
  aspera L.
    var. ***velutina*** (Hook. & Arn.) C.C. Towns., 36
  velutina Hook. & Arn., 36
Acourtia
  formosa D. Don, 178
  fruticosa (LaLlave & Lex.) B.L. Turner, 178
Adenophorus
  pinnatifidus Gaud., 190
Adenopodia
  patens (Hook. & Arn.) J. Dixon ex Brenan, 117
Adenostoma Hook. & Arn., 36
  fasciculatum Hook. & Arn., 36, 205
Adesmia
  angustifolia Hook. & Arn., 37
  conferta Hook. & Arn., 37
  glutinosa Hook. & Arn., 37
  microphylla Hook. & Arn., 37, 204
  tenella Hook. & Arn., 37, 38
Adinandra
  millettii (Hook. & Arn.) Hance, 73
Aegiceras
  minus Gaertn., 75
Aegochloa
  atractyloides Benth., 137
  cotulaefolia Benth., 138
  pubescens Benth., 138
Ageratina
  lasioneura (Hook. & Arn.) R.M. King & H. Rob., 96
Ageratum
  petiolatum (Hook. & Arn.) Hemsl., 58
Aglaia
  odorata Lour., 206
Agoseris
  apargioides (Less.) Greene, 52, 131

Alisma
  andrieuxii Hook. & Arn., 38
  virgata Hook. & Arn., 39
Allium
  falcifolium Hook. & Arn., 39
Allocarpus
  scabrifolius Hook. & Arn., 39
Aloysia
  salviifolia (Hook. & Arn.) Moldenke, 181
Alphitonia
  zizyphoides (Spreng.) A. Gray, 152
Alsia
  californica (Hook. & Arn.) Sull., 194
Alyxia
  stellata (J.R. & G. Forster) Roem. & Schult., 39
  sulcata Hook. & Arn., 39
Amellus
  villosa Pursh, 88
Amirola
  glandulosa Hook. & Arn., 39
Ampelopsis
  cantoniensis (Hook. & Arn.) K. Koch, 72
Amsinckia
  vernicosa Hook. & Arn., 40
Andropogon
  tahitensis Hook. & Arn., 40
  vachellii Nees, 40
    var. *perfectior* Hook. & Arn., 40
Anemia
  californica Nutt., 41
Anemone
  narcissiflora L.
    subsp. ***sibirica*** (L.) Hultén, 41
      var. *uniflora* Hook. & Arn., 41
Anemopsis Hook. & Arn., 41
  californica (Nutt.) Hook. & Arn., 41
"*Anguria dubia* Hook. & Arn.", 41
Anisopappus Hook. & Arn., 41
  chinensis Hook. & Arn., 41
Anoda
  lanceoloata Hook. & Arn., 42
Anodendron
  affine (Hook. & Arn.) Druce, 114
Anthistiria
  caudata Nees, 42

Antigonon
   cordatum Mart. & Galleoti, 43
   leptopus Hook. & Arn., 18, 42
   platypus Hook. & Arn., 43
Antirrhinum
   kelloggii Greene, 132
Antrophyum
   lessonii Bory, 187
   plantagineum (Cav.) Kaulf., 187
      var. *lessonii* (Bory) Hook. & Arn., 187
Aquilegia
   caerulea Torr. & A. Gray, 43
   "*macrantha* Hook. & Arn.", 43
Arabis
   blepharophylla Hook. & Arn., 43
Aralia
   octophylla Lour., 144
Arbutus
   furiens Hook. & Arn., 43, 209
   punctata Hook. & Arn., 43, 209
   pungens Hook. & Arn., 44
Archidendron
   clypearia (Jack) I.C. Nielsen
      subsp. ***clypearia***, 116
Arctostaphylos
   hookeri G. Don, 44
Aristeguietia
   salvia (Colla) R.M. King & H. Rob., 97
Aristolochia
   taliscana Hook. & Arn., 44
Artemisia
   borealis Pallas, 44
      var. *lanuginosa* Hook. & Arn., 44
Arundinella
   glabra Hook. & Arn., 45, 210
   nepalensis Trin., 45
Arundo
   henslowiana Hook. & Arn., 45, 210
Asclepias
   vestita Hook. & Arn., 45
Aspidium
   cyatheoides Kaulf., 190
   molle Sw.
      var. *paucisorum* Hook. & Arn., 187
   subintegerrimum Hook. & Arn., 187
Asplenium
   acuminatum Hook. & Arn., 187
   diplazioides Hook. & Arn., 187
   formosum Willd., 188
   subalatum Hook. & Arn., 188

Aster
   filaginifolius Hook. & Arn., 45
   subulatus Michx.
      var. ***parviflorus*** (Nees) Sundberg, 92
   tomentellus Hook. & Arn., 45, 209
Astragalus
   amatus Clos, 46
   berteri Colla, 46
   berterianus (Moris) Reiche, 46
   didymocarpus Hook. & Arn., 46
   ervoides Hook. & Arn., 46
   leucophyllus Torr., 148
   macrodon (Hook. & Arn.) A. Gray, 148
   procumbens Hook. & Arn., 46
   prostratus Hook. & Arn., 46
Astrephia
   mexicana Hook. & Arn., 47
Astrogyne
   crotonoides Benth., 112
Atenia Hook. & Arn., 47
   gairdneri Hook. & Arn., 47
Azorella
   spinosa (Ruiz & Pavon) Pers., 136

Baccharis
   absinthioides Hook. & Arn., 48
   linearis (Ruiz & Pavon) Pers.
      subsp. ***linearis***, 49
   mucronata Hook. & Arn., 48
   oblongifolia (Ruiz & Pavon) Pers., 49
   obovata Hook. & Arn., 49
   rigida Hook. & Arn., 49, 209
   rosmarinifolia Hook. & Arn., 49
Bahia
   gracilis Hook. & Arn., 49, 210
Baltimora
   recta L., 184
Barnadesia
   ulicina Hook. & Arn., 50
Bartonia
   micrantha Hook. & Arn., 50
Batis
   fruticosa Roxb., 179
Berberis
   andrieuxii Hook. & Arn., 50
   glomerata Hook. & Arn., 51
Berchemia
   lineata DC., 206
Bernardia
   mexicana (Hook. & Arn.) Müll. Arg., 112
Bidens
   australis Spreng., 51
   paniculata Hook. & Arn., 51

Index of Scientific Names

Bignonia
  obovata Hook. & Arn., 51
Bikkia
  tetrandra (L.f.) A. Rich., 147
Blepharipappus
  glandulosus Hook., 122
Blumea
  chinensis Hook. & Arn., 51
Boehmeria
  albida Hook. & Arn., 52
  densiflora Hook. & Arn., 52
  grandis (Hook. & Arn.) A. Heller, 180
Borkhausia
  lessingii Hook. & Arn., 52
Bothriochloa
  bladhii (Retz.) S.T. Blake, 40, 41
Bouvardia
  discolor Hook. & Arn., 52
  scabra Hook. & Arn., 53
  ternifolia (Cav.) Schlecht., 53
  tolucana Hook. & Arn., 53
  xylosteoides Hook. & Arn., 53
Bradleia
  sinica Gaertn., 105
Brickellia
  lanata (DC.) A. Gray, 57
Bridelia
  collina (Roxb.) Hook. & Arn., 54
  diversifolia (Roxb.) Hook. & Arn., 54
  loureiroi Hook. & Arn., 54
  oblongifolia (Roxb.) Hook. & Arn., 54
  patula (Roxb.) Hook. & Arn., 55
  stipularis (L.) Blume, 55
  "*stipularis* (L.) Hook. & Arn.", 55
  tomentosa Blume, 54
Briza
  subaristatum Lam., 61
Brizopyrum
  douglasii (Nees) Hook. & Arn., 55
  spicatum (L.) Hook. & Arn., 55
Bromus
  carinatus Hook. & Arn., 55
Brongniartia
  glabrata Hook. & Arn., 55
Brunellia
  quadrilocularis Hook. & Arn., 56
  sandwicensis Gaud. ex Hook. & Arn., 56, 209
Bryonia
  attenuata Hook. & Arn., 41, 56
Buchnera
  cruciata D. Don, 57
  densiflora Hook. & Arn., 56

Buddleja
  curviflora Hook. & Arn., 57, 209
  japonica Hemsl., 57
Bulbostylis
  rigida Hook. & Arn., 57

Cacalia
  cirsiifolia Hook. & Arn., 57
  denticulata Hook. & Arn., 57, 209
  sessilifolia Hook. & Arn., 57
Caelestina
  petiolata Hook. & Arn., 58
Caesalpinia
  angulata (Hook. & Arn.) Baill., 185
  millettii Hook. & Arn., 25, 58
Calandrinia
  compressa Schrad. ex DC., 59
  monandra (Ruiz & Pavon) DC., 77
  tenella Hook. & Arn., 58
Calea
  scabrifolia (Hook. & Arn.) Hemsl., 39
Callicarpa
  nudiflora Hook. & Arn., 59
  parvifolia Hook. & Arn., 59
  subpubescens Hook. & Arn., 60
Calliglossa Hook. & Arn., 60
  douglasii Hook. & Arn., 60
Calochortus
  tolmiei Hook. & Arn., 60
  uniflorus Hook. & Arn., 60
Calopogonium Desv., 82
  caeruleum (Benth.) Hemsl., 82
Calotheca
  stricta Hook. & Arn., 61, 209
Calycanthus
  occidentalis Hook. & Arn., 61
Calystegia
  subacaulis Hook. & Arn., 61
Camissonia
  bistorta (Nutt. ex Torr. & A. Gray) P.H. Raven, 140
  boothii (Douglas) P.H. Raven
    subsp. **alyssoides** (Hook. & Arn.) P.H. Raven, 140
    subsp. **decorticans** (Hook. & Arn.) P.H. Raven, 104
  graciliflora (Hook. & Arn.) P.H. Raven, 140
Canavalia
  multiflora (Hook. & Arn.) Hook. & Arn., 61
  pubescens Hook. & Arn., 62
  villosa Benth., 61, 139

Canthium
  beecheyi Steud., 62
  lucidum Hook. & Arn., 62
  lucidum R. Br., 62
Cardamine
  tenuirostris Hook. & Arn., 62
Carex
  bispicata Hook. & Arn., 62
  boottiana Hook. & Arn., 17, 62
  gmelinii Hook. & Arn., 63
  hebecarpa Hook. & Arn., 63
  hookeri Kunth, 63
  longirostrata C.A. Mey.
    var. *longirostrata*, 62
Carica
  papaya L., 63
  peltata Hook. & Arn., 63
Casearia
  impunctata Hook. & Arn., 64, 209
Cassia
  gaudichaudii Hook. & Arn., 64
  pauciflora Kunth, 64
  punctulata Hook. & Arn., 64
Castilleja
  affinis Hook. & Arn., 7, 64
  ambigua Hook. & Arn., 65
  foliolosa Hook. & Arn., 64, 65
  laciniata Hook. & Arn., 66, 209
  latifolia Hook. & Arn., 66
  miniata Hook., 65
Caturus
  scandens Lour., 179
Caucalis
  microcarpa Hook. & Arn., 66
Caulanthus
  lasiophyllus (Hook. & Arn.) Payson, 180
Cayaponia
  attenuata (Hook. & Arn.) Cogn., 41, 56
Ceanothus
  cuneatus (Hook.) Nutt.
    var. *cinerascens* Hook. & Arn., 67
    var. *rufescens* Hook. & Arn., 66
  cuneatus sensu Nutt., non (Hook.) Nutt., 67
  incanus Torr. & A. Gray
    var. *minor* Hook. & Arn., 67
  integerrimus Hook. & Arn., 67
  oliganthus Nutt., 67
    var. *sorediatus* (Hook. & Arn.) Hoover, 68
  sorediatus Hook. & Arn., 67
Centaurium
  centaurioides (Roxb.) R. Rao & Hemadri, 94
  madrense (Hemsl.) B.L. Rob., 95

  quitense (Kunth) B.L. Rob., 95
  tenuifolium (M. Martens & Galeotti) B.L. Rob., 95
Cephaelis
  fragrans Hook. & Arn., 68
Cephalophora
  decurrens Less., 110
Cerasus
  ilicifolius Nutt. ex Hook. & Arn., **29, 30**, 68, 207
Cercocarpus
  montanus Raf., 69
  parvifolius Nutt. ex Hook. & Arn., 68
Chaenactis
  achilleifolia Hook. & Arn., 69
  douglasii (Hook.) Hook. & Arn., 69
  stevioides Hook. & Arn., 69
Chaetogastra
  ferruginea Hook. & Arn., 69
Chaetymenia Hook. & Arn., 70
  peduncularis Hook. & Arn., 70
Chamaecrista
  hispidula (Vahl) Irwin & Barneby, 64
  punctulata (Hook. & Arn.) H.S. Irwin & Barneby, 64
Chamaesyce
  arnottiana (Endl.) Deg. & Deg., 98
Chascolytrum
  subaristatum (Lam.) Desv., 61
Cheilanthes
  dissecta Hook. & Arn., 188
Cheirodendron
  platyphyllum (Hook. & Arn.) Seem., 143
  trigynum (Gaud.) A. Heller, 142
Chenopodium
  acuminatum Willd., 70
  spinosum Hook., 106
  vachellii Hook. & Arn., 70
Chiococca
  barbata G. Forst., 204
  odorata Hook. & Arn., 70
Chironia
  centaurioides Roxb., 94
Chlamysperma
  arenarioides Hook. & Arn., 71
Christella
  cyatheoides (Kaulf.) Holttum, 190
Chromolaena
  collina (DC.) R.M. King & H. Rob., 96
  glaberrima (DC.) R.M. King & H. Rob., 96
Chryseis Lindl., non Cass., 71
  californica (Cham.) Lindl., 71
  "*californica* (Cham.) Hook. & Arn.", 71

Index of Scientific Names

Chrysopsis
  scabra Hook. & Arn., 71
Chuquiraga
  revoluta Fielding & Gardner, 50
  ulicina (Hook. & Arn.) Hook. & Arn., 50
Cissus
  cantoniensis Hook. & Arn., 72
Citharexylum
  cyanocarpum Hook. & Arn., 72, 204
Cleistanthus
  collinus (Roxb.) Benth., 54
  diversifolius (Roxb.) Müll. Arg., 54
  oblongifolius (Roxb.) Müll. Arg., 54
  patulus (Roxb.) Müll. Arg., 55
  stipularis (Kuntze) Müll. Arg., 55
Clematis
  acapulcensis Hook. & Arn., 73
Clerodendrum
  castaneifolium Hook. & Arn., 73
  fortunatum L., 73
  lividum Lindl., 73
Cleyera
  millettii Hook. & Arn., 25, 73, 205
Clinostigma
  savoryana (Rehder & E.H. Wilson) H.E. Moore & Fosberg, 17
Cluytia
  collina Roxb., 54
  diversifolia Roxb., 54
  monoica Lour., 54
  oblongifolia Roxb., 54
  patula Roxb., 55
  semperflorens Roxb., 170
  stipularis L., 55
Cnestis
  monadelpha Roxb., 75
Cocculus
  diantherus Hook. & Arn., 73
  orbiculatus (L.) DC., 74
Coffea
  chamissonis Hook. & Arn., 74
Collea Lindl., 7
Collema
  turneri Hook. & Arn., 194
Collomia
  biflora (Ruiz & Pavon) Brand, 74
  cavanillesii Hook. & Arn., 74
  linearis Nutt., 74
  nudicaulis Hook. & Arn., 74
Connarus
  juglandifolius Hook. & Arn., 75
  microphyllus Hook. & Arn., 75
  roxburghii Hook. & Arn., 75
Convolvulus
  densiflorus Hook. & Arn., 76
  filifolius Hook. & Arn., 76, 209
Conyza
  chinensis L., 52
  spiculosa (Hook. & Arn.) Zardini, 92
Cordia
  decandra Hook. & Arn., 19, 76
Corethrogyne
  filaginifolia (Hook. & Arn.) Nutt., 45
Cornutia
  quinata Lour., 184
Corrigiola
  deltoidea Hook. & Arn., 77
Crassula
  connata (Ruiz & Pavon) A. Berger, 175
Crepidium Blume, 155
  resupinatum (G. Forst.) Szlach., 156
Cristaria
  aspera Gay, 77
  pinnatifida Hook. & Arn., 77
Critonia
  hebebotrya DC., 109
Crossopetalum
  scoparium (Hook. & Arn.) Kuntze, 136
Crotalaria
  acapulcensis Hook. & Arn., 77
  longirostrata Hook. & Arn., 77
  pumila Ort., 78
  tepicana Hook. & Arn., 78
  uncinella Lam., 78
  vachellii Hook. & Arn., 78
Croton
  gracilis Kunth, 112
Crusea
  parviflora Hook. & Arn., 78, 79
  subulata Hook. & Arn., 79
Cryptantha
  circumscissa (Hook. & Arn.) I.M. Johnston, 126
  muricata (Hook. & Arn.) Nelson & J.F. Macbr., 137
Ctenitis
  squamigera (Hook. & Arn.) Copel., 190
Cuphea
  arnottiana (Standl.) R.C. Foster, 80
  barbigera Hook. & Arn., 79
  bracteata Hook. & Arn., 79
  floribunda Hook. & Arn., 80
  hookeriana Walp., 80
  llavea Lex., 79

Cuphea
   lobophora Koehne
      var. ***occidentalis*** S.A. Graham, 80
   mimuloides Cham. & Schlchtdl., 81
   tenella Hook. & Arn., 80
Cupia
   mollissima Hook. & Arn., 81
Cuscuta
   australis R. Br., 81
   californica Hook. & Arn., 81
   millettii Hook. & Arn., 81
Cyanostremma Benth. ex Hook. & Arn., 81
   caeruleum (Benth.) Benth. ex Hook. & Arn., 82
Cyclophorus
   angustatus (Sw.) Desv., 190
Cyclophyllum
   barbatum (G. Forst.) N. Hallé & J. Florence, 70
Cymbopogon
   refractus (R. Br.) A. Camus, 40
Cynanchum
   birostratum Hook. & Arn., 82
Cynoglossum
   paniculatum Hook. & Arn., 82
   penicillatum Hook. & Arn., 83
Cyperus
   caricifolius Hook. & Arn., 83
   javanicus Houtt., 83
   multiceps Hook. & Arn., 83
   odoratus L., 83
   prescottianus Hook. & Arn., 83
   trachysanthos Hook. & Arn., 84
Cyrtandra
   menziesii Hook. & Arn., 84

Dalea
   argyrostachys Hook. & Arn., 84
   crenulata Hook. & Arn., 84
   elata Hook. & Arn., 84
   gracilis Hook. & Arn., 85
   versicolor Zucc.
      subsp. ***argyrostachys*** (Hook. & Arn.) Barneby
      var. ***argyrostachys***, 84
Davallia
   macraeana Hook. & Arn., 188
Delphinium
   nudicaule Torr. & A. Gray, 85
   sarcophyllum Hook. & Arn., 85
Desmodium
   heterocarpon (L.) DC., 86
   heterophyllum Hook. & Arn., 85
   hookerianum D. Dietr., 86

   podocarpum Hook. & Arn., 86
   purpureum Hook. & Arn., 86
Dianella
   sandwicensis Hook. & Arn., 86
Dicentra
   chrysantha (Hook. & Arn.) Walp., 87
Dictyota
   spinulosa Hook. & Arn., 17, 192
Dielytra
   chrysantha Hook. & Arn., 87
Diodia
   barbigera Hook. & Arn., 87, 209
Dioscorea
   gracilis Hook. & Arn., 87
   humifusa Poepp.
      var. ***gracilis*** (Hook. & Arn.) L.E. Navas, 87
   obtusifolia Hook. & Arn., 87
Diplandra Hook. & Arn., 88
   lopezioides Hook. & Arn., 88
Diplazium
   arnottii Brack., 188
Diplolepis
   ovata Lindl., 180
Diplopappus
   ericoides Less., 108
   occidentalis Hook. & Arn., 88
   villosus (Pursh) Hook. & Arn., 88
Distasis
   concinna Hook. & Arn., 88
Distichlis
   spicata (L.) Greene, 55
Dolia
   vermiculata Lindl., 100
Dothidea
   granulosa Hook. & Arn., 194
Drosera
   loureiroi Hook. & Arn., 89, 205
   spatulata Labill., 89
Dryopteris
   crinalis (Hook. & Arn.) C. Chr., 191
   parasitica (L.) Kuntze, 187
   sandwicensis (Hook. & Arn.) C. Chr., 191
   unidentata (Hook. & Arn.) C. Chr., 192
Dubautia
   laxa Hook. & Arn., 89
Dubreulia
   peploides Gaud., 150
Duhaldea
   chinensis DC., 52

Ecdysanthera Hook. & Arn., 89
   rosea Hook. & Arn., 89

Index of Scientific Names

Echinodorus
  subalatus (Mart.) Griseb.
    subsp. ***andrieuxii*** (Hook. & Arn.) R.R. Haynes & Holm-Niels., 38
  virgatus (Hook. & Arn.) Micheli, 39
Echites
  pubescens Hook. & Arn., 90
Ectropothecium
  sandvicense (Hook. & Arn.) Mitt., 193
Elaeocarpus
  bifidus Hook. & Arn., 90
  photiniifolius Hook. & Arn., 90, 207
Elatostema
  sessile J.R. & G. Forst., 154
Elytropus
  chilensis (A. DC.) Müll. Arg., 90
Emmenanthe
  lutea (Hook. & Arn.) A. Gray, 100
Emmenanthus Hook. & Arn., 90
  chinensis Hook. & Arn., 91
Eragrostis
  millettii Hook. & Arn., 91
  pilosissima Link, 91
Ericameria
  ericoides (Less.) Jepson, 108
Erigeron
  concinnus (Hook. & Arn.) Torr. & A. Gray, 89
  foliosus Nutt., 88
  multiflorus Hook. & Arn., 91
  pauciflorus Hook. & Arn., 92
  spiculosus Hook. & Arn., 92
  velutipes Hook. & Arn., 92
Eriocaulon
  cantoniensis Hook. & Arn., 93
  sexangulare L., 93
Eriodyction
  californicum (Hook. & Arn.) Torr., 185
Eriophyllum
  lanatum (Pursh) J. Forbes, 49
Erodium
  macrophyllum Hook. & Arn., 93
Eryngium
  beecheyanum Hook. & Arn., 93
  tenue Hook. & Arn., 93, 209
Erysimum
  glaberrimum Hook. & Arn., 94
Erythraea
  centaurioides (Roxb.) Hook. & Arn., 94
  macrantha Hook. & Arn., 94
    var. *macrantha*, 95
    var. *major* Hook. & Arn., 95
  "*mexicana* Griseb. ex. Hook. & Arn.", 95
  texensis Griseb., 94
Eschscholzia
  californica Cham., 71
  crocea Benth., 71
Eugenia
  temu Hook. & Arn., 96, 209
Eunanus
  douglasii Benth., 134
  tolmiaei Benth., 134
Eupatorium
  lasioneuron Hook. & Arn., 96
  nigrescens Hook. & Arn., 96
  ovalifolium Hook. & Arn., 96
  reticulatum Hook. & Arn., 96
Euphorbia
  arnottiana Endl., 98
  bifida Hook. & Arn., 97, 99
  clusiifolia Hook. & Arn., 97
  engelmannii Boiss., 98
  hookeri Steud., 98
  lathyrus L., 97
    var. *minor* Hook. & Arn., 97
  multiformis Gaud. ex Hook. & Arn., 97
  myrtifolia Hook. & Arn., 98
  ramosissima Hook. & Arn., 98
  rotundifolia Hook. & Arn., 98
  sparrmanni Boiss., 98
  strigosa Hook. & Arn., 99
  vachellii Hook. & Arn., 99
Eutoca
  aretioides Hook. & Arn., 99
    var. *perpusilla* Hook. & Arn., 99
  lutea Hook. & Arn., 100

Fabiana
  lanuginosa Hook. & Arn., 100
  viscosa Hook. & Arn., 100
Fedia
  laxa Hook. & Arn., 101, 209
Ferula
  caruifolia Hook. & Arn., 101
  macrocarpa Hook. & Arn., 101
  parvifolia Hook. & Arn., 101
Ficus
  beecheyana Hook. & Arn., 102
  erecta Thunb., 102
    var. *sieboldiana* Miq., 102
    var. *beecheyana* (Hook. & Arn.) King, 102
  hirta Vahl, 103
  lancifolia Hook. & Arn., 102
  pertusa L. f., 102

Ficus
   pyriformis Hook. & Arn., 102
   setosa Hook. & Arn., 103
Filago
   californica Nutt., 105
Fimbristylis
   affinis Hook. & Arn., 103
   dichotoma (L.) Vahl, 103
Flagellaria
   repens Lour., 153
Flourensia
   thurifera (Molina) DC., 111
Fraxinus
   dipetala Hook. & Arn., 103
Fritillaria
   kamtschatcensis Fisch. ex Hook., 17
Funastrum
   bilobum (Hook. & Arn.) J.F. Macbr., 166

Gaillardia Foug., 177
"*Galardia* Lam.", 177
Galeana
   pratensis (Kunth) Rydb., 71
Galinsoga
   resinosa Hook. & Arn., 104
Galium
   californicum Hook. & Arn., 104
Gaultheria
   insana (Molina) D.J. Middleton, 43
Gaura
   decorticans Hook. & Arn., 104
Gilia
   squarrosa (Eschsch.) Hook. & Arn., 105
Glochidion
   molle Hook. & Arn., 105
   puberum (L.) Hutch., 105
   sinicum (Gaertn.) Hook. & Arn., 105
   zeylanicum (Gaertn.) A. Juss.
      var. ***talbotii*** (Hook. f.) Haines, 105
Gnaphalium
   cheiranthifolium Lam., 105
   chilense Spreng., 106
   citrinum Hook. & Arn., 105
   cymatoides Kunze ex DC., 106
   filaginoides Hook. & Arn., 105
   sprengelii Hook. & Arn., 106
   stramineum Kunth, 106
   ulophyllum Hook. & Arn., 106
Grammica
   aphylla Lour., 81
Grammitis
   hookeri (Brack.) Copel., 191

Grayia Hook. & Arn., 106
   polygonoides Hook. & Arn., 106
   spinosa (Hook.) Moq., 107
Grindelia
   hirsutula Hook. & Arn., 107
   humilis Hook. & Arn., 107
Grumilea
   reevesii (Wall.) Hook. & Arn., 107
Guardiola Cerv. ex Bonpl., 179
   tulocarpus A. Gray, 179
Guarea
   glabra Vahl, 166
Gunnera
   scabra Ruiz & Pavon, 9
Gutierrezia
   resinosa (Hook. & Arn.) S.F. Blake, 104
Gymnocoronis
   latifolia Hook. & Arn., 108
Gymnosteris
   nudicaulis (Hook. & Arn.) Greene, 75

Haplopappus
   ericoides (Less.) Hook. & Arn., 108
   mucronatus (Hook. & Arn.) B.D. Jacks., 49
   squarrosus Hook. & Arn., 108
Hartmannia
   pungens Hook. & Arn., 108
Hazardia
   squarrosa (Hook. & Arn.) Greene, 108
Hebeclinium
   tepicanum Hook. & Arn., 109
Hedyotis
   coriacea Sm., 120
   macrostemon Hook. & Arn., 109
   uncinella Hook. & Arn., 109
   vachellii Hook. & Arn., 109
Hedysarum
   striatum Thunb., 124
Helenium
   puberulum DC., 110
   pubescens Ait., 110
   pubescens Hook. & Arn., 110
Helianthus
   glutinosus Hook. & Arn., 110
Heliotropium
   anomalum Hook. & Arn., 13, 111
   stenophyllum Hook. & Arn., 111, 209
   strigosum Willd., 126
Helodium
   blandowii (Web. & Mohr) Warnst., 193
Helosciadium
   californicum Hook. & Arn., 111

Index of Scientific Names

Hemizonia
  congesta DC.
    subsp. *luzulifolia* (DC.) Babc. & H.M. Hall, 112
  filipes Hook. & Arn., 111
  multicaulis Hook. & Arn., 112
  pungens (Hook. & Arn.) Torr. & A. Gray, 108
  sericea Hook. & Arn., 112, 210
Hendecandra
  crotonoides Hook. & Arn., 112
Hermesia
  mexicana Hook. & Arn., 112
Heterocentron Hook. & Arn., 112
  mexicana Hook. & Arn., 113
Heteropteris
  beecheyana A. Juss., 113
  brachiata (L.) DC., 113
  tomentosa A. Juss., 113
  tomentosa Hook. & Arn., 113
Heterotheca
  villosa (Pursh) Shinners, 88
Heuchera
  hispida Hook. & Arn., 113
  pilossisima Fisch. & Mey., 113
Hisutsua
  serrata Hook. & Arn., 114
Hofmeisteria
  dissecta (Hook. & Arn.) R.M. King & H. Rob., 149
  urenifolia (Hook. & Arn.) Walp., 149
Hoita
  strobilina (Hook. & Arn.) Rydb., 155
Hoitzia
  amplectens Hook. & Arn., 114
  elata Hook. & Arn., 114, 210
  lupulina Hook. & Arn., 114
  squarrosa Eschsch., 105, 138
Holarrhena
  affinis Hook. & Arn., 114
Holozonia
  filipes (Hook. & Arn.) Greene, 111
Horkelia
  californica Cham. & Schlecht., 115
  fusca Lindl.
    subsp. *parviflora* (Nutt. ex Hook. & Arn.) Keck, 115
  grandis Hook. & Arn., 115, 210
  parviflora Nutt. ex Hook. & Arn., 115
Hosackia
  tomentosa Hook. & Arn., 115
Huperzia
  phyllantha (Hook. & Arn.) Holub, 189
Hymenopappus
  douglasii Hook., 69

Hymenophyllum
  lanceolatum Hook. & Arn., 188
  obtusum Hook. & Arn., 188
Hypnum
  fuscescens Hook. & Arn., 193
  laricinum Wilson, 193
  sandvicense Hook. & Arn., 193
Hypochaeris
  apargioides Hook. & Arn., 115
Hypolepis
  tenuifolia (G. Forst.) Bernh., 188
Ilex
  anomala Hook. & Arn., 115
  asprella (Hook. & Arn.) Champion ex Benth., 154
  integra Thunb.
    var. *beecheyi* Loes., 154
  pubescens Hook. & Arn., 116, 206
Indigofera
  constricta Rydb., 116
  torulosa Hook. & Arn., 116
Inga
  dimidiata Hook. & Arn., 116
  guatemalensis Hook. & Arn., 116
  patens Hook. & Arn., 117
Ipomoea
  cruckshanksii Choisy, 76
  filifolia (Hook. & Arn.) G. Don, 76
Iris
  beecheyana Herb., 117
  douglasiana Herb., 117, 118
    var. *bracteata* Herb., 118
    var. *nuda* Herb., 118
  haematophylla Fisch. ex Link
    var. *valametica* Herb., 118
  longipetala Herb., 118
  missouriensis Nutt., 119
  tolmieana Herb., 118
Ischaemum
  aureum (Hook. & Arn.) Hack., 172
  barbatum Retz., 133
  sieboldii Miq., 172
Isocoma
  menziesii (Hook. & Arn.) G.L. Nesom, 156
Isopyrum
  occidentale Hook. & Arn., 119
Itea
  chinensis Hook. & Arn., 119, 206
Ixonanthes Jack, 90
  chinensis (Hook. & Arn.) Champ., 91
  reticulata Jack, 91

Ixora
  fragrans (Hook. & Arn.) A. Gray, 68

Jaegeria
  pedunculata Hook. & Arn., 119
Juncus
  longistylis Torr., 119
  menziesii R. Br.
    var. *californicus* Hook. & Arn., 119
Jungermannia
  conchifolia Hook. & Arn., 193
Juniperus
  chinensis L.
    var. *chinensis*, 186
  taxifolia Hook. & Arn., 186
  thunbergii Hook. & Arn., 186
  virginiana sensu Thunb., non L., 186
  "*virginica* Thunb.", 186

Kadua
  affinis Cham. & Schltdl., 147
  centranthoides Hook. & Arn., 120
  coriacea (Sm.) W.L. Wagner & Lorence, 120
  glomerata Hook. & Arn., 120
  smithii Hook. & Arn., 120
Kalimeris
  indicus (L.) Schultz-Bip., 114
Kallstroemia
  maxima (L.) Hook. & Arn., 120
Krameria
  cistoidea Hook. & Arn., 19, 120

Lantana
  lippioides Hook. & Arn., 121
Laportea
  interrupta (L.) Chew, 180
Lasianthera
  macrocephala (Hook. & Arn.) K. Becker, 125
Lathyrus
  decaphyllus Hook.
    var. *minor* Hook. & Arn., 121, 209
  macraei Hook. & Arn., 121
  magellanicus Lam., 121
  pubescens Hook. & Arn., 121, 209
  sessilifolius Hook. & Arn., 121, 209
  venosus Muhl. ex Willd., 121
Laurus
  caustica Molina, 159
Layia Hook. & Arn., 121
"*Layia* Hook. & Arn.", 122

Layia Hook. & Arn. ex DC., 60, 121, 122
  chrysanthemoides (DC.) A. Gray, 60
  douglasii Hook. & Arn., 122
  emarginata Hook. & Arn., **ix**, 16, 122, 206
  gaillardioides (Hook. & Arn.) DC., 177
  glandulosa (Hook.) Hook. & Arn., 122
  heterotricha (DC.) Hook. & Arn., 123
  hieracioides (DC.) Hook. & Arn., 123
Lepidium
  corymbosum Hook. & Arn., 123
  leiocarpum Hook. & Arn., 123
  montanum Nutt., 123
  nitidum Torr. & A. Gray, 123
  virginicum L., 168
Leptodactylon Hook. & Arn., 123
  californicum Hook. & Arn., 123
Leptogium
  phyllocarpum
    var. *turneri* (Hook. & Arn.) Zahlbr., 194
  sp., 194
Leptopetalum Hook. & Arn., 124
  mexicanum Hook. & Arn., **viii**, 124
Leptostomum
  splachnoideum Hook. & Arn., 193
Lespedeza
  striata (Thunb.) Hook. & Arn., 124
Lessingia
  filaginifolia (Hook. & Arn.) M.A. Lane, 45
Leucas
  benthamiana Hook. & Arn., 124
  mollissima Wall. ex Benth., 124
Leucheria
  senecioides Hook. & Arn., 125
Liabum
  discolor (Hook. & Arn.) Hemsl., 171
Libertia
  sessiliflora (Poepp.) Skottsb., 171
Lindsaea
  repens (Bory) Thw.
    var. *macraeana* (Hook. & Arn.) C. Chr., 188
  variabilis Hook. & Arn., 189
"*Linum oligophyllum* Hook. & Arn.", 125
Liparis
  revoluta Hook. & Arn., 125
Lipochaeta
  lobata (Gaud.) DC., 181
  macrocephala Hook. & Arn., 125
  succulenta (Hook. & Arn.) DC., 182
Lippia
  sp., 121
Lithocarpus
  densiflorus (Hook. & Arn.) Rehder, 157

Index of Scientific Names

Lithophragma
   heterophyllum (Hook. & Arn.) Torr. & A. Gray, 174
Lithospermum
   chinense Hook. & Arn., 126
   circumscissum Hook. & Arn., 126
Lithraea
   caustica (Molina) Hook. & Arn., 159
Llagunoa
   glandulosa (Hook. & Arn.) G. Don, 40
Lobelia
   angulatodentata Hook. & Arn., 126
   arabidoides Hook. & Arn., 126
   carnosula Hook. & Arn., 127
   cordifolia Hook. & Arn., 127
   divaricata Hook. & Arn., 127
   flexuosa (C. Presl) A. DC.
      subsp. *flexuosa*, 127
   lanceolata Hook. & Arn., 127
   laxiflora Kunth
      subsp. *laxiflora*, 126, 128
   macrostachys Hook. & Arn., 128
   ovalifolia Hook. & Arn., 128
   polyphylla Hook. & Arn., 128, 209
Loeselia
   glandulosa (Cav.) G. Don, 114
   involucrata G. Don, 114
Lomaria
   longifolia Hook. & Arn., 189
Lomatium
   caruifolium (Hook. & Arn.) Coult. & Rose, 101
   macrocarpum (Hook. & Arn.) Coult. & Rose, 101
   parvifolium (Hook. & Arn.) Jepson, 102
Lonicera
   affinis Hook. & Arn., 128
   confusa (Sweet) DC., 129
   subspicata Hook. & Arn., 129
   telfairii Hook. & Arn., 129
Lopezia Cav., 88, 167
   lopezioides (Hook. & Arn.) Plitmann, P.H. Raven & Breedlove, 88
   semeiandra Plitmann, P.H. Raven & Breedlove, 167, 168
Loranthus
   cactorum Hook. & Arn., 19, 129, 209
Lotus
   eriophorus Greene, 115
Lucuma
   ferruginea Hook. & Arn., 130

Lupinus
   arboreus Sims, 130
   macrocarpus Hook. & Arn., 130, 209
   parviflorus Nutt., 130
   truncatus Nutt., 130
Lycopodium
   phyllanthum Hook. & Arn., 189
Lysimachia
   glaucophylla Hook. & Arn., 131
   lineariloba Hook. & Arn., 131
   mauritiana Lam., 131

Maclura
   fruticosa (Roxb.) Corner, 179
Macrorhynchus
   lessingii Hook. & Arn., 131
Madaraglossa
   heterotricha DC., 123
   hieracioides DC., 123
Mahonia
   andrieuxii (Hook. & Arn.) Fedde, 50
Malacothrix
   saxatilis (Nutt.) Torr. & A. Gray, 172
Mallotus
   philippensis (Lam.) Müll. Arg., 161
Malva
   malachroides Hook. & Arn., 131
Marina
   crenulata (Hook. & Arn.) Barneby
      var. *crenulata*, 84
   diffusa (Moric.) Barneby
      var. *diffusa*, 85
Maurandya
   stricta Hook. & Arn., 132
Melampodium
   tenellum Hook. & Arn., 132
Melochia
   hispida Hook. & Arn., 132, 209
Memecylon
   nigrescens Hook. & Arn., 132
Mentzelia
   micrantha (Hook. & Arn.) Torr. & A. Gray, 50
Meoschium
   lodiculare Nees, 133
Merremia
   umbellata (L.) Hall. f., 76
Metrosideros
   macropus Hook. & Arn., 133
   obovata Hook. & Arn., 13, 133, 204
Mimosa
   caven Molina, 36
   cavenia Molina, 35
   guatemalensis (Hook. & Arn.) Benth., 117

Index of Scientific Names

Mimulus
  douglasii (Benth.) A. Gray, 135
  nanus Hook. & Arn.
    var. ***nanus***, 134
    var. *pluriflorus* Hook. & Arn., 133
    var. *subuniflorus* Hook. & Arn., 134
Mitracarpus
  hirtus (L.) DC., 135
  pallidus Hook. & Arn., 135
Monnina
  linearifolia Ruiz & Pavon, 204
Monochoria
  ovata (Hook. & Arn.) Kunth, 152
  vaginalis (Burm. f.) Kunth, 153
Mulinum
  cuneatum Hook. & Arn., 135
Mycinema
  flava Hook. & Arn., 192
Myginda
  scoparia Hook. & Arn., 136
Myoporum
  euphrasioides Hook. & Arn., 13, 136
Myosotis
  fulva Hook. & Arn., 136
  muricata Hook. & Arn., 137
Myrceugenia
  exsucca (DC.) O. Berg, 96
Myrsine
  ardisioides Hook. & Arn., 137, 209

Nama
  aretioides (Hook. & Arn.) Brand, 99, 100
Navarretia
  atractyloides (Benth.) Hook. & Arn., 137
  cotulifolia (Benth.) Hook. & Arn., 138
  pubescens (Benth.) Hook. & Arn., 138
  squarrosa (Eschsch.) Hook. & Arn., 105, 138
Neckera
  californica Hook. & Arn., 194
Nemophila
  menziesii Hook. & Arn., 138
Neogaerrhinum
  strictum (Hook. & Arn.) Rothm., 132
Nephrodium
  apiifolium Hook. & Arn., 189
  dubrueilianum (Gaud.) Hook. & Arn., 189
  squamigerum Hook. & Arn., 190
Nesogenes
  euphrasioides (Hook. & Arn.) A. DC., 136
Neurocarpum
  multiflorum Hook. & Arn., 61, 138

Neyraudia
  reynaudiana (Kunth) Keng ex Hitchc., 45
Niphobolus
  macrocarpus Hook. & Arn., 190, 204
Nolana
  sedifolia Poepp.
    subsp. ***sedifolia***, 100
Notholaena
  hirsuta (Poir.) Desv., 190
  pilosa Hook. & Arn., 190
Nuttallia Torr. & A. Gray ex Hook. & Arn., 139
  cerasiformis Torr. & A. Gray ex Hook. & Arn., 139

Odontotrichum
  pringlei (S. Watson) Rydb., 57
Oemleria Rchb., 139
  cerasiformis (Hook. & Arn.) J.W. Landon, 139
Oenanthe
  sarmentosa J. Presl, 111
Oenothera
  alyssoides Hook. & Arn., 139
  caespitosa Nutt.
    subsp. ***marginata*** (Nutt. ex Hook. & Arn.) Munz, 141
  graciliflora Hook. & Arn., 140
  heterophylla Nutt. ex Hook. & Arn., 140
  marginata Nutt. ex Hook. & Arn., 141
Oldenlandia
  hedyotidea (DC.) Hand.-Mazz., 109
  vachellii (Hook. & Arn.) Kuntze, 110
Oligotrichum
  canaliculatum (Hook. & Arn.) Mitt., 194
Ophioglossum
  crotalophoroides Walter, 190
  tuberosum Hook. & Arn., 190
Ormosia
  emarginata (Hook. & Arn.) Benth., **ix**, 17, 122
Orthocarpus
  tolmiei Hook. & Arn., 141
Osmorhiza
  chilense Hook. & Arn., 141, 209
Oxalis
  glomerata Hook. & Arn., 142
  laxa Hook. & Arn., 142
  tortuosa Lindl., 142
Oxypappus
  seemannii (Schultz-Bip.) Blake, 72
Oxyura
  chrysanthemoides sensu Lindl., non DC., 60

Index of Scientific Names

Panax
   ovatum Hook. & Arn., 142
   platyphyllum Hook. & Arn., 143
Panicum
   affine Hook. & Arn., 143
   beecheyi Hook. & Arn., 14, 143
   colliei Endl., 7, 143
   gossypinum Hook. & Arn., 143
   pellitum Trin., 143
   tenuifolium Hook. & Arn., 143
   torridum Gaud., 143
Paratropia
   cantoniensis Hook. & Arn., 144
Parmelia
   calicarpa Hook. & Arn., 194
Parsonsia
   alboflavescens (Dennst.) Mabberley, 144
   arnottiana Standl., 80
   helicandra Hook. & Arn., 144, 209
   "*Passiflora pannosa* Hook. & Arn.", 144
Pavonia
   pleurantha (DC.) Fryxell, 145
   racemifera Hook. & Arn., 144
Pectis
   diffusa Hook. & Arn., 145
   taliscana Hook. & Arn., 145
   uniaristata DC., 145
Pectocarya
   anisocarpa Veno, 83
   penicillata (Hook. & Arn.) A. DC., 83
Penstemon
   laricifolius Hook. & Arn., 145
Peperomia
   blanda Kunth
      var. *floribunda* (Miq.) Hüber, 146
   leptostachya Hook. & Arn, 145
   membranacea Hook. & Arn., 146
   "*pallida* (Spreng.) Hook. & Arn.", 146
   reflexa (L.) A. Dietr., 147
   rhomboidea Hook. & Arn., 146
   tetraphylla Hook. & Arn., 146
Pergularia
   divaricata Lour., 173
Pericalia
   sessilifolia (Hook. & Arn.) Rydb., 58
Perideridia Rchb., 47
   gairdneri (Hook. & Arn.) Mathias, 47
Perotis
   longiflora Nees, 147
   patula Nees, 147
   rara R. Br., 147

Petesia
   carnosa Hook. & Arn., 147, 209
   coriacea Hook. & Arn., 147
   terminalis Hook. & Arn., 147
Petunia
   parviflora Juss., 162
Phaca
   leucophylla (Torr.) Hook. & Arn., 148
   macrodon Hook. & Arn., 148
Phacelia
   "*brunoniana* Gillies", 148
   cumingii (Benth.) A. Gray, 148
   lutea (Hook. & Arn.) J.T. Howell, 100
   ramosissima Dougl. ex Lehm., 148
      var. *brunoniana* A. DC., 148
Phalaris
   californica Hook. & Arn., 148
Phallus
   daemona, 5
Phania
   dissecta Hook. & Arn., 149
   urenifolia Hook. & Arn., 149
Phaseolus
   micranthus Hook. & Arn., 149, 209
Phoradendron
   sp., 183
Photinia
   prunifolia (Hook. & Arn.) Lindl., 149
   serrulata DC.
      var. *obovata* Hook. & Arn., 150
      var. *prunifolia* Hook. & Arn., 149
Phyllanthus
   cinerascens Hook. & Arn., 150
   cochinchinensis Spreng., 150
   distichus Hook. & Arn., 150
Pilea
   peploides (Gaud.) Hook. & Arn., 150
Pinus
   radiata D. Don
      var. **radiata**, 186
   sinclairii Hook. & Arn., 186
Piper
   arboreum Aublet
      subsp. **tuberculatum** (Jacq.) Tebbs, 151
   begoniifolium Hook. & Arn., 150, 210
   ellipticum Hook. & Arn., 151
   methysticum G. Forst., 16
   microstachyum Vahl., 151
   nervosum C. DC., 151
   patens Hook. & Arn., 151, 210
   scabrifolium Hook. & Arn., 151, 210
Pipturus
   albidus (Hook. & Arn.) A. Gray, 52

Pittosporum
  glabrum Hook. & Arn., 151
  pauciflorum Hook. & Arn., 151, 205
Plagiobothrys
  fulvus (Hook. & Arn.) I.M. Johnston, 137
Plantago
  mollis Hook. & Arn., 152, 210
  patagonica Jacq., 152
Pleurozia
  conchifolia (Hook. & Arn.) Aust. var. *conchifolia*, 193
Pneumatopteris
  sandwicensis (Brack.) Holttum, 191
Poa
  douglasii Nees, 55
Polygala
  aparinoides Hook. & Arn., 152
Polypodium
  adenophorus Hook. & Arn., 190
  californicum Kaulf., 191
  crinale Hook. & Arn., 191
  intermedium Hook. & Arn., 191
  polycarpon Hook. & Arn., 191
  sandwicense Hook. & Arn., 191
  setigerum Hook. & Arn., 191
  subtriphyllum Hook. & Arn., 191
  unidentatum Hook. & Arn., 191
Polystichum
  dubrueilianum Gaud., 189
  subintegerrimum (Hook. & Arn.) R. Rodr., 187
Polystomella
  granulosa (Hook & Arn.) Theiss. & Syd., 194
Polytrichum
  canaliculatum Hook. & Arn., 194
Pomaderris
  zizyphoides (Spreng.) Hook. & Arn., 152
Pontederia
  ovata Hook. & Arn., 152
"*Poppigia cyanocarpa* Bert.", 72
Porterella
  carnosula (Hook. & Arn.) Torr., 127
Potentilla
  villosa Pallas
    var. *gracilis* Hook. & Arn., 153
Pothos
  loureiroi Hook. & Arn., 153
  repens (Lour.) Druce, 153
Pottsia Hook. & Arn., 153
  cantonensis Hook. & Arn., 153
  laxiflora (Blume) Kuntze, 154

Pouteria
  obovata (R. Br.) Baehni, 130, 170
Premna
  serratifolia L., 182
Prinos
  asprellus Hook. & Arn., 154, 206
  integra Hook. & Arn., 154
Procris
  glabra Hook. & Arn., 154
  sessilis (J.R. & G. Forst.) Hook. & Arn., 154
Proustia
  ilicifolia Hook. & Arn., 155
Prunus
  ilicifolius (Nutt. ex Hook. & Arn.) Walp., 68
Psacalium
  pringlei (S. Watson) H. Rob. & Brettell, 57
Psoralea
  strobilina Hook. & Arn., 155
Psychotria
  asiatica L., 108
  kaduana (Cham. & Schltdl.) Fosberg, 74
  reevesii Wall., 108
  scandens Hook. & Arn., 155
  serpens L., 155
Psydrax
  odorata (G. Forst.) A.C. Sm. & S. Darwin, 62
Pterochilus Hook. & Arn., 155
  plantaginea Hook. & Arn., 156
Pyrrocoma
  menziesii Hook. & Arn., 156

Quercus
  aristata Hook. & Arn., 156
  densiflora Hook. & Arn., 156
  douglasii Hook. & Arn., 157
Quinchamalium
  chilense Molina
    var. *gracilis* Hook. & Arn., 157
    var. *robustior* Hook. & Arn., 157
  gracile Brongn., 158
  majus Brongn., 157

Ranunculus
  aquatilis L.
    var. *capillaceus* (Thuill.) DC., 158
    var. *brachypus* Hook. & Arn., 158
  bonariensis Poir.
    var. *trisepalus* (Gillies ex Hook. & Arn.) Lourteig, 159
  californicus Benth., 158
  dissectus Hook. & Arn., 158
  hebecarpus Hook. & Arn., 158
  humilis Collie ex Hook. & Arn., 158

Index of Scientific Names

Raphiolepis
   integerrima Hook. & Arn., 159
   umbellata (Thunb.) Makino, 159
Rhamnus
   cuneatus Hook., 66
   ziziphoides Spreng., 152
Rhaphithamnus
   cyanocarpus Miers
      var. *pallidus* Miers, 72
   spinosus (Juss.) Moldenke, 72
Rhus
   caustica (Molina) Hook. & Arn., 159
   macrophylla Hook. & Arn., 160, 210
   succedanea L., 75
Rhynchosia
   grandiflora Schlchtdl. & Cham., 207
   mexicana Hook. & Arn., 160
   minima (L.) DC., 160
Rhynchospora
   sclerioides Hook. & Arn., 160
Ribes
   californicum Hook. & Arn., 160
   occidentale Hook. & Arn., 160
      menziesii Pursh, 161
   speciosum Pursh, 7, 16
   subvestitum Hook. & Arn., 161
Roldana
   sessilifolia (Hook. & Arn.) H. Rob. & Brettell, 58
Rondeletia
   dubia Hemsl., 53
   leucophylla Kunth, 53
Rottlera
   aurantiaca Hook. & Arn., 161
Rourea
   glabra Kunth
      var. **glabra**, 161
   microphylla Planch., 75
   millettii Planch., 75
   minor (Gaertn.) Leenh., 76
   oblongifolia Hook. & Arn., 161, 210
Rubus
   parviflorus Nutt.
      var. **velutinus** (Hook. & Arn.) Greene, 162
   velutinus Hook. & Arn., 162, 210
Rytidostylis Hook. & Arn., 162
   gracilis Hook. & Arn., 162, 210

Sabia
   limoniacea Wall. ex Hook. f. & Thomson, 137
      var. *ardisioides* L. Chen, 137

Sadleria
   pallida Hook. & Arn., 192
Salix
   alaxensis (Anders.) Coville, 162
   speciosa Hook. & Arn., 162
Salpiglossis
   prostrata Hook. & Arn., 162
Salvia
   lasiocephala Hook. & Arn., 162
Sanicula
   arctopoides Hook. & Arn., 163
   bipinnata Hook. & Arn., 163
   crassicaulis DC., 164
   laciniata Hook. & Arn., 163
   menziesii Hook. & Arn., 164
   nudicaulis Hook. & Arn., 164
Santalum
   paniculatum Hook. & Arn., 164
Sapindus
   drummondii Hook. & Arn., 165
   glabrescens Hook. & Arn., 165
   marginatus Willd., 165
   saponaria L.
      var. **drummondii** (Hook. & Arn.) L.D. Benson, 165
Sarcostemma
   bilobum Hook. & Arn., 166
Saxifraga
   cernua L.
      var. *multiflora* Hook. & Arn., 166
   sibirica L., 166
Scaevola
   gaudichaudii Hook. & Arn., 166
   glabra Hook. & Arn., 166
   mollis Hook. & Arn., 167
   montana Gaud., 166
Schefflera
   heptaphylla (L.) Frodin, 144
Schizoloma
   heterophyllum (Dryand.) J. Sm., 189
Schoenocrambe
   linifolia (Nutt.) Greene, 94
Schoenoplectus
   pungens (Vahl) Palla
      var. **pungens**, 167
Scirpus
   longifolius Hook. & Arn., 167, 210
Scleria
   neesiana Hook. & Arn., 167
   scrobiculata Nees & Meyen, 167
Sedum
   uniflorum Hook. & Arn., 167

Semeiandra Hook. & Arn., 167
   grandiflora Hook. & Arn., 167, 207
     var. *subhirsuta* Hook. & Arn., 168
Senebiera
   mexicana Hook. & Arn., 168, 210
Senecio
   arnicoides Hook. & Arn., 168, 210
   beecheyanus Schultz-Bip., 58
   bipinnatifidus Hook. & Arn., 168, 210
   bridgesii Hook. & Arn., 168
   glabratus Hook. & Arn., 169, 210
   nigrescens Hook. & Arn., 169
   yegua (Colla) Cabrera, 57
Senna
   gaudichaudii (Hook. & Arn.) H.S. Irwin & Barneby, 64
Sequoia
   sempervirens Endl., 22
Sesbania
   tomentosa Hook. & Arn., 169, 210
Sicyos
   microcarpus Mann, 169
   pachycarpus Hook. & Arn., 16, 169
   waimanaloensis H. St John, 169
Sida
   albida Willd., 35
   grossulariifolia Hook. & Arn., 170, 210
Sidalcea
   malachroides (Hook. & Arn.) A. Gray, 132
Sideroxylon
   ferrugineum Hook. & Arn., 170
   wightianum Hook. & Arn., 170
   "*Silvaea* Hook. & Arn.", 170
     "*semperflorens* (Roxb.) Hook. & Arn.", 171
   Sinclairia Hook. & Arn., 171
     discolor Hook. & Arn., 171, 210
Sisyrhinchium
   sessiliflorum Hook. & Arn., 171
Solanum
   refractum Hook. & Arn., 171
   sandwicense Hook. & Arn., 171
Sonchus
   californicus Hook. & Arn., 172
Sphaeralcea
   grossulariifolia (Hook. & Arn.) Rydb., 170
Sphaerocionium
   lanceolatum (Hook. & Arn.) Copel., 188
   obtusum (Hook. & Arn.) Copel., 188
Sphagneticola
   calendulacea (L.) Pruski, 182, 185
Spodiopogon
   aureus Hook. & Arn., 172
   ischaemoides Hook. & Arn., 172
"*Stachys biflora* Hook. & Arn.", 172

Stemmadenia
   pubescens Benth., 51
Stemodia
   peduncularis Benth., 176
Stenolobium
   caeruleum Benth., 82
Stevia
   caracasana DC., 173
   elliptica Hook. & Arn., 173
   glandulosa Hook. & Arn., 173
Strophanthus
   divaricatus (Lour.) Hook. & Arn., 173
Styrax
   suberifolius Hook. & Arn., 173
Syzygium
   buxifolium Hook. & Arn., 173

Tabernaemontana
   mollis Hook. & Arn., 174
   pandacaqui Poir., 174
Tagetes
   congesta Hook. & Arn., 174, 210
   micrantha Cav., 174
Tarenna
   mollissima (Hook. & Arn.) B.L. Rob., 81
Tectaria
   gaudichaudii (Mett.) Maxon, 189
   subtriphylla (Hook. & Arn.) Copel., 191
Tellima
   heterophylla Hook. & Arn., 174
Tessaria
   absinthioides (Hook. & Arn.) DC., 48
Tetradymia
   spinosa Hook. & Arn., 174
Tetramolopium
   lepidotum (Less.) Sherff, 92
Tetranthera
   californica Hook. & Arn., 175
Tetrapterys
   mexicana Hook. & Arn., 175
Themeda
   caudata (Nees) A. Camus, 42
Thermopsis
   macrophylla Hook. & Arn., 175
Tibouchina
   longifolia (Vahl) Baill., 69
Tillaea
   erecta Hook. & Arn., 175, 210
Tithonia
   angustifolia Hook. & Arn., 175
   pachycephala DC., 175

Index of Scientific Names

Tofieldia
   coccinea Richardson, 205
Toxocarpus
   wightianus Hook. & Arn., 176
Trematolobelia
   macrostachys (Hook. & Arn.) Zahlbr. ex Rock, 128
Trentopohlia
   flava (Hook. & Arn.) De Toni, 192
Trevirana
   parviflora Hook. & Arn., 176
Tribulus
   maximus L., 120
Tridax
   gaillardioides Hook. & Arn., 176
Trifolium
   chilense Hook. & Arn., 177, 210
   dichotomum Hook. & Arn., 177
   grandiflorum Hook. & Arn., 178, 210
   melananthum Hook. & Arn., 178
   polymorphum Poir. ex Lam. & Poir., 178
   variegatum Nutt.
      var. ***variegatum***, 178
Trigonostemon Blume, 170
Tristerix
   aphyllus (Miers ex DC.) Barlow & Wiens, 129
Triumfetta
   paniculata Hook. & Arn., 178
Trixis
   latifolia Hook. & Arn., 178
   michuacana Lex.
      var. ***longifolia*** (D. Don) C. Anderson, 179
   obvallata Hook. & Arn., 179
Trophis
   fruticosa (Roxb.) Hook. & Arn., 179
   scandens (Lour.) Hook. & Arn., 179
Troximon
   apargioides Less., 52, 131
Tulocarpus Hook. & Arn., 179
   mexicanus Hook. & Arn., 179
Turritis
   lasiophylla Hook. & Arn., 179
Tweedia
   birostrata (Hook. & Arn.) Hook. & Arn., 82
Tylophora
   ovata (Lindl.) Hook. & Arn., 180

Umbellularia
   californica (Hook. & Arn.) Nutt., 175
Uniola
   spicata L., 55

Urceola Roxb., 89
   rosea (Hook. & Arn.) D.J. Middleton, 90
Urera
   glabra (Hook. & Arn.) Wedd., 154
Urtica
   affinis Hook. & Arn., 180
   grandis Hook. & Arn., 180
   millettii Hook. & Arn., 180, 210

Vaccinium
   ovatum Pursh, 181
      var. *angustifolium* Hook. & Arn., 181
Vachellia
   caven (Molina) Seigler & Ebinger, 36
Valeriana
   apiifolia A. Gray, 47
   ceratophylla Kunth, 47
   crispa Ruiz & Pav., 181
   "*pterocarpa* Hook. & Arn.", 181
Valerianella
   sp., 101
Verbena
   salviifolia Hook. & Arn., 181
Verbesina
   chinensis L., 42
   hastulata Hook. & Arn., 181
   prostrata Hook. & Arn., 182, 185
   succulenta Hook. & Arn., 182
Vesicularia
   inflectens (Brid.) C. Muell., 193
Viburnum
   chinense Hook. & Arn., 182
   nervosum D. Don, 182
   nervosum Hook. & Arn., 182
   sempervirens K. Koch, 183
Vicia
   linearifolia Hook. & Arn., 183
   micrantha Hook. & Arn., 183
   nigricans Hook. & Arn., 121, 183
   parviflora Hook. & Arn., 183
Viguiera
   angustifolia (Hook. & Arn.) S.F. Blake, 176
   cordata (Hook. & Arn.) D'Arcy, 184, 185
Viscum
   chilense Hook. & Arn., 183, 210
Vitex
   loureiroi Hook. & Arn., 183
   quinata (Lour.) F.N. Williams, 184

Wedelia
   acapulcensis Kunth, 184

Index of Scientific Names

Wedelia
cordata Hook. & Arn., 184
populifolia Hook. & Arn., 184
strigosa Hook. & Arn., 184
subflexuosa Hook. & Arn., 185
Wigandia
californica Hook. & Arn., 185
Wollastonia
prostrata Hook. & Arn., 185
Woodwardia
orientalis Sw., 192
prolifera Hook. & Arn., 192

Yabea
microcarpa (Hook. & Arn.) Koso-Pol., 66

Zippelia
begoniaefolium Blume, 151
Zuccagnia
angulata Hook. & Arn., 185